THE BIBLE
IN MY EVERYDAY LIFE

•

By
EUGENE FRANKLIN REESE
Contributor to
"The System Bible Study"

Introduction by
DR. A. T. ROBERTSON
Author of
"Word Pictures in the New Testament," "A Grammar of the Greek New
Testament in the Light of Historical Research," etc.

A Verse for Each Day selected by
DR. CHARLES G. TRUMBULL
Editor,
"The Sunday School Times";
Author of
"Taking Men Alive," "Genesis and Yourself," "The Life Story of
C. I. Scofield," etc. (Begins on Page 421)

•

A PRACTICAL APPLICATION OF THE BIBLE
TO EVERYDAY LIFE
Based on the Authorized
(King James) Version of the Bible
(*Without Comment*)

THE SYSTEM BIBLE COMPANY
Kansas City, Missouri
U. S. A.

TO MY MOTHER

INTRODUCTION

It is a pleasure to write a few introductory words to "The Bible in My Everyday Life," by Mr. E. F. Reese. At once one notes that the selection of Scripture passages here is for a practical purpose. Mr. Reese is not trying to prove theological doctrines by bringing together these selections, but to put in handy form passages calculated to strengthen one's faith in Christ as Lord and Saviour and to brighten one's path in the midst of trials and temptations and to increase one's loyalty to Christ and usefulness in the kingdom of God. It is primarily a personal experience with these Scriptures in his own life that Mr. Reese gives us. They have helped him and he naturally feels that they will render a like service to others. It is not an exhaustive concordance that we have here, but a choice among many like passages is made that reveal the personal equation. Readers will often think of other Scriptures that have helped them and that will be all to the good. Mr. Reese has not aimed to be exhaustive, but to give for the busy man and woman an adequate collection of Scripture passages on various vital matters that concern our thinking and life. In doing this he has, of course, often taken verses out of the context, but he has tried to do no violence to the context. Jesus said that his very words are spirit and life and it is true.

These wonderful words of life help men live and help them die.

Unfortunately not all persons read the Bible regularly, though nearly every one has a copy, one is glad to think. Not long ago a lady was travelling on the train who told me this incident. She was quietly reading her New Testament. In the section of the Pullman with her sat a mother and her son who watched her reading with some interest. Presently the mother asked: "Is that the New Testament that you are reading? Do you read it every day? Do you like to read it? Do you know how to find what you want in it?" The last question was wistful and soon the stranger learned that this mother had been called to her old home by her father's death, taking her son with her. She was in great need of comfort, but did not know how to find it in God's Word. She was very grateful when the stranger helped her with a short list of passages and was glad to use the pocket Testament to read them. This incident throws light upon the actual condition of many people who do not read the Bible systematically, who do not study it book by book, who hear sermons on isolated verses, who even study the Sunday school lessons which do not by any means cover the whole Bible. In a given emergency they are at a loss to find the words needed, even when they have hid it in their hearts. They do not know where to turn for the daily manna for their souls.

Dr. J. Rendel Harris, the Quaker scholar of England, has shown that the Jews and later the

Christians used *Testiomonia* (*Testimonies*), books of selected Scripture quotations which were very useful. Paul apparently quotes from one of these collections in Romans 3:9 to 18 (Psalms 14:1ff.; 53:1ff.; 5:9; 140:3; 10:7; Isaiah 59:7f.; Psalms 36:1). See another in Hebrews 1:7 to 13 (Psalms 104:4; 45:6f.; 102:25f.; 110:1). It is not an unheard of thing, therefore, that Mr. Reese has here done, but one that was tried long ago and found useful.

Books are cheaper now that in the old days, but people have less leisure that ever, and they need the comfort and strength to be derived from the knowledge of the Word of God. Hence there is a distinct place for "The Bible in My Everyday Life." Give the Bible the place that it deserves. Even the Bible student who knows his Bible will be glad to have in handy form these selected passages that a business man like Mr. Reese has found of special service and blessing.

There is no danger that this method of Bible use will displace the reading of the Bible as a whole. It will have precisely the opposite effect. Many will be stimulated by the aptness and pertinency of these Bible passages to read each verse in its context to get the flavor of the whole. There is a good deal of senseless criticism today on the use of verses of the Bible. It has been abused, no doubt, and can be. Judas went and hanged himself. Go thou and do likewise. And what thou doest do quickly. These are all Scripture quotations, but taken out of their context and

7

put together thus they make utterly erroneous justification for suicide. There is a right way to use the Sword of the Spirit. Jesus quoted words from Deuteronomy to answer the tempter. One does not always have to quote the entire context to make use of the truth of Scripture. So one wishes God's blessing on this effort to put in convenient form ready for immediate use the Bible truths that feed the soul and build one up in the faith of Christ our Lord.

A. T. Robertson

Louisville, Ky.

FOREWORD

This book is the outgrowth of the author's ever increasing realization of his own need for such guidance as it provides in the various walks of everyday life.

Many scholarly classifications of Scripture have been compiled and published, and the best of such classifications have been consulted in the preparation of this work. But the greatest objection which the average individual finds to such compilations, is that they are not limited to *those passages of the Bible which apply especially to him as an individual of today.* It is the purpose of this book to eliminate that objection, thereby facilitating the *practical* application of the Bible to one's everyday life.

In order to avoid possible influencing of the reader's mind through a special arrangement of verses, the verses under each subject are presented in the order in which they appear, respectively, in the Bible. In each case the reference is given, showing where the passage quoted may be found in the Bible.

It is hoped that the study of this book will stimulate the reading of the Bible itself. The student is urged to turn to his Bible frequently and study the Biblical setting of those verses which strike him with particular force. In the author's opinion, enough of such setting has been given herein to insure proper understanding of the lessons involved, but a broader reading of the Bible often will provide a background against which the lesson will stand out with greater clearness and power.

For the sake of clarity, words sometimes have been omitted from the verses quoted (all such omissions being indicated thus: . . .). Almost all of these omissions have consisted merely in dropping conjunctions ("and," "for," "therefore," etc.) which might be somewhat confusing. In no case has any word been omitted which might be considered essential to a correct interpretation of the passage in its bearing on the subject.

In the text of the book, the subjects have been arranged alphabetically, for convenience in locating them. In the front of the book (Page 11) will be found an index classifying the various subjects according to their relation to the everyday life of the individual. In the back of the book (Page 459) is given an index listing the subjects alphabetically.

It is believed that this book overcomes the greatest obstacles in the way of the average busy person of today in his efforts to regulate his life according to the one authoritative standard—that of the Bible. The subjects covered, and the verses quoted, are those which seem to have the greatest significance for the individual of today who desires to be a good citizen of his country and of the vastly greater realm of his Maker.

E. F. R.

Chicago, Illinois.

CLASSIFIED INDEX

When looking for some certain subject, consult the
☞ALPHABETICAL INDEX in the back of the book
(Page 459).

CLASSIFIED INDEX—*Continued*

12

CLASSIFIED INDEX—*Continued*

13

CLASSIFIED INDEX—*Continued*

CLASSIFIED INDEX—*Continued*

15

CLASSIFIED INDEX—*Continued*

CLASSIFIED INDEX—*Continued*

17

CLASSIFIED INDEX—*Continued*

THE BIBLE IN MY EVERYDAY LIFE

ACCUSATION, False

Matt. 5: 11 Blessed are ye, when *men* shall revile you, and persecute *you*, and shall say all manner of evil against you falsely, for my sake.

Luke 3: 14 And the soldiers likewise demanded of him, saying, And what shall we do? And he said unto them, Do violence to no man, neither accuse *any* falsely; and be content with your wages.

II. Tim. 3: 3 Without natural affection, trucebreakers, false accusers, incontinent, fierce, despisers of those that are good, 5 Having a form of godliness, but denying the power thereof: from such turn away.

I. Pet. 4: 14 If ye be reproached for the name of Christ, happy *are ye;* for the Spirit of glory and of God resteth upon you: on their part he is evil spoken of, but on your part he is glorified.

See DECEIT; FALSEHOOD; INJUSTICE; SLANDER.

AFFLICTED, Duty to

Job 6: 14 To him that is afflicted pity *should be shewed* from his friend; . . .

Matt. 25: 34 Then shall the King say unto them on his right hand, Come, ye blessed of my Father, inherit the kingdom prepared for you from the foundation of the world: 35 For I was a hungered, and ye gave me meat: I was thirsty, and ye gave me drink: I was a stranger, and ye took me in: 36 Naked, and ye clothed me: I was sick, and ye visited me: I was in prison, and ye came unto me. 37 Then shall the righteous an-

21

swer him, saying, Lord, when saw we thee a hungered, and fed *thee?* or thirsty, and gave *thee* drink? 38 When saw we thee a stranger, and took *thee* in? or naked, and clothed *thee?* 39 Or when saw we thee sick, or in prison, and came unto thee? 40 And the King shall answer and say unto them, Verily I say unto you, Inasmuch as ye have done *it* unto one of the least of these my brethren, ye have done *it* unto me. 41 Then shall he say also unto them on the left hand, Depart from me, ye cursed, into everlasting fire, prepared for the devil and his angels: 42 For I was a hungered, and ye gave me no meat: I was thirsty, and ye gave me no drink: 43 I was a stranger, and ye took me not in: naked, and ye clothed me not: sick, and in prison, and ye visited me not. 44 Then shall they also answer him, saying, Lord, when saw we thee a hungered, or athirst, or a stranger, or naked, or sick, or in prison, and did not minister unto thee? 45 Then shall he answer them, saying, Verily I say unto you, Inasmuch as ye did *it* not to one of the least of these, ye did *it* not to me.

Luke 10: 30 . . . Jesus . . . said, A certain *man* went down from Jerusalem to Jericho, and fell among thieves, which stripped him of his raiment, and wounded *him*, and departed, leaving *him* half dead. 31 And by chance there came down a certain priest that way; and when he saw him, he passed by on the other side. 32 And likewise a Levite, when he was at the place, came and looked *on him*, and passed by on the other side. 33 But a certain Samaritan, as he journeyed, came where he was; and when he saw him, he had compassion *on him*, 34 And went to *him*, and bound up his wounds, pouring in oil and wine, and set him on his own beast, and brought him to an

inn, and took care of him.   35 And on the morrow when he departed, he took out two pence, and
gave *them* to the host, and said unto him, Take
care of him: and whatsoever thou spendest more,
when I come again, I will repay thee.   36 Which
now of these three, thinkest thou, was neighbour
unto him that fell among the thieves?   37 And
he said, He that shewed mercy on him. Then said
Jesus unto him, Go, and do thou likewise.

Jas. 1:   27 Pure religion and undefiled before
God and the Father is this, To visit the fatherless
and widows in their affliction, *and* to keep himself
unspotted from the world.

See AFFLICTION; ALMS; BEREAVEMENT; JESUS,
Compassion of; SYMPATHY.

AFFLICTION

Job 5:   17 Behold, happy *is* the man whom God
correcteth: therefore despise not thou the chastening of the Almighty: 18 For he maketh sore,
and bindeth up: he woundeth, and his hands make
whole.

Job 36:   15 He delivereth the poor in his affliction, and openeth their ears in oppression.

Psa. 23:   4 Yea, though I walk through the valley of the shadow of death, I will fear no evil: for
thou *art* with me; thy rod and thy staff they comfort me.

Psa. 55:   22 Cast thy burden upon the Lord,
and he shall sustain thee: he shall never suffer the
righteous to be moved.

Psa. 103:   13 Like as a father pitieth *his* children, *so* the Lord pitieth them that fear him.

Psa. 140:   12 I know that the Lord will maintain the cause of the afflicted, *and* the right of the
poor.

Psa. 147:   3 He healeth the broken in heart,

and bindeth up their wounds.

Prov. 3: 11 My son, despise not the chastening of the Lord; neither be weary of his correction: 12 For whom the Lord loveth he correcteth; even as a father the son *in whom* he delighteth.

Hos. 6: 1 Come, and let us return unto the Lord: for he hath torn, and he will heal us; he hath smitten, and he will bind us up.

Nah. 1: 7 The Lord *is* good, a strong hold in the day of trouble; and he knoweth them that trust in him.

Matt. 5: 3 Blessed *are* the poor in spirit: for theirs is the kingdom of heaven. 4 Blessed *are* they that mourn: for they shall be comforted. 10 Blessed *are* they which are persecuted for righteousness' sake: for theirs is the kingdom of heaven. 11 Blessed are ye, when *men* shall revile you, and persecute *you*, and shall say all manner of evil against you falsely, for my sake. 12 Rejoice, and be exceeding glad: for great *is* your reward in heaven: for so persecuted they the prophets which were before you.

Matt. 11: 28 Come unto me, all *ye* that labour and are heavy laden, and I will give you rest.

John 14: 1 Let not your heart be troubled: ye believe in God, believe also in me. 16 And I will pray the Father, and he shall give you another Comforter, that he may abide with you forever; 18 I will not leave you comfortless: I will come to you.

John 15: 2 Every branch in me that beareth not fruit he taketh away: and every *branch* that beareth fruit, he purgeth it, that it may bring forth more fruit. 18 If the world hate you, ye know that it hated me before *it hated* you. 20 Remember the word that I said unto you, The servant is not greater than his lord. If they have persecuted me, they will also persecute you; if they have kept my saying, they will keep yours also.

John 16: 20 . . . Ye shall weep and lament, but the world shall rejoice; and ye shall be sorrowful, but your sorrow shall be turned into joy.

Rom. 5: 3 . . . We glory in tribulations also; knowing that tribulation worketh patience; 4 And patience, experience; and experience, hope:

Rom. 8: 28 . . . We know that all things work together for good to them that love God, to them who are the called according to *his* purpose. 35 Who shall separate us from the love of Christ? *shall* tribulation, or distress, or persecution, or famine, or nakedness, or peril, or sword? 37 Nay, in all these things we are more than conquerors through him that loved us.

II. Cor. 1: 3 Blessed *be* God, even the Father of our Lord Jesus Christ, the Father of mercies, and the God of all comfort; 4 Who comforteth us in all our tribulation, that we may be able to comfort them which are in any trouble, by the comfort wherewith we ourselves are comforted of God. 5 For as the sufferings of Christ abound in us, so our consolation also aboundeth by Christ. 7 And . . . as ye are partakers of the sufferings, so *shall ye be* also of the consolation.

II. Cor. 4: 8 *We are* troubled on every side, yet not distressed; *we are* perplexed, but not in despair; 9 Persecuted, but not forsaken; cast down, but not destroyed; 10 Always bearing about in the body the dying of the Lord Jesus, that the life also of Jesus might be made manifest in our body.

II. Cor. 12: 9 . . . He said unto me, My grace is sufficient for thee: for my strength is made perfect in weakness. Most gladly therefore will

I rather glory in my infirmities, that the power of Christ may rest upon me.

II. Tim. 2: 12 If we suffer, we shall also reign with *him*: if we deny *him*, he also will deny us:

Heb. 12: 3 . . . Consider him that endured such contradiction of sinners against himself, lest ye be wearied and faint in your minds. 4 Ye have not yet resisted unto blood, striving against sin. 6 For whom the Lord loveth he chasteneth, and scourgeth every son whom he receiveth. 7 If ye endure chastening, God dealeth with you as with sons; for what son is he whom the father chasteneth not? 8 But if ye be without chastisement, whereof all are partakers, then are ye bastards, and not sons. 9 Furthermore, we have had fathers of our flesh which corrected *us*, and we gave *them* reverence: shall we not much rather be in subjection unto the Father of spirits, and live? 10 For they verily for a few days chastened *us* after their own pleasure; but he for *our* profit, that *we* might be partakers of his holiness. 11 Now no chastening for the present seemeth to be joyous, but grievous: nevertheless, afterward it yieldeth the peaceable fruit of righteousness unto them which are exercised thereby.

Heb. 13: 5 . . . He hath said, I will never leave thee, nor forsake thee. 6 . . . The Lord *is* my helper, and I will not fear what man shall do unto me.

Jas. 1: 12 Blessed *is* the man that endureth temptation: for when he is tried, he shall receive the crown of life, which the Lord hath promised to them that love him. 27 Pure religion and undefiled before God and the Father is this, To visit the fatherless and widows in their affliction, *and* to keep himself unspotted from the world.

Jas. 5: 13 Is any among you afflicted? let him

pray . . . 14 Is any sick among you? let him
call for the elders of the church; and let them pray
over him, anointing him with oil in the name of
the Lord: 15 And the prayer of faith shall save
the sick, and the Lord shall raise him up; and if
he have committed sins, they shall be forgiven
him.

I. Pet. 4: 14 If ye be reproached for the name
of Christ, happy *are ye;* for the Spirit of glory
and of God resteth upon you: on their part he is
evil spoken of, but on your part he is glorified.

Rev. 2: 10 Fear none of those things which
thou shalt suffer: . . . be thou faithful unto death,
and I will give thee a crown of life.

Rev. 3: 19 As many as I love, I rebuke and
chasten: be zealous therefore, and repent.

See AFFLICTED, Duty to; BEREAVEMENT.

ALMS (Charity)

Prov. 21: 13 Whoso stoppeth his ears at the
cry of the poor, he also shall cry himself, but shall
not be heard.

Prov. 22: 9 He that hath a bountiful eye shall
be blessed; for he giveth of his bread to the poor.

Prov. 28: 27 He that giveth unto the poor
shall not lack: but he that hideth his eyes shall
have many a curse.

Prov. 29: 14 The king that faithfully judgeth
the poor, his throne shall be established for ever.

Matt. 5: 42 Give to him that asketh thee, and
from him that would borrow of thee turn not thou
away.

Matt. 6: 1 Take heed that ye do not your
alms before men, to be seen of them: otherwise ye have no reward of your Father which is
in heaven. 3 But when thou doest alms, let not
thy left hand know what thy right hand doeth:

27

4 That thine alms may be in secret: and thy
Father which seeth in secret himself shall reward
thee openly.

Matt. 25: 34 Then shall the King say unto
them on his right hand, Come, ye blessed of my
Father, inherit the kingdom prepared for you
from the foundation of the world: 35 For I was
a hungered, and ye gave me meat: I was thirsty,
and ye gave me drink: I was a stranger, and ye
took me in: 36 Naked, and ye clothed me: I was
sick, and ye visited me: I was in prison, and ye
came unto me. 40 . . . Verily I say unto you,
Inasmuch as ye have done *it* unto one of the least
of these my brethren, ye have done *it* unto me.
41 Then shall he say also unto them on the left
hand, Depart from me, ye cursed, into everlasting fire, prepared for the devil and his angels:
42 For I was a hungered, and ye gave me no meat:
I was thirsty, and ye gave me no drink: 43 I
was a stranger, and ye took me not in: naked, and
ye clothed me not: sick, and in prison, and ye
visited me not. 45 . . . Verily I say unto you,
Inasmuch as ye did *it* not to one of the least of
these, ye did *it* not to me. 46 And these shall go
away into everlasting punishment: but the righteous into life eternal.

Luke 3: 11 . . . He that hath two coats, let
him impart to him that hath none; and he that
hath meat, let him do likewise.

Luke 11: 41 . . . Give alms of such things as
ye have; . . .

Luke 12: 33 Sell that ye have, and give alms;
provide yourselves bags which wax not old, a
treasure in the heavens that faileth not, where no
thief approacheth, neither moth corrupteth. 34
For where your treasure is, there will your heart
be also.

28

Acts 20: 35 . . . Ye ought to support the weak, and to remember the words of the Lord Jesus, how he said, It is more blessed to give than to receive.

Rom. 12: 8 . . . He that giveth, *let him do it* with simplicity; . . . 10 *Be* kindly affectioned one to another with brotherly love; . . . 13 Distributing to the necessity of saints; given to hospitality. 20 . . . If thine enemy hunger, feed him; if he thirst, give him drink: for in so doing thou shalt heap coals of fire on his head.

II. Cor. 9: 6 . . . He which soweth sparingly shall reap also sparingly; and he which soweth bountifully shall reap also bountifully. 7 Every man according as he purposeth in his heart, *so let him give;* not grudgingly, or of necessity: for God loveth a cheerful giver.

Eph. 4: 28 Let him that stole steal no more: but rather let him labour, working with *his* hands the thing which is good, that he may have to give to him that needeth.

I. John 3: 17 . . . Whoso hath this world's good, and seeth his brother have need, and shutteth up his bowels *of compassion* from him, how dwelleth the love of God in him?

See BENEFICENCE; LIBERALITY; MERCY; POOR; TITHES.

AMBITION

Matt. 4: 8 . . . The devil taketh him up into an exceeding high mountain, and sheweth him all the kingdoms of the world, and the glory of them; 9 And saith unto him, All these things will I give thee, if thou wilt fall down and worship me. 10 Then saith Jesus unto him, Get thee hence, Satan: for it is written, Thou shalt worship the Lord thy God, and him only shalt thou serve.

Matt. 6:   26 . . . What is a man profited,
if he shall gain the whole world, and lose his own
soul? or what shall a man give in exchange for his
soul?

Matt. 18:   1 At the same time came the disciples unto Jesus, saying, Who is the greatest in
the kingdom of heaven?   2 And Jesus called a
little child unto him, and set him in the midst of
them,   3 And said, Verily I say unto you, Except ye be converted, and become as little children,
ye shall not enter into the kingdom of heaven.   4
Whosoever therefore shall humble himself as this
little child, the same is greatest in the kingdom of
heaven.   5 And whoso shall receive one such little child in my name receiveth me.

Matt. 23:   12 . . . Whosoever shall exalt himself shall be abased; and he that shall humble himself shall be exalted.

Mark 10:   35 . . . James and John, the sons
of Zebedee, come unto him, saying, Master, we
would that thou shouldest do for us whatsoever
we shall desire.   36 And he said unto them,
What would ye that I should do for you?   37
They said unto him, Grant unto us that
we may sit, one on thy right hand, and the
other on thy left hand, in thy glory.   38 But
Jesus said unto them, Ye know not what ye ask:
can ye drink of the cup that I drink of? and be
baptized with the baptism that I am baptized
with?   39 And they said unto him, We can.   And
Jesus said unto them, Ye shall indeed drink of the
cup that I drink of; and with the baptism that I
am baptized withal shall ye be baptized: 40 But
to sit on my right hand and on my left hand is not
mine to give; but *it shall be given to them* for
whom it is prepared.   41 And when the ten heard

it, they began to be much displeased with James and John.   42 But Jesus called them *to him*, and saith unto them, Ye know that they which are accounted to rule over the Gentiles exercise lordship over them; and their great ones exercise authority upon them.   43 But so shall it not be among you: but whosoever will be great among you, shall be your minister: 44 And whosoever of you will be the chiefest, shall be servant of all.   45 For even the Son of man came not to be ministered unto, but to minister, and to give his life a ransom for many.

Luke 22: 24 . . . There was . . . a strife among them, which of them should be accounted the greatest.   25 And he said unto them, The kings of the Gentiles exercise lordship over them; and they that exercise authority upon them are called benefactors.   26 But ye *shall* not *be* so: but he that is greatest among you, let him be as the younger; and he that is chief, as he that doth serve.   27 For whether *is* greater, he that sitteth at meat, or he that serveth? *is* not he that sitteth at meat? but I am among you as he that serveth. 28 Ye are they which have continued with me in my temptations.   29 And I appoint unto you a kingdom, as my Father hath appointed unto me; 30 That ye may eat and drink at my table in my kingdom, and sit on thrones judging the twelve tribes of Israel.

John 13: 3 Jesus knowing that the Father had given all things into his hands, and that he was come from God, and went to God; 4 He riseth from supper, and laid aside his garments; and took a towel, and girded himself.   5 After that he poureth water into a basin, and began to wash the disciples' feet, and to wipe *them* with the

31

towel wherewith he was girded. 6 Then cometh he to Simon Peter: and Peter saith unto him, Lord, dost thou wash my feet? 7 Jesus answered and said unto him, What I do thou knowest not now; but thou shalt know hereafter. 8 Peter saith unto him, Thou shalt never wash my feet. Jesus answered him, If I wash thee not, thou hast no part with me. 9 Simon Peter saith unto him, Lord, not my feet only, but also *my* hands and *my* head. 10 Jesus saith to him, He that is washed needeth not save to wash *his* feet, but is clean every whit: and ye are clean, but not all. 11 For he knew who should betray him; therefore said he, Ye are not all clean. 12 So after he had washed their feet, and had taken his garments, and was set down again, he said unto them, Know ye what I have done to you? 13 Ye call me Master and Lord: and ye say well; for *so* I am. 14 If I then, *your* Lord and Master, have washed your feet; ye also ought to wash one another's feet. 15 For I have given you an example, that ye should do as I have done to you. 16 Verily, verily, I say unto you, The servant is not greater than his lord; neither he that is sent greater than he that sent him. 17 If ye know these things, happy are ye if ye do them.

I. John 2: 16 . . . All that *is* in the world, the lust of the flesh, and the lust of the eyes, and the pride of life, is not of the Father, but is of the world.

See COVETOUSNESS; SELF-EXALTATION.

ANGER

Prov. 15: 1 A soft answer turneth away wrath: but grievous words stir up anger. 18 A wrathful man stirreth up strife: but *he that is* slow to anger appeaseth strife.

Prov. 16: 32 *He that is* slow to anger *is* better than the mighty; and he that ruleth his spirit than he that taketh a city.

Prov. 19: 11 The discretion of a man deferreth his anger; and *it is* his glory to pass over a transgression.

Prov. 22: 24 Make no friendship with an angry man; and with a furious man thou shalt not go; 25 Lest thou learn his ways, and get a snare to thy soul.

Prov. 27: 4 Wrath *is* cruel, and anger *is* outrageous; . . .

Prov. 30: 33 Surely the churning of milk bringeth forth butter, and the wringing of the nose bringeth forth blood: so the forcing of wrath bringeth forth strife.

Ecc. 7: 9 Be not hasty in thy spirit to be angry: for anger resteth in the bosom of fools.

Matt. 5: 22 . . . Whosoever is angry with his brother without a cause shall be in danger of the, judgment: and whosoever shall say to his brother, Raca, shall be in danger of the council: but whosoever shall say, Thou fool, shall be in danger of hell fire.

Eph. 4: 26 Be ye angry, and sin not: let not the sun go down upon your wrath:

Col. 3: 8 . . . Put off all these; anger, wrath, malice, blasphemy, filthy communication out of your mouth.

I. Tim. 2: 8 I will . . . that men pray every where, lifting up holy hands, without wrath and doubting.

Jas. 1: 19 . . . Let every man be swift to hear, slow to speak, slow to wrath: 20 For the wrath of man worketh not the righteousness of God.

See HATRED; MALICE; RETALIATION; also CHAR-

ITABLENESS; TOLERANCE.

ANTICHRISTS

Matt. 7: 15 Beware of false prophets, which come to you in sheep's clothing, but inwardly they are ravening wolves. 16 Ye shall know them by their fruits. Do men gather grapes of thorns, or figs of thistles? 17 Even so every good tree bringeth forth good fruit; but a corrupt tree bringeth forth evil fruit. 18 A good tree cannot bring forth evil fruit, neither *can* a corrupt tree bring forth good fruit. 19 Every tree that bringeth not forth good fruit is hewn down, and cast into the fire. 20 Wherefore by their fruits ye shall know them.

Matt. 24: 23 . . . If any man shall say unto you, Lo, here *is* Christ, or there; believe *it* not. 24 For there shall arise false Christs, and false prophets, and shall shew great signs and wonders; insomuch that, if *it were* possible, they shall deceive the very elect.

Luke 21: 8 . . . Take heed that ye be not deceived: for many shall come in my name, saying, I am *Christ;* and the time draweth near: go ye not therefore after them.

II. Thess. 2: 3 Let no man deceive you by any means: for *that day shall not come,* except there come a falling away first, and that man of sin be revealed, the son of perdition; 4 Who opposeth and exalteth himself above all that is called God, or that is worshipped; so that he as God sitteth in the temple of God, shewing himself that he is God.

I. John 2: 18 Little children, it is the last time: and as ye have heard that antichrist shall come, even now are there many antichrists; where-

by we know that it is the last time. 19 They
went out from us, but they were not of us; for if
they had been of us, they would *no doubt* have
continued with us: but *they went out*, that they
might be made manifest that they were not all of
us. 20 But ye have an unction from the Holy
One, and ye know all things. 21 I have not written unto you because ye know not the truth, but
because ye know it, and that no lie is of the truth.
22 Who is a liar but he that denieth that Jesus is
the Christ? He is antichrist, that denieth the
Father and the Son.

I. John 4: 3 . . . Every spirit that confesseth
not that Jesus Christ is come in the flesh is not of
God: and this is that *spirit* of antichrist, whereof
ye have heard that it should come; and even now
already is it in the world.

II. John: 7 . . . Many deceivers are entered
into the world, who confess not that Jesus Christ
is come in the flesh. This is a deceiver and an
antichrist.

See WICKED.

ATHEISM

Psa. 10: 4 The wicked, through the pride of
his countenance, will not seek *after God*: God *is*
not in all his thoughts.

Psa. 14: 1 The fool hath said in his heart,
There is no God. . . .

See SKEPTICISM; UNBELIEF.

AVARICE

Ecc. 5: 10 He that loveth silver shall not be
satisfied with silver; nor he that loveth abundance
with increase: this *is* also vanity. 11 When
goods increase, they are increased that eat them:
and what good *is there* to the owners thereof, sav-

ing the beholding *of them* with their eyes?

Luke 12: 15 . . . Take heed, and beware of covetousness: for a man's life consisteth not in the abundance of the things which he possesseth. 16 . . . The ground of a certain rich man brought forth plentifully: 17 And he thought within himself, saying, What shall I do, because I have no room where to bestow my fruits? 18 And he said, This will I do: I will pull down my barns, and build greater; and there will I bestow all my fruits and my goods. 19 And I will say to my soul, Soul, thou has much goods laid up for many years; take thine ease, eat, drink, *and* be merry. 20 But God said unto him, *Thou* fool, this night thy soul shall be required of thee: then whose shall those things be, which thou hast provided? 21 So *is* he that layeth up treasure for himself, and is not rich toward God.

I. Tim. 3: 2 A bishop then must be blameless, . . . 3 Not given to wine, no striker, not greedy of filthy lucre; but patient, not a brawler, not covetous;

I. Tim. 6: 5 Perverse disputings of men of corrupt minds, and destitute of the truth, supposing that gain is godliness: from such withdraw thyself. 10 For the love of money is the root of all evil: which while some coveted after, they have erred from the faith, and pierced themselves through with many sorrows.

I. John 3: 17 . . . Whoso hath this world's good, and seeth his brother have need, and shutteth up his bowels *of compassion* from him, how dwelleth the love of God in him?

See COVETOUSNESS; SELFISHNESS; UNJUST GAIN.

BACKBITING

Psa. 15: 1 Lord, who shall abide in thy tabernacle? who shall dwell in thy holy hill? 3 *He that* backbiteth not with his tongue, nor doeth evil to his neighbour, nor taketh up a reproach against his neighbour.

Rom. 1: 30 Backbiters, haters of God, despiteful, proud, boasters, inventors of evil things, disobedient to parents, 32 . . . They which commit such things are worthy of death, . . .

See ACCUSATION, False; GOSSIP; MALICE; SLANDER.

BACKSLIDING

Psa. 44: 20 If we have forgotten the name of our God, or stretched out our hands to a strange god; 21 Shall not God search this out? for he knoweth the secrets of the heart.

Prov. 14: 14 The backslider in heart shall be filled with his own ways: . . .

Prov. 24: 16 . . . A just *man* falleth seven times, and riseth up again: but the wicked shall fall into mischief.

Matt. 5: 13 Ye are the salt of the earth: but if the salt have lost his savour, wherewith shall it be salted? it is thenceforth good for nothing, but to be cast out, and to be trodden under foot of men.

Matt. 24: 12 . . . Because iniquity shall abound, the love of many shall wax cold. 13 But he that shall endure unto the end, the same shall be saved.

Mark 4: 14 The sower soweth the word. 15 And these are they by the way side, where the word is sown; but when they have heard, Satan cometh immediately, and taketh away the word that was sown in their hearts. 16 And these are

37

they likewise which are sown on stony ground;
who, when they have heard the word, immediately
receive it with gladness; 17 And have no root in
themselves, and so endure but for a time: afterward, when affliction or persecution ariseth for
the word's sake, immediately they are offended.
18 And these are they which are sown among
thorns; such as hear the word, 19 And the cares
of this world, and the deceitfulness of riches, and
the lusts of other things entering in, choke the'
word, and it becometh unfruitful.

Mark 8: 38 Whosoever . . . shall be ashamed
of me and of my words, in this adulterous and sinful generation, of him also shall the Son of man
be ashamed, when he cometh in the glory of his
Father with the holy angels.

Luke 9: 62 . . . Jesus said unto him, No man,
having put his hand to the plough, and looking
back, is fit for the kingdom of God.

Luke 17: 32 Remember Lot's wife.

John 15: 6 If a man abide not in me, he is
cast forth as a branch, and is withered; and men
gather them, and cast them into the fire, and they
are burned.

I. Cor. 10: 12 . . . Let him that thinketh he
standeth take heed lest he fall. 13 There hath no
temptation taken you but such as is common to
man: but God is faithful, who will not suffer you
to be tempted above that ye are able; but will with
the temptation also make a way to escape, that ye
may be able to bear it.

I. Tim. 1: 19 Holding faith, and a good conscience; which some having put away, concerning
faith have made shipwreck:

I. Tim. 6: 10 . . . The love of money is the
root of all evil: which while some coveted after,
they have erred from the faith, and pierced them-

38

selves through with many sorrows.

II. Tim. 2: 12 If we suffer, we shall also reign
with *him*: if we deny *him*, he also will deny us:

Heb. 3: 12 Take heed, brethren, lest there be
in any of you an evil heart of unbelief, in departing from the living God.

Heb. 6: 4 . . . *It is* impossible for those who
were once enlightened, and have tasted of the
heavenly gift, and were made partakers of the
Holy Ghost, 5 And have tasted the good word
of God, and the powers of the world to come,
6 If they shall fall away, to renew them again
unto repentance; seeing they crucify to themselves
the Son of God afresh, and put *him* to an open
shame.

Heb. 10: 26 . . . If we sin wilfully after that
we have received the knowledge of the truth, there
remaineth no more sacrifice for sins, 27 But a
certain fearful looking for of judgment and fiery
indignation, which shall devour the adversaries.
28 He that despised Moses' law died without mercy
under two or three witnesses: 29 Of how much
sorer punishment, suppose ye, shall he be thought
worthy, who hath trodden under foot the Son of
God, and hath counted the blood of the covenant,
wherewith he was sanctified, an unholy thing,
and hath done despite unto the Spirit of grace?

II. Pet. 2: 20 . . . If after they have escaped
the pollutions of the world through the knowledge
of the Lord and Saviour Jesus Christ, they are
again entangled therein, and overcome, the latter
end is worse with them than the beginning. 21
For it had been better for them not to have known
the way of righteousness, than, after they have
known *it*, to turn from the holy commandment
delivered unto them. 22 But it is happened unto
them according to the true proverb, The dog *is*

turned to his own vomit again; and, The sow that was washed to her wallowing in the mire. See STEADFASTNESS.

BAPTISM

Matt. 3: 16 . . . Jesus, when he was baptized, went up straightway out of the water: and, lo, the heavens were opened unto him, and he saw the Spirit of God descending like a dove, and lighting upon him: 17 And lo a voice from heaven, saying, This is my beloved Son, in whom I am well pleased.

Matt. 28: 19 Go ye . . . , and teach all nations, baptizing them in the name of the Father, and of the Son, and of the Holy Ghost:

Mark 1: 4 John did baptize in the wilderness, and preach the baptism of repentance for the remission of sins. 5 And there went out unto him all the land of Judea, and they of Jerusalem, and were all baptized of him in the river of Jordan, confessing their sins. 6 And John was clothed with camel's hair, and with a girdle of a skin about his loins; and he did eat locusts and wild honey; 7 And preached, saying, There cometh one mightier than I after me, the latchet of whose shoes I am not worthy to stoop down and unloose 8 I indeed have baptized you with water: but he shall baptize you with the Holy Ghost.

John 3: 5 Jesus answered, . . . Except a man be born of water and *of* the Spirit, he cannot enter into the kingdom of God.

Acts 2: 38 . . . Peter said unto them, Repent, and be baptized every one of you in the name of Jesus Christ for the remission of sins, and ye shall receive the gift of the Holy Ghost. 39 For the promise is unto you, and to your children, and to all that are afar off, *even* as many as the Lord our God shall call.

Rom. 6: 3 Know ye not, that so many of us as were baptized into Jesus Christ were baptized into his death? 4 Therefore we are buried with him by baptism into death: that like as Christ was raised up from the dead by the glory of the Father, even so we also should walk in newness of life.

I. Cor. 12: 13 . . . By one Spirit are we all baptized into one body, whether *we be* Jews or Gentiles, whether *we be* bond or free; and have been all made to drink into one Spirit.

Gal. 3: 27 . . . As many of you as have been baptized into Christ have put on Christ.

Eph. 4: 4 *There is* one body, and one Spirit, even as ye are called in one hope of your calling; 5 One Lord, one faith, one baptism, 6 One God and Father of all, who *is* above all, and through all, and in you all.

Col. 2: 12 Buried with him in baptism, wherein also ye are risen with *him* through the faith of the operation of God, who hath raised him from the dead.

I. Pet. 3: 20 . . . Once the longsuffering of God waited in the days of Noah, while the ark was a preparing, wherein few, that is, eight souls were saved by water. 21 The like figure whereunto *even* baptism doth also now save us, (not the putting away of the filth of the flesh, but the answer of a good conscience toward God,) by the resurrection of Jesus Christ:

See HOLY GHOST; REPENTANCE; SALVATION.

BENEFICENCE

Psa. 41: 1 Blessed *is* he that considereth the poor: the Lord will deliver him in time of trouble.

Prov. 3: 27 Withhold not good from them to

whom it is due, when it is in the power of thine hand to do *it*. 28 Say not unto thy neighbour, Go, and come again, and to morrow I will give; when thou hast it by thee.

Prov. 22: 9 He that hath a bountiful eye shall be blessed; for he giveth of his bread to the poor.

Prov. 25: 21 If thine enemy be hungry, give him bread to eat; and if he be thirsty, give him water to drink:

Ezek. 18: 5 . . . If a man be just, and do that which is lawful and right, 7 And hath not oppressed any, *but* hath restored to the debtor his pledge, hath spoiled none by violence, hath given his bread to the hungry, and hath covered the naked with a garment; 9 Hath walked in my statutes, and hath kept my judgments, to deal truly; he *is* just, he shall surely live, saith the Lord God.

Matt. 5: 42 Give to him that asketh thee, and from him that would borrow of thee turn not thou away.

Matt. 19: 21 Jesus said unto him, If thou wilt be perfect, go *and* sell that thou hast, and give to the poor, and thou shalt have treasure in heaven: and come *and* follow me.

Mark 9: 41 . . . Whosoever shall give you a cup of water to drink in my name, because ye belong to Christ, verily I say unto you, he shall not lose his reward.

Luke 3: 11 . . . He that hath two coats, let him impart to him that hath none; and he that hath meat, let him do likewise.

I. Cor. 13: 3 . . . Though I bestow all my goods to feed *the poor*, and though I give my body to be burned, and have not charity, it profiteth me nothing.

II. Cor. 8: 9 . . . Ye know the grace of our

Lord Jesus Christ, that, though he was rich, yet for your sakes he became poor, that ye through his poverty might be rich.

II. Cor. 9: 6 . . . He which soweth sparingly shall reap also sparingly; and he which soweth bountifully shall reap also bountifully.

I. Tim. 5: 8 . . . If any provide not for his own, and specially for those of his own house, he hath denied the faith, and is worse than an infidel. 16 If any man or woman that believeth have widows, let them relieve them, and let not the church be charged; that it may relieve them that are widows indeed.

I. Tim. 6: 17 Charge them that are rich in this world, . . . 18 That they do good, that they be rich in good works, ready to distribute, willing to communicate;

Heb. 6: 10 . . . God is not unrighteous to forget your work and labour of love, which ye have shewed toward his name, in that ye have ministered to the saints, and do minister.

Jas. 2: 15 If a brother or sister be naked, and destitute of daily food, 16 And one of you say unto them, Depart in peace, be ye warmed and filled; notwithstanding ye give them not those things which are needful to the body; what doth it profit?

I. John 3: 17 . . . Whoso hath this world's good, and seeth his brother have need, and shutteth up his bowels of compassion from him, how dwelleth the love of God in him? 18 . . . Let us not love in word, neither in tongue; but in deed and in truth.

See ALMS; GIVING; KINDNESS; LIBERALITY; MERCY; PERSONAL CHRISTIAN WORK; POOR; UNSELFISHNESS.

BEREAVEMENT

Ecc. 7: 2 *It is* better to go to the house of mourning, than to go to the house of feasting: for that *is* the end of all men; and the living will lay *it* to his heart.

Rom. 12: 15 Rejoice with them that do rejoice, and weep with them that weep.

I. Thess. 4: 13 . . . I would not have you to be ignorant, brethren, concerning them which are asleep, that ye sorrow not, even as others which have no hope. 14 For if we believe that Jesus died and rose again, even so them also which sleep in Jesus will God bring with him. 15 For this we say unto you by the word of the Lord, that we which are alive *and* remain unto the coming of the Lord shall not prevent them which are asleep. 16 For the Lord himself shall descend from heaven with a shout, with the voice of the archangel, and with the trump of God: and the dead in Christ shall rise first: 17 Then we which are alive *and* remain shall be caught up together with them in the clouds, to meet the Lord in the air: and so shall we ever be with the Lord. 18 Wherefore comfort one another with these words.

See AFFLICTED, Duty to; AFFLICTION; DEATH; SYMPATHY; WIDOWS—ORPHANS.

BIGOTRY

Mark. 2: 15 . . . As Jesus sat at meat in his house, many publicans and sinners sat also together with Jesus and his disciples; . . . 16 And when the scribes and Pharisees saw him eat with publicans and sinners, they said unto his disciples, How is it that he eateth and drinketh with publicans and sinners?

Luke 9: 49 . . . John . . . said, Master, we saw one casting out devils in thy name; and we

THE BIBLE IN MY EVERYDAY LIFE

forbade him, because he followeth not with us. 50 And Jesus said unto him, Forbid *him* not: for he that is not against us is for us.

Luke 18: 10 Two men went up into the temple to pray; the one a Pharisee, and the other a publican. 11 The Pharisee stood and prayed thus with himself, God, I thank thee, that I am not as other men *are*, extortioners, unjust, adulterers, or even as this publican. 12 I fast twice in the week, I give tithes of all that I possess. 13 And the publican, standing afar off, would not lift up so much as *his* eyes unto heaven, but smote upon his breast, saying, God be merciful to me a sinner. 14 I tell you, this man went down to his house justified *rather* than the other: for every one that exalteth himself shall be abased; and he that humbleth himself shall be exalted.

Rom. 3: 9 What then? are we better *than they?* No, in no wise: for we have before proved both Jews and Gentiles, that they are all under sin; 10 As it is written, There is none righteous, no, not one: 22 . . . The righteousness of God . . . . *is* by faith of Jesus Christ unto all and upon all them that believe; for there is no difference: 23 For all have sinned, and come short of the glory of God;

III. John: 9 I wrote unto the church: but Diotrephes, who loveth to have the preeminence among them, receiveth us not. 10 Wherefore, if I come, I will remember his deeds which he doeth, prating against us with malicious words: and not content therewith, neither doth he himself receive the brethren, and forbiddeth them that would, and casteth *them* out of the church.

See CONCEIT; SELF-RIGHTEOUSNESS; also TOL-ERANCE.

BIRTH

Ecc. 11: 5 As thou knowest not what *is* the way of the spirit, *nor* how the bones *do grow* in the womb of her that is with child: even so thou knowest not the works of God who maketh all.

Luke 1: 24 . . . His wife Elisabeth conceived, and hid herself five months, saying, 25 Thus hath the Lord dealt with me in the days wherein he looked on *me*, to take away my reproach among men. 58 And her neighbors and her cousins heard how the Lord had shewed great mercy upon her; and they rejoiced with her.

Luke 2: 4 . . . Joseph . . . went up from Galilee, out of the city of Nazareth, into Judea, unto the city of David, which is called Bethlehem, (because he was of the house and lineage of David,) 5 To be taxed with Mary his espoused wife, being great with child. 6 And so it was, that, while they were there, the days were accomplished that she should be delivered. 7 And she brought forth her firstborn son, and wrapped him in swaddling clothes, and laid him in a manger; because there was no room for them in the inn. 8 And there were in the same country shepherds abiding in the field, keeping watch over their flock by night. 9 And, lo, the angel of the Lord came upon them, and the glory of the Lord shone round about them; and they were sore afraid. 10 And the angel said unto them, Fear not: for, behold, I bring you good tidings of great joy, which shall be to all people. 11 For unto you is born this day in the city of David a Saviour, which is Christ the Lord. 12 And this *shall be* a sign unto you; Ye shall find the babe wrapped in swaddling clothes, lying in a manger. 13 And suddenly there was with the angel a multitude of

the heavenly host praising God, and saying, 14
Glory to God in the highest, and on earth peace,
good will toward men.

John 16: 21 A woman when she is in travail
hath sorrow, because her hour is come: but as
soon as she is delivered of the child, she remem-
bereth no more the anguish, for joy that a man
is born into the world.

I. Tim. 2: 15 . . . She shall be saved in child-
bearing, if they continue in faith and charity and
holiness with sobriety.

See CHILDREN; PARENTS.

BLASPHEMY

Exod. 20: 7 Thou shalt not take the name of
the Lord thy God in vain: for the Lord will not
hold him guiltless that taketh his name in vain.

Prov. 30: 8 Remove far from me vanity and
lies; give me neither poverty nor riches; feed me
with food convenient for me: 9 Lest I be full,
and deny *thee*, and say, Who *is* the Lord? or lest
I be poor, and steal, and take the name of my
God *in vain*.

Isa. 29: 15 Woe unto them that seek deep to
hide their counsel from the Lord, and their works
are in the dark, and they say, Who seeth us? and
who knoweth us? 16 Surely your turning of
things upside down shall be esteemed as the pot-
ter's clay: for shall the work say of him that
made it, He made me not? or shall the thing
framed say of him that framed it, He had no
understanding?

Matt. 5: 33 . . . Ye have heard that it hath
been said by them of old time, Thou shalt not
forswear thyself, but shalt perform unto the
Lord thine oaths: 34 But I say unto you, Swear
not at all; neither by heaven; for it is God's

throne: 35 Nor by the earth; for it is his footstool: neither by Jerusalem; for it is the city of the great King. 36 Neither shalt thou swear by thy head, because thou canst not make one hair white or black. 37 But let your communication be, Yea, yea; Nay, nay: for whatsoever is more than these cometh of evil.

Matt. 12: 31 . . . All manner of sin and blasphemy shall be forgiven unto men: but the blasphemy *against* the *Holy* Ghost shall not be forgiven unto men. 32 And whosoever speaketh a word against the Son of man, it shall be forgiven him: but whosoever speaketh against the Holy Ghost, it shall not be forgiven him, neither in this world, neither in the *world* to come.

Mark 7: 21 . . . From within, out of the heart of men, proceed evil thoughts, adulteries, fornications, murders, 22 Thefts, covetousness, wickedness, deceit, lasciviousness, an evil eye, blasphemy, pride, foolishness: 23 All these evil things come from within, and defile the man.

Heb. 10: 28 He that despised Moses' law died without mercy under two or three witnesses: 29 Of how much sorer punishment, suppose ye, shall he be thought worthy, who hath trodden under foot the Son of God, and hath counted the blood of the covenant, wherewith he was sanctified, an unholy thing, and hath done despite unto the Spirit of grace?

Jas. 3: 10 Out of the same mouth proceedeth blessing and cursing. My brethren, these things ought not so to be.

See REVERENCE.

BOASTING

I. Kings 20: 11 . . . Let not him that girdeth on *his harness* boast himself as he that putteth it off.

Psa. 49: 6 They that trust in their wealth, and boast themselves in the multitude of their riches; 7 None *of them* can by any means redeem his brother nor give to God a ransom for him:

Psa. 52: 1 Why boastest thou thyself in mischief, O mighty man? the goodness of God *endureth* continually.

Prov. 25: 14 Whoso boasteth himself of a false gift *is like* clouds and wind without rain. 27 *It is* not good to eat much honey: so *for men* to search their own glory *is not* glory.

Prov. 27: 1 Boast not thyself of to morrow; for thou knowest not what a day may bring forth. 2 Let another man praise thee, and not thine own mouth; a stranger, and not thine own lips.

I. Cor. 4: 7 . . . Who maketh thee to differ *from another?* and what hast thou that thou didst not receive? now if thou didst receive *it,* why dost thou glory, as if thou hadst not received *it?*

II. Cor. 10: 17 . . . He that glorieth, let him glory in the Lord. 18 For not he that commendeth himself is approved, but whom the Lord commendeth.

Eph. 2: 8 . . . By grace are ye saved through faith; and that not of yourselves: *it is* the gift of God: 9 Not of works, lest any man should boast.

See CONCEIT; SELF-EXALTATION; also HUMILITY; MEEKNESS.

BORROWING—LENDING

Psa. 37: 21 The wicked borroweth, and payeth not again: but the righteous sheweth mercy, and giveth. 25 I have been young, and *now* am old; yet have I not seen the righteous forsaken, nor his seed begging bread. 26 *He is* ever merciful, and lendeth; and his seed *is* blessed.

Prov. 19: 17 He that hath pity upon the poor lendeth unto the Lord; and that which he hath given will he pay him again.

Prov. 22: 7 . . . The borrower *is* servant to the lender.

Prov. 28: 8 He that by usury and unjust gain increaseth his substance, he shall gather it for him that will pity the poor.

Matt. 5: 42 Give to him that asketh thee, and from him that would borrow of thee turn not thou away.

Luke 6: 34 . . . If ye lend *to them* of whom ye hope to receive, what thank have ye? for sinners also lend to sinners, to receive as much again. 35 But love ye your enemies, and do good, and lend, hoping for nothing again; and your reward shall be great, and ye shall be the children of the Highest: . . .

See BENEFICENCE; LIBERALITY; UNSELFISHNESS.

BREACH OF TRUST

Luke 16: 12 . . . If ye have not been faithful in that which is another man's, who shall give you that which is your own?

See CONTRACTS; DISHONESTY; FALSEHOOD.

BRIBERY

Prov. 17: 23 A wicked *man* taketh a gift out of the bosom to pervert the ways of judgment.

Prov. 28: 21 To have respect of persons *is* not good: for, for a piece of bread *that* man will transgress.

Prov. 29: 4 The king by judgment establisheth the land: but he that receiveth gifts overthroweth it.

Isa. 5: 22 Woe unto *them that are* mighty to drink wine, and men of strength to mingle strong drink: 23 Which justify the wicked for reward, and take away the righteousness of the righteous from him!

Isa. 33: 15 He that walketh righteously, and speaketh uprightly; he that despiseth the gain of oppressions, that shaketh his hands from holding of bribes, that stoppeth his ears from hearing of blood, and shutteth his eyes from seeing evil; 16 He shall dwell on high; his place of defence *shall be* the munitions of rocks: bread shall be given him; his waters *shall be* sure.

Matt. 28: 11 . . . Behold, some of the watch came into the city, and shewed unto the chief priests all the things that were done. 12 And when they were assembled with the elders, and had taken counsel, they gave large money unto the soldiers, 13 Saying, Say ye, His disciples came by night, and stole him *away* while we slept. 14 And if this come to the governor's ears, we will persuade him, and secure you. 15 So they took the money, and did as they were taught: and this saying is commonly reported among the Jews until this day.

Acts 8: 18 . . . When Simon saw that through laying on of the apostles' hands the Holy Ghost was given, he offered the money, 19 Saying, Give me also this power, that on whomsoever I lay hands, he may receive the Holy Ghost. 20 But Peter said unto him, Thy money perish with thee, because thou hast thought that the gift of God may be purchased with money.

See AVARICE; BREACH OF TRUST; DISHONESTY; TEMPTATION; UNJUST GAIN; also HONESTY; INTEGRITY.

BUSYBODY

Prov. 20: 3 *It is* an honour for a man to cease from strife: but every fool will be meddling.

II. Thess. 3: 11 . . . We hear that there are some which walk among you disorderly, working not at all, but are busybodies. 12 Now them that are such we command and exhort by our Lord Jesus Christ, that with quietness they work, and eat their own bread.

I. Pet. 4: 15 . . . Let none of you suffer as a murderer, or *as* a thief, or *as* an evil doer, or as a busybody in other men's matters.

See GOSSIP.

CHARACTER

Prov. 24: 21 My son, fear thou the Lord and the king: *and* meddle not with them that are given to change: 22 For their calamity shall rise suddenly; and who knoweth the ruin of them both?

Matt. 10: 22 . . . Ye shall be hated of all *men* for my name's sake: but he that endureth to the end shall be saved.

Luke 9: 62 . . . Jesus said unto him, No man, having put his hand to the plough, and looking back, is fit for the kingdom of God.

Rom. 8: 29 . . . Whom he did foreknow, he also did predestinate *to be* conformed to the image of his Son, that he might be the first born among many brethren. 30 Moreover, whom he did predestinate, them he also called: and whom he called, them he also justified: and whom he justified, them he also glorified.

Eph. 4: 14 That we *henceforth* be no more children, tossed to and fro, and carried about with every wind of doctrine, by the sleight of men, *and* cunning craftiness, whereby they lie in wait to deceive; 15 But speaking the truth in love, may

52

grow up into him in all things, which is the head, *even* Christ:

II. Tim. 2:   15 Study to shew thyself approved unto God, a workman that needeth not to be ashamed, rightly dividing the word of truth.   16 But shun profane *and* vain babblings: for they will increase unto more ungodliness.   21 If a man therefore purge himself from these, he shall be a vessel unto honour, sanctified, and meet for the master's use, *and* prepared unto every good work.   22 Flee also youthful lusts: but follow righteousness, faith, charity, peace, with them that call on the Lord out of a pure heart.

See   INTEGRITY;   MANHOOD;   REPUTATION; WOMANHOOD; also GRACES, Christian.

CHARITABLENESS—UNCHARITABLENESS

Prov.17:   9 He that covereth a transgression seeketh love; but he that repeateth a matter separateth *very* friends.

Prov. 19:   11 The discretion of a man deferreth his anger; and *it is* his glory to pass over a transgression.

Prov. 24:   17 Rejoice not when thine enemy falleth, and let not thine heart be glad when he stumbleth: 29 Say not, I will do so to him as he hath done to me: I will render to the man according to his work.

Ecc. 7:   21 . . . Take no heed unto all words that are spoken; lest thou hear thy servant curse thee: 22 For oftentimes also thine own heart knoweth that thou thyself likewise hast cursed others.

Matt. 5:   7 Blessed are the merciful: for they shall obtain mercy.   43 Ye have heard that it hath been said, Thou shalt love thy neighbour, and hate thine enemy.   44 But I say unto you, Love

53

your enemies, bless them that curse you, do good
to them that hate you, and pray for them which
despitefully use you, and persecute you; 45 That
ye may be the children of your Father which is in
heaven: for he maketh his sun to rise on the evil
and on the good, and sendeth rain on the just and
on the unjust. 46 For if ye love them which love
you, what reward have ye? do not even the publicans the same? 47 And if ye salute your brethren only, what do ye more *than others?* do not
even the publicans so?

Matt. 6: 12 . . . Forgive us our debts, as we
forgive our debtors. 14 For if ye forgive men
their trespasses, your heavenly Father will also
forgive you: 15 But if ye forgive not men their
trespasses, neither will your Father forgive your
trespasses.

Matt. 7: 1 Judge not, that ye be not judged.
2 For with what judgment ye judge, ye shall be
judged: and with what measure ye mete, it shall
be measured to you again. 3 And why beholdest thou the mote that is in thy brother's eye, but
considerest not the beam that is in thine own eye?
4 Or how wilt thou say to thy brother, Let me pull
out the mote out of thine eye; and, behold, a beam
is in thine own eye? 5 Thou hypocrite, first cast
out the beam out of thine own eye; and then shalt
thou see clearly to cast out the mote out of thy
brother's eye.

Matt. 18: 21 Then came Peter to him, and
said, Lord, how oft shall my brother sin against
me, and I forgive him? till seven times? 22 Jesus
saith unto him, I say not unto thee, Until seven
times: but, Until seventy times seven. 23 Therefore is the kingdom of heaven likened unto a certain king, which would take account of his servants. 24 And when he had begun to reckon, one

was brought unto him, which owed him ten thousand talents. 25 But forasmuch as he had not to pay, his lord commanded him to be sold, and his wife, and children, and all that he had, and payment to be made. 26 The servant therefore fell down, and worshipped him, saying, Lord, have patience with me, and I will pay thee all. 27 Then the lord of that servant was moved with compassion, and loosed him, and forgave him the debt. 28 But the same servant went out, and found one of his fellow servants, which owed him a hundred pence: and he laid hands on him, and took *him* by the throat, saying, Pay me that thou owest. 29 And his fellow servant fell down at his feet, and besought him, saying, Have patience with me, and I will pay thee all. 30 And he would not: but went and cast him into prison, till he should pay the debt. 31 So when his fellow servants saw what was done, they were very sorry, and came and told unto their lord all that was done. 32 Then his lord, after that he had called him, said unto him, O thou wicked servant, I forgave thee all that debt, because thou desiredst me: 33 Shouldest not thou also have had compassion on thy fellow servant, even as I had pity on thee? 34 And his lord was wroth, and delivered him to the tormentors, till he should pay all that was due unto him. 35 So likewise shall my heavenly Father do also unto you, if ye from your hearts forgive not every one his brother their trespasses.

Mark 11: 25 . . . When ye stand praying, forgive, if ye have aught against any; that your Father also which is in heaven may forgive you your trespasses.

Luke 6: 31 . . . As ye would that men should do to you, do ye also to them likewise. 36 Be ye therefore merciful, as your Father also is merciful. 37 Judge not, and ye shall not be judged: condemn not, and ye shall not be condemned: forgive, and ye shall be forgiven:

Luke 17: 3 Take heed to yourselves: If thy brother trespass against thee, rebuke him; and if he repent, forgive him. 4 And if he trespass against thee seven times in a day, and seven times in a day turn again to thee, saying, I repent; thou shalt forgive him.

John 7: 24 Judge not according to the appearance, but judge righteous judgment.

Rom. 2: 1 . . . Thou art inexcusable, O man, whosoever thou art that judgest: for wherein thou judgest another, thou condemnest thyself; for thou that judgest doest the same things. 2 But we are sure that the judgment of God is according to truth against them which commit such things.

Rom. 12: 14 Bless them which persecute you: bless, and curse not. 17 Recompense to no man evil for evil. . . . 18 If it be possible, as much as lieth in you, live peaceably with all men. 19 Dearly beloved, avenge not yourselves, but *rather* give place unto wrath: for it is written, Vengeance *is* mine; I will repay, saith the Lord. 20 Therefore if thine enemy hunger, feed him; if he thirst, give him drink: for in so doing thou shalt heap coals of fire on his head. 21 Be not overcome of evil, but overcome evil with good.

Rom. 14: 10 . . . Why dost thou judge thy brother? or why dost thou set at nought thy brother? for we shall all stand before the judgment seat of Christ. 13 Let us not therefore judge one another any more: but judge this rather, that no man put a stumblingblock or an occasion to fall in *his* brother's way. 19 Let us . . . follow after the things which make for peace, and things wherewith one may edify another.

I. Cor. 10:   32 Give none offence, neither to the Jews, nor to the Gentiles, nor to the church of God:

Gal. 6:   1 . . . . If a man be overtaken in a fault, ye which are spiritual, restore such a one in the spirit of meekness; considering thyself, lest thou also be tempted.   2 Bear ye one another's burdens, and so fulfill the law of Christ.

Eph. 4:   32 . . . Be ye kind one to another, tenderhearted, forgiving one another, even as God for Christ's sake hath forgiven you.

Col. 3:   12 Put on . . . , as the elect of God, holy and beloved, bowels of mercies, kindness, humbleness of mind, meekness, longsuffering;   13 Forbearing one another, and forgiving one another, if any man have a quarrel against any: even as Christ forgave you, so also *do* ye.

Jas. 2:   13 . . . He shall have judgment without mercy, that hath shewed no mercy; and mercy rejoiceth against judgment.

Jas. 4:   11 Speak not evil one of another, brethren. He that speaketh evil of *his* brother, and judgeth his brother, speaketh evil of the law, and judgeth the law: but if thou judge the law, thou art not a doer of the law, but a judge.   12 There is one lawgiver, who is able to save and to destroy: who art thou that judgest another?

I. Pet. 3:   8 Finally, *be ye* all of one mind, having compassion one of another; love as brethren, *be* pitiful, *be* courteous: 9 Not rendering evil for evil, or railing for railing: but contrariwise blessing; knowing that ye are thereunto called, that ye should inherit a blessing.

See GOLDEN RULE; KINDNESS; MERCY; UNSELFISHNESS.

CHILDREN

Psa. 27:   10 When my father and my mother forsake me, then the Lord will take me up.

Psa. 103:   17 . . . The mercy of the Lord *is* from everlasting to everlasting upon them that fear him, and his righteousness unto children's children;

Psa. 127:   3 Lo, children *are* a heritage of the Lord: *and* the fruit of the womb *is his* reward. 4 As arrows *are* in the hand of a mighty man; so *are* children of the youth.   5 Happy *is* the man that hath his quiver full of them: they shall not be ashamed, . . .

Prov. 8:   17 I love them that love me; and those that seek me early shall find me.

Prov. 10:   1 . . . A wise son maketh a glad father: but a foolish son *is* the heaviness of his mother.

Prov. 17:   6 Children's children *are* the crown of old men; and the glory of children *are* their fathers.   21 He that begetteth a fool *doeth it* to his sorrow: and the father of a fool hath no joy.   25 A foolish son *is* a grief to his father, and bitterness to her that bare him.

Prov. 20:   7 The just *man* walketh in his integrity: his children *are* blessed after him.

Prov. 22:   15 Foolishness *is* bound in the heart of a child; *but* the rod of correction shall drive it far from him.

Prov. 23:   24 The father of the righteous shall greatly rejoice: and he that begetteth a wise *child* shall have joy of him.   25 Thy father and thy mother shall be glad, and she that bare thee shall rejoice.

Prov. 29:   3 Whoso loveth wisdom rejoiceth his father: but he that keepeth company with har-

lots spendeth *his* substance. 15 . . . A child left
to himself bringeth his mother to shame.

Ecc. 4: 13 Better *is* a poor and a wise child,
than an old and foolish king, who will no more be
admonished.

Matt. 18: 2 . . . Jesus called a little child
unto him, and set him in the midst of them, 3
And said, Verily I say unto you, Except ye be converted, and become as little children, ye shall not
enter into the kingdom of heaven. 4 Whosoever
therefore shall humble himself as this little child,
the same is greatest in the kingdom of heaven.
5 And whoso shall receive one such little child in
my name receiveth me. 6 But whoso shall offend
one of these little ones which believe in me, it were
better for him that a millstone were hanged about
his neck, and *that* he were drowned in the depth of
the sea. 10 Take heed that ye despise not one of
these little ones; for I say unto you, That in
heaven their angels do always behold the face of
my Father which is in heaven.

Mark 10: 14 . . . Jesus . . . said unto them,
Suffer the little children to come unto me, and
forbid them not; for of such is the kingdom of
God.

Acts 2: 38 . . . Peter said unto them, Repent, and be baptized every one of you in the name
of Jesus Christ for the remission of sins, and ye
shall receive the gift of the Holy Ghost. 39 For
the promise is unto you, and to your children, and
to all that are afar off, *even* as many as the Lord
our God shall call.

I. John 2: 12 I write unto you, little children,
because your sins are forgiven you for his name's
sake. 13 . . . I write unto you, little chldren,
because ye have known the Father.

See PARENTS, Duties of; WIDOWS—ORPHANS;

YOUTH.

Duties of: Exod. 20 12 Honour thy father and thy mother: that thy days may be long upon the land which the Lord thy God giveth thee.

Psa. 148: 12 Both young men, and maidens; old men, and children: 13 Let them praise the name of the Lord: for his name alone is excellent; his glory *is* above the earth and heaven.

Prov. 1: 8 My son, hear the instruction of thy father, and forsake not the law of thy mother:

Prov. 3: 1 My son, forget not my law; but let thine heart keep my commandments: 2 For length of days, and long life, and peace, shall they add to thee. 3 Let not mercy and truth forsake thee: bind them about thy neck; write them upon the table of thine heart:

Prov. 13: 1 A wise son *heareth* his father's instruction: but a scorner heareth not rebuke.

Prov. 19: 26 He that wasteth *his* father, *and* chaseth away *his* mother, *is* a son that causeth shame, and bringeth reproach.

Prov. 23: 22 Hearken unto thy father that begat thee, and despise not thy mother when she is old.

Prov. 28: 7 Whoso keepeth the law *is* a wise son: but he that is a companion of riotous *men* shameth his father. 24 Whoso robbeth his father or his mother, and saith, *It is* no transgression; the same *is* the companion of a destroyer.

Matt. 15: 4 . . . God commanded, saying, Honour thy father and mother: and, He that curseth father or mother, let him die the death.

Eph. 6: 1 Children, obey your parents in the Lord: for this is right. 2 Honour thy father and mother; which is the first commandment with promise; 3 That it may be well with thee, and thou mayest live long on the earth. ,

Col. 3: 20 Children, obey *your* parents in all things: for this is well pleasing unto the Lord.

See PARENTS.

CHURCH

Matt. 16: 18 . . . Thou art Peter, and upon this rock I will build my church; and the gates of hell shall not prevail against it. 19 And I will give unto thee the keys of the kingdom of heaven: and whatsoever thou shalt bind on earth shall be bound in heaven; and whatsoever thou shalt loose on earth shall be loosed in heaven.

Matt. 18: 19 . . . If two of you shall agree on earth as touching any thing that they shall ask, it shall be done for them of my Father which is in heaven. 20 For where two or three are gathered together in my name, there am I in the` midst of them.

Acts 20: 28 Take heed . . . unto yourselves, and to all the flock, over the which the Holy Ghost hath made you overseers, to feed the church of God, which he hath purchased with his own blood.

Rom. 12: 4 . . . As we have many members in one body, and all members have not the same office: 5 So we, *being* many, are one body in Christ, and every one members one of another.

I. Cor. 12: 5 . . . There are differences of administrations, but the same Lord. 6 And there are diversities of operations, but it is the same God which worketh all in all. 13 . . . By one Spirit are we all baptized into one body, whether *we be* Jews or Gentiles, whether *we be* bond or free; and have been all made to drink into one Spirit. 14 For the body is not one member, but many. 25 . . . There should be no schism in

the body; . . . the members should have the same
care one for another.   26 And whether one member suffer, all the members suffer with it; or one
member be honoured, all the members rejoice with
it.   27 Now ye are the body of Christ, and members in particular.

Gal. 3: 26 . . . Ye are all the children of
God by faith in Christ Jesus.   27 For as many
of you as have been baptized into Christ have put
on Christ.   28 There is neither Jew nor Greek,
there is neither bond nor free, there is neither
male nor female: for ye are all one in Christ Jesus.

Eph. 1: 17 . . . The God of our Lord Jesus
Christ . . . 22 . . . hath put all *things* under
his feet, and gave him *to be* the head over all
things to the church,   23 Which is his body, the
fulness of him that filleth all in all.

Eph. 2: 19 . . . Ye are no more strangers
and foreigners, but fellow citizens with the saints,
and of the household of God;   20 And are built
upon the foundation of the apostles and prophets,
Jesus Christ himself being the chief corner *stone;*
21 In whom all the building fitly framed together
groweth unto a holy temple in the Lord: 22 In
whom ye also are builded together for a habitation
of God through the Spirit.

Eph. 4: 4 *There is* one body, and one Spirit,
even as ye are called in one hope of your calling;
5 One Lord, one faith, one baptism,   6 One God
and Father of all, who *is* above all, and through all,
and in you all.

Eph. 5: 23 . . . The husband is the head of
the wife, even as Christ is the head of the church:
and he is the Saviour of the body.   24 Therefore
as the church is subject unto Christ, so *let* the
wives *be* to their own husbands in every thing.

25 Husbands, love your wives, even as Christ also loved the church, and gave himself for it; 26 That he might sanctify ·and cleanse it with the washing of water by the word,   27 That he might present it to himself a glorious church, not having spot, or wrinkle, or any such thing; but that it should be holy and without blemish. 28 So ought men to love their wives as their own bodies. He that loveth his wife loveth himself. 29 For no man ever yet hated his own flesh; but nourisheth and cherisheth it, even as the Lord the church: 30 For we are members of his body, of his flesh, and of his bones. 31 For this cause shall a man leave his father and mother, and shall be joined unto his wife, and they two shall be one flesh. 32 This is a great mystery: but I speak concerning Christ and the church.

Col. 1: 12 Giving thanks unto the Father, which hath made us meet to be partakers of the inheritance of the saints in light: 13 Who hath delivered us from the power of darkness, and hath translated *us* into the kingdom of his dear Son: 14 In whom we have redemption through his blood, *even* the forgiveness of sins: 15 Who is the image of the invisible God, the firstborn of every creature: 18 And he is the head of the body, the church: . . .

I. Tim. 3:   14 These things write I unto thee, . . . 15 . . . that thou mayest know how thou oughtest to behave thyself in the house of God, which is the church of the living God, the pillar and ground of the truth.

See MINISTER.

Activity: Luke 13: 6 . . . A certain *man* had a fig tree planted in his vineyard; and he came and sought fruit thereon, and found none. 7

Then said he unto the dresser of his vineyard, Behold, these three years I come seeking fruit on this fig tree, and find none: cut it down; why cumbereth it the ground? 8 And he answering said unto him, Lord, let it alone this year also, till I shall dig about it, and dung *it*: 9 And if it bear fruit, *well*: and if not, *then* after that thou shalt cut it down.

' John 15: 1 I am the true vine, and my Father is the husbandman. 2 Every branch in me that beareth not fruit he taketh away: and every *branch* that beareth fruit, he purgeth it; that it may bring forth more fruit. 3 Now ye are clean through the word which I have spoken unto you. 4 Abide in me, and I in you. As the branch cannot bear fruit of itself, except it abide in the vine; no more can ye, except ye abide in me. 5 I am the vine, ye *are* the branches. He that abideth in me, and I in him, the same bringeth forth much fruit; for without me ye can do nothing. 6 If a man abide not in me, he is cast forth as a branch, and is withered; and men gather them, and cast *them* into the fire, and they are burned. 7 If ye abide in me, and my words abide in you, ye shall ask what ye will, and it shall be done unto you. 8 Herein is my Father glorified, that ye bear much fruit; so shall ye be my disciples.

Acts 1: 14 These all continued with one accord in prayer and supplication, with the women, and Mary the mother of Jesus, and with his brethren.

Acts 2: 1 . . . When the day of Pentecost was fully come, they were all with one accord in one place. 46 And they, continuing daily with one accord in the temple, and breaking bread from house to house, did eat their meat with gladness and singleness of heart, 47 Praising God, and having favour with all the people. And the Lord added to the church daily such as should be saved.

I. Cor. 3: 8 . . . Every man shall receive his own reward according to his own labour. 9 For we are labourers together with God:. . .

Gal. 6: 9 . . . Let us not be weary in well doing: for in due season we shall reap, if we faint not.

Heb. 10: 24 . . . Let us consider one another to provoke unto love and to good works: 25 Not forsaking the assembling of ourselves together, as the manner of some *is;* but exhorting *one another*: and so much the more, as ye see the day approaching.

Heb. 12: 28 . . . Let us have grace, whereby we may serve God acceptably with reverence and godly fear:

Heb. 13: 16 . . . To do good and to communicate forget not: for with such sacrifices God is well pleased.

Jas. 1: 22 . . . Be ye doers of the word, and not hearers only, deceiving your own selves.

See PERSONAL CHRISTIAN WORK.

Attendance: Psa. 84: 4 Blessed *are* they that dwell in thy house: . . . 10 For a day in thy courts *is* better than a thousand. I had rather be a doorkeeper in the house of my God, than to dwell in the tents of wickedness.

Matt. 5: 16 Let your light so shine before men, that they may see your good works, and glorify your Father which is in heaven.

Heb. 10: 24 . . . Let us consider one another to provoke unto love and to good works: 25 Not forsaking the assembling of ourselves together, . . .

House: Matt. 21: 13 . . . My house shall be called the house of prayer; . . .

Matt. 23: 16 Woe unto you, *ye* blind guides, which say, Whosoever shall swear by the temple, it is nothing; but whosoever shall swear by the gold of the temple, he is a debtor! 17 *Ye* fools and blind: for whether is greater, the gold, or the temple that sanctifieth the gold? 21 . . . Whoso shall swear by the temple, sweareth by it, and by him that dwelleth therein.

John 2: 16 . . . Make not my Father's house a house of merchandise.

I. Tim. 3: 14 These things write I unto thee, . . . 15 . . . that thou mayest know how thou oughtest to behave thyself in the house of God, which is the church of the living God, the pillar and ground of the truth.

Support: Psa. 76: 11 Vow, and pay unto the Lord your God: let all that be round about him bring presents unto him that ought to be feared.

Prov. 3: 9 Honour the Lord with thy substance, and with the firstfruits of all thine increase: 10 So shall thy barns be filled with plenty, and thy presses shall burst out with new wine.

Ecc. 11: 1 Cast thy bread upon the waters: for thou shalt find it after many days.

Acts 20: 28 Take heed therefore unto yourselves, and to all the flock, over the which the Holy Ghost hath made you overseers, to feed the church of God, which he hath purchased with his own blood.

I. Cor. 16: 2 Upon the first *day* of the week let every one of you lay by him in store, as *God* hath prospered him, . . .

II. Cor. 8: 1 . . . We do you to wit of the grace of God bestowed on the churches of Mace-

donia; 2 How that in a great trial of affliction,
the abundance of their joy and their deep poverty
abounded unto the riches of their liberality. 3
For to *their* power, I bear record, yea, and beyond
their power *they were* willing of themselves;
4 Praying us ·with much entreaty that we
would receive the gift, and *take upon us* the
fellowship of the ministering to the saints. 5
And *this they did*, not as we hoped, but first gave
their own selves to the Lord, and unto us by the
will of God. 6 Insomuch that we desired Titus,
that as he had begun, so he would also finish in
you the same grace also. 7 Therefore, as ye
abound in every *thing, in* faith, and utterance, and
knowledge, and *in* all diligence, and *in* your love
to us, *see* that ye abound in this grace also. 8
I speak not by commandment, but by occasion of
the forwardness of others, and to prove the sincerity of your love. 9 For ye know the grace of
our Lord Jesus Christ, that, though he was rich,
yet for your sakes he became poor, that ye through
his poverty might be rich. 20 Avoiding this, that
no man should blame us in this abundance which
is administered by us: 21 Providing for honest
things, not only in the sight of the Lord, but also
in the sight of men. 24 Wherefore shew ye to
them, and before the churches, the proof of your
love, and of our boasting on your behalf.

II. Cor. 9: 4 Lest haply if they of Macedonia
come with me, and find you unprepared, we (that
we say not, ye) should be ashamed in this same
confident boasting. 7 Every man according as
he purposeth in his heart, *so let him give;* not
grudgingly, or of necessity: for God loveth a
cheerful giver.

I. Tim. 6: 17 Charge them that are rich in

67

this world, that they be not highminded, nor trust in uncertain riches, but in the living God, who giveth us richly all things to enjoy; 18 That they do good, that they be rich in good works, ready to distribute, willing to communicate; 19 Laying up in store for themselves a good foundation against the time to come, that they may lay hold on eternal life.

Tit. 3: 8 *This is* a faithful saying, and these things I will that thou affirm constantly, that they which have believed in God might be careful to maintain good works. These things are good and profitable unto men.

Heb. 6: 10 . . . God *is* not unrighteous to forget your work and labour of love, which ye have shewed toward his name, in that ye have ministered to the saints, and do minister.

See ALMS; BENEFICENCE; GIVING; LIBERALITY; TITHES.

CITIZEN, Duties of

Prov. 22: 11 He that loveth pureness of heart, *for* the grace of his lips the king *shall be* his friend.

Ecc. 8: 2 I *counsel thee* to keep the king's commandment, and *that* in regard of the oath of God.

Ecc. 10: 4 If the spirit of the ruler rise up against thee, leave not thy place; for yielding pacifieth great offences.

Mark 12: 17 . . . Jesus . . . said unto them, Render to Cesar the things that are Cesar's, and to God the things that are God's. . . .

Rom. 13: 1 Let every soul be subject unto the higher powers. For there is no power but of God: the powers that be are ordained of God. 2 Whosoever therefore resisteth the power, resisteth the ordinance of God: and they that resist shall receive to themselves damnation. 3 For rulers are not a terror to good works, but to the evil. Wilt thou then not be afraid of the power? do that which is good, and thou shalt have praise of the same: 4 For he is the minister of God to thee for good. But if thou do that which is evil, be afraid; for he beareth not the sword in vain: for he is the minister of God, a revenger to *execute* wrath upon him that doeth evil. 5 Wherefore *ye* must needs be subject, not only for wrath, but also for conscience' sake. 6 For, for this cause pay ye tribute also: for they are God's ministers, attending continually upon this very thing. 7 Render therefore to all their dues: tribute to whom tribute *is due;* custom to whom custom; fear to whom fear; honour to whom honour. 8 Owe no man any thing, but to love one another: for he that loveth another hath fulfilled the law.

I. Tim. 2: 1 I exhort . . . , that, first of all, supplications, prayers, intercessions, *and* giving of thanks, be made for all men; 2 For kings, and *for* all that are in authority; that we may lead a quiet and peaceable life in all godliness and honesty.

Tit. 3: 1 Put them in mind to be subject to principalities and powers, to obey magistrates, to be ready to every good work, 2 To speak evil of no man, to be no brawlers, *but* gentle, shewing all meekness unto all men.

I. Pet. 2: 13 Submit yourselves to every ordinance of man for the Lord's sake: whether it be to the king, as supreme; 14 Or unto governors, as unto them that are sent by him for the punishment of evil doers, and for the praise of them that do well. 15 For so is the will of God, that with well doing ye may put to silence the ignorance of foolish men: 16 As free, and not using *your* liberty for a cloak of maliciousness, but as the servants of God. 17 Honour all *men*. Love the brotherhood. Fear God. Honour the king. 18 Servants, *be* subject to *your* masters with all fear; not only to the good and gentle, but also to the froward. 19 For this *is* thankworthy, if a man for conscience toward God endure grief, suffering wrongfully.

See CITIZENSHIP in Classified Index (Page 18).

COMMANDMENTS

The New: John 13: 34 A new commandment I give unto you, That ye love one another; as I have loved you, that ye also love one another. 35 By this shall all *men* know that ye are my disciples, if ye have love one to another.

Rom. 13. 8 Owe no man any thing, but to love one another: for he that loveth another hath fulfilled the law. 9 For this, Thou shalt not commit adultery, Thou shalt not kill, Thou shalt not steal, Thou shalt not bear false witness, Thou shalt not covet; and if *there be* any other commandment, it is briefly comprehended in this saying, namely, Thou shalt love thy neighbour as thyself. 10 Love worketh no ill to his neighbour: therefore love *is* the fulfilling of the law.

1

The Ten: Exod. 20: 3 T H O U   S H A L T HAVE NO OTHER GODS BEFORE ME.

Mark 12: 29 . . . Jesus answered him, The first of all the commandments *is*, Hear, O Israel; The Lord our God is one Lord: 30 And thou shalt love the Lord thy God with all thy heart, and with all thy soul, and with all thy mind, and with all thy strength: this *is* the first com-

70

mandment. 31 And the second *is* like, *namely* this, Thou shalt love thy neighbour as thyself. There is none other commandment greater than these.

See GOD.

2

Exod. 20: 4 THOU SHALT NOT MAKE UNTO THEE ANY GRAVEN IMAGE, or any likeness *of any thing* that *is* in heaven above, or that *is* in the earth beneath, or that *is* in the water under the earth: 5 Thou shalt not bow down thyself to them, nor serve them: . . .

John 4: 24 God *is* a Spirit: and they that worship him must worship *him* in spirit and in truth.

I. Cor. 6: 9 . . . Be not deceived: neither fornicators, nor idolaters, . . . 10 . . . shall inherit the kingdom of God.

Rev. 21: 8 . . . Idolaters, and all liars, shall have their part in the lake which burneth with fire and brimstone: which is the second death.

3

Exod. 20: 7 THOU SHALT NOT TAKE THE NAME OF THE LORD THY GOD IN VAIN: for the Lord will not hold him guiltless that taketh his name in vain.

Matt. 5: 33 . . . Ye have heard that it hath been said by them of old time, Thou shalt not forswear thyself, but shalt perform unto the Lord thine oaths: 34 But I say unto you, Swear not at all; neither by heaven; for it is God's throne: 35 Nor by the earth; for it is his footstool: neither by Jerusalem; for it is the city of the great King. 36 Neither shalt thou swear by thy head, because thou canst not make one hair white or black.   37 But let your communication be, Yea, yea; Nay,

nay: for whatsoever is more than these cometh
of evil.

Luke 1: 49 . . . Holy *is* his name.

See BLASPHEMY; REVERENCE.

4

Exod. 20: 8 REMEMBER THE SABBATH
DAY, TO KEEP IT HOLY. 9 Six days shalt
thou labour, and do all thy work: 10 But the
seventh day *is* the sabbath of the Lord thy God:
in it thou shalt not do any work, thou, nor thy
son, nor thy daughter, thy manservant, nor thy
maidservant, nor thy cattle, nor thy stranger that
is within thy gates: 11 For *in* six days the Lord
made heaven and earth, the sea, and all that in
them *is,* and rested the seventh day: wherefore
the Lord blessed the sabbath day, and hallowed it.

Mark. 2: 27 . . . The sabbath was made for
man, and not man for the sabbath: 28 Therefore
the Son of man is Lord also of the sabbath.

See SABBATH.

5

Exod. 20: 12 HONOUR T H Y F A T H E R
AND THY MOTHER: that thy days may be long
upon the land which the Lord thy God giveth thee.

Matt. 15: 4 . . . God commanded, saying,
Honour thy father and mother: and, He that curseth father or mother, let him die the death.

See CHILDREN, Duties of.

6

Exod. 20: 13 THOU SHALT NOT KILL.

Matt. 5: 21 Ye have heard that it was said by
them of old time, Thou shalt not kill; and whosoever shall kill shall be in danger of the judgment:
22 But I say unto you, That whosoever is angry

with his brother without a cause shall be in danger of the judgment: and whosoever shall say to his brother, Raca, shall be in danger of the council: but whosoever shall say, Thou fool, shall be in danger of hell fire.
See MURDER.

7

Exod. 20: 14 THOU SHALT NOT COMMIT ADULTERY.
Matt. 5: 27 Ye have heard that it was said by them of old time, Thou shalt not commit adultery: 28 But I say unto you, That whosoever looketh on a woman to lust after her hath committed adultery with her already in his heart.
See LASCIVIOUSNESS.

8

Exod. 20: 15 THOU SHALT NOT STEAL.
Mark 10: 19 Thou knowest the commandments, Do not commit adultery, Do not kill, Do not steal, Do not bear false witness, Defraud not, Honour thy father and mother.
See THEFT.

9

Exod. 20: 16 THOU SHALT NOT BEAR FALSE WITNESS AGAINST THY NEIGHBOUR.
Matt. 12: 36 . . . Every idle word that men shall speak, they shall give account thereof in the day of judgment. 37 For by thy words thou shalt be justified, and by thy words thou shalt be condemned.
See ACCUSATION, False.

10

Exod. 20: 17 THOU SHALT NOT COVET

thy neighbour's house, thou shalt not covet thy neighbour's wife, nor his manservant, nor his maidservant, nor his ox, nor his ass, nor any thing that *is* thy neighbours'.

Luke 12: 15 . . . Take heed, and beware of covetousness: for a man's life consisteth not in the abundance of the things which he possesseth.

See COVETOUSNESS.

COMMUNION—LORD'S SUPPER

Matt. 26: 26 . . . As they were eating, Jesus took bread, and blessed *it*, and brake *it*, and gave *it* to the disciples, and said, Take, eat; this is my body. 27 And he took the cup, and gave thanks, and gave *it* to them, saying, Drink ye all of it; 28 For this is my blood of the new testament, which is shed for many for the remission of sins. 29 But I say unto you, I will not drink henceforth of this fruit of the vine, until that day when I drink it new with you in my Father's kingdom. 30 And when they had sung a hymn, they went out into the mount of Olives.

Acts 2: 42 . . . They continued steadfastly in the apostles' doctrine and fellowship, and in breaking of bread, and in prayers. 46 And they, continuing daily with one accord in the temple, and breaking bread from house to house, did eat their meat with gladness and singleness of heart.

Acts 20: 7 . . . Upon the first *day* of the week, when the disciples came together to break bread, Paul preached unto them, . . .

I. Cor. 10: 16 The cup of blessing which we bless, is it not the communion of the blood of Christ? The bread which we break, is it not the communion of the body of Christ? 17 For we *being* many are one bread, *and* one body: for we

74

are all partakers of that one bread. 21 Ye cannot drink the cup of the Lord, and the cup of devils: ye cannot be partakers of the Lord's table, and of the table of devils. 22 Do we provoke the Lord to jealousy? are we stronger than he?

I. Cor. 11: 20 When ye come together . . . into one place, *this* is not to eat the Lord's supper. 21 For in eating every one taketh before *other* his own supper: and one is hungry, and another is drunken. 22 What! have ye not houses to eat and to drink in? or despise ye the church of God, and shame them that have not? What shall I say to you? shall I praise you in this? I praise *you* not. 23 For I have received of the Lord that which also I delivered unto you, That the Lord Jesus, the *same* night in which he was betrayed, took bread: 24 And when he had given thanks, he brake *it*, and said, Take, eat; this is my body, which is broken for you: this do in remembrance of me. 25 After the same manner also *he took* the cup, when he had supped, saying, This cup is the new testament in my blood: this do ye, as oft as ye drink *it*, in remembrance of me. 26 For as often as ye eat this bread, and drink this cup, ye do shew the Lord's death till he come. 27 Wherefore whosoever shall eat this bread, and drink *this* cup of the Lord, unworthily, shall be guilty of the body and blood of the Lord. 28 But let a man examine himself, and so let him eat of *that* bread, and drink of *that* cup. 29 For he that eateth and drinketh unworthily, eateth and drinketh damnation to himself, not discerning the Lord's body. 30 For this cause many *are* weak and sickly among you, and many sleep. 31 For if we would judge ourselves, we should not be judged. 32 But when we are judged, we are chastened of the Lord,

75

that we should not be condemned with the world.
33 Wherefore, my brethren, when ye come together to eat, tarry one for another. 34 And if
any man hunger, let him eat at home; that ye
come not together unto condemnation . . . .

CONCEIT

Prov. 3: 5 Trust in the Lord with all thine
heart; and lean not unto thine own understanding.
7 Be not wise in thine own eyes: fear the Lord,
and depart from evil.

Prov. 12: 15 The way of a fool *is* right in his
own eyes: but he that hearkeneth unto counsel *is*
wise.

Prov. 26: 5 Answer a fool according to his
folly, lest he be wise in his own conceit. 12 Seest
thou a man wise in his own conceit? *there is* more
hope of a fool than of him. 16 The sluggard *is*
wiser in his own conceit than seven men that can
render a reason.

Prov. 28: 11 The rich man *is* wise in his own
conceit; but the poor that hath understanding
searcheth him out. 26 He that trusteth in his
own heart is a fool: but whoso walketh wisely, he
shall be delivered.

Isa. 5: 21 Woe unto *them that are* wise in
their own eyes, and prudent in their own sight!

Jer. 9: 23 Thus saith the Lord, Let not the wise
man glory in his wisdom, neither let the mighty
man glory in his might, let not the rich *man* glory
in his riches: 24 But let him that glorieth glory
in this, that he understandeth and knoweth me,
that I *am* the Lord which exercise loving kindness,
judgment, and righteousness, in the earth: . . .

Matt. 18: 1 At the same time came the disciples unto Jesus, saying, Who is the greatest in
the kingdom of heaven? 2 And Jesus called a

little child unto him, and set him in the midst of them,   3 And said, Verily I say unto you, Except ye be converted, and become as little children, ye shall not enter into the kingdom of heaven.   4 Whosoever therefore shall humble himself as this little child, the same is greatest in the kingdom of heaven.   5 And whoso shall receive one such little child in my name receiveth me.

Luke 18:   10 Two men went up into the temple to pray; the one a Pharisee, and the other a publican.   11 The Pharisee stood and prayed thus with himself, God, I thank thee, that I am not as other men *are*, extortioners, unjust, adulterers, or even as this publican.   12 I fast twice in the week, I give tithes of all that I possess.   13 And the publican, standing afar off, would not lift up so much as *his* eyes unto heaven, but smote upon his breast, saying, God be merciful to me a sinner.   14 I tell you, this man went down to his house justified *rather* than the other: for every one that exalteth himself shall be abased; and he that humbleth himself shall be exalted.

Rom. 12:   3 . . . I say, through the grace given unto me, to every man that is among you, not to think *of himself* more highly than he ought to think; but to think soberly, according as God hath dealt to every man the measure of faith.   16 . . . Mind not high things, but condescend to men of low estate.   Be not wise in your own conceits.

See BOASTING; PRESUMPTION; PRIDE; SELF-EX-ALTATION; SELF-RIGHTEOUSNESS.

CONFIDENCE

Psa. 20:   7 Some *trust* in chariots, and some in horses: but we will remember the name of the Lord our God.

Psa. 23:   4 Yea, though I walk through the

valley of the shadow of death, I will fear no evil: for thou *art* with me; thy rod and thy staff they comfort me. 6 Surely goodness and mercy shall follow me all the days of my life: and I will dwell in the house of the Lord for ever.

Psa. 27: 1 The Lord *is* my light and my salvation; whom shall I fear? the Lord *is* the strength of my life; of whom shall I be afraid?

Psa. 49: 6 They that trust in their wealth, and boast themselves in the multitude of their riches; 7 None *of them* can by any means redeem his brother, nor give to God a ransom for him:

Psa. 56: 4 . . . In God I have put my trust; I will not fear what flesh can do unto me.

Prov. 28: 1 The wicked flee when no man pursueth: but the righteous are bold as a lion. 26 He that trusteth in his own heart is a fool: . . .

Zech. 4: 6 . . . Not by might, nor by power, but by my Spirit, saith the Lord of hosts.

Mark 10: 24 . . . How hard is it for them that trust in riches to enter into the kingdom of God!

Luke 12: 19 . . . I will say to my soul, Soul, thou hast much goods laid up for many years; take thine ease, eat, drink, *and* be merry. 20 But God said unto him, *Thou* fool, this night thy soul shall be required of thee: then whose shall those things be, which thou has provided?

II. Cor. 1: 9 . . . We should not trust in ourselves, but in God which raiseth the dead:

Gal. 6: 7 Be not deceived; God is not mocked: for whatsoever a man soweth, that shall he also reap.

I. Thess. 5: 2 . . . The day of the Lord so

cometh as a thief in the night. 3 For when they shall say, Peace and safety; then sudden destruction cometh upon them, as travail upon a woman with child; and they shall not escape.

Heb. 3: 12 Take heed, brethren, lest there be in any of you an evil heart of unbelief, in departing from the living God. 14 For we are made partakers of Christ, if we hold the beginning of our confidence steadfast unto the end;

Heb. 10: 35 Cast not away . . . your confidence, which hath great recompense of reward. 36 For ye have need of patience, that, after ye have done the will of God, ye might receive the promise.

Heb. 13: 5 . . . He hath said, I will never leave thee, nor forsake thee. 6 So that we may boldly say, The Lord is my helper, and I will not fear what man shall do unto me.

Jas. 4: 13 Go to now, ye that say, To day or to morrow we will go into such a city, and continue there a year, and buy and sell, and get gain: 14 Whereas ye know not what *shall be* on the morrow. For what *is* your life? It is even a vapour, that appeareth for a little time, and then vanisheth away. 15 For that ye *ought* to say, If the Lord will, we shall live, and do this, or that.

See COURAGE; FAITH.

CONSCIENCE

Prov. 28: 1 The wicked flee when no man pursueth: but the righteous are bold as a lion.

Acts. 24: 16 . . . Herein do I exercise myself, to have always a conscience void of offence toward God, and *toward* men.

Rom. 14: 5 One man esteemeth one day above another: another esteemeth every day *alike*. Let every man be fully persuaded in his own mind.

6 He that regardeth the day, regarded *it* unto the Lord; and he that regardeth not the day, to the Lord he doth not regard *it*. He that eateth, eateth to the Lord, for he giveth God thanks; and he that eateth not, to the Lord he eateth not, and giveth God thanks. 14 I know, and am persuaded by the Lord Jesus, that *there is* nothing unclean of itself: but to him that esteemeth any thing to be unclean, to him *it is* unclean. 15 But if thy brother be grieved with *thy* meat, now walkest thou not charitably. Destroy not him with thy meat, for whom Christ died. 23 And he that doubteth is damned if he eat, because *he eateth* not of faith: for whatsoever *is* not of faith is sin.

I. Cor. 10: 27 If any of them that believe not bid you *to a feast*, and ye be disposed to go; whatsoever is set before you, eat, asking no question for conscience' sake.

II. Cor. 1: 12 . . . Our rejoicing is this, the testimony of our conscience, that in simplicity and godly sincerity, not with fleshly wisdom, but by the grace of God, we have had our conversation in the world, . . .

I. Tim. 1: 5 Now the end of the commandment is charity out of a pure heart, and *of* a good conscience, and *of* faith unfeigned:

Tit. 1: 15 Unto the pure all things *are* pure: but unto them that are defiled and unbelieving *is* nothing pure; but even their mind and conscience is defiled.

Heb. 10: 22 Let us draw near with a true heart in full assurance of faith, having our hearts sprinkled from an evil conscience, and our bodies washed with pure water. 26 . . . If we sin wilfully after that we have received the knowledge of the truth, there remaineth no more sacrifice for sins,   27 But a certain fearful looking for of judgment and fiery indignation, which shall devour the adversaries.

Heb. 13 :   18 Pray for us : for we trust we have a good conscience, in all things willing to live honestly.

I. Pet. 2 :   19 . . . This *is* thankworthy, if a man for conscience toward God endure grief, suffering wrongfully.

I. Pet. 3 :   15 . . . Sanctify the Lord God in your hearts : . . . 16 Having a good conscience;

. . . 21 . . . Baptism doth also now save us, (not the putting away of the filth of the flesh, but the answer of a good conscience toward God,) by the resurrection of Jesus Christ:

I. John 3 :   20 . . . If our heart condemn us, God is greater than our heart, and knoweth all things.   21 Beloved, if our heart condemn us not, *then* have we confidence toward God.

See HEART; MIND.

CONSECRATION

Matt. 13 :   44 . . . The kingdom of heaven is like unto treasure hid in a field; the which when a man hath found, he hideth, and for joy thereof goeth and selleth all that he hath, and buyeth that field.   45 Again, the kingdom of heaven is like unto a merchantman, seeking goodly pearls: 46 Who, when he had found one pearl of great price, went and sold all that he had, and bought it.

Rom. 6 :   12 Let not sin . . . reign in your mortal body, that ye should obey it in the lusts thereof.   13 Neither yield ye your members *as* instruments of unrighteousness unto sin: but yield yourselves unto God, as those that are alive from the dead, and your members *as* instruments of righteousness unto God.   16 Know ye not, that tc whom ye yield yourselves servants to obey, his servants ye are to whom ye obey; whether of sin unto death, or of obedience unto righteousness? 19 I speak after the manner of men because of the infirmity of your flesh: for as ye have yielded your members servants to uncleanness and to iniquity unto iniquity; even so now yield your members servants to righteousness unto holiness.

Rom. 12: 1 I beseech you . . . , brethren, by the mercies of God, that ye present your bodies a living sacrifice, holy, acceptable unto God, *which is* your reasonable service. 2 And be not conformed to this world: but be ye transformed by the renewing of your mind, that ye may prove what *is* that good, and acceptable, and perfect will of God.

See SPIRITUAL.

CONSISTENCY

Matt. 6: 24 No man can serve two masters: for either he will hate the one, and love the other; or else he will hold to the one, and despise the other. Ye cannot serve God and mammon.

Matt. 7: 3 . . . Why beholdest thou the mote that is in thy brother's eye, but considerest not the beam that is in thine own eye? 4 Or how wilt thou say to thy brother, Let me pull out the mote out of thine eye; and, behold, a beam *is* in thine own eye? 5 Thou hypocrite, first cast out the beam out of thine own eye; and then shalt thou see clearly to cast out the mote out of thy brother's eye.

Rom. 14: 22 . . . Happy *is* he that condemneth not himself in that thing which he alloweth.

I. Cor. 10: 21 Ye cannot drink the cup of the Lord, and the cup of devils: ye cannot be partakers of the Lord's table, and of the table of

82

devils.

See STEADFASTNESS; also INCONSISTENCY.

CONTENTMENT

Psa. 37: 7 Rest in the Lord, and wait patiently for him: fret not thyself because of him who prospereth in his way, because of the man who bringeth wicked devices to pass. 16 A little that a righteous man hath *is* better than the riches of many wicked.

Prov. 16. 8 Better *is* a little with righteousness, than great revenues without right.

Prov. 17: 1 Better *is* a dry morsel, and quietness therewith, than a house full of sacrifices *with* strife. 22 A merry heart doeth good *like* a medicine: . . .

Prov. 30: 8 . . . Give me neither poverty nor riches; feed me with food convenient for me: 9 Lest I be full, and deny *thee*, and say, Who *is* the Lord? or lest I be poor, and steal, and take the name of my God *in vain.*

Ecc. 2: 24 *There is* nothing better for a man, *than* that he should eat and drink, and *that* he should make his soul enjoy good in his labour. This also I saw, that it *was* from the hand of God.

Ecc. 4: 6 Better *is* a handful *with* quietness, than both the hands full *with* travail and vexation of spirit.

Ecc. 5: 12 The sleep of a labouring man *is* sweet, whether he eat little or much: but the abundance of the rich will not suffer him to sleep.

Ecc. 6: 9 Better *is* the sight of the eyes than the wandering of the desire: . . .

Ecc. 9: 7 Go thy way, eat thy bread with joy, and drink thy wine with a merry heart; for God now accepteth thy works. 8 Let thy garments be always white; and let thy head lack no ointment.

9 Live joyfully with the wife whom thou lovest all the days of the life of thy vanity, which he hath given thee under the sun, all the days of thy vanity: for that *is* thy portion in *this* life, and in thy labour which thou takest under the sun. 10 Whatsoever thy hand findeth to do, do *it* with thy might; for *there is* no work, nor device, nor knowledge, nor wisdom, in the grave, whither thou goest.

I. Cor. 7: 17 . . . As God hath distributed to every man, as the Lord hath called every one, so let him walk. . . . 20 Let every man abide in the same calling wherein he was called.

Gal. 5: 26 Let us not be desirous of vainglory, provoking one another, envying one another.

Philip. 4: 11 . . . I have learned, in whatsoever state I am, *therewith* to be content. 12 I know both how to be abased, and I know how to abound: every where and in all things I am instructed both to be full and to be hungry, both to abound and to suffer need. 13 I can do all things through Christ which strengtheneth me.

I. Tim. 6: 6 . . . Godliness with contentment is great gain. 7 For we brought nothing into *this* world, *and it is* certain we can carry nothing out. 8 And having food and raiment, let us be therewith content.

Heb. 13: 5 *Let your* conversation *be* without covetousness; *and be* content with such things as ye have: for he hath said, I will never leave thee, nor forsake thee. 6 So that we may boldly say, The Lord *is* my helper, and I will not fear what man shall do unto me.

See HAPPINESS; PEACE.

CONTRACTS

Gal. 3: 15. . . Though *it be* but a man's covenant, yet *if it be* confirmed, no man disannulleth, or addeth thereto.
See SURETYSHIP.

COUNSEL

Prov. 1: 5 A wise *man* will hear, and will increase learning; and a man of understanding shall attain unto wise counsels: 24 Because I have called, and ye refused; I have stretched out my hand, and no man regarded; 25 But ye have set at nought all my counsel, and would none of my reproof: 26 I also will laugh at your calamity; I will mock when your fear cometh; 27 When your fear cometh as desolation, and your destruction cometh as a whirlwind; when distress and anguish cometh· upon you. 28 Then shall they call upon me, but I will not answer; they shall seek me early, but they shall not find me: 29 For that they hated knowledge, and did not choose the fear of the Lord: 30 They would none of my counsel: they despised all my reproof. 31 Therefore shall they eat of the fruit of their own way, and be filled with their own devices. 32 For the turning away of the simple shall slay them, and the prosperity of fools shall destroy them. 33 But whoso hearkeneth unto me shall dwell safely, and shall be quiet from fear of evil.

Prov. 9: 8 Reprove not a scorner, lest he hate thee: rebuke a wise man, and he will love thee. 9 Give *instruction* to a wise *man,* and he will be yet wiser: teach a just *man,* and he will increase in learning.

Prov. 11: 14 Where no counsel *is,* the people fall: but in the multitude of counsellors *there is* safety.

Prov. 12:   15 The way of a fool *is* right in his own eyes: but he that hearkeneth unto counsel *is* wise.

Prov. 15:   22 Without counsel purposes are disappointed: but in the multitude of counsellors they are established.

Prov. 19: 20 Hear counsel, and receive instruction, that thou mayest be wise in thy latter end. 21 *There are* many devices in a man's heart; nevertheless the counsel of the Lord, that shall stand.

Prov. 27:   9 Ointment and perfume rejoice the heart: so *doth* the sweetness of a man's friend by hearty counsel.

See INSTRUCTION; PRUDENCE.

COURAGE

Prov. 28:   1 The wicked flee when no man pursueth: but the righteous are bold as a lion.

Mark 5:   36 . . . Be not afraid, only believe.

I. Cor. 16:   13 Watch ye, stand fast in the faith, quit you like men, be strong.

Philip. 1:   27 . . . Let your conversation be as it becometh the gospel of Christ: . . . that ye stand fast in one spirit, with one mind striving together for the faith of the gospel; 28 And in nothing terrified by your adversaries: which is to them an evident token of perdition, but to you of salvation, and that of God.   29 For unto you it is given in the behalf of Christ, not only to believe on him, but also to suffer for his sake;

II. Tim. 1:   7 . . . God hath not given us the spirit of fear; but of power, and of love, and of a sound mind.   8 Be not thou therefore ashamed of the testimony of our Lord, . . .

I. Pet. 3:   13 . . . Who *is* he that will harm you, if ye be followers of that which is good?

I. Pet. 5:   8 Be sober, be vigilant; because your

adversary the devil, as a roaring lion, walketh about, seeking whom he may devour: 9 Whom resist steadfast in the faith, knowing that the same afflictions are accomplished in your brethren that are in the world.

See CONFIDENCE.

COURTESY

Luke 6: 31 . . . As ye would that men should do to you, do ye also to them likewise.

I. Cor. 10: 27 If any of them that believe not bid you *to a feast,* and ye be disposed to go; whatsoever is set before you, eat, asking no question for conscience' sake.

I. Pet. 3: 8 . . . *Be ye* all of one mind, having compassion one of another; love as brethren, *be* pitiful, *be* courteous:

See DIPLOMACY; TACT.

COVETOUSNESS

Exod. 20: 17 Thou shalt not covet . . . any thing that *is* thy neighbour's.

Job 31: 24 If I have made gold my hope, or have said to the fine gold, *Thou art* my confidence; 28 This also *were* an iniquity *to be punished by* the judge: for I should have denied the God *that is* above.

Psa. 10: 3 . . . The wicked boasteth of his heart's desire, and blesseth the covetous, *whom* the Lord abhorreth.

Prov. 21: 25 The desire of the slothful killeth him; for his hands refuse to labour. 26 He coveteth greedily all the day long: but the righteous giveth and spareth not.

Prov. 23. 4 Labour not to be rich: cease from thine own wisdom. 5 Wilt thou set thine eyes upon that which is not? for *riches* certainly make themselves wings; they fly away as an eagle toward heaven.

Ecc. 5: 10 He that loveth silver shall not be satisfied with silver; nor he that loveth abundance with increase: this *is* also vanity. 11 When goods increase, they are increased that eat them: and what good *is there* to the owners thereof, saving the beholding *of them* with their eyes?

Isa. 5: 8 Woe unto them that join house to house, *that* lay field to field, till *there be* no place, that they may be placed alone in the midst of the earth!

Matt. 6: 19 Lay not up for yourselves treasures upon earth, where moth and rust doth corrupt, and where thieves break through and steal: 20 But lay up for yourselves treasures in heaven, where neither moth nor rust doth corrupt, and where thieves do not break through nor steal: 21 For where your treasure is, there will your heart be also. 24 No man can serve two masters: for either he will hate the one, and love the other; or else he will hold to the one, and despise the other. Ye cannot serve God and mammon. 25 Therefore I say unto you, Take no thought for your life, what ye shall eat, or what ye shall drink; nor yet for your body, what ye shall put on. Is not the life more than meat, and the body than raiment? 33 But seek ye first the kingdom of God, and his righteousness; and all these things shall be added unto you.

Matt. 13: 22 He . . . that received seed among the thorns is he that heareth the word; and the care of this world, and the deceitfulness of riches, choke the word, and he becometh unfruitful.

Matt. 16: 26 . . . What is a man profited, if

88

he shall gain the whole world, and lose his own soul? or what shall a man give in exchange for his soul?

Mark 7: 21 . . . From within, out of the heart of men, proceed evil thoughts, . . . 22 . . . covetousness, . . . 23 All these evil things come from within, and defile the man.

Luke 12: 15 . . . Take heed, and beware of covetousness: for a man's life consisteth not in the abundance of the things which he possesseth.

Rom. 13: 9 . . . Thou shalt not commit adultery, Thou shalt not kill, Thou shalt not steal, Thou shalt not bear false witness, Thou shalt not covet; and if *there be* any other commandment, it is briefly comprehended in this saying, namely, Thou shalt love thy neighbour as thyself.

I. Cor. 5: 11 . . . If any man that is called a brother be a fornicator, or covetous, or an idolater, or a railer, or a drunkard, or an extortioner; with such a one no not to eat.

Eph. 5: 3 . . . Fornication, and all uncleanness, or covetousness, let it not be once named among you, as becometh saints;

Col. 3: 2 Set your affection on things above, not on things on the earth. 5 Mortify therefore your members which are upon the earth; fornication, uncleanness, inordinate affection, evil concupiscence, and covetousness, which is idolatry: 6 For which things' sake the wrath of God cometh on the children of disobedience:

I. Tim. 6: 7 . . . We brought nothing into *this* world, *and it is* certain we can carry nothing out. 8 And having food and raiment, let us be therewith content. 9 But they that will be rich fall into temptation and a snare, and *into* many foolish and hurtful lusts, which drown men in destruction

and perdition. 10 For the love of money is the
root of all evil: which while some coveted after,
they have erred from the faith, and pierced themselves through with many sorrows. 11 But thou,
O man of God, flee these things; and follow after
righteousness, godliness, faith, love, patience,
meekness.

II. Tim. 3: 2 . . . Men shall be lovers of their
own selves, covetous, . . . 5 Having a form of
godliness, but denying the power thereof: from
such turn away.

Heb. 13: 5 *Let your* conversation *be* without
covetousness; *and be* content with such things as
ye have: for he hath said, I will never leave thee,
nor forsake thee.

I. Pet. 5: 1 The elders which are among you I
exhort, . . . 2 Feed the flock of God which is
among you, taking the oversight *thereof,* not by
constraint, but willingly; not for filthy lucre, but
of a ready mind;

I. John 2: 15 Love not the world, neither the
things *that are* in the world. If any man love the
world, the love of the Father is not in him. 16
For all that *is* in the world, the lust of the flesh,
and the lust of the eyes, and the pride of life, is
not of the Father, but is of the world. 17 And
the world passeth away, and the lust thereof: but
he that doeth the will of God abideth for ever.

See AVARICE; SELFISHNESS; UNJUST GAIN.

CRIMINAL OFFENSES

Matt. 15: 19 . . . Out of the heart proceed
evil thoughts, murders, adulteries, fornications,
thefts, false witness, blasphemies: 20 These are
the things which defile a man: . . .

Rom. 1: 18 . . . The wrath of God is revealed
from heaven against all ungodliness and unright-

eousness of men, who hold the truth in unrighteousness; 28 And even as they did not like to
retain God in *their* knowledge, God gave them
over to a reprobate mind, to do those things which
are not convenient; 29 Being filled with all unrighteousness, fornication, wickedness, covetousness, maliciousness; full of envy, murder, debate,
deceit, malignity; whisperers, 30 Backbiters,
haters of God, despiteful, proud, boasters, inventors of evil things, disobedient to parents, 31
Without understanding, covenant-breakers, without natural affection, implacable, unmerciful:
32 Who, knowing the judgment of God, that they
which commit such things are worthy of death,
not only do the same, but have pleasure in them
that do them.

Rom. 13. 9 . . . Thou shalt not commit adultery, Thou shalt not kill, Thou shalt not steal,
Thou shalt not bear false witness, Thou shalt not
covet; and if *there be* any other commandment, it
is briefly comprehended in this saying, namely,
Thou shalt love thy neighbour as thyself.

I. Cor. 5: 11 . . . I have written unto you not
to keep company, if any man that is called a
brother be a fornicator, or covetous, or an idolater, or a railer, or a drunkard, or an extortioner;
with such a one no not to eat.

Gal. 5: 19 . . . The works of the flesh are
manifest, which are *these*, Adultery, fornication,
uncleanness, lasciviousness, 20 Idolatry, witchcraft, hatred, variance, emulations, wrath, strife,
seditions, heresies, 21 Envyings, murders,
drunkenness, revellings, and such like: of the
which I tell you before, as I have also told *you* in
time past, that they which do such things shall
not inherit the kingdom of God.

See LASCIVIOUSNESS; WICKED; also ACCUSATION, False; EXTORTION; MURDER, etc.

DEATH

The Last Sleep: Psa. 23: 4 Yea, though I walk through the valley of the shadow of death, I will fear no evil: for thou *art* with me; thy rod and thy staff they comfort me.

Psa. 37: 35 I have seen the wicked in great power, and spreading himself like a green bay tree. 36 Yet he passed away, and, lo, he *was* not: yea, I sought him, but he could not be found. 37 Mark the perfect *man,* and behold the upright: for the end of *that* man *is* peace.

Psa. 49: 10 . . . Wise men die, likewise the fool and the brutish person perish, and leave their wealth to others.

Psa. 89: 48 What man *is he that* liveth, and shall not see death? shall he deliver his soul from the hand of the grave? . . .

Psa. 103: 15 *As for* man, his days *are* as grass: as a flower of the field, so he flourisheth. 16 For the wind passeth over it, and it is gone; and the place thereof shall know it no more.

Psa. 116: 15 Precious in the sight of the Lord *is* the death of his saints.

Prov. 11: 7 When a wicked man dieth, *his* expectation shall perish: and the hope of unjust *men* perisheth.

Ecc. 9: 10 Whatsoever thy hand findeth to do, do *it* with thy might; for *there is* no work, nor device, nor knowledge, nor wisdom, in the grave, whither thou goest.

Ecc. 12: 7 Then shall the dust return to the earth as it was: and the spirit shall return unto God who gave it.

Luke 12: 19 . . . I will say to my soul, Soul,

thou hast much goods laid up for many years; take thine ease, eat, drink, *and* be merry. 20 But God said unto him, *Thou* fool, this night thy soul shall be required of thee: then whose shall those things be, which thou hast provided? 21 So *is* he that layeth up treasure for himself, and is not rich toward God.

Luke 20: 34 . . . Jesus . . . said unto them, The children of this world marry, and are given in marriage: 35 But they which shall be accounted worthy to obtain that world, and the resurrection from the dead, neither marry, nor are given in marriage: 36 Neither can they die any more: for they are equal unto the angels; and are the children of God, being the children of the resurrection. 37 Now that the dead are raised, even Moses shewed at the bush, when he calleth the Lord the God of Abraham, and the God of Isaac, and the God of Jacob. 38 For he is not a God of the dead, but of the living: for all live unto him.

John 5: 21 . . . As the Father raiseth up the dead, and quickeneth *them;* even so the Son quickeneth whom he will. 28 Marvel not at this: for the hour is coming, in the which all that are in the graves shall hear his voice, 29 And shall come forth; they that have done good, unto the resurrection of life; and they that have done evil, unto the resurrection of damnation.

John 9: 4 I must work the works of him that sent me, while it is day: the night cometh, when no man can work.

John 15: 13 Greater love hath no man than this, that a man lay down his life for his friends.

Rom. 5: 12 Wherefore, as by one man sin entered into the world, and death by sin; and so

death passed upon all men, for that all have
sinned: 20 Moreover the law entered, that the
offence might abound. But where sin abounded,
grace did much more abound: 21 That as sin
hath reigned unto death, even so might grace
reign through righteousness unto eternal life by
Jesus Christ our Lord.

Rom. 14: 7 . . . None of us liveth to himself,
and no man dieth to himself. 8 For whether we
live, we live unto the Lord; and whether we die,
we die unto the Lord: whether we live therefore,
or die, we are the Lord's. 9 For to this end
Christ both died, and rose, and revived, that he
might be Lord both of the dead and living.

I. Cor. 15: 20 . . . Now is Christ risen from
the dead, *and* become the firstfruits of them that
slept. 21 For since by man *came* death, by man
came also the resurrection of the dead. 22 For
as in Adam all die, even so in Christ shall all be
made alive. 26 The last enemy *that* shall be destroyed *is* death. 51 Behold, I shew you a mystery; We shall not all sleep, but we shall all be
changed, 52 In a moment, in the twinkling of an
eye, at the last trump: for the trumpet shall sound,
and the dead shall be raised incorruptible, and we
shall be changed. 53 For this corruptible must
put on incorruption, and this mortal *must* put on
immortality. 54 So when this corruptible shall
have put on incorruption, and this mortal shall
have put on immortality, then shall be brought
to pass the saying that is written, Death is swallowed up in victory. 55 O death, where *is* thy
sting? O grave, where *is* thy victory? 56 The
sting of death *is* sin; and the strength of sin *is*
the law. 57 But thanks *be* to God, which giveth
us the victory through our Lord Jesus Christ.

II. Cor. 5: 1 . . . We know that, if our earthly house of *this* tabernacle were dissolved, we have a building of God, a house not made with hands, eternal in the heavens. 8 We are confident, *I say,* and willing rather to be absent from the body, and to be present with the Lord.

Philip. 1: 20 According to my earnest expectation and *my* hope, that in nothing I shall be ashamed, but *that* with all boldness, as always, *so* now also Christ shall be magnified in my body, whether *it be* by life, or by death. 21 For to me to live *is* Christ, and to die *is* gain.

I. Thess. 4: 13 . . . I would not have you to be ignorant, brethren, concerning them which are asleep, that ye sorrow not, even as others which have no hope. 14 For if we believe that Jesus died and rose again, even so them also which sleep in Jesus will God bring with him.

I. Thess. 5: 9 . . . God hath not appointed us to wrath, but to obtain salvation by our Lord Jesus Christ, 10 Who died for us, that, whether we wake or sleep, we should live together with him.

I. Tim. 6: 7 . . . We brought nothing into *this* world, *and it is* certain we can carry nothing out.

Heb. 2: 9 . . . Jesus . . . was made a little lower than the angels for the suffering of death, crowned with glory and honour; that he by the grace of God should taste death for every man. 14 Forasmuch then as the children are partakers of flesh and blood, he also himself likewise took part of the same; that through death he might destroy him that had the power of death, that is, the devil; 15 And deliver them, who through fear of death were all their lifetime subject to bondage.

Heb. 9: 27 . . . It is appointed unto men once to die, but after this the judgment:

I. Pet. 1: 24 . . . All flesh *is* as grass, and all the glory of man as the flower of grass. The grass withereth, and the flower thereof falleth away:

Rev. 14: 13 . . . Blessed *are* the dead which die in the Lord from henceforth: Yea, saith the Spirit, that they may rest from their labours; and their works do follow them.

Rev. 20: 12 . . . I saw the dead, small and great, stand before God; and the books were opened: and another book was opened, which is *the book* of life: and the dead were judged out of those things which were written in the·books, according to their works. 13 And the sea gave up the dead which were in it; and death and hell ·delivered up the dead which were in them: and they were judged every man according to their works.

Rev. 21: 4 . . . God shall wipe away all tears from their eyes; and there shall be no more death, neither sorrow, nor crying, neither shall there be any more pain: for the former things are passed away.

See HEAVEN; HELL; IMMORTALITY.

The Second: Prov. 14: 12 There is a way which seemeth right unto a man; but the end thereof *are* the ways of death.

Ezek. 18: 4 .. . . The soul that sinneth, it shall die. 21 But if the wicked will turn from all his sins that he hath committed, and keep all my statutes, and do that which is lawful and right, he shall surely live, he shall not die.· 23 Have I any pleasure at all that the wicked should die? saith the Lord God: *and* not that he should

return from his ways, and live? 24 But when the
righteous turneth away from his righteousness,
and committeth iniquity, *and* doeth according to
all the abominations that the wicked *man* doeth,
shall he live? All his righteousness that he hath
done shall not be mentioned: in his trespass that
he hath trespassed, and in his sin that he hath
sinned, in them shall he die.

Ezek. 33: 8 When I say unto the wicked, O
wicked *man*, thou shalt surely die; if thou dost not
speak to warn the wicked from his way, that
wicked *man* shall die in his iniquity; but his blood
will I require at thine hand. 9 Nevertheless, if
thou warn the wicked of his way to turn from
it; if he do not turn from his way, he shall die in
his inquity; but thou hast delivered thy soul.

Matt. 7: 13 Enter ye in at the strait gate: for
wide *is* the gate, and broad *is* the way, that leadeth
to destruction, and many there be which go in
thereat:

Matt. 10: 28 . . . Fear not them which kill
the body, but are not able to kill the soul: but
rather fear him which is able to destroy both soul
and body in hell.

Matt. 25: 31 When the Son of man shall come
in his glory, and all the holy angels with him,
then shall he sit upon the throne of his glory:
41 Then shall he say . . . unto them on the left
hand, Depart from me, ye cursed, into everlasting
fire, prepared for the devil and his angels: 42
For I was a hungered, and ye gave me no meat:
I was thirsty, and ye gave me no drink: 43 I
was a stranger, and ye took me not in: naked, and
ye clothed me not: sick, and in prison, and ye
visited me not. 44 Then shall they . . . answer
him, saying, Lord, when saw we thee a hungered,

or athirst, or a stranger, or naked, or sick, or in
prison, and did not minister unto thee? 45 Then
shall he answer them, saying, Verily I say unto
you, Inasmuch as ye did *it* not to one of the least
of these, ye did *it* not to me. 46 And these shall
go away into everlasting punishment: but the
righteous into life eternal.

Mark 9: 43 . . . If thy hand offend thee, cut
it off: it is better for thee to enter into life maimed,
than having two hands to go into hell, into the
fire that never shall be quenched:

Rom. 1: 18 . . . The wrath of God is revealed from heaven against all ungodliness and
unrighteousness of men, who hold the truth in unrighteousness; 29 Being filled with all unrighteousness, fornication, wickedness, covetousness,
maliciousness; full of envy, murder, debate, deceit,
malignity; whisperers, 30 Backbiters, haters of
God, despiteful, proud, boasters, inventors of evil
things, disobedient to parents, 31 Without understanding, covenant-breakers, without natural
affection, implacable, unmerciful: 32 Who,
knowing the judgment of God, that they which
commit such things are worthy of death, not only
do the same, but have pleasure in them that do
them.

Rom. 6: 16 Know ye not, that to whom ye
yield yourselves servants to obey, his servants ye
are to whom ye obey; whether of sin unto death,
or of obedience unto righteousness? 23 . . . The
wages of sin *is* death; but the gift of God *is* eternal
life through Jesus Christ our Lord.

Rom. 8: 6 . . . To be carnally minded *is*
death; but to be spiritually minded *is* life and
peace. 13 For if ye live after the flesh, ye shall
die: but if ye through the Spirit do mortify the

98

deeds of the body, ye shall live.

II. Thess. 1: 7 . . . The Lord Jesus shall be revealed from heaven with his mighty angels, 8 In flaming fire taking vengeance on them that know not God, and that obey not the gospel of our Lord Jesus Christ: 9 Who shall be punished with everlasting destruction from the presence of the Lord, and from the glory of his power;

Jas. 1: 15 . . . When lust hath conceived, it bringeth forth sin; and sin, when it is finished, bringeth forth death.

Jas. 4: 12 There is one lawgiver, who is able to save and to destroy: who art thou that judgest another?

Rev. 2: 11 . . . He that overcometh shall not be hurt of the second death.

Rev. 20: 14 . . . Death and hell were cast into the lake of fire. This is the second death. 15 And whosoever was not found written in the book of life was cast into the lake of fire.

Rev. 21: 8 . . . The fearful, and unbelieving, and the abominable, and murderers, and whoremongers, and sorcerers, and idolaters, and all liars, shall have their part in the lake which burneth with fire and brimstone: which is the second death.

See HELL; IMMORTALITY; WICKED.

DECEIT

Prov. 11: 18 The wicked worketh a deceitful work: but to him that soweth righteousness *shall be* a sure reward.

Prov. 12: 17 *He that* speaketh truth sheweth forth righteousness: but a false witness deceit.

Prov. 24: 28 Be not a witness against thy neighbour without cause; and deceive *not* with thy lips.

Prov. 26: 24 He that hateth dissembleth with his lips, and layeth up deceit within him; 25 When he speaketh fair, believe him not: for *there are* seven abominations in his heart. 26 *Whose* hatred is covered by deceit, his wickedness shall be shewed before the *whole* congregation. 27 Whoso diggeth a pit shall fall therein: and he that rolleth a stone, it will return upon him. 28 A lying tongue hateth *those that are* afflicted by it; and a flattering mouth worketh ruin.

Matt. 19: 18 . . . Jesus said, . . . Thou shalt not bear false witness,

Mark 7: 20 . . . That which cometh out of the man, that defileth the man. 21 For from within, out of the heart of men, proceed evil thoughts, . . . 22 . . . deceit, . . .

II. Cor. 4: 1 . . . Seeing we have this ministry, as we have received mercy, we faint not; 2 But have renounced the hidden things of dishonesty, not walking in craftiness, nor handling the word of God deceitfully; but, by manifestation of the truth, commending ourselves to every man's conscience in the sight of God.

Eph. 5: 6 Let no man deceive you with vain words: for because of these things cometh the wrath of God upon the children of disobedience.

Col. 2: 8 Beware lest any man spoil you through philosophy and vain deceit, after the tradition of men, after the rudiments of the world, and not after Christ.

I. Pet. 2: 1 . . . Laying aside all malice, and all guile, and hypocrisies, and envies, and all evil speakings, 2 As newborn babes, desire the sincere milk of the word, that ye may grow thereby:

I. Pet. 3: 10 . . . He that will love life, and

see good days, let him refrain his tongue from evil, and his lips that they speak no guile:

See ACCUSATION, False; FALSEHOOD; HYPOCRISY.

DEPRAVITY

Psa. 14: 1 The fool hath said in his heart, *There is* no God. . . .

Psa. 94: 11 The Lord knoweth the thoughts of man, that they *are* vanity.

Psa. 130: 3 If thou, Lord, shouldest mark iniquities, O Lord, who shall stand?

Prov. 20: 6 Most men will proclaim every one his own goodness: but a faithful man who can find? 9 Who can say, I have made my heart clean, I am pure from my sin?

Ecc. 7: 20 . . . *There is* not a just man upon earth, that doeth good, and sinneth not. 29 Lo, this only have I found, that God hath made man upright; but they have sought out many inventions.

Ecc. 8: 11 Because sentence against an evil work is not executed speedily, therefore the heart of the sons of men is fully set in them to do evil.

Isa. 53: 6 All we like sheep have gone astray; we have turned every one to his own way; and the Lord hath laid on him the iniquity of us all.

Jer. 17: 9 The heart *is* deceitful above all *things*, and desperately wicked: who can know it?

Matt. 7: 17 . . . Every good tree bringeth forth good fruit; but a corrupt tree bringeth forth evil fruit. 18 A good tree cannot bring forth evil fruit, neither *can* a corrupt tree bring forth good fruit. 19 Every tree that bringeth not forth good fruit is hewn down, and cast into the fire. 20 Wherefore by their fruits ye shall know them.

Matt. 12 :   34 . . . How can ye, being evil, speak good things? for out of the abundance of the heart the mouth speaketh.   35 A good man out of the good treasure of the heart bringeth forth good things: and an evil man out of the evil treasure bringeth forth evil things.

Matt. 15 :   19 . . . Out of the heart proceed evil thoughts, murders, adulteries, fornications, thefts, false witness, blasphemies: 20 These are *the things* which defile a man: . . .

John 3 :   19 . . . This is the condemnation, that light is come into the world, and men loved darkness rather than light, because their deeds were evil.

Rom. 2 :   1 . . . Thou art inexcusable, O man, whosoever thou art that judgest: for wherein thou judgest another, thou condemnest thyself; for thou that judgest doest the same things.

Rom. 3 :   9 What then? are we better *than they?* No, in no wise: for we have before proved both Jews and Gentiles, that they are all under sin; 10 As it is written, There is none righteous, no, not one: 23 For all have sinned, and come short of the glory of God;

Rom. 6 :   19 I speak after the manner of men because of the infirmity of your flesh: for as ye have yielded your members servants to uncleanness and to iniquity unto iniquity; even so now yield your members servants to righteousness unto holiness.   20 For when ye were the servants of sin, ye were free from righteousness.

Rom. 7 :   14 . . . We know that the law is spiritual: but I am carnal, sold under sin.   18 For I know that in me (that is, in my flesh,) dwelleth no good thing: for to will is present with

102

me; but *how* to perform that which is good I find not. 19 For the good that I would, I do not: but the evil which I would not, that I do. 20 Now if I do that I would not, it is no more I that do it, but sin that dwelleth in me. 21 I find then a law, that, when I would do good, evil is present with me. 22 For I delight in the law of God after the inward man: 23 But I see another law in my members, warring against the law of my mind, and bringing me into captivity to the law of sin which is in my members. 24 O wretched man that I am! who shall deliver me from the body of this death? 25 I thank God through Jesus Christ our Lord. So then with the mind I myself serve the law of God; but with the flesh the law of sin.

Rom. 8: 5 . . . They that are after the flesh do mind the things of the flesh; but they that are after the Spirit, the things of the Spirit. 6 For to be carnally minded *is* death; but to be spiritually minded *is* life and peace. 7 Because the carnal mind *is* enmity against God: for it is not subject to the law of God, neither indeed can be. 8 So then they that are in the flesh cannot please God. 13 . . . If ye live after the flesh, ye shall die: but if ye through the Spirit do mortify the deeds of the body, ye shall live.

I. Cor. 2: 14 . . . The natural man receiveth not the things of the Spirit of God: for they are foolishness unto him: neither can he know *them*, because they are spiritually discerned. 15 But he that is spiritual judgeth all things, yet he himself is judged of no man.

I. Cor. 3: 3 . . . Whereas *there is* among you envying, and strife, and divisions, are ye not carnal, and walk as men?

103

I. Cor. 5: 9 I wrote unto you in an epistle not to company with fornicators: 10 Yet not altogether with the fornicators of this world, or with the covetous, or extortioners, or with idolaters; for then must ye needs go out of the world. 11 But now I have written unto you not to keep company, if any man that is called a brother be a fornicator, or covetous, or an idolater, or a railer, or a drunkard, or an extortioner; with such a one no not to eat.

II. Cor. 3: 5 Not that we are sufficient of ourselves to think any thing as of ourselves; but our sufficiency *is* of God;

Gal. 5: 17 . . . The flesh lusteth against the Spirit, and the Spirit against the flesh: and these are contrary the one to the other; so that ye cannot do the things that ye would. 19 Now the works of the flesh are manifest, which are *these*, Adultery, fornication, uncleanness, lasciviousness, 20 Idolatry, witchcraft, hatred, variance, emulations, wrath, strife, seditions, heresies, 21 Envyings, murders, drunkenness, revellings, and such like: of the which I tell you before, as I have also told *you* in time past, that they which do such things shall not inherit the kingdom of God.

Eph. 2: 1 . . . You *hath he quickened*, who were dead in trespasses and sins; 2 Wherein in time past ye walked according to the course of this world, according to the prince of the power of the air, the spirit that now worketh in the children of disobedience: 3 Among whom also we all had our conversation in times past in the lusts of our flesh, fulfilling the desires of the flesh and of the mind; and were by nature the children of wrath, even as others.

Eph. 4: 17 This I say . . . and testify in the

104

Lord, that ye henceforth walk not as other Gentiles walk, in the vanity of their mind, 18 Having the understanding darkened, being alienated from the life of God through the ignorance that is in them, because of the blindness of their heart: 19 Who being past feeling have given themselves over unto lasciviousness, to work all uncleanness with greediness. 22 . . . Put off concerning the former conversation the old man, which is corrupt according to the deceitful lusts;

Col. 3: 5 Mortify . . . your members which are upon the earth; fornication, uncleanness, inordinate affection, evil concupiscence, and covetousness, which is idolatry: 6 For which things' sake the wrath of God cometh on the children of disobedience: 8 . . . Also put off all these; anger, wrath, malice, blasphemy, filthy communication out of your mouth. 9 Lie not one to another, . . .

Jas. 4: 1 From whence *come* wars and fightings among you? *come they* not hence, *even* of your lusts that war in your members? 2 Ye lust, and have not: ye kill, and desire to have, and cannot obtain: ye fight and war, yet ye have not, because ye ask not. 3 Ye ask, and receive not, because ye ask amiss, that ye may consume *it* upon your lusts. 4 Ye adulterers and adulteresses, know ye not that the friendship of the world is enmity with God? whosoever therefore will be a friend of the world is the enemy of God.

I. Pet. 2: 9 . . . Ye should shew forth the praises of him who hath called you out of darkness into his marvellous light: 25 For ye were as sheep going astray; but are now returned unto the Shepherd and Bishop of your souls.

I. John 1: 8 If we say that we have no sin, we

deceive ourselves, and the truth is not in us. 10
If we say that we have not sinned, we make him
a liar, and his word is not in us.

I. John 2: 15 . . . If any man love the world,
the love of the Father is not in him. 16 For all
that *is* in the world, the lust of the flesh, and the
lust of the eyes, and the pride of life, is not of the
Father, but is of the world.

I. John 3: 10 In this the children of God are
manifest, and the children of the devil: whosoever
doeth not righteousness is not of God, neither he
that loveth not his brother.

Rev. 3: 17 Because thou sayest, I am rich, and
increased with goods, and have need of nothing;
and knowest not that thou art wretched, and miserable, and poor, and blind, and naked: 18 I
counsel thee to buy of me gold tried in the fire,
that thou mayest be rich; and white raiment, that
thou mayest be clothed, and *that* the shame of thy
nakedness do not appear; and anoint thine eyes
with eyesalve, that thou mayest see.

See EVIL COMPANY; INFLUENCE, Evil; LASCIV-
IOUSNESS; "SOWING WILD OATS"; WICKED; WORLD-
LINESS.

DILIGENCE

Prov. 4: 23 Keep thy heart with all diligence;
for out of it *are* the issues of life.

Prov. 10: 4 He becometh poor that dealeth
with a slack hand: but the hand of the diligent
maketh rich. 5 He that gathereth in summer *is*
a wise son: *but* he that sleepeth in harvest *is* a
son that causeth shame.

Prov. 12: 24 The hand of the diligent shall
bear rule: but the slothful shall be under tribute.

Prov. 13: 4 The soul of the sluggard desireth,
and *hath* nothing: but the soul of the diligent shall

be made fat.

Prov. 27: 23 Be thou diligent to know the state of thy flocks, *and* look well to thy herds:

John 9: 4 I must work the works of him that sent me, while it is day: the night cometh, when no man can work.

II. Tim. 4: 2 Preach the word; be instant in season, out of season; reprove, rebuke, exhort with all longsuffering and doctrine.

Heb. 6: 10 . . . God *is* not unrighteous to forget your work and labour of love, which ye have shewed toward his name, in that ye have ministered to the saints, and do minister. 11 And we desire that every one of you do shew the same diligence to the full assurance of hope unto the end: 12 That ye be not slothful, but followers of them who through faith and patience inherit the promises.

Heb. 12: 14 Follow peace with all *men*, and holiness, without which no man shall see the Lord: 15 Looking diligently lest any man fail of the grace of God; lest any root of bitterness springing up trouble *you*, and thereby many be defiled;

II. Pet. 1: 5 . . . Giving all diligence, add to your faith virtue; and to virtue, knowledge; 6 And to knowledge, temperance; and to temperance, patience; and to patience, godliness; 7 And to godliness, brotherly kindness; and to brotherly kindness, charity. 10 . . . Give diligence to make your calling and election sure: for if ye do these things, ye shall never fall:

II. Pet. 3: 14 . . . Be diligent that ye may be found of him in peace, without spot, and blameless.

See INDUSTRY; STEADFASTNESS.

DIPLOMACY

I. Cor. 9: 19 . . . Though I be free from all *men*, yet have I made myself servant unto all, that I might gain the more. 20 And unto the Jews I became as a Jew, that I might gain the Jews; to them that are under the law, as under the law, that I might gain them that are under the law; 21 To them that are without law, as without law, (being not without law to God, but under the law to Christ,) that I might gain them that are without law. 22 To the weak became I as weak, that I might gain the weak: I am made all things to all *men*, that I might by all means save some.

See COURTESY; PRUDENCE; TACT.

DISHONESTY

Exod. 20: 15 Thou shall not steal.

Lev. 19: 13 Thou shalt not defraud thy neighbour, neither rob *him:* . . . 35 Ye shall do no unrighteousness in judgment, in meteyard, in weight, or in measure.

Psa. 37: 21 The wicked borroweth, and payeth not again: but the righteous sheweth mercy, and giveth.

Psa. 62: 10 Trust not in oppression, and become not vain in robbery: if riches increase, set not your heart *upon them.*

Prov. 3: 28 Say not unto thy neighbour, Go, and come again, and to morrow I will give; when thou hast it by thee.

Prov. 20: 14 *It is* naught, *it is* naught, saith the buyer: but when he is gone his way, then he boasteth. 17 Bread of deceit *is* sweet to a man; but afterwards his mouth shall be filled with gravel.

Jer. 22: 13 Woe unto him that buildeth his house by unrighteousness, and his chambers by wrong; *that* useth his neighbour's service without wages, and giveth him not for his work;

Mark 10: 19 . . . Do not steal, Do not bear false witness, Defraud not, . . .

Eph. 4: 28 Let him that stole steal no more: but rather let him labour, working with *his* hands the thing which is good, that he may have to give to him that needeth.

I. Thess. 4: 3 . . . This is the will of God, . . . 6 That no *man* go beyond and defraud his brother in *any* matter: because that the Lord *is* the avenger of all such, as we also have forewarned you and testified.

Jas. 5: 4 Behold, the hire of the labourers who have reaped down your fields, which is of you kept back by fraud, crieth: and the cries of them which have reaped are entered into the ears of the Lord of Sabaoth.

See BREACH OF TRUST; BRIBERY; DECEIT; EXTORTION; FALSEHOOD; HYPOCRISY; INJUSTICE; THEFT; UNJUST GAIN.

DISPENSATIONS, Old and New

Matt. 5: 17 Think not that I am come to destroy the law, or the prophets: I am not come to destroy, but to fulfill.

Matt. 11: 27 All things are delivered unto me of my Father: and no man knoweth the Son, but the Father; neither knoweth any man the Father, save the Son, and *he* to whomsoever the Son will reveal *him*.

Matt. 26: 27 . . . He took the cup, and gave thanks, and gave *it* to them, saying, Drink ye all of it; 28 For this is my blood of the new testament, which is shed for many for the remission of sins.

Luke 16: 16 The law and the prophets *were*

until John: since that time the kingdom of God is preached, and every man presseth into it.

John 4: 23 . . . The hour cometh, and now is, when the true worshippers shall worship the Father in spirit and in truth: for the Father seeketh such to worship him.

John 5: 25 Verily, verily, I say unto you, The hour is coming, and now is, when the dead shall hear the voice of the Son of God: and they that hear shall live.

John 6: 32 . . . Jesus said unto them, Verily, verily, I say unto you, Moses gave you not that bread from heaven; but my Father giveth you the true bread from heaven. 33 For the bread of God is he which cometh down from heaven, and giveth life unto the world. 48 I am that bread of life. 49 Your fathers did eat manna in the wilderness, and are dead. 51 I am the living bread which came down from heaven: if any man eat of this bread, he shall live for ever: and the bread that I will give is my flesh, which I will give for the life of the world.

Acts 13: 38 Be it known unto you . . . that through this man is preached unto you the forgiveness of sins: 39 And by him all that believe are justified from all things, from which ye could not be justified by the law of Moses.

DIVORCE

Matt. 5: 31 It hath been said, whosoever shall put away his wife, let him give her a writing of divorcement: 32 But I say unto you, That whosoever shall put away his wife, saving for the cause of fornication, causeth her to commit adultery: and whosoever shall marry her that is divorced committeth adultery.

Matt. 19: 4 . . . Have ye not read, that he

which made *them* at the beginning made them male and female, 5 And said, For this cause shall a man leave father and mother, and shall cleave to his wife: and they twain shall be one flesh? 6 Wherefore they are no more twain, but one flesh. What therefore God hath joined together, let not man put asunder.

Mark 10: 11 . . . Whosoever shall put away his wife, and marry another, committeth adultery against her. 12 And if a woman shall put away her husband, and be married to another, she committeth adultery.

I. Cor. 7: 10 . . . Let not the wife depart from *her* husband: 11 But and if she depart, let her remain unmarried, or be reconciled to *her* husband: and let not the husband put away *his* wife.

See HUSBAND—WIFE; MARRIAGE.

ECONOMY

Prov. 10: 4 He becometh poor that dealeth *with* a slack hand: but the hand of the diligent maketh rich.

Prov. 21: 17 He that loveth pleasure *shall be* a poor man: he that loveth wine and oil shall not be rich.

Prov. 23: 21 . . . The drunkard and the glutton shall come to poverty: and drowsiness shall clothe *a man* with rags.

See FRUGALITY; also EXTRAVAGANCE.

EMPLOYER—EMPLOYEE

Deut. 24: 14 Thou shalt not oppress a hired servant *that is* poor and needy, *whether he be* of thy brethren, or of thy strangers that *are* in thy land within thy gates: 15 At his day thou shalt give *him* his hire, neither shall the sun go down upon it; for he *is* poor, and setteth his heart upon it: lest he cry against thee unto the Lord, and it be sin unto thee.

Job 31: 13 If I did despise the cause of my manservant or of my maidservant, when they contended with me; 14 What then shall I do when God riseth up? and when he visiteth, what shall I answer him? 15 Did not he that made me in the womb make him? and did not one fashion us in the womb?

Prov. 13: 17 A wicked messenger falleth into mischief: but a faithful ambassador *is* health.

Prov. 22: 16 He that oppresseth the poor to increase his *riches, and* he that giveth to the rich, *shall* surely *come to want.*

Prov. 25: 13 As the cold of snow in the time of harvest, *so is* a faithful messenger to them that send him: for he refresheth the soul of his masters.

Prov. 27: 18 Whoso keepeth the fig tree shall eat the fruit thereof: so he that waiteth on his master shall be honoured.

Prov. 29: 21 He that delicately bringeth up his servant from a child shall have him become *his* son at the length.

Prov. 30: 21 For three *things* the earth is disquieted, and for four *which* it cannot bear: 22 For a servant when he reigneth; and a fool when he is filled with meat; 23 For an odious *woman* when she is married; and a handmaid that is heir to her mistress.

Ecc. 7: 21 . . . Take no heed unto all words that are spoken; lest thou hear thy servant curse thee: 22 For oftentimes also thine own heart knoweth that thou thyself likewise hast cursed others.

Jer. 22: 13 Woe unto him that buildeth his house by unrighteousness, and his chambers by wrong; *that* useth his neighbour's service without wages, and giveth him not for his work;

Matt. 10: 10 . . . The workman is worthy of his meat.

Luke 12: 42 . . . The Lord said, Who then is that faithful and wise steward, whom *his* lord shall make ruler over his household, to give *them their* portion of meat in due season? 43 Blessed *is* that servant, whom his lord when he cometh shall find so doing. 47 And that servant, which knew his lord's will, and prepared not *himself*, neither did according to his will, shall be beaten with many *stripes.* 48 But he that knew not, and did commit things worthy of stripes, shall be beaten with few *stripes.* For unto whomsoever much is given, of him shall be much required; and to whom men have committed much, of him they will ask the more.

Luke 16: 10 He that is faithful in that which is least is faithful also in much: and he that is unjust in the least is unjust also in much. 12 And if ye have not been faithful in that which is another man's, who shall give you that which is your own? 13 No servant can serve two masters: for either he will hate the one, and love the other; or else he will hold to the one, and despise the other. . . .

I. Cor. 4: 2 . . . It is required in stewards, that a man be found faithful.

I. Cor. 7: 22 . . . He that is called in the Lord, *being* a servant, is the Lord's freeman: likewise also he that is called, *being* free, is Christ's servant. 23 Ye are bought with a price; be not ye the servants of men. 24 Brethren, let every

113

man, wherein he is called, therein abide with God.

Eph. 6: 5 Servants, be obedient to them that are *your* masters according to the flesh, with fear and trembling, in singleness of your heart, as unto Christ; 7 With good will doing service, as to the Lord, and not to men: 9 And, ye masters, do the same things unto them, forbearing threatening: knowing that your Master also is in heaven; neither is there respect of persons with him.

Col. 3: 22 Servants, obey in all things *your* masters according to the flesh; not with eyeservice, as menpleasers; but in singleness of heart, fearing God: 23 And whatsoever ye do, do *it* heartily, as to the Lord, and not unto men; 24 Knowing that of the Lord ye shall receive the reward of the inheritance: for ye serve the Lord Christ. 25 But he that doeth wrong shall receive for the wrong which he hath done: and there is no respect of persons.

Col. 4: 1 Masters, give unto *your*. servants that which is just and equal; knowing that ye also have a Master in heaven.

I. Tim. 6: 1 Let as many servants as are under the yoke count their own masters worthy of all honour, that the name of God and *his* doctrine be not blasphemed. 2 And they that have believing masters, let them not despise *them*, because they are brethren; but rather do *them* service, because they are faithful and beloved, partakers of the benefit. These things teach and exhort.

Tit. 2: 9 *Exhort* servants to be obedient unto their own masters, *and* to please *them* well in all things; not answering again; 10 Not purloining, but shewing all good fidelity; that they may adorn the doctrine of God our Saviour in all things.

Jas. 5:   4 Behold, the hire of the labourers who have reaped down your fields, which is of you kept back by fraud, crieth: and the cries of them which have reaped are entered into the ears of the Lord of Sabaoth.

I. Pet. 2:   18 Servants, be subject to *your* masters with all fear; not only to the good and gentle, but also to the froward.   19 For this *is* thankworthy, if a man for conscience toward God endure grief, suffering wrongfully.

See SERVICE; WAGES.

ENEMY

Prov. 25:   21 If thine enemy be hungry, give him bread to eat; and if he be thirsty, give him water to drink: 22 For thou shalt heap coals of fire upon his head, and the Lord shall reward thee.

Matt. 5:   43 Ye have heard that it hath been said, Thou shalt love thy neighbour, and hate thine enemy.   44 But I say unto you, Love your enemies, bless them that curse you, do good to them that hate you, and pray for them which despitefully use you, and persecute you;   45 That ye may be the children of your Father which is in heaven: for he maketh his sun to rise on the evil and on the good, and sendeth rain on the just and on the unjust.   46 For if ye love them which love you, what reward have ye? do not even the publicans the same?   47 And if ye salute your brethren only, what do ye more *than others?* do not even the publicans so?   48 Be ye therefore perfect, even as your Father which is in heaven is perfect.

Luke 6:   31 . . . As ye would that men should do to you, do ye also to them likewise.

Rom. 12:   14 Bless them which persecute you:

bless, and curse not.

See HATRED; MALICE; RETALIATION.

ENVY

Job. 5: 2 . . . Wrath killeth the foolish man, and envy slayeth the silly one.

Psa. 37: 1 Fret not thyself because of evil doers, neither be thou envious against the workers of iniquity.

Prov. 3: 31 Envy thou not the oppressor, and choose none of his ways.

Prov. 14: 30 A sound heart *is* the life of the flesh: but envy the rottenness of the bones.

Prov. 27: 4 Wrath *is* cruel, and anger *is* outrageous; but who *is* able to stand before envy?

Rom. 13: 13 Let us walk honestly, as in the day; not in rioting and drunkenness, not in chambering and wantonness, not in strife and envying:

I. Cor. 3: 3 . . . Whereas *there is* among you envying, and strife, and divisions, are ye not carnal, and walk as men?

I. Cor. 13: 4 Charity suffereth long, *and* is kind; charity envieth not; . . .

Gal. 5: 19 . . . The works of the flesh are manifest, which are *these*, . . . 21 Envyings, murders, drunkenness, revellings, and such like: of the which I tell you before, as I have also told *you* in time past, that they which do such things shall not inherit the kingdom of God. 26 Let us not be desirous of vainglory, provoking one another, envying one another.

Phil. 1: 15 Some indeed preach Christ even of envy and strife; and some also of good will: 16 The one preach Christ of contention, not sincerely, supposing to add affliction to my bonds: 17 But the other of love, knowing that I am set for the defence of the gospel. 18 What 'then? notwithstanding, every way, whether in pretence, or in truth, Christ is preached; and I therein do rejoice, yea, and will rejoice.

I. Tim. 6:   4 He is proud, knowing nothing, but doting about questions and strifes of words, whereof cometh envy, strife, railings, evil surmisings,   5 Perverse disputings of men of corrupt minds, and destitute of the truth, supposing that gain is godliness: from such withdraw thyself.

Jas. 3: 14 . . . If ye have bitter envying and strife in your hearts, glory not, and lie not against the truth.   16 For where envying, and strife *is*, there *is* confusion and every evil work.

Jas. 5:   9 Grudge not one against another, brethren, lest ye be condemned: behold, the judge standeth before the door.

See COVETOUSNESS; JEALOUSY.

EQUALITY OF PERSONS

Job. 31: 13 If I did despise the cause of my manservant or of my maidservant, when they contended with me;   14 What then shall I do when God riseth up? and when he visiteth, what shall I answer him?   15 Did not he that made me in the womb make him? and did not one fashion us in the womb?

Psa. 33:   13 The Lord looketh from heaven; he beholdeth all the sons of men.   15 He fashioneth their hearts alike; he considereth all their works.

Prov. 22:   2 The rich and poor meet together: the Lord *is* the maker of them all.

Matt. 23:   8 . . . Be not ye called Rabbi: for one is your Master, *even* Christ; and all ye are brethren.

117

Acts 10: 28 . . . God hath shewed me that I should not call any man common or unclean.

Acts 17: 24 God . . . made the world and all things therein, . . . 26 And hath made of one blood all nations of men for to dwell on all the face of the earth, . . .

Jas. 1: 9 Let the brother of low degree rejoice in that he is exalted: 10 But the rich, in that he is made low: because as the flower of the grass he shall pass away. 11 For the sun is no sooner risen with a burning heat, but it withereth the grass, and the flower thereof falleth, and the grace of the fashion of it perisheth: so also shall the rich man fade away in his ways.

See FELLOWSHIP with Persons; HUMILITY; TOLERANCE.

EVIL COMPANY

Exod. 23: 2 Thou shalt not follow a multitude to *do* evil; . . .

Psa. 84: 10 . . . I had rather be a doorkeeper in the house of my God, than to dwell in the tents of wickedness.

Prov. 1: 10 My son, if sinners entice thee, consent thou not. 11 If they say, Come with us, let us lay wait for blood, let us lurk privily for the innocent without cause: 14 Cast in thy lot among us; let us all have one purse: 15 My son, walk not thou in the way with them; refrain thy foot from their path:

Prov. 2: 11 Discretion shall preserve thee, understanding shall keep thee: 12 To deliver thee from the way of the evil *man*, from the man that speaketh froward things; 16 To deliver thee from the strange woman, *even* from the stranger *which* flattereth with her words; 19 None that go unto her return again, neither take they hold of the paths of life.

Prov. 12: 11 He that tilleth his land shall be satisfied with bread: but he that followeth vain *persons is* void of understanding.

Prov. 13: 20 He that walketh with wise *men* shall be wise: but a companion of fools shall be destroyed.

Prov. 16: 29 A violent man enticeth his neighbour, and leadeth him into the way *that is* not good.

Prov. 17: 12 Let a bear robbed of her whelps meet a man, rather than a fool in his folly.

Prov. 20: 19 He that goeth about *as* a tale-bearer revealeth secrets: therefore meddle not with him that flattereth with his lips.

Prov. 22: 10 Cast out the scorner, and contention shall go out; yea, strife and reproach shall cease. 24 Make no friendship with an angry man; and with a furious man thou shalt not go; 25 Lest thou learn his ways, and get a snare to thy soul.

Prov. 23: 6 Eat thou not the bread of *him that hath* an evil eye, neither desire thou his dainty meats: 7 For as he thinketh in his heart, so *is* he: Eat and drink, saith he to thee; but his heart *is* not with thee. 20 Be not among winebibbers; among riotous eaters of flesh: 21 For the drunkard and the glutton shall come to poverty: and drowsiness shall clothe *a man* with rags.

Prov. 28: 7 Whoso keepeth the law *is* a wise son: but he that is a companion of riotous *men* shameth his father. 19 He that tilleth his land shall have plenty of bread: but he that followeth after vain *persons* shall have poverty enough.

Prov. 29: 24 Whoso is partner with a thief hateth his own soul: he heareth cursing, and bewrayeth *it* not.

Ecc. 9: 18 Wisdom *is* better than weapons of war: but one sinner destroyeth much good.

Matt. 24: 12 . . . Because iniquity shall abound, the love of many shall wax cold. 13 But he that shall endure unto the end, the same shall be saved.

Rom. 16: 17 . . . Mark them which cause divisions and offences contrary to the doctrine which ye have learned; and avoid them. 18 For they that are such serve not our Lord Jesus Christ, but their own belly; and by good words and fair speeches deceive the hearts of the simple.

I. Cor. 5: 6 . . . . Know ye not that a little leaven leaveneth the whole lump? 9 I wrote unto you in an epistle not to company with fornicators: 10 Yet not altogether with the fornicators of this world, or with the covetous, or extortioners, or with idolaters; for then must ye needs go out of the world. 11 But now I have written unto you not to keep company, if any man that is called a brother be a fornicator, or covetous, or an idolater, or a railer, or a drunkard, or an extortioner; with such a one no not to eat.

I. Cor. 15: 33 Be not deceived: evil communications corrupt good manners.

II. Cor. 6: 14 Be ye not unequally yoked together with unbelievers: for what fellowship hath righteousness with unrighteousness? and what communion hath light with darkness? 15 And what concord hath Christ with Belial? or what part hath he that believeth with an infidel? 17 Wherefore come out from among them, and be ye separate, saith the Lord, and touch not the unclean *thing;* and I will receive you,

Eph. 5: 11 . . . Have no fellowship with the

unfruitful works of darkness, but rather reprove *them.* 12 For it is a shame even to speak of those things which are done of them in secret.

I. Tim. 5: 22 Lay hands suddenly on no man, neither be partaker of other men's sins: keep thyself pure.

I. Tim. 6: 3 If any man teach otherwise, and consent not to wholesome words, *even* the words of our Lord Jesus Christ, and to the doctrine which is according to godliness; 4 He is proud, knowing nothing, but doting about questions and strifes of words, whereof cometh envy, strife, railings, evil surmisings, 5 Perverse disputings of men of corrupt minds, and destitute of the truth, supposing that gain is godliness: from such withdraw thyself. 9 . . . They that will be rich fall into temptation and a snare, and *into* many foolish and hurtful lusts, which drown men in destruction and perdition. 10 For the love of money is the root of all evil: which while some coveted after, they have erred from the faith, and pierced themselves through with many sorrows. 11 But thou, O man of God, flee these things; and follow after righteousness, godliness, faith, love, patience, meekness.

II. Tim. 3: 2 . . . Men shall be lovers of their own selves, covetous, boasters, proud, blasphemers, disobedient to parents, unthankful, unholy, 3 Without natural affection, trucebreakers, false accusers, incontinent, fierce, despisers of those that are good, 4 Traitors, heady, highminded, lovers of pleasures more than lovers of God; 5 Having a form of godliness, but denying the power thereof: from such turn away.

See INFLUENCE, Evil; WICKED.

EXAMPLE

Matt. 5: 16 Let your light so shine before men, that they may see your good works, and glorify your Father which is in heaven. 48 Be ye . . . perfect, even as your Father which is in heaven is perfect.

Luke 6: 36 Be ye . . . merciful, as your Father also is merciful.

John 13: 15 . . . I have given you an example, that ye should do as I have done to you.

Rom. 15: 2 Let every one of us please *his* neighbour for *his* good to edification.

I. Cor. 8: 8 . . . Meat commendeth us not to God: for neither, if we eat, are we the better; neither, if we eat not, are we the worse. 9 But take heed lest by any means this liberty of yours become a stumblingblock to them that are weak. 13 Wherefore, if meat make my brother to offend, I will eat no flesh while the world standeth, lest I make my brother to offend.

I. Cor. 11: 1 Be yet followers of me, even as I also *am* of Christ.

Phil. 3: 17 Brethren, be followers together of me, and mark them which walk so as ye have us for an ensample.

II. Thess. 3: 7 . . . Ye ought to follow us: for we behaved not ourselves disorderly among you; 8 Neither did we eat any man's bread for nought; but wrought with labour and travail night and day, that we might not be chargeable to any of you: 9 Not because we have not power, but to make ourselves an ensample unto you to follow us. 10 For even when we were with you, this we commanded you, that if any would not work, neither should he eat.

I. Tim. 1: 15 . . . Christ Jesus came into the

world to save sinners; of whom I am chief. 16 Howbeit for this cause I obtained mercy, that in me first Jesus Christ might shew forth all long-suffering, for a pattern to them which should hereafter believe on him to life everlasting.

I. Tim. 4: 12 Let no man despise thy youth; but be thou an example of the believers, in word, in conversation, in charity, in spirit, in faith, in purity.

Tit. 2: 1 . . . Speak thou the things which become souna doctrine: 7 In all things shewing thyself a pattern of good works: in doctrine *shewing* uncorruptness, gravity, sincerity, 8 Sound speech, that cannot be condemned; that he that is of the contrary part may be ashamed, having no evil thing to say of you.

Jas. 5: 10 Take, my brethren, the prophets, who have spoken in the name of the Lord, for an example of suffering affliction, and of patience. 11 Behold, we count them happy which endure. Ye have heard of the patience of Job, and have seen the end of the Lord; that the Lord is very pitiful, and of tender mercy.

I. Pet. 2: 11 Dearly beloved, I beseech *you* as strangers and pilgrims, abstain from fleshly lusts, which war against the soul; 12 Having your conversation honest among the Gentiles: that, whereas they speak against you as evil doers, they may by *your* good works, which they shall behold, glorify God in the day of visitation. 13 Submit yourselves to every ordinance of man for the Lord's sake: whether it be to the king, as supreme; 14 Or unto governors, as unto them that are sent by him for the punishment of evil doers, and for the praise of them that do well. 15 For so is the will of God, that with well doing ye

may put to silence the ignorance of foolish men:
I. Pet. 5: 2 Feed the flock of God which is
among you, taking the oversight *thereof*, not by
constraint, but willingly; not for filthy lucre, but
of a ready mind; 3 Neither as being lords over
God's heritage, but being ensamples to the flock.
See INFLUENCE; JESUS as Example.

EXCUSE

Matt. 25: 24 Then he which had received the
one talent came and said, Lord, I knew thee that
thou art a hard man, reaping where thou hast not
sown, and gathering where thou hast not strewed:
25 And I was afraid, and went and hid thy talent
in the earth: lo, *there* thou hast *that is* thine.
26 His lord answered and said unto him, *Thou*
wicked and slothful servant, thou knewest that I
reap where I sowed not, and gather where I have
not strewed: 27 Thou oughtest therefore to have
put my money to the exchangers, and *then* at my
coming I should have received mine own with
usury. 28 Take therefore the talent from him,
and give *it* unto him which hath ten talents. 29
For unto every one that hath shall be given, and
he shall have abundance: but from him that hath
not shall be taken away even that which he hath.
30 And cast ye the unprofitable servant into outer
darkness: there shall be weeping and gnashing of
teeth.

Luke 9: 59 . . . He said unto another, Follow
me. But he said, Lord, suffer me first to go and
bury my father. 60 Jesus said unto him, Let the
dead bury their dead: but go thou and preach the
kingdom of God. 61 And another also said,
Lord, I will follow thee; but let me first go bid
them farewell, which are at home at my house.
62 And Jesus said unto him, No man, having put

his hand to the plough, and looking back, is fit for the kingdom of God.

Rom. 1: 20 . . . They are without excuse: 21 Because that, when they knew God, they glorified *him* not as God, neither were thankful; but became vain in their imaginations, and their foolish heart was darkened.

Rom. 2: 1 . . . Thou art inexcusable, O man, whosoever thou art that judgest: for wherein thou judgest another, thou condemnest thyself; for thou that judgest doest the same things.

EXPEDIENCY

Rom. 14: 14 I know, and am persuaded by the Lord Jesus, that *there is* nothing unclean of itself: but to him that esteemeth any thing to be unclean, to him *it is* unclean. 15 But if thy brother be grieved with *thy* meat, now walkest thou not charitably. Destroy not him with thy meat, for whom Christ died. 21 *It is* good neither to eat flesh, nor to drink wine, nor *any thing* whereby thy brother stumbleth, or is offended, or is made weak.

I. Cor. 8: 8 . . . Meat commendeth us not to God: for neither, if we eat, are we the better; neither, if we eat not, are we the worse. 9 But take heed lest by any means this liberty of yours become a stumblingblock to them that are weak. 13 Wherefore, if meat make my brother to offend, I will eat no flesh while the world standeth, lest I make my brother to offend.

I. Cor. 9: 19 . . . Though I be free from all *men*, yet have I made myself servant unto all, that I might gain the more. 20 And unto the Jews I became as a Jew, that I might gain the Jews; to them that are under the law, as under the law, that I might gain them that are under

the law; 21 To them that are without law, as
without law, (being not without law to God, but
under the law to Christ,) that I might gain them
that are without law. 22 To the weak became I as
weak, that I might gain the weak: I am made all
things to all *men*, that I might by all means save
some.

I. Cor. 10: 23 All things are lawful for me,
but all things are not expedient: all things are
lawful for me, but all things edify not. 27 If any
of them that believe not bid you *to a feast*, and ye
be disposed to go; whatsoever is set before you,
eat, asking no question for conscience' sake. 32
Give none offence, neither to the Jews, nor to the
Gentiles, nor to the church of God: 33 Even as I
please all *men* in all *things*, not seeking mine own
profit, but the *profit* of many, that they may be
saved.

See DIPLOMACY; PRUDENCE; TACT.

EXTORTION

I. Cor. 5: 9 I wrote unto you in an epistle not
to company with fornicators: 10 Yet not altogether with the fornicators of this world, or with
the covetous, or extortioners, or with idolaters;
for then must ye needs go out of the world. 11
But now I have written unto you not to keep company, if any man that is called a brother be a
fornicator, or covetous, or an idolater, or a railer,
or a drunkard, or an extortioner; with such a one
no not to eat.

I. Cor. 6: 9 Know ye not that the unrighteous
shall not inherit the kingdom of God? Be not deceived; neither fornicators, . . . 10 . . . nor
extortioners, shall inherit the kingdom of God.

See OPPRESSION; UNJUST GAIN.

EXTRAVAGANCE

Prov. 10: 4 He becometh poor that dealeth *with* a slack hand: but the hand of the diligent maketh rich.

Prov. 21: 17 He that loveth pleasure *shall be* a poor man: he that loveth wine and oil shall not be rich. 20 *There is* treasure to be desired and oil in the dwelling of the wise; but a foolish man spendeth it up.

Luke 12: 19 . . . I will say to my soul, Soul, thou hast much goods laid up for many years; take thine ease, eat, drink, *and* be merry. 20 But God said unto him, *Thou* fool, this night thy soul shall be required of thee: then whose shall those things be, which thou hast provided?

Luke 15: 12 . . . The younger of them said to *his* father, Father, give me the portion of goods that falleth *to me*. And he divided unto them *his* living. 13 And not many days after the younger son gathered all together, and took his journey into a far country, and there wasted his substance with riotous living. 14 And when he had spent all, there arose a mighty famine in that land; and he began to be in want. 15 And he went and joined himself to a citizen of that country; and he sent him into his fields to feed the swine. 16 And he would fain have filled his belly with the husks that the swine did eat: and no man gave unto him. 17 And when he came to himself, he said, How many hired servants of my father's have bread enough and to spare, and I perish with hunger!

See FOLLY; PLEASURE; also ECONOMY.

FAITH

Psa. 27: 14 Wait on the Lord: be of good

courage, and he shall strengthen thine heart: wait,
I say, on the Lord.

Psa. 33: 18 Behold, the eye of the Lord *is*
upon them that fear him, upon them that hope in
his mercy; 19 To deliver their soul from death,
and to keep them alive in famine.

Psa. 34: 22 The Lord redeemeth the soul of
his servants: and none of them that trust in him
shall be desolate.

Psa. 112: 5 A good man sheweth favour, and
lendeth: he will guide his affairs with discretion.
7 He shall not be afraid of evil tidings: his heart
is fixed, trusting in the Lord.

Psa. 118: 8 *It is* better to trust in the Lord
than to put confidence in man. 9 *It is* better to
trust in the Lord than to put confidence in princes.

Prov. 3: 5 Trust in the Lord with all thine
heart; and lean not unto thine own understanding.

Prov. 29: 25 The fear of man bringeth a
snare: but whoso putteth his trust in the Lord
shall be safe.

Isa. 26: 3 Thou wilt keep *him* in perfect
peace, *whose* mind *is* stayed *on thee:* because he
trusteth in thee. 4 Trust ye in the Lord for
ever: for in the Lord JEHOVAH *is* everlasting
strength.

Jer. 17: 7 Blessed *is* the man that trusteth in
the Lord, and whose hope the Lord is.

Nah. 1: 7 The Lord *is* good, a strong hold in
the day of trouble; and he knoweth them that
trust in him.

Hab. 2: 4 . . . The just shall live by his
faith.

Matt. 6: 31 . . . Take no thought, saying,
What shall we eat? or, What shall we drink? or,

Wherewithal shall we be clothed? 32 (For after all these things do the Gentile seek:) for your heavenly Father knoweth that ye have need of all these things. 33 But seek ye first the kingdom of God, and his righteousness; and all these things shall be added unto you.

Matt. 9: 22 . . . Jesus . . . said, Daughter, be of good comfort; thy faith hath made thee whole. And the woman was made whole from that hour.

Matt. 17: 18 . . . Jesus rebuked the devil; and he departed out of him: and the child was cured from that very hour. 19 Then came the disciples to Jesus apart, and said, Why could not we cast him out? 20 And Jesus said unto them, Because of your unbelief: for verily I say unto you, If ye have faith as a grain of mustard seed, ye shall say unto this mountain, Remove hence to yonder place; and it shall remove: and nothing shall be impossible unto you.

Matt. 21: 21 Jesus . . . said unto them, Verily I say unto you, If ye have faith, and doubt not, ye shall not only do this *which is done* to the fig tree, but also if ye shall say unto this mountain, Be thou removed, and be thou cast into the sea; it shall be done. 22 And all things, whatsoever ye shall ask in prayer, believing, ye shall receive.

Mark 9: 23 Jesus said unto him, If thou canst believe, all things *are* possible to him that believeth.

Mark 11: 22 . . . Jesus . . . saith unto them, Have faith in God.

Mark 16: 16 He that believeth and is baptized shall be saved; but he that believeth not shall be damned. 17 And these signs shall follow them that believe; In my name shall they cast out

129

devils; they shall speak with new tongues; 18
They shall take up serpents; and if they drink
any deadly thing, it shall not hurt them; they
shall lays hands on the sick, and they shall recover.

John 3: 16 . . . God so loved the world, that
he gave his only begotten Son, that whosoever
believeth in him should not perish, but have everlasting life. 18 He that believeth on him is not
condemned: but he that believeth not is condemned already, because he hath not believed in
the name of the only begotten Son of God. 36
He that believeth on the Son hath everlasting life:
and he that believeth not the Son shall not see
life; but the wrath of God abideth on him.

John 5: 24 Verily, verily, I say unto you, He
that heareth my word, and believeth on him that
sent me, hath everlasting life, and shall not come
into condemnation; but is passed from death unto
life.

John 6: 35 . . . Jesus said unto them, I am
the bread of life: he that cometh to me shall never
hunger; and he that believeth on me shall never
thirst.

John 11: 25 Jesus said unto her, I am the
resurrection, and the life: he that believeth in me,
though he were dead, yet shall he live: 26 And
whosoever liveth and believeth in me shall never
die. . . .

John 12: 46 I am come a light into the world,
that whosoever believeth on me should not abide
in darkness.

John 14: 1 Let not your heart be troubled: ye
believe in God, believe also in me. 11 Believe
me that I *am* in the Father, and the Father in me:
or else believe me for the very works' sake. 12
Verily, verily, I say unto you, He that believeth
on me, the works that I do shall he do also; and

greater *works* than these shall he do; because I go unto my Father.

John 20: 27 Then saith he to Thomas, Reach hither thy finger, and behold my hands; and reach hither thy hand, and thrust *it* into my side; and be not faithless, but believing. 28 And Thomas answered and said unto him, My Lord and my God. 29 Jesus saith unto him, Thomas, because thou hast seen· me, thou hast believed: blessed *are* they that have not seen, and *yet* have believed.

Acts 3: 6 . . . Peter said, Silver and gold have I none; but such as I have give I thee: In the name of Jesus Christ of Nazareth rise up and walk. 8 And he leaping up stood, and walked, and entered with them into the temple, walking, and leaping, and praising God. 12 . . . Peter . . . answered unto the people, Ye men of Israel, why marvel ye at this? or why look ye so earnestly on us, as though by our own power or holiness we had made this man to walk? 13 The God of Abraham, and of Isaac, and of Jacob, the God of our fathers, hath glorified his Son Jesus; . . . 16 And his name, through faith in his name, hath made this man strong, whom ye see and know: yea, the faith which is by him hath given him this perfect soundness in the presence of you all.

Acts 10: 43 To him give all the prophets witness, that through his name whosoever believeth in him shall receive remission of sins.

Rom. 1: 16 . . . I am not ashamed of the gospel of Christ: for it is the power of God unto salvation to every one that believeth; to the Jew first, and also to the Greek. 17 For therein is the righteousness of God revealed from faith to faith: as it is written, The just shall live by faith.

Rom. 3: 22 Even the righteousness of God *which is* by faith of Jesus Christ unto all and upon all them that believe; for there is no difference: 23 For all have sinned, and come short of the glory of God; 24 Being justified freely by his grace through the redemption that is in Christ Jesus: 25 Whom God hath set forth *to be* a propitiation through faith in his blood, to declare his righteousness for the remission of sins that are past, through the forbearance of God; 26 To declare, *I say,* at this time his righteousness: that he might be just, and the justifier of him which believeth in Jesus. 27 Where *is* boasting then? It is excluded. By what law? of works? Nay; but by the law of faith. 28 Therefore we conclude that a man is justified by faith without the deeds of the law. 29 *Is he* the God of the Jews only? *is he* not also of the Gentiles? Yes, of the Gentiles also: 30 Seeing *it is* one God, which shall justify the circumcision by faith, and uncircumcision through faith. 31 Do we then make void the law through faith? God forbid: yea, we establish the law.

Rom. 4: 4 . . . To him that worketh is the reward not reckoned of grace, but of debt. 5 But to him that worketh not, but believeth on him that justifieth the ungodly, his faith is counted for righteousness.

Rom. 5: 1 . . . Being justified by faith, we have peace with God through our Lord Jesus Christ: 2 By whom also we have access by faith into this grace wherein we stand, and rejoice in hope of the glory of God.

Rom. 9: 31 . . . Israel, which followed after the law of righteousness, hath not attained to the law of righteousness. 32 Wherefore? Because *they sought it* not by faith, but as it were by the works of the law. For they stumbled at that stumblingstone; 33 As it is written, Behold, I lay in Sion a stumblingstone and rock of offence: and whosoever believeth on him shall not be ashamed.

Rom. 10: 4 . . . Christ *is* the end of the law for righteousness to every one that believeth. 9 . . . If thou shalt confess with thy mouth the Lord Jesus, and shalt believe in thine heart that God hath raised him from the dead, thou shalt be saved. 10 For with the heart man believeth unto righteousness; and with the mouth confession is made unto salvation.

Rom. 15: 13 Now the God of hope fill you with all joy and peace in believing, that ye may abound in hope, through the power of the Holy Ghost.

I. Cor. 2: 5 . . . Your faith should not stand in the wisdom of men, but in the power of God.

I. Cor. 12: 8 . . . To one is given by the Spirit the word of wisdom; . . . 9 To another faith by the same Spirit; . . .

I. Cor. 13: 13 . . . Now abideth faith, hope, charity, these three; but the greatest of these *is* charity.

II. Cor. 5: 7 (. . . We walk by faith, not by sight:)

Gal. 2: 16 Knowing that a man is not justified by the works of the law, but by the faith of Jesus Christ, even we have believed in Jesus Christ, that we might be justified by the faith of Christ, and not by the works of the law: for by the works of the law shall no flesh be justified.

Gal. 3: 7 Know ye . . . that they which are of faith, the same are the children of Abraham.

9 So then they which be of faith are blessed
with faithful Abraham. 13 Christ hath redeemed us from the curse of the law, being made
a curse for us: for it is written, Cursed *is* every
one that hangeth on a tree: 14 That the blessing
of Abraham might come on the Gentiles through
Jesus Christ; that we might receive the promise
of the Spirit through faith.

Gal. 5: 22 . . . The fruit of the Spirit is love,
joy, peace, longsuffering, gentleness, goodness,
faith, 23 Meekness, temperance: against such
there is no law.

Eph. 2: 8 . . . By grace are ye saved through
faith; and that not of yourselves: *it is* the gift
of God:

Eph. 6: 11 Put on the whole armour of God,
that ye may be able to stand against the wiles of
the devil. 16 Above all, taking the shield of faith,
wherewith ye shall be able to quench all the fiery
darts of the wicked.

Col. 2: 6 As ye have . . . received Christ
Jesus the Lord, *so* walk ye in him: 12 Buried
with him in baptism, wherein also ye are risen
with *him* through the faith of the operation of
God, who hath raised him from the dead.

I. Thess. 5: 8 . . . Let us, who are of the day,
be sober, putting on the breastplate of faith and
love; and for a helmet, the hope of salvation.

I. Tim. 1: 5 . . . The end of the commandment is charity out of a pure heart, and *of* a good
conscience, and *of* faith unfeigned: 18 This
charge I commit unto thee, son Timothy, according to the prophecies which went before on thee,
that thou by them mightest war a good warfare;
19 Holding faith, and a good conscience; which
some having put away, concerning faith have

made shipwreck:

I. Tim. 6: 11 . . . Thou, O man of God, . . . follow after righteousness, godliness, faith, love, patience, meekness. 12 Fight the good fight of faith, lay hold on eternal life, whereunto thou art also called, and hast professed a good profession before many witnesses. 17 Charge them that are rich in this world, that they be not high-minded, nor trust in uncertain riches, but in the living God, who giveth us richly all things to enjoy;

II. Tim. 3: 15 . . . From a child thou hast known the holy Scriptures, which are able to make thee wise unto salvation through faith which is in Christ Jesus.

II. Tim. 4: 7 I have fought a good fight, I have finished *my* course, I have kept the faith: 8 Henceforth there is laid up for me a crown of righteousness, which the Lord, the righteous judge, shall give me at that day: and not to me only, but unto all them also that love his appearing.

Heb. 10: 22 Let us draw near with a true heart in full assurance of faith, having our hearts sprinkled from an evil conscience, and our bodies washed with pure water. 23 Let us hold fast the profession of *our* faith without wavering; for he *is* faithful that promised;

Heb. 11: 1 . . . Faith is the substance of things hoped for, the evidence of things not seen. 3 Through faith we understand that the worlds were framed by the word of God, so that things which are seen were not made of things which do appear. 6 But without faith *it is* impossible to please *him*: for he that cometh to God must believe that he is, and *that* he is a rewarder of them

135

that diligently seek him.

Heb. 13: 5 *Let your* conversation *be* without covetousness; *and be* content with such things as ye have: for he hath said, I will never leave thee, nor forsake thee. 6 So that we may boldly say, The Lord *is* my helper, and I will not fear what man shall do unto me.

Jas. 2: 26 . . . As the body without the spirit is dead, so faith without works is dead also.

I. John 3: 23 . . . This is his commandment, That we should believe on the name of his Son Jesus Christ, and love one another, as he gave us commandment.

I. John 5: 4 . . . Whatsoever is born of God overcometh the world: and this is the victory that overcometh the world, *even* our faith. 5 Who is he that overcometh the world, but he that believeth that Jesus is the Son of God? 10 He that believeth on the Son of God hath the witness in himself: he that believeth not God hath made him a liar; because he believeth not the record that God gave of his Son. 13 These things have I written unto you that believe on the name of the Son of God; that ye may know that ye have eternal life, and that ye may believe on the name of the Son of God.

See FAITHFULNESS; SALVATION.

FAITHFULNESS—UNFAITHFULNESS

Psa. 31: 23 O love the Lord, all ye his saints: *for* the Lord preserveth the faithful, and plentifully rewardeth the proud doer.

Prov. 28: 20 A faithful man shall abound with blessings: but he that maketh haste to be rich shall not be innocent.

Matt. 10: 22 . . . Ye shall be hated of all *men* for my name's sake: but he that endureth to the end shall be saved.

Matt. 24: 45 Who then is a faithful and wise servant, whom his lord hath made ruler over his household, to give them meat in due season? 46 Blessed *is* that servant, whom his lord when he cometh shall find so doing.

Matt. 25: 13 Watch . . .; for ye know neither the day nor the hour wherein the Son of man cometh. 14 For *the kingdom of heaven is* as a man travelling into a far country, *who* called his own servants, and delivered unto them his goods. 15 And unto one he gave five talents, to another two, and to another one; to every man according to his several ability; and straightway took his journey. 16 Then he that had received the five talents went and traded with the same, and made *them* other five talents. 17 And likewise he that *had received* two, he also gained other two. 18 But he that had received one went and digged in the earth, and hid his lord's money. 19 After a long time the lord of those servants cometh, and reckoneth with them. 20 And so he that had received five talents came and brought other five talents, saying, Lord, thou deliveredst unto me five talents: behold, I have gained beside them five talents more. 21 His lord said unto him, Well done, *thou* good and faithful servant: thou hast been faithful over a few things, I will make thee ruler over many things: enter thou into the joy of thy lord. 22 He also that had received two talents came and said, Lord, thou deliveredst unto me two talents: behold, I have gained two other talents beside them. 23 His lord said unto him, Well done, good and faithful servant; thou hast been faithful over a few things, I will make thee ruler over many things: enter thou into the joy of thy lord. 24 Then he which had received the one talent came and said, Lord, I knew thee that thou art a hard man, reaping where thou hast not sown, and gathering where thou hast not strewed: 25 And I was afraid, and went and hid thy talent in the earth: lo, *there* thou hast *that is* thine. 26 His lord answered and said unto him, *Thou* wicked and slothful servant, thou knewest that I reap where I sowed not, and gather where I have not strewed: 27 Thou oughtest therefore to have put my money to the exchangers, and *then* at my coming I should have received mine own with usury. 28 Take therefore the talent from him, and give *it* unto him which hath ten talents. 29 For unto every one that hath shall be given, and he shall have abundance: but from him that hath not shall be taken away even that which he hath. 30 And cast ye the unprofitable servant into outer darkness: there shall be weeping and gnashing of teeth.

Luke 16: 10 He that is faithful in that which is least is faithful also in much: and he that is unjust in the least is unjust also in much. 11 If therefore ye have not been faithful in the unrighteous mammon, who will commit to your trust the true *riches?* 12 And if ye have not been faithful in that which is another man's, who shall give you that which is your own?

John 15: 4 Abide in me, and I in you. As the branch cannot bear fruit of itself, except it abide in the vine; no more can ye, except ye abide in me. 5 I am the vine, ye *are* the branches. He that abideth in me, and I in him, the same bringeth forth much fruit; for without me ye can do nothing. 6 If a man abide not in me, he is

138

cast forth as a branch, and is withered; and men gather them, and cast *them* into the fire, and they are burned.   7 If ye abide in me, and my words abide in you, ye shall ask what ye will, and it shall be done unto you.   8 Herein is my Father glorified, that ye bear much fruit; so shall ye be my disciples.

I. Cor. 4:   2 . . . It is required in stewards, that a man be found faithful.

Col. 3:   22 Servants, obey in all things *your* masters according to the flesh; not with eyeservice, as menpleasers; but in singleness of heart, fearing God: 23 And whatsoever ye do, do *it* heartily, as to the Lord, and not unto men;   24 Knowing that of the Lord ye shall receive the reward of the inheritance: for ye serve the Lord Christ.

Rev. 2:   10 Fear none of those things which thou shalt suffer: . . . be thou faithful unto death, and I will give thee a crown of life.

See BREACH OF TRUST; FAITH; OBEDIENCE; STEADFASTNESS; STEWARDSHIP.

FALSEHOOD

Exod. 20:   16 Thou shalt not bear false witness against thy neighbour.

Psa. 34:   13 Keep thy tongue from evil, and thy lips from speaking guile.

Psa. 101:   5 Whoso privily slandereth his neighbour, him will I cut off: him that hath a high look and a proud heart will not I suffer. 7 He that worketh deceit shall not dwell within my house: he that telleth lies shall not tarry in my sight.

Prov. 6:   16 These six *things* doth the Lord hate; yea, seven *are* an abomination unto him: 17 A proud look, a lying tongue, and hands that shed innocent blood, 18 A heart that deviseth wicked imaginations, feet that be swift in running to mischief, 19 A false witness *that* speaketh lies, and he that soweth discord among brethren.

Prov. 10: 18 He that hideth hatred *with* lying lips, and he that uttereth a slander, *is* a fool.

Prov. 12: 19 The lip of truth shall be established for ever: but a lying tongue *is* but for a moment. 22 Lying lips *are* abomination to the Lord: but they that deal truly *are* his delight.

Prov. 13: 5 A righteous *man* hateth lying: but a wicked *man* is loathsome, and cometh to shame.

Prov. 14: 8 The wisdom of the prudent *is* to understand his way: but the folly of fools *is* deceit.

Prov. 17: 7 Excellent speech becometh not a fool: much less do lying lips a prince.

Prov. 19: 5 A false witness shall not be unpunished; and *he that* speaketh lies shall not escape. 22 The desire of a man *is* his kindness: and a poor man *is* better than a liar.

Prov. 20: 17 Bread of deceit *is* sweet to a man; but afterwards his mouth shall be filled with gravel.

Prov. 21: 6 The getting of treasures by a lying tongue *is* a vanity tossed to and fro of them that seek death.

Prov. 24: 28 Be not a witness against thy neighbour without cause; and deceive *not* with thy lips.

Prov. 26: 18 As a mad. *man* who casteth firebrands, arrows, and death, 19 So *is* the man *that* deceiveth his neighbour, and saith, Am not I in sport? 24 He that hateth dissembleth with his lips, and layeth up deceit within him; 25 When

he speaketh fair, believe him not: for *there are*
seven abominations in his heart. 26 *Whose*
hatred is covered by deceit, his wickedness shall
be shewed before the *whole* congregation. 27
Whoso diggeth a pit shall fall therein: and he
that rolleth a stone, it will return upon him.
28 A lying tongue hateth *those that are* afflicted
by it; and a flattering mouth worketh ruin.

Matt. 15: 19 . . . Out of the heart proceed
evil thoughts, murders, adulteries, fornications,
thefts, false witness, blasphemies: 20 These are
the things which defile a man: . . .

Matt. 19: 18 . . . Jesus said, . . . Thou shalt
not bear false witness,

Luke 3: 14 . . . The soldiers . . . demanded
of him, saying, And what shall we do? And he
said unto them, Do violence to no man, neither
accuse *any* falsely; and be content with your
wages.

John 8: 43 Why do ye not understand my
speech? *even* because ye cannot hear my word.
44 Ye are of *your* father the devil, and the lusts
of your father ye will do: he was a murderer from
the beginning, and abode not in the truth, because
there is no truth in him. When he speaketh a lie,
he speaketh of his own: for he is a liar, and the
father of it. 45 And because I tell *you* the truth,
ye believe me not.

Eph. 4: 25 . . . Putting away lying, speak
every man truth with his neighbour: for we are
members one of another. 29 Let no corrupt communication proceed out of your mouth, but that
which is good to the use of edifying, that it may
minister grace unto the hearers.

I. Tim. 1: 9 . . . The law is not made for a
righteous man, but for the lawless and disobedient, . . . 10 . . . for liars, for perjured per-

sons, and if there be any other thing that is contrary to sound doctrine;

Rev. 21: 8 . . . All liars, shall have their part in the lake which burneth with fire and brimstone: which is the second death.

See ACCUSATION, False; DECEIT; HYPOCRISY; also SINCERITY; TRUTH.

FAMILY

Love: Psa. 133: 1 Behold, how good and how pleasant *it is* for brethren to dwell together in unity!

Prov. 15: 17 Better *is* a dinner of herbs where love is, than a stalled ox and hatred therewith.

See LOVE.

Loyalty: Prov. 27: 8 As a bird that wandereth from her nest, so *is* a man that wandereth from his place. 10 Thine own friend, and thy father's friend, forsake not; neither go into thy brother's house in the day of thy calamity: *for* better *is* a neighbour *that is* near than a brother far off.

Mark 10: 6 . . . From the beginning of the creation God made them male and female. 7 For this cause shall a man leave his father and mother, and cleave to his wife; 8 And they twain shall be one flesh: so then they are no more twain, but one flesh. 9 What therefore God hath joined together, let not man put asunder.

I. Tim. 5: 16 If any man or woman that believeth have widows, let them relieve them, and let not the church be charged; that it may relieve them that are widows indeed.

See LOYALTY.

Worship: Josh. 24: 15 . . . Choose you this day whom ye will serve; . . . as for me and my house, we will serve the Lord.

Prov. 22: 6 Train up a child in the way he should go: and when he is old, he will not depart from it.

Matt. 18: 20 . . . Where two or three are gathered together in my name, there am I in the midst of them.

FEAR

Job 15: 20 The wicked man travaileth with pain all *his* days, and the number of years is hidden to the oppressor. 24 Trouble and anguish shall make him afraid; they shall prevail against him, as a king ready to the battle.

Prov. 1: 24 Because I have called, and ye refused; I have stretched out my hand, and no man regarded; 25 But ye have set at nought all my counsel, and would none of my reproof: 26 I also will laugh at your calamity; I will mock when your fear cometh; 27 When your fear cometh as desolation, and your destruction cometh as a whirlwind; when distress and anguish cometh upon you.

Prov. 28: 1 The wicked flee when no man pursueth: but the righteous are bold as a lion.

Matt. 10: 28 . . . Fear not them which kill the body, but are not able to kill the soul: but rather fear him which is able to destroy both soul and body in hell.

Philip. 2: 12 . . . Work out your own salvation with fear and trembling. ·

Jas. 2: 19 Thou believest that there is one God; thou doest well: the devils also believe, and tremble.

I. John 4: 18 There is no fear in love; but perfect love casteth out fear: because fear hath tor-

ment. He that feareth is not made perfect in love.
See REVERENCE; also COURAGE.

FELLOWSHIP

With God, Jesus and the Holy Spirit: Isa. 57:
15 . . . Thus saith the high and lofty One that
inhabiteth eternity, whose name *is* Holy; I dwell
in a high and holy *place*, with him also *that is*
of a contrite and humble spirit, to revive the
spirit of the humble, and to revive the heart of
the contrite ones.

Matt. 12: 50 . . . Whosoever shall do the will
of my Father which is in heaven, the same is my
brother, and sister, and mother.

Matt. 18: 20 . . . Where two or three are
gathered together in my name, there am I in the
midst of them.

Mark 9: 36 . . . He took a child, and set him
in the midst of them: and when he had taken
him in his arms, he said unto them, 37 Whosoever shall receive one of such children in my name,
receiveth me; and whosoever shall receive me, receiveth not me, but him that sent me.

John 6: 53 . . . Jesus said unto them, Verily,
verily, I say unto you, Except ye eat the flesh of
the Son of man, and drink his blood, ye have no
life in you. 56 He that eateth my flesh, and
drinketh my blood, dwelleth in me, and I in him.

John 14: 23 Jesus . . . said unto him, If a
man love me, he will keep my words: and my
Father will love him, and we will come unto him,
and make our abode with him.

John 15: 4 Abide in me, and I in you. As
the branch cannot bear fruit of itself, except it
abide in the vine; no more can ye, except ye abide
in me. 5 I am the vine, ye *are* the branches. He
that abideth in me, and I in him, the same bring-

eth forth much fruit; for without me ye can do nothing. 7 If ye abide in me, and my words abide in you, ye shall ask what ye will, and it shall be done unto you. 14 Ye are my friends, if ye do whatsoever I command you.

John 17: 20 Neither pray I for these alone, but for them also which shall believe on me through their word; 21 That they all may be one; as thou, Father, *art* in me, and I in thee, that they also may be one in us: that the world may believe that thou hast sent me. 22 And the glory which thou gavest me I have given them; that they may be one, even as we are one: 23 I in them, and thou in me, that they may be made perfect in one; and that the world may know that thou hast sent me, and hast loved them, as thou hast loved me. 24 Father, I will that they also, whom thou hast given me, be with me where I am; that they may behold my glory, which thou hast given me: for thou lovedst me before the foundation of the world. 25 O righteous Father, the world hath not known thee: but I have known thee, and these have known that thou hast sent me. 26 And I have declared unto them thy name, and will declare *it;* that the love wherewith thou hast loved me may be in them, and I in them.

Rom. 7: 4 . . . Ye . . . are become dead to the law by the body of Christ; that ye should be married to another, *even* to him who is raised from the dead, that we should bring forth fruit unto God.

Rom. 8: 1 *There is* . . . no condemnation to them which are in Christ Jesus, who walk not after the flesh, but after the Spirit. 9 . . . Ye are not in the flesh, but in the Spirit, if so be that the Spirit of God dwell in you. Now if any

145

man have not the Spirit of Christ, he is none of his. 10 And if Christ *be* in you, the body *is* dead because of sin; but the Spirit *is* life because of righteousness. 11 But if the Spirit of him that raised up Jesus from the dead dwell in you, he that raised up Christ from the dead shall also quicken your mortal bodies by his Spirit that dwelleth in you. 16 The Spirit itself beareth witness with our spirit, that we are the children of God: 17 And if children, then heirs; heirs of God, and joint heirs with Christ; if so be that we suffer with *him*, that we may be also glorified together.

Rom. 12: 5 . . . We, *being* many, are one body in Christ, and every one members one of another.

I. Cor. 1: 9 God *is* faithful, by whom ye were called unto the fellowship of his Son Jesus Christ our Lord.

I. Cor. 3: 16 Know ye not that ye are the temple of God, and *that* the Spirit of God dwelleth in you?

I. Cor. 6: 15 Know ye not that your bodies are the members of Christ? shall I then take the members of Christ, and make *them* the members of a harlot? God forbid. 17 . . . He that is joined unto the Lord is one spirit.

I. Cor. 10: 16 The cup of blessing which we bless, is it not the communion of the blood of Christ? The bread which we break, is it not the communion of the body of Christ?

I. Cor. 12: 12 . . . As the body is one, and hath many members, and all the members of that one body, being many, are one body: so also *is* Christ. 13 For by one Spirit are we all baptized into one body, whether *we be* Jews or Gentiles, whether *we be* bond or free; and have been all made to drink into one Spirit. 27 Now ye are the body of Christ, and members in particular.

II. Cor. 6: 16 . . . What agreement hath the temple of God with idols? for ye are the temple of the living God; as God hath said, I will dwell. in them, and walk in *them;* and I will be their God, and they shall be my people. 17 Wherefore come out from among them, and be ye separate, saith the Lord, and touch not the unclean *thing;* and I will receive you, 18 And will be a Father unto you, and ye shall be my sons and daughters, saith the Lord Almighty.

II. Cor. 13: 5 Examine yourselves, whether ye be in the faith; prove your own selves. Know ye not your own selves, how that Jesus Christ is in you, except ye be reprobates? 11 . . . Be perfect, be of good comfort, be of one mind, live in peace; and the God of love and peace shall be with you.

Eph. 2: 18 . . . Through him we both have access by one Spirit unto the Father. 19 Now therefore ye are no more strangers and foreigners, but fellow citizens with the saints, and of the household of God; 20 And are built upon the foundation of the apostles and prophets, Jesus Christ himself being the chief corner *stone;* 21 In whom all the building fitly framed together groweth unto a holy temple in the Lord: 22 In whom ye also are builded together for a habitation of God through the Spirit.

Eph. 5: 30 . . . We are members of his body, of his flesh, and of his bones. 32 This is a great mystery: but I speak concerning Christ and the church.

Col. 3: 1 If ye . . . be risen with Christ, seek those things which are above, where Christ sitteth on the right hand of God. 3 For ye are dead, and your life is hid with Christ in God. 4 When Christ, *who is* our life, shall appear, then shall ye also appear with him in glory.

I. Thess. 5: 9 . . . God hath not appointed us to wrath, but to obtain salvation by our Lord Jesus Christ, 10 Who died for us, that, whether we wake or sleep, we should live together with him.

Heb. 2: 11 . . . Both he that sanctifieth and they who are sanctified *are* all of one: for which cause he is not ashamed to call them brethren,

I. John 1: 5 . . . God is light, and in him is no darkness at all. 6 If we say that we have fellowship with him, and walk in darkness, we lie, and do not the truth:

I. John 2: 5 . . . Whoso keepeth his word, in him verily is the love of God perfected: hereby know we that we are in him. 6 He that saith he abideth in him ought himself also so to walk, even as he walked.

I. John 3: 24 . . . He that keepeth his commandments dwelleth in him, and he in him. And hereby we know that he abideth in us, by the Spirit which he hath given us.

I. John 4: 15 Whosoever shall confess that Jesus is the Son of God, God dwelleth in him, and he in God. 16 . . . God is love; and he that dwelleth in love dwelleth in God, and God in him. 19 We love him, because he first loved us.

I. John 5: 20 . . . We know that the Son of God is come, and hath given us an understanding, that we may know him that is true; and we are in him that is true, *even* in his Son Jesus Christ. This is the true God, and eternal life.

II. John: 9 Whosoever transgresseth, and abideth not in the doctrine of Christ, hath not

God. He that abideth in the doctrine of Christ, he hath both the Father and the Son.

Rev. 3: 20 Behold, I stand at the door, and knock: if any man hear my voice, and open the door, I will come in to him, and will sup with him, and he with me.

Rev. 21: 3 . . . I heard a great voice out of heaven saying, Behold, the tabernacle of God *is* with men, and he will dwell with them, and they shall be his people, and God himself shall be with them, *and be* their God.

With Persons: Psa. 1: 1 Blessed *is* the man that walketh not in the counsel of the ungodly, nor standeth in the way of sinners, nor sitteth in the seat of the scornful.

Psa. 133: 1 Behold, how good and how pleasant *it is* for brethren to dwell together in unity!

Prov. 4: 14 Enter not into the path of the wicked, and go not in the way of evil *men.* 15 Avoid it, pass not by it, turn from it, and pass away.

Prov. 9: 6 Forsake the foolish, and live; and go in the way of understanding.

Prov. 14: 7 Go from the presence of a foolish man, when thou perceivest not *in him* the lips of knowledge.

Prov. 28: 19 He that tilleth his land shall have plenty of bread: but he that followeth after vain *persons* shall have poverty enough.

Prov. 29: 24 Whoso is partner with a thief hateth his own soul: he heareth cursing, and bewrayeth *it* not.

Ecc. 4: 9 Two *are* better than one; because they have a good reward for their labour. 10 For if they fall, the one will lift up his fellow: but woe to him *that is* alone when he falleth; for *he hath* not another to help him up. 11 Again,

149

if two lie together, then they have heat: but how can one be warm *alone?* 12 And if one prevail against him, two shall withstand him; and a threefold cord is not quickly broken.

Amos 3: 3 Can two walk together, except they be agreed?

Matt. 23: 8 Be not ye called Rabbi: for one is your Master, *even* Christ; and all ye are brethren.

John 13: 34 A new commandment I give unto you, That ye love one another; as I have loved you, that ye also love one another.

Acts 20: 35 I have shewed you all things, how that so labouring ye ought to support the weak, and to remember the words of the Lord Jesus, how he said, It is more blessed to give than to receive.

Rom. 14: 10 . . . Why dost thou judge thy brother? or why dost thou set at nought thy brother? for we shall all stand before the judgment seat of Christ. 13 Let us not therefore judge one another any more: but judge this rather, that no man put a stumblingblock or an occasion to fall in *his* brother's way. 19 Let us therefore follow after the things which make for peace, and things wherewith one may edify another. 21 *It is* good neither to eat flesh, nor to drink wine, nor *any thing* whereby thy brother stumbleth, or is offended, or is made weak.

Rom. 15: 1 We . . . that are strong ought to bear the infirmities of the weak, and not to please ourselves. 2 Let every one of us please *his* neighbour for *his* good to edification. 3 For even Christ pleased not himself; but, as it is written, The reproaches of them that reproached thee fell on me. 5 Now the God of patience and consolation grant you to be likeminded one toward another according to Christ Jesus: 6 That ye may with one mind *and* one mouth glorify God, even the Father of our Lord Jesus Christ. 7 Wherefore receive ye one another, as Christ also received us, to the glory of God.

Rom. 16: 17 . . . Mark them which cause divisions and offences contrary to the doctrine which ye have learned; and avoid them.

I. Cor. 5: 11 . . . I have written unto you not to keep company, if any man that is called a brother be a fornicator, or covetous, or an idolater, or a railer, or a drunkard, or an extortioner; with such a one no not to eat.

I. Cor. 15: 33 Be not deceived: evil communications corrupt good manners.

II. Cor. 6: 14 Be ye not unequally yoked together with unbelievers: for what fellowship hath righteousness with unrighteousness? and what communion hath light with darkness? 15 And what concord hath Christ with Belial? or what part hath he that believeth with an infidel?

Gal. 6: 2 Bear ye one another's burdens, and so fulfil the law of Christ. 10 As we have therefore opportunity, let us do good unto all *men*, especially unto them who are of the household of faith.

Eph. 5: 11 . . . Have no fellowship with the unfruitful works of darkness, but rather reprove *them*.

Philip. 2: 1 If *there be* . . . any consolation in Christ, if any comfort of love, if any fellowship of the Spirit, if any bowels and mercies, 2 Fulfil ye my joy, that ye be likeminded, having the same love, *being* of one accord, of one mind. 3 *Let* nothing *be done* through strife or vainglory; but in lowliness of mind let each esteem other better than themselves. 4 Look not every

151

man on his own things, but every man also on the things of others.

Col. 3: 16 Let the word of Christ dwell in you richly in all wisdom; teaching and admonishing one another in psalms and hymns and spiritual songs, singing with grace in your hearts to the Lord. 18 Wives, submit yourselves unto your own husbands, as it is fit in the Lord. 19 Husbands, love *your* wives, and be not bitter against them. 20 Children, obey *your* parents in all things: for this is well pleasing unto the Lord. 21 Fathers, provoke not your children *to anger*, lest they be discouraged. 22 Servants, obey in all things *your* masters according to the flesh; not with eyeservice, as menpleasers; but in singleness of heart, fearing God:

I. Thess. 5: 11 . . . Comfort yourselves together, and edify one another, even as also ye do. 14 . . . Warn them that are unruly, comfort the feebleminded, support the weak, be patient toward all *men*.

II. Tim. 3: 2 . . . Men shall be lovers of their own selves, covetous, boasters, proud, blasphemers, disobedient to parents, unthankful, unholy, 3 Without natural affection, trucebreakers, false accusers, incontinent, fierce, despisers of those that are good, 4 Traitors, heady, highminded, lovers of pleasures more than lovers of God; 5 Having a form of godliness, but denying the power thereof: from such turn away.

Heb. 10: 24 . . . Let us consider one another to provoke unto love and to good works: 25 Not forsaking the assembling of ourselves together, as the manner of some *is;* but exhorting *one another:* and so much the more, as ye see the day approaching.

Heb. 13: 1 Let brotherly love continue. 2 Be not forgetful to entertain strangers: for thereby some have entertained angels unawares. 3 Remember them that are in bonds, as bound with them; *and* them which suffer adversity, as being yourselves also in the body.

Jas. 5: 16 Confess *your* faults one to another, and pray one for another, that ye may be healed. The effectual fervent prayer of a righteous man availeth much.

I. Pet. 2: 17 Honour all *men*. Love the brotherhood. Fear God. Honour the king. 18 Servants, *be* subject to *your* masters with all fear; not only to the good and gentle, but also to the froward.

I. Pet. 3: 8 . . . *Be ye* all of one mind, having compassion one of another; love as brethren, *be* pitiful, *be* courteous: 9 Not rendering evil for evil, or railing for railing: but contrariwise blessing; knowing that ye are thereunto called, that ye should inherit a blessing.

I. John 1: 7 . . . If we walk in the light, as he is in the light, we have fellowship one with another, and the blood of Jesus Christ his Son cleanseth us from all sin.

I. John 4: 7 Beloved, let us love one another: for love is of God; . . .

See FRIEND.

FLATTERY

Prov. 14: 20 The poor is hated even of his own neighbour: but the rich *hath* many friends.

Prov. 20: 19 He that goeth about *as* a talebearer revealeth secrets: therefore meddle not with him that flattereth with his lips.

Prov. 24: 24 He that saith unto the wicked, Thou *art* righteous; him shall the people curse, nations shall abhor him:

Prov. 26: 28 A lying tongue hateth *those that are* afflicted by it; and a flattering mouth worketh ruin.

Prov. 28: 23 He that rebuketh a man, afterwards shall find more favour than he that flattereth with the tongue.

Prov. 29: 5 A man that flattereth his neighbour spreadeth a net for his feet.

Luke 6: 26 Woe unto you, when all men shall speak well of you! for so did their fathers to the false prophets.

Gal. 1: 10 . . . Do I seek to please men? for if I yet pleased men, I should not be the servant of Christ.

I. Thess. 2: 4 . . . As we were allowed of God to be put in trust with the gospel, even so we speak; not as pleasing men, but God, which trieth our hearts. 5 For neither at any time used we flattering words, as ye know, nor a cloak of covetousness; God *is* witness:

FOLLY

Psa. 14: 1 The fool hath said in his heart, *There is* no God. . . .

Psa. 107: 17 Fools, because of their transgression, and because of their iniquities, are afflicted.

Prov. 1: 7 The fear of the Lord *is* the beginning of knowledge: *but* fools despise wisdom and instruction. 22 How long, ye simple ones, will ye love simplicity? and the scorners delight in their scorning, and fools hate knowledge?

Prov. 9: 6 Forsake the foolish, and live; and go in the way of understanding. 13 A foolish woman *is* clamorous: *she is* simple, and knoweth nothing. 14 For she sitteth at the door of her

house, on a seat in the high places of the city,
15 To call passengers who go right on their ways:
16 Whoso *is* simple, let him turn in hither: . . .

Prov. 10: 1 . . . A wise son maketh a glad
father: but a foolish son *is* the heaviness of his
mother. 8 The wise in heart will receive commandments: but a prating fool shall fall. 18 He
that hideth hatred *with* lying lips, and he that
uttereth a slander, *is* a fool.

Prov. 14: 7 Go from the presence of a foolish
man, when thou perceivest not *in him* the lips of
knowledge. 8 The wisdom of the prudent *is* to
understand his way: but the folly of fools *is* deceit. 9 Fools make a mock at sin: but among
the righteous *there is* favour. 15 The simple believeth every word: but the prudent *man* looketh
well to his going. 16 A wise *man* feareth, and
departeth from evil: but the fool rageth, and is
confident. 17 *He that is* soon angry dealeth fool-
ishly: and a man of wicked devices is hated.
29 *He that is* slow to wrath *is* of great understanding: but *he that is* hasty of spirit exalteth
folly.

Prov. 15: 21 Folly *is* joy to *him that is* desti-
titute of wisdom: but a man of understanding
walketh uprightly.

Prov. 17: 25 A foolish son *is* a grief to his
father, and bitterness to her that bare him.

Prov. 18: 6 A fool's lips enter into contention,
and his mouth calleth for strokes. 7 A fool's
mouth *is* his destruction, and his lips *are* the snare
of his soul.

Prov. 20: 3 *It is* an honour for a man to
cease from strife: but every fool will be meddling.

Prov. 21: 20 *There is* treasure to be desired
and oil in the dwelling of the wise; but a foolish

man spendeth it up.

Prov. 26:   3 A whip for the horse, a bridle for the ass, and a rod for the fool's back.   10 The great *God* that formed all *things* both rewardeth the fool, and rewardeth transgressors.   12 Seest thou a man wise in his own conceit? *there is* more hope of a fool than of him.

Prov. 29:   11 A fool uttereth all his mind: but a wise *man* keepeth it in till afterwards.

Ecc. 7:   9 Be not hasty in thy spirit to be angry: for anger resteth in the bosom of fools.

Ecc. 10:   11 Surely the serpent will bite without enchantment; and a babbler is no better.

Matt. 7:   26 . . . Every one that heareth these sayings of mine, and doeth them not, shall be likened unto a foolish man, which built his house upon the sand: 27 And the rain descended, and the floods came, and the winds blew, and beat upon that house; and it fell: and great was the fall of it.

Luke 12:. 20 . . . God said unto him, *Thou* fool, this night thy soul shall be required of thee: then whose shall those things be, which thou hast provided?   21 So *is* he that layeth up treasure for himself, and is not rich toward God.

See LASCIVIOUSNESS; PLEASURE; "SOWING WILD OATS"; WICKED.

FOOD

Psa. 23:   1 The Lord *is* my shepherd; I shall not want.   5 Thou preparest a table before me in the presence of mine enemies: . . .

Psa. 104:   14 He causeth the grass to grow for the cattle, and herb for the service of man: that he may bring forth food out of the earth;   15 And wine *that* maketh glad the heart of man, . . . and bread *which* strengtheneth man's heart.

Psa. 111: 5 He hath given meat unto them that fear him: he will ever be mindful of his covenant.

John 4: 32 . . . He said unto them, I have meat to eat that ye know not of. 34 Jesus saith unto them, My meat is to do the will of him that sent me, and to finish his work.

John 6: 31 Our fathers did eat manna in the desert; as it is written, He gave them bread from heaven to eat. 32 Then Jesus said unto them, Verily, verily, I say unto you, Moses gave you not that bread from heaven; but my Father giveth you the true bread from heaven. 33 For the bread of God is he which cometh down from heaven, and giveth life unto the world. 34 Then said they unto him, Lord, evermore give us this bread. 35 And Jesus said unto them, I am the bread of life: he that cometh to me shall never hunger; and he that believeth on me shall never thirst. 36 But I said unto you, That ye also have seen me, and believe not. 37 All that the Father giveth me shall come to me; and him that cometh to me I will in no wise cast out. 38 For I came down from heaven, not to do mine own will, but the will of him that sent me. 39 And this is the Father's will which hath sent me, that of all which he hath given me I should lose nothing, but should raise it up again at the last day. 40 And this is the will of him that sent me, that every one which seeth the Son, and believeth on him, may have everlasting life: and I will raise him up at the last day. 41 The Jews then murmured at him, because he said, I am the bread which came down from heaven. 54 Whoso eateth my flesh, and drinketh my blood, hath eternal life; and I will raise him up at the last day. 55 For my flesh is meat indeed, and

157

my blood is drink indeed.   56 He that eateth my
flesh, and drinketh my blood, dwelleth in me, and
I in him.   57 As the living Father hath sent me,
and I live by the Father; so he that eateth me,
even he shall live by me.   58 This is that bread
which came down from heaven: not as your
fathers did eat manna, and are dead: he that
eateth of this bread shall live for ever.

Rom. 14:   14 I know, and am persuaded by the
Lord Jesus, that *there is* nothing unclean of itself:
but to him that esteemeth any thing to be unclean, to him *it is* unclean.   21 *It is* good neither
to eat flesh, nor to drink wine, nor *any thing*
whereby thy brother stumbleth, or is offended, or
is made weak.

I. Cor. 8:   13 . . . If meat make my brother
to offend, I will eat no flesh while the world
standeth, lest I make my brother to offend.

. I. Cor. 10:   17 . . . We *being* many are one
bread, *and* one body: for we are all partakers of
that one bread.   21 Ye cannot drink the cup of
the Lord, and the cup of devils: ye cannot be
partakers of the Lord's table, and of the table of
devils.   27 If any of them that believe not bid
you *to a feast*, and ye be disposed to go; whatsoever is set before you, eat, asking no question for
conscience' sake.   28 But if any man say unto
you, This is offered in sacrifice unto idols, eat not
for his sake that shewed it, and for conscience'
sake: for the earth *is* the Lord's, and the fulness
thereof: 29 Conscience, I say, not thine own,
but of the other: for why is my liberty judged of
another *man's* conscience?   30 For if I by grace
be a partaker, why am I evil spoken of for that
for which I give thanks?   31 Whether therefore
ye eat, or drink, or whatsoever ye do, do all to the

glory of God.

I. Tim. 4: 1 . . . The Spirit speaketh expressly, that in the latter times some shall depart from the faith, ... 3 Forbidding to marry, *and commanding* to abstain from meats, which God hath created to be received with thanksgiving of them which believe and know the truth. 4 For every creature of God *is* good, and nothing to be refused, if it be received with thanksgiving: 5 For it is sanctified by the word of God and prayer.

FRIEND—FRIENDSHIP

Prov. 11: 13 A talebearer revealeth secrets: but he that is of a faithful spirit concealeth the matter.

Prov. 17: 9 He that covereth a transgression seeketh love; but he that repeateth a matter separateth *very* friends. 17 A friend loveth at all times, and a brother is born for adversity.

Prov. 18: 24 A man *that hath* friends must shew himself friendly: and there is a friend *that* sticketh closer than a brother.

Prov. 22: 24 Make no friendship with an angry man; and with a furious man thou shalt not go; 25 Lest thou learn his ways, and get a snare to thy soul.

Prov. 25: 17 Withdraw thy foot from thy neighbour's house; lest he be weary of thee, and *so* hate thee. 19 Confidence in an unfaithful man in time of trouble *is like* a broken tooth, and a foot out of joint.

Prov. 27: 6 Faithful *are* the wounds of a friend; but the kisses of an enemy *are* deceitful. 9 Ointment and perfume rejoice the heart: so *doth* the sweetness of a man's friend by hearty counsel. 10 Thine own friend, and thy father's friend, forsake not; neither go into thy brother's house in the day of thy calamity: *for* better *is* a neighbour *that is* near than a brother far off. 19 As in water face *answereth* to face, so the heart of man to man.

Ecc. 4: 9 Two *are* better than one; because they have a good reward for their labour. 10 For if they fall, the one will lift up his fellow: but woe to him *that is* alone when he falleth; for *he hath* not another to help him up. 11 Again, if two lie together, then they have heat: but how can one be warm *alone?* 12 And if one prevail against him, two shall withstand him; and a threefold cord is not quickly broken.

Amos 3: 3 Can two walk together, except they be agreed?

John 15: 12 This is my commandment, That ye love one another, as I have loved you. 13 Greater love hath no man than this, that a man lay down his life for his friends. 14 Ye are my friends, if ye do whatsoever I command you. 15 Henceforth I call you not servants; for the servant knoweth not what his lord doeth: but I have called you friends; for all things that I have heard of my Father I have made known unto you.

See FELLOWSHIP.

FRUGALITY

Prov. 11: 16 A gracious woman retaineth honour: and strong *men* retain riches.

Prov. 12: 27 The slothful *man* roasteth not that which he took in hunting: but the substance of a diligent man *is* precious.

Prov. 13: 22 A good *man* leaveth an inheritance to his children's children: and the wealth of the sinner *is* laid up for the just. 23 Much food *is in* the tillage of the poor: but there is *that is* destroyed for want of judgment.

Prov. 21: 17 He that loveth pleasure *shall be* a poor man: he that loveth wine and oil shall not be rich. 20 *There is* treasure to be desired and oil in the dwelling of the wise; but a foolish man spendeth it up.

Prov. 23: 20 Be not among winebibbers; among riotous eaters of flesh: 21 For the drunkard and the glutton shall come to poverty: and drowsiness shall clothe *a man* with rags.

Prov. 31: 10 Who can find a virtuous woman? for her price *is* far above rubies. 27 She looketh well to the ways of her household, and eateth not the bread of idleness.

See ECONOMY; also EXTRAVAGANCE.

GIVING

I. Cor. 9: 11 If we have sown unto you spiritual things, *is it* a great thing if we shall reap your carnal things? 12 If others be partakers of *this* power over you, *are* not we rather? Nevertheless we have not used this power; but suffer all things, lest we should hinder the gospel of Christ. 13 Do ye not know that they which minister about holy things live *of the things* of the temple? and they which wait at the altar are partakers with the altar? 14 Even so hath the Lord ordained that they which preach the gospel should live of the gospel.

II. Cor. 8: 1 . . . We do you to wit of the grace of God bestowed on the churches of Macedonia; 2 How that in a great trial of affliction, the abundance of their joy and their deep poverty abounded unto the riches of their liberality. 3 For to *their* power, I bear record, yea, and beyond *their* power *they were* willing of themselves; 4 Praying us with much entreaty that we would receive the gift, and *take upon us* the fellowship

161

of the ministering to the saints. 5 And *this they did*, not as we hoped, but first gave their own selves to the Lord, and unto us by the will of God. 6 Insomuch that we desired Titus, that as he had begun, so he would also finish in you the same grace also. 7 Therefore, as ye abound in every *thing, in* faith, and utterance, and knowledge, and *in* all diligence, and *in* your love to us, *see* that ye abound in this grace also. 8 I speak not by commandment, but by occasion of the forwardness of others, and to prove the sincerity of your love. 9 For ye know the grace of our Lord Jesus Christ, that, though he was rich, yet for your sakes he became poor, that ye through his poverty might be rich. 11 Now therefore perform the doing *of it;* that as *there was* a readiness to will, so *there may be* a performance also out of that which ye have. 12 For if there be first a willing mind, *it is* accepted according to that a man hath, *and* not according to that he hath not.

II. Cor. 9: 15 Thanks *be* unto God for his unspeakable gift.

Gal. 6: 6 Let him that is taught in the word communicate unto him that teacheth in all good things.

Phil. 4: 10 . . . I rejoice in the Lord greatly, that now at the last your care of me hath flourished again; wherein ye were also careful, but ye lacked opportunity. 11 Not that I speak in respect of want: for I have learned, in whatsoever state I am, *therewith* to be content. 12 I know both how to be abased, and I know how to abound: every where and in all things I am instructed both to be full and to be hungry, both to abound and to suffer need. 13 I can do all things through Christ which strengtheneth me. 14 Notwith-

standing, ye have well done, that ye did communicate with my affliction.   15 Now ye Philippians
know also, that in the beginning of the gospel,
when I departed from Macedonia, no church com-
municated with me as concerning giving and receiving, but ye only.   16 For even in Thessalonica
ye sent once and again unto my necessity.   17
Not because I desire a gift: but I desire fruit that
may abound to your account.   18 But I have all,
and abound: I am full, having received of Epa-
phroditus the things *which were sent* from you,
an odour of a sweet smell, a sacrifice acceptable,
well pleasing to God.   19 But my God shall supply all your need according to his riches in glory
by Christ Jesus.

See ALMS; BENEFICENCE; CHURCH Support;
LIBERALITY; POOR.

GLUTTONY

Prov. 23: 20 Be   not   among   winebibbers;
among riotous eaters of flesh: 21 For the drunkard and the glutton shall come to poverty: and
drowsiness shall 'clothe *a man* with rags.

Prov. 30: 21 For three *things* the earth is disquieted, and for four *which* it cannot bear: 22
For a servant when he reigneth; and a fool when
he is filled with meat; 23 For an odious *woman*
when she is married; and a handmaid that is heir
to her mistress.

Luke 12: 19 . . . I will say to my soul, Soul,
thou hast much goods laid up for many years;
take thine ease, eat, drink, *and* be merry.   20 But
God said unto him, *Thou* fool, this night thy soul
shall be required of thee: then whose shall those
things be, which thou hast provided?

Luke 21: 34 . . . Take heed to yourselves,

lest at any time your hearts be overcharged with
surfeiting, and drunkenness, and cares of this
life, and *so* that day come upon you unawares.

Rom. 13: 13 Let us walk honestly, as in the
day; not in rioting and drunkenness, not in
chambering and wantonness, not in strife and
envying: 14 But put ye on the Lord Jesus
Christ, and make not provision for the flesh, to
fulfil the lusts *thereof.*

Philip. 3: 18 (. . . Many walk, of whom I
have told you often, and now tell you even weeping, *that they are* the enemies of the cross of
Christ: 19 Whose end *is* destruction, whose God
is their belly, and *whose* glory *is* in their shame,
who mind earthly things.)

See TEMPERANCE.

GOD

Gen. 1: 1 In the beginning God created the
heaven and the earth. 27 . . . God created man
in his *own* image, in the image of God created he
him; male and female created he them.

Deut. 10: 17 . . . The Lord your God *is* God
of gods, and Lord of lords, a great God, a mighty,
and a terrible, which regardeth not persons, nor
taketh reward:

Psa. 19: 1 The heavens declare the glory of
God; and the firmament sheweth his handywork.
7 The law of the Lord *is* perfect, converting the
soul: the testimony of the Lord *is* sure, making
wise the simple. 8 The statutes of the Lord *are*
right, rejoicing the heart: the commandment of
the Lord *is* pure, enlightening the eyes. 9 The
fear of the Lord *is* clean, enduring for ever: the
judgments of the Lord *are* true *and* righteous
altogether.

Psa. 24: 1 The earth *is* the Lord's, and the

fulness thereof; the world, and they that dwell therein.

Psa. 46: 1 God *is* our refuge and strength, a very present help in trouble.

Psa. 103: 8 The Lord *is* merciful and gracious, slow to anger, and plenteous in mercy. 13 Like as a father pitieth *his* children, *so* the Lord pitieth them that fear him. 17 . . . The mercy of the Lord *is* from everlasting to everlasting upon them that fear him, and his righteousness unto children's children; 18 To such as keep his covenant, and to those that remember his commandments to do them.

Psa. 111: 3 . . . His righteousness endureth for ever. 7 The works of his hands *are* verity and judgment; all his commandments *are* sure. 9 He sent redemption unto his people: he hath commanded his covenant for ever: holy and reverend *is* his name. 10 The fear of the Lord *is* the beginning of wisdom: a good understanding have all they that do *his commandments:* his praise endureth for ever.

Psa. 145: 18 The Lord *is* nigh unto all them that call upon him, to all that call upon him in truth.

Psa. 146: 8 The Lord openeth *the eyes of* the blind: the Lord raiseth them that are bowed down: the Lord loveth the righteous: 9 The Lord preserveth the strangers; he relieveth the fatherless and widow: but the way of the wicked he turneth upside down.

Prov. 3: 6 In all thy ways acknowledge him, and he shall direct thy paths.

Prov. 15: 3 The eyes of the Lord *are* in every place, beholding the evil and the good.

Prov. 21: 2 . . . The Lord pondereth the

hearts. 3 To do justice and judgment *is* more acceptable to the Lord than sacrifice.

Prov. 26: 10 The great *God* that formed all *things* both rewardeth the fool, and rewardeth transgressors.

Ecc. 3: 14 I know that, whatsoever God doeth, it shall be for ever: nothing can be put to it, nor any thing taken from it: and God doeth *it*, that *men* should fear before him.

Isa. 44: 6 Thus saith the Lord . . . I *am* the first, and I *am* the last; and besides me *there is* no God.

Dan. 4: 3 How great *are* his signs! and how mighty *are* his wonders! his kingdom *is* an everlasting kingdom, and his dominion *is* from generation to generation.

Matt. 6: 8 . . . Your Father knoweth what things ye have need of, before ye ask him. 14 . . . If ye forgive men their trespasses, your heavenly Father will also forgive you: 15 But if ye forgive not men their trespasses, neither will your Father forgive your trespasses.

Matt. 7: 11 If ye . . ., being evil, know how to give good gifts unto your children, how much more shall your Father which is in heaven give good things to them that ask him?

Matt. 10: 28 . . . Fear not them which kill the body, but are not able to kill the soul: but rather fear him which is able to destroy both soul and body in hell.

Matt. 11: 27 All things are delivererd unto me of my Father: and no man knoweth the Son, but the Father; neither knoweth any man the Father, save the Son, and *he* to whomsoever the Son will reveal *him*.

Matt. 19: 24 . . . I say unto you, It is easier

for a camel to go through the eye of a needle, than for a rich man to enter into the kingdom of God. 25 When his disciples heard *it*, they were exceedingly amazed, saying, Who then can be saved? 26 But Jesus beheld *them*, and said unto them, With men this is impossible; but with God all things are possible.

Mark 10: 18 . . . , Jesus said unto him, Why callest thou me good? *there is* none good but one, *that is*, God.

Luke 6: 36 Be ye therefore merciful, as your Father also is merciful.

John 1: 18 No man hath seen God at any time; the only begotten Son, which is in the bosom of the Father, he hath declared *him*.

John 3: 16 . . . God so loved the world, that he gave his only begotten Son, that whosoever believeth in him should not perish, but have everlasting life.

John 4: 24 God *is* a Spirit: and they that worship him must worship *him* in spirit and in truth.

John 14: 6 Jesus saith unto him, I am the way, the truth, and the life: no man cometh unto the Father, but by me. 7 If ye had known me, ye should have known my Father also: and from henceforth ye know him, and have seen him. 8 Philip saith unto him, Lord, shew us the Father, and it sufficeth us. 9 Jesus saith unto him, Have I been so long time with you, and yet hast thou not known me, Philip? he that hath seen me hath seen the Father; and how sayeth thou *then*, Shew us the Father? 10 Believest thou not that I am in the Father, and the Father in me? the words that I speak unto you I speak not of myself: but the Father that dwelleth in me, he doeth the works.

11 Believe me that I *am* in the Father, and the Father in me: or else believe me for the very works' sake.

Acts 10: 34 . . . Peter . . . said, Of a truth I perceive that God is no respecter of persons: 35 But in every nation he that feareth him, and worketh righteousness, is accepted with him.

Acts 17: 24 God that made the world and all things therein, seeing that he is Lord of heaven and earth, dwelleth not in temples made with hands; 25 Neither is worshipped with men's hands, as though he needed any thing, seeing he giveth to all life, and breath, and all things; 28 For in him we live, and move, and have our being; as certain . . . poets have said, For we are also his offspring. 31 . . . He hath appointed a day, in the which he will judge the world in righteousness by *that* man whom he hath ordained; *whereof* he hath given assurance unto all *men*, in that he hath raised him from the dead.

Rom. 3: 29 *Is he* the God of the Jews only? *is he* not also of the Gentiles? Yes, of the Gentiles also:

Rom. 8: 28 . . . We know that all things work together for good to them that love God, to them who are the called according to *his* purpose. 31 . . . If God *be* for us, who *can be* against us?

Rom. 11: 33 O the depth of the riches both of the wisdom and knowledge of God! how unsearchable *are* his judgments, and his ways past finding out! 36 For of him, and through him, and to him, *are* all things: to whom *be* glory for ever. Amen.

I. Cor. 6: 14 . . . God hath both raised up the Lord, and will also raise up us by his own power. 19 What! know ye not that your body is the temple of the Holy Ghost *which is* in you, which ye have of God, and ye are not your own? 20 For ye are bought with a price: therefore glorify God in your body, and in your spirit, which are God's.

II. Cor. 1: 3 Blessed *be* God, even the Father of our Lord Jesus Christ, the Father of mercies, and the God of all comfort; 4 Who comforteth us in all our tribulation, that we may be able to comfort them which are in any trouble, by the comfort wherewith we ourselves are comforted of God.

II. Cor. 9: 7 Every man according as he purposeth in his heart, *so let him give;* not grudgingly, or of necessity: for God loveth a cheerful giver.

I. Tim. 2: 5 . . . *There is* one God, and one mediator between God and men, the man Christ Jesus;

Heb. 10: 30 . . . Vengeance *belongeth* unto me, I will recompense, saith the Lord. And again, The Lord shall judge his people. 31 *It is* a fearful thing to fall into the hands of the living God.

Heb. 12: 9 . . . We have had fathers of our flesh which corrected *us*, and we gave *them* reverence: shall we not much rather be in subjection unto the Father of spirits, and live?

Jas. 1: 17 Every good gift and every perfect gift is from above, and cometh down from the Father of lights, with whom is no variableness, neither shadow of turning.

Jas. 4: 8 Draw nigh to God, and he will draw nigh to you. . . . 10 Humble yourselves in the sight of the Lord, and he shall lift you up.

I. Pet. 3: 18 . . . Christ . . . once suffered for sins, the just for the unjust, that he might bring us to God, being put to death in the flesh, but quickened by the Spirit:

II. Pet. 3: 9 The Lord is not slack concerning his promise, as some men count slackness; but is longsuffering to us-ward, not willing that any should perish, but that all should come to repentance.

I. John 1: 9 If we confess our sins, he is faithful and just to forgive us *our* sins, and to cleanse us from all unrighteousness.

I. John 3: 1 Behold, what manner of love the Father hath bestowed upon us, that we should be called the sons of God: . . .

I. John 4: 8 He that loveth not, knoweth not God; for God is love. 9 In this was manifested the love of God toward us, because that God sent his only begotten Son into the world, that we might live through him. 15 Whosoever shall confess that Jesus is the Son of God, God dwelleth in him, and he in God. 16 . . . God is love; and he that dwelleth in love dwelleth in God, and God in him. 19 We love him, because he first loved us.

See HOLY GHOST; JESUS; also SALVATION.

Duty to: Exod. 20: 3 Thou shalt have no other gods before me. 7 Thou shalt not take the name of the Lord thy God in vain: for the Lord will not hold him guiltless that taketh his name in vain.

Psa. 37: 3 Trust in the Lord, and do good; *so* shalt thou dwell in the land, and verily thou shalt be fed.

Ecc. 12: 1 Remember now thy Creator in the days of thy youth, while the evil days come not, nor the years draw nigh, when thou shalt say, I have no pleasure in them;

Matt. 4: 10 Then saith Jesus unto him, Get

thee hence, Satan: for it is written, Thou shalt worship the Lord thy God, and him only shalt thou serve.

Matt. 12: 50 . . . Whosoever shall do the will of my Father which is in heaven, the same is my brother, and sister, and mother.

Matt. 22: 21 . . . Render . . .unto Cesar the things which are Cesar's; and unto God the things that are God's. 37 Jesus said unto him, Thou shalt love the Lord thy God with all thy heart, and with all thy soul, and with all thy mind. 38 This is the first and great commandment. 39 And the second *is* like unto it, Thou shalt love thy neighbour as thyself. 40 On these two commandments hang all the law and the prophets.

Luke 17: 10 . . . When ye shall have done all those things which are commanded you, say, We are unprofitable servants: we have done that which was our duty to do.

Luke 21: 3 . . . Of a truth I say unto you, that this poor widow hath cast in more than they all: 4 For all these have of their abundance cast in unto the offerings of God: but she of her penury hath cast in all the living that she had.

Acts 5: 29 . . . Peter and the *other* apostles . . . said, We ought to obey God rather than men.

Jude: 21 Keep yourselves in the love of God, looking for the mercy of our Lord Jesus Christ unto eternal life.

GOLDEN RULE

Matt. 7: 12 . . . All things whatsoever ye would that men should do to you, do ye even so to them: for this is the law and the prophets.

Luke 6: 31 . . . As ye would that men should do to you, do ye also to them likewise.

See COMMANDMENT, The New.

GOSSIP

Lev. 19: 16 Thou shalt not go up and down *as* a talebearer among thy people; . . .

Psa. 15: 1 Lord, who shall abide in thy tabernacle? who shall dwell in thy holy hill? 2 He that walketh uprightly, and worketh righteousness, and speaketh the truth in his heart. 3 *He that* backbiteth not with his tongue, nor doeth evil to his neighbour, nor taketh a reproach against his neighbour.

Prov. 11: 13 A talebearer revealeth secrets: but he that is of a faithful spirit concealeth the matter.

Prov. 16: 28 A froward man soweth strife: and a whisperer separateth chief friends.

Prov. 17: 9 He that covereth a transgression seeketh love; but he that repeateth a matter separateth *very* friends.

Prov. 20: 19 He that goeth about *as* a talebearer revealeth secrets: therefore meddle not with him that flattereth with his lips.

Prov. 26: 20 Where no wood is, *there* the fire goeth out: so where *there is* no talebearer, the strife ceaseth. 22 The words of a talebearer *are* as wounds, and they go down into the innermost parts of the belly.

Prov. 29: 11 A fool uttereth all his mind: but a wise *man* keepeth it in till afterwards.

Ecc. 10: 11 Surely the serpent will bite without enchantment; and a babbler is no better.

Matt. 12: 34 . . . Out of the abundance of the heart the mouth speaketh. 35 A good man out of the good treasure of the heart bringeth forth good things: and an evil man out of the evil treasure bringeth forth evil things. 36 But I say unto you, That every idle word that men

172

shall speak, they shall give account thereof in the day of judgment. 37 For by thy words thou shalt be justified, and by thy words thou shalt be condemned.

See BACKBITING; BUSYBODY; SLANDER.

GRACES, Christian

Matt. 5: 3 Blessed *are* the poor in spirit: for theirs is the kingdom of heaven. 4 Blessed *are* they that mourn: for they shall be comforted. 5 Blessed *are* the meek: for they shall inherit the earth. 6 Blessed *are* they which do hunger and thirst after righteousness: for they shall be filled. 7 Blessed *are* the merciful: for they shall obtain mercy. 8 Blessed *are* the pure in heart: for they shall see God. 9 Blessed *are* the peacemakers: for they shall be called the children of God. 10 Blessed *are* they which are persecuted for righteousness' sake: for theirs is the kingdom of heaven. 11 Blessed are ye, when *men* shall revile you, and persecute *you,* and shall say all manner of evil against you falsely, for my sake.

Rom. 5: 1 . . . Being justified by faith, we have peace with God through our Lord Jesus Christ: 2 By whom also we have access by faith into this grace wherein we stand, and rejoice in hope of the glory of God. 3 And not only *so,* but we glory in tribulations also; knowing that tribulation worketh patience; 4 And patience, experience; and experience, hope: 5 And hope maketh not ashamed; because the love of God is shed abroad in our hearts by the Holy Ghost which is given unto us.

I. Cor. 13: 1 Though I speak with the tongues of men and of angels, and have not charity, I am become *as* sounding brass, or a tinkling cymbal. 2 And though I have *the gift of* prophecy,

173

and understand all mysteries, and all knowledge; and though I have all faith, so that I could remove mountains, and have not charity, I am nothing. 3 And though I bestow all my goods to feed *the* ° *poor*, and though I give my body to be burned, and have not charity, it profiteth me nothing. 4 Charity suffereth long, *and* is kind; charity envieth not; charity vaunteth not itself, is not puffed up, 5 Doth not behave itself unseemly, seeketh not her own, is not easily provoked, thinketh no evil; 6 Rejoiceth not in iniquity, but rejoiceth in the truth; 7 Beareth all things, believeth all things, hopeth all things, endureth all things. 8 Charity never faileth: but whether *there be* prophecies, they shall fail; whether *there be* tongues, they shall cease; whether *there be* knowledge, it shall vanish away. 13 And now abideth faith, hope, charity, these three; but the greatest of these *is* charity.

Gal. 5: 22 . . . The fruit of the Spirit is love, joy, peace, longsuffering, gentleness, goodness, faith, 23 Meekness, temperance: against such there is no law.

Col. 3: 12 Put on . . . , as the elect of God, holy and beloved, bowels of mercies, kindness, humbleness of mind, meekness, longsuffering; 13 Forbearing one another, and forgiving one another, if any man have a quarrel against any: even as Christ forgave you, so also *do* ye. 14 And above all these things *put on* charity, which is the bond of perfectness. 15 And let the peace of God rule in your hearts, to the which also ye are called in one body; and be ye thankful. 16 Let the word of Christ dwell in you richly in all wisdom; teaching and admonishing one another in psalms and hymns and spiritual songs, singing

174

with grace in your hearts to the Lord. 17 And whatsoever ye do in word or deed, *do* all in the name of the Lord Jesus, giving thanks to God and the Father by him.

II. Pet. 1: 5 . . . Giving all diligence, add to your faith virtue; and to virtue, knowledge; 6 And to knowledge, temperance; and to temperance, patience; and to patience, godliness; 7 And to godliness, brotherly kindness; and to brotherly kindness, charity. 8 For if these things be in you, and abound, they make *you that ye shall* neither *be* barren nor unfruitful in the knowledge of our Lord Jesus Christ.

See CHARACTER; RIGHTEOUS.

HAPPINESS

Job 5: 17 Behold, happy *is* the man whom God correcteth: therefore despise not thou the chastening of the Almighty: 18 For he maketh sore, and bindeth up: he woundeth, and his hands make whole.

Psa. 128: 1 Blessed *is* every one that feareth the Lord; that walketh in his ways. 2 For thou shalt eat the labour of thine hands: happy *shalt* thou *be*, and *it shall be* well with thee.

Psa. 133: 1 Behold, how good and how pleasant *it is* for brethren to dwell together in unity!

Psa. 144: 15 Happy *is that* people, that is in such a case: *yea,* happy *is that* people, whose God *is* the Lord.

Prov. 3: 13 Happy *is* the man *that* findeth wisdom, and the man *that* getteth understanding: 14 For the merchandise of it *is* better than the merchandise of silver, and the gain thereof than fine gold. 15 She *is* more precious than rubies: and all the things thou canst desire are not to be compared unto her. 16 Length of days *is* in her right hand; *and* in her left hand riches and honour. 17 Her ways *are* ways of pleasantness, and all her paths *are* peace. 18 She *is* a tree of life to them that lay hold upon her: and happy *is every one* that retaineth her.

Prov. 14: 21 He that despiseth his neighbour sinneth: but he that hath mercy on the poor, happy *is* he.

Prov. 15: 13 A merry heart maketh a cheerful countenance: but by sorrow of the heart the spirit is broken. 15 All the days of the afflicted *are* evil: but he that is of a merry heart *hath* a continual feast. 20 A wise son maketh a glad father: but a foolish man despiseth his mother.

Prov. 17: 22 A merry heart doeth good *like* a medicine: but a broken spirit drieth the bones.

Prov. 29: 18 Where *there is* no vision, the people perish: but he that keepeth the law, happy *is* he.

Ecc. 3: 1 To every *thing there is* a season, and a time to every purpose under the heaven: 4 A time to weep, and a time to laugh; a time to mourn, and a time to dance; 11 He hath made every *thing* beautiful in his time: also he hath set the world in their heart, so that no man can find out the work that God maketh from the beginning to the end. 12 I know that *there is* no good in them, but for *a man* to rejoice, and to do good in his life. 13 And also that every man should eat and drink, and enjoy the good of all his labour, it *is* the gift of God. 22 Wherefore I perceive that *there is* nothing better, than that a man should rejoice in his own works; for that *is* his portion: for who shall bring him to see what shall be after him?

Matt. 5: 3 Blessed *are* the poor in spirit: for

theirs is the kingdom of heaven. 4 Blessed *are* they that mourn: for they shall be comforted. 5 Blessed *are* the meek: for they shall inherit the earth. 6 Blessed *are* they which do hunger and thirst after righteousness: for they shall be filled. 7 Blessed *are* the merciful: for they shall obtain mercy. 8 Blessed *are* the pure in heart: for they shall see God. 9 Blessed *are* the peacemakers: for they shall be called the children of God. 10 Blessed *are* they which are persecuted for righteousness' sake: for theirs is the kingdom of heaven. 11 Blessed are ye, when *men* shall revile you, and persecute *you*, and shall say all manner of evil against you falsely, for my sake. 12 Rejoice, and be exceeding glad: for great *is* your reward in heaven: for so persecuted they the prophets which were before you.

John 20: 29 Jesus saith unto him, Thomas, because thou hast seen me, thou hast believed: blessed *are* they that have not seen, and *yet* have believed.

Rom. 5: 1 . . . Being justified by faith, we have peace with God through our Lord Jesus Christ: 2 By whom also we have access by faith into this grace wherein we stand, and rejoice in hope of the glory of God.

Gal. 5: 22 . . . The fruit of the Spirit is love, joy, peace, longsuffering, gentleness, goodness, faith, 23 Meekness, temperance: against such there is no law.

I. Pet. 3: 14 . . . If ye suffer for righteousness' sake, happy *are ye:* . . .

I. Pet. 4: 12 Beloved, think it not strange concerning the fiery trial which is to try you, as though some strange thing happened unto you: 13 But rejoice, inasmuch as ye are partakers of

Christ's sufferings; that, when his glory shall be revealed, ye may be glad also with exceeding joy. 14 If ye be reproached for the name of Christ, happy *are ye;* for the Spirit of glory and of God resteth upon you: . . .

Rev. 14: 13 . . . I heard a voice from heaven saying unto me, Write, Blessed *are* the dead which die in the Lord from henceforth: Yea, saith the Spirit, that they may rest from their labours; and their works do follow them.

Rev. 22: 14 Blessed *are* they that do his commandments, that they may have right to the tree of life, and may enter in through the gates into the city.

See CONTENTMENT; PEACE; PLEASURE.

HATRED

Lev. 19: 17 Thou shalt not hate thy brother in thine heart: . . .

Prov. 10: 12 Hatred stirreth up strifes: but love covereth all sins. 18 He that hideth hatred *with* lying lips, and he that uttereth a slander, *is* a fool.

Prov. 15: 17 Better *is* a dinner of herbs where love is, than a stalled ox and hatred therewith.

Prov. 26: 24 He that hateth dissembleth with his lips, and layeth up deceit within him; 25 When he speaketh fair, believe him not: for *there are* seven abominations in his heart. 26 *Whose* hatred is covered by deceit, his wickedness shall be shewed before the *whole* congregation. 27 Whoso diggeth a pit shall fall therein: and he that rolleth a stone, it will return upon him. 28 A lying tongue hateth *those that are* afflicted by it; and a flattering mouth worketh ruin.

178

Matt. 5:   43 Ye have heard that it hath been said, Thou shalt love thy neighbour, and hate thine enemy.   44 But I say unto you, Love your enemies, bless them that curse you, do good to them that hate you, and pray for them which despitefully use you, and persecute you;

Matt. 6:   15 . . . If ye forgive not men their trespasses, neither will your father forgive your trespasses.

Matt. 10:   22 . . . Ye shall be hated of all *men* for my name's sake: but he that endureth to the end shall be saved.

Luke 14:   26 If any *man* come to me, and hate not his father, and mother, and wife, and children, and brethren, and sisters, yea, and his own life also, he cannot be my disciple.

John 15:   18 If the world hate you, ye know that it hated me before *it hated* you.   19 If ye were of the world, the world would love his own; but because ye are not of the world, but I have chosen you out of the world, therefore the world hateth you.   23 He that hateth me hateth my Father also.

Gal. 5:   19 . . . The works of the flesh are manifest, which are *these*, . . . 20 . . . hatred, . . . wrath, strife, . . .   21 . . . and such like: of the which I tell you before, as I have also told *you* in time past, that they which do such things shall not inherit the kingdom of God.

Eph. 4:   31 Let all bitterness, and wrath, and anger, and clamour, and evil speaking, be put away from you, with all malice:

Col. 3:   8 . . . Put off all these; anger, wrath, malice, blasphemy, filthy communication out of your mouth.

I. John 2:   9 He that saith he is in the light,

179

and hateth his brother, is in darkness even until
now.

I. John 3: 14 . . . He that loveth not *his*
brother abideth in death. 15 Whosoever hateth
his brother is a murderer: and ye know that no
murderer hath eternal life abiding in him.

I. John 4: 20 If a man say, I love God, and
hateth his brother, he is a liar: for he that loveth
not his brother whom he hath seen, how can he
love God whom he hath not seen?

See ANGER; ENEMY; MALICE; RETALIATION.

HEART

I. Sam. 16: 7 . . . *The Lord seeth* not as man
seeth; for man looketh on the outward appearance, but the Lord looketh on the heart.

Psa. 34: 18 The Lord *is* nigh unto them that
are of a broken heart; and saveth such as be of a
contrite spirit.

Psa. 51: 10 Create in me a clean heart, O
God; and renew a right spirit within me. 17
The sacrifices of God *are* a broken spirit: a
broken and a contrite heart, O God, thou wilt not
despise.

Prov. 4: 23 Keep thy heart with all diligence;
for out of it *are* the issues of life.

Prov. 14: 30 A sound heart *is* the life of the
flesh: but envy the rottenness of the bones.

Prov. 15: 13 A merry heart maketh a cheerful countenance: but by sorrow of the heart the
spirit is broken. 14 The heart of him that hath
understanding seeketh knowledge: but the mouth
of fools feedeth on foolishness. 15 All the days
of the afflicted *are* evil: but he that is of a merry
heart *hath* a continual feast.

Prov. 21: 2 Every way of a man *is* right in
his own eyes: but the Lord pondereth the hearts.

Jer. 17:   10 I the Lord search the heart, *I* try the reins, even to give every man according to his ways, *and* according to the fruit of his doings.

Matt. 5:   8 Blessed *are* the pure in heart: for they shall see God.

Matt. 12:   34 . . . How can ye, being evil, speak good things? for out of the abundance of the heart the mouth speaketh.   35 A good man out of the good treasure of the heart bringeth forth good things: and an evil man out of the evil treasure bringeth forth evil things.

Matt. 15:´ 18 . . . Those things which proceed out of the mouth come forth from the heart; and they defile the man.   19 For out of the heart proceed evil thoughts, murders, adulteries, fornications, thefts, false witness, blasphemies: 20 These are *the things* which defile a man: . . .

Matt. 23:   26 . . . Cleanse first that *which is* within the cup and platter, that the outside of them may be clean also.

Mark 12:   30 . . . Thou shalt love the Lord thy God with all thy heart, and with all thy soul, and with all thy mind, and with all thy strength: this *is* the first commandment.

Luke 16:   15 . . . He said unto them, Ye are they which justify yourselves before men; but God knoweth your hearts: for that which is highly esteemed among men is abomination in the sight of God.

Heb. 3:   7 . . . The Holy Ghost saith, To day if ye will hear his voice,   8 Harden not your hearts, . . .   12 Take heed, brethren, lest there be in any of you an evil heart of unbelief, in departing from the living God.

Heb. 4:   12 . . . The word of God *is* quick, and powerful, and sharper than any twoedged

181

sword, piercing even to the dividing asunder of
soul and spirit, and of the joints and marrow, and
is a discerner of the thoughts and intents of the
heart.

Rev. 2: 23 . . . All the churches shall know
that I am he which searcheth the reins and hearts:
and I will give unto every one of you according
to your works.

See CONSCIENCE; KINDNESS; MERCY; MIND;
SPIRIT.

HEAVEN

Psa. 11: 4 The Lord *is* in his holy temple, the
Lord's throne *is* in heaven: his eyes behold, his
eyelids try, the children of men.

Matt. 5: 3 Blessed *are* the poor in spirit: for
theirs is the kingdom of heaven. 10 Blessed *are*
they which are persecuted for righteousness'
sake: for theirs is the kingdom of heaven. 11
Blessed are ye, when *men* shall revile you, and
persecute *you,* and shall say all manner of evil
against you falsely, for my sake. 12 Rejoice, and
be exceeding glad: for great *is* your reward in
heaven: . . . 34 . . . I say unto you, Swear not
at all; neither by heaven; for it is God's throne:

Matt. 6: 19 Lay not up for yourselves treasures upon earth, where moth and rust doth corrupt, and where thieves break through and steal:
20 But lay up for yourselves treasures in heaven,
where neither moth nor rust doth corrupt, and
where thieves do not break through nor steal:

Matt. 18: 10 Take heed that ye despise not
one of these little ones; for I say unto you, That
in heaven their angels do always behold the face
of my Father which is in heaven.

Matt. 19: 21 Jesus said unto him, If thou wilt
be perfect, go *and* sell that thou hast, and give to

the poor, and thou shalt have treasure in heaven: and come *and* follow me.

Matt. 25: 34 Then shall the King say unto them on his right hand, Come, ye blessed of my Father, inherit the kingdom prepared for you from the foundation of the world:

Mark 16: 19 . . . After the Lord had spoken unto them, he was received up into heaven, and sat on the right hand of God.

Luke 15: 7 I say unto you, that . . . joy shall be in heaven over one sinner that repenteth, more than over ninety and nine just persons, which need no repentance.

Luke 20: 34 . . . Jesus . . . said unto them, The children of this world marry, and are given in marriage: 35 But they which shall be accounted worthy to obtain that world, and the resurrection from the dead, neither marry, nor are given in marriage: 36 Neither can they die any more: for they are equal unto the angels; and are the children of God, being the children of the resurrection.

John 14: 2 In my Father's house are many mansions: if *it were* not *so,* I would have told you. I go to prepare a place for you. 3 And if I go and prepare a place for you, I will come again, and receive you unto myself; that where I am, *there* ye may be also.

II. Cor. 5: 1 . . . We know that, if our earthly house of *this* tabernacle were dissolved, we have a building of God, a house not made with hands, eternal in the heavens.

I. Thess. 4: 16 . . . The Lord himself shall descend from heaven with a shout, with the voice of the archangel, and with the trump of God: and the dead in Christ shall rise first: 17 Then we which are alive *and* remain shall be caught up together with them in the clouds, to meet the Lord in the air: and so shall we ever be with the Lord.

Heb. 11: 16 . . . They desire a better *country*, that is, a heavenly: wherefore God is not ashamed to be called their God: for he hath prepared for them a city.

Heb. 13: 14 . . . Here have we no continuing city, but we seek one to come.

I. Pet. 1: 3 Blessed *be* the God and Father of our Lord Jesus Christ, which according to his abundant mercy hath begotten us again unto a lively hope by the resurrection of Jesus Christ from the dead, 4 To an inheritance incorruptible, and undefiled, and that fadeth not away, reserved in heaven for you, 5 Who are kept by the power of God through faith unto salvation ready to be revealed in the last time.

Rev. 3: 21 To him that overcometh will I grant to sit with me in my throne, even as I also overcame, and am set down with my Father in his throne.

Rev. 7: 9 . . . I beheld, . . . lo, a great multitude, which no man could number, of all nations, and kindreds, and people, and tongues, stood before the throne, and before the Lamb, clothed with white robes and palms in their hands; 13 And one of the elders answered, saying unto me, What are these which are arrayed in white robes? and whence came they? 14 And I said unto him, Sir, thou knowest. And he said to me, These are they which came out of great tribulation, and have washed their robes, and made them white in the blood of the Lamb. 15 Therefore are they before the throne of God, and serve him day and night in his temple: and he that sitteth on the throne

shall dwell among them. 16 They shall hunger
no more, neither thirst any more; neither shall
the sun light on them, nor any heat. 17 For the
Lamb which is in the midst of the throne shall
feed them, and shall lead them unto living fountains of waters: and God shall wipe away all tears
from their eyes.

Rev. 14: 2 . . . I heard a voice from heaven,
as the voice of many waters, and as the voice of a
great thunder: and I heard the voice of harpers
harping with their harps: 3 And they sung as it
were a new song before the throne, . . .

Rev. 21: 1 And I saw a new heaven and a new
earth: for the first heaven and the first earth were
passed away; and there was no more sea. 2 And
I John saw the holy city, new Jerusalem, coming
down from God out of heaven, prepared as a bride
adorned for her husband. 3 And I heard a great
voice out of heaven saying, Behold, the tabernacle of God *is* with men, and he will dwell with
them, and they shall be his people, and God himself shall be with them, *and be* their God. 4 And
God shall wipe away all tears from their eyes;
and there shall be no more death, neither sorrow,
nor crying, neither shall there be any more pain:
for the former things are passed away. 5 And
he that sat upon the throne said, Behold, I make
all things new. . . . 9 And there came unto me
one of the seven angels . . . 10 And he carried
me away in the spirit to a great and high mountain, and shewed me that great city, the holy
Jerusalem, descending out of heaven from God,
11 Having the glory of God: . . . 22 And I
saw no temple therein: for the Lord God Almighty
and the Lamb are the temple of it. 23 And the
city had no need of the sun, neither of the moon,

to shine in it: for the glory of God did lighten it, and the Lamb *is* the light thereof. 24 And the nations of them which are saved shall walk in the light of it: and the kings of the earth do bring their glory and honour into it. 25 And the gates of it shall not be shut at all by day: for there shall be no night there. 26 And they shall bring the glory and honour of the nations into it. 27 And there shall in no wise enter into it any thing that defileth, neither *whatsoever* worketh abomination, or *maketh* a lie: but they which are written in the Lamb's book of life.

Rev. 22: 1 And he shewed me a pure river of water of life, clear as crystal, proceeding out of the throne of God and of the Lamb. 2 In the midst of the street of it, and on either side of the river, *was there* the tree of life, which bare twelve *manner of* fruits, *and* yielded her fruit every month: and the leaves of the tree *were* for the healing of the nations. 3 And there shall be no more curse: but the throne of God and of the Lamb shall be in it; and his servants shall serve him: 4 And they shall see his face; and his name *shall be* in their foreheads. 5 And there shall be no night there; and they need no candle, neither light of the sun; for the Lord God giveth them light: and they shall reign for ever and ever. 14 Blessed *are* they that do his commandments, that they may have right to the tree of life, and may enter in through the gates into the city. 19 And if any man shall take away from the words of the book of this prophecy, God shall take away his part out of the book of life, and out of the holy city, and *from* the things which are written in this book.

See IMMORTALITY; RIGHTEOUS; SALVATION; - also HELL.

HELL

Psa. 9: 17 The wicked shall be turned into hell, *and* all the nations that forget God.

Prov. 15: 24 The way of life *is* above to the wise, that he may depart from hell beneath.

Prov. 27: 20 Hell and destruction are never full; so the eyes of man are never satisfied.

Matt. 5: 22 . . . I say unto you, That whosoever is angry with his brother without a cause shall be in danger of the judgment: and whosoever shall say to his brother, Raca, shall be in danger of the council: but whosoever shall say, Thou fool, shall be in danger of hell fire. 29 . . . If thy right eye offend thee, pluck it out, and cast *it* from thee: for it is profitable for thee that one of thy members should perish, and not *that* thy whole body should be cast into hell. 30 And if thy right hand offend thee, cut it off, and cast *it* from thee: for it is profitable for thee that one of thy members should perish, and not *that* thy whole body should be cast into hell.

Matt. 10: 28 . . . Fear not them which kill the body, but are not able to kill the soul: but rather fear him which is able to destroy both soul and body in hell.

Matt. 16: 18 . . . Thou art Peter, and upon this rock I will build my church; and the gates of hell shall not prevail against it.

Matt. 18: 8 . . . If thy hand or thy foot offend thee, cut them off, and cast *them* from thee: it is better for thee to enter into life halt or maimed, rather than having two hands or two feet to be cast into everlasting fire. 9 And if thine eye offend thee, pluck it out, and cast *it* from thee: it is better for thee to enter into life with one eye, rather than having two eyes to be cast into hell fire.

Mark 9: 48 Where their worm dieth not, and the fire is not quenched.

Luke 16: 23 . . . In hell he lifted up his eyes, being in torments, and seeth Abraham afar off, and Lazarus in his bosom. 24 And he cried and said, Father Abraham, have mercy on me, and send Lazarus, that he may dip the tip of his finger in water, and cool my tongue; for I am tormented in this flame. 25 But Abraham said, Son, remember that thou in thy lifetime receivedst thy good things, and likewise Lazarus evil things: but now he is comforted, and thou art tormented. 26 And beside all this, between us and you there is a great gulf fixed: so that they which would pass from hence to you cannot; neither can they pass to us, that *would come* from thence.

II. Pet. 2: 4 . . . God spared not the angels that sinned, but cast *them* down to hell, and delivered *them* into chains of darkness, to be reserved unto judgment;

Rev. 20: 10 . . . The devil that deceived them was cast into the lake of fire and brimstone, . . . and shall be tormented day and night for ever and ever. 13 And the sea gave up the dead which were in it; and death and hell delivered up the dead which were in them: and they were judged every man according to their works. 14 And death and hell were cast into the lake of fire. This is the second death. 15 And whosoever was not found written in the book of life was cast into the lake of fire.

Rev. 21: 8 . . . The fearful, and unbelieving, and the abominable, and murderers, and whoremongers, and sorcerers, and idolaters, and all liars, shall have their part in the lake which burneth with fire and brimstone: which is the second death.

Rev. 22: 15 . . . Without *are* dogs, and sorcerers, and whoremongers, and murderers, and idolaters, and whosoever loveth and maketh a lie.

See DEATH, The Second; UNBELIEF; WICKED; also HEAVEN.

HOLY GHOST—HOLY SPIRIT—COMFORTER

Job 32: 8 . . . *There is* a spirit in man: and the inspiration of the Almighty giveth them understanding.

Job. 33: 4 The Spirit of God hath made me, and the breath of the Almighty hath given me life.

Psa. 139: 7 Whither shall I go from thy Spirit? or whither shall I flee from thy presence?

Zech. 4: 6 . . . Not by might, nor by power, but by my Spirit, saith the Lord of hosts.

Matt. 1: 18 Now the birth of Jesus Christ was on this wise: When as his mother Mary was espoused to Joseph, before they came together, she was found with child of the Holy Ghost.

Matt. 3: 16 . . . Jesus, when he was baptized, went up straightway out of the water: and, lo, the heavens were opened unto him, and he saw the Spirit of God descending like a dove, and lighting upon him; 17 And lo a voice from heaven, saying, This is my beloved Son, in whom I am well pleased.

Matt. 12: 31 . . . I say unto you, All manner of sin and blasphemy shall be forgiven unto men: but the blasphemy *against* the *Holy* Ghost shall not be forgiven unto men. 32 And whosoever speaketh a word against the Son of man, it shall be forgiven him: but whosoever speaketh against the

189

Holy Ghost, it shall not be forgiven him, neither in this world, neither in the *world* to come.

Matt. 28: 19 Go ye . . . and teach all nations, baptizing them in the name of the Father, and of the Son, and of the Holy Ghost:

Luke 11: 13 If ye . . ., being evil, know how to give good gifts unto your children; how much more shall *your* heavenly Father give the Holy Spirit to them that ask him?

John 3: 5 Jesus answered, Verily, verily, I say unto thee, Except a man be born of water and *of* the Spirit, he cannot enter into the kingdom of God. 6 That which is born of the flesh is flesh; and that which is born of the Spirit is spirit. 7 Marvel not that I said unto thee, Ye must be born again. 8 The wind bloweth where it listeth, and thou hearest the sound thereof, but canst not tell whence it cometh, and whither it goeth: so is every one that is born of the Spirit.

John 4: 24 God *is* a Spirit: and they that worship him must worship *him* in spirit and in truth.

John 6: 63 It is the Spirit that quickeneth; the flesh profiteth nothing: the words that I speak unto you, *they* are spirit, and *they* are life.

John 7: 38 He that believeth on me, as the Scripture hath said, out of his belly shall flow rivers of living water. 39 (But this spake he of the Spirit, which they that believe on him should receive: for the Holy Ghost was not yet *given;* because that Jesus was not yet glorified.)

John 14: 16 . . . I will pray the Father, and he shall give you another Comforter, that he may abide with you for ever; 17 *Even* the Spirit of truth; whom the world cannot receive, because it seeth him not, neither knoweth him: but ye know him; for he dwelleth with you, and shall be in you. 26 . . . The Comforter, *which is* the Holy Ghost, whom the Father will send in my name, he shall teach you all things, and bring all things to your remembrance, whatsoever I have said unto you.

John 15: 26 . . . When the Comforter is come, whom I will send unto you from the Father, *even* the Spirit of truth, which proceedeth from the Father, he shall testify of me:

John 16: 7 . . . It is expedient for you that I go away: for if I go not away, the Comforter will not come unto you; but if I depart, I will send him unto you. 8 And when he is come, he will reprove the world of sin, and of righteousness, and of judgment: 9 Of sin, because they believe not on me; 10 Of righteousness, because I go to my Father, and ye see me no more; 11 Of judgment, because the prince of this world is judged. 13 . . . When he, the Spirit of truth, is come, he will guide you into all truth: for he shall not speak of himself; but whatsoever he shall hear, *that* shall he speak: and he will shew you things to come. 14 He shall glorify me: for he shall receive of mine, and shall shew *it* unto you. ·

Acts 1: 5 . . . John truly baptized with water; but ye shall be baptized with the Holy Ghost not many days hence. 8 . . . Ye shall receive power, after that the Holy Ghost is come upon you: . . . 16 Men *and* brethren, this Scripture must needs have been fulfilled, which the Holy Ghost by the mouth of David spake before concerning Judas, which was guide to them that took Jesus.

Acts 2: 1 . . . When the day of Pentecost was fully come, they were all with one accord in one place. 2 And suddenly there came a sound from heaven as of a rushing mighty wind, and it filled all the house where they were sitting. 3 And there appeared unto them cloven tongues like as of fire, and it sat upon each of them. 4 And they were all filled with the Holy Ghost, and began to speak with other tongues, as the Spirit gave them utterance. 32 . . . Jesus hath God raised up, whereof we all are witnesses. 33 Therefore being by the right hand of God exalted, and having received of the Father the promise of the Holy Ghost, he hath shed forth this, which ye now see and hear. 38 Then Peter said unto them, Repent, and be baptized every one of you in the name of Jesus Christ for the remission of sins, and ye shall receive the gift of the Holy Ghost. .

Acts 4: 31 . . . When they had prayed, the place was shaken where they were assembled together; and they were all filled with the Holy Ghost, and they spake the word of God with boldness.

Acts 5: 30 The God of our fathers raised up Jesus, whom ye slew and hanged on a tree. 31 Him hath God exalted with his right hand *to be* a Prince and a Saviour, for to give repentance to Israel, and forgiveness of sins. 32 And we are his witnesses of these things; and *so is* also the Holy Ghost, whom God hath given to them that obey him.

Acts 8: 14 . . . When the apostles which were at Jerusalem heard that Samaria had received the word of God, they sent unto them Peter and John: 15 Who, when they were come down, prayed for them, that they might receive the Holy Ghost: 16 (For as yet he was fallen upon none of them: only they were baptized in the name of

the Lord Jesus.)   17 Then laid they *their* hands
on them, and they received the Holy Ghost.   18
And when Simon saw that through laying on of
the apostles' hands the Holy Ghost was given, he
offered them money,   19 Saying, Give me also
this power, that on whomsoever I lay hands, he
may receive the Holy Ghost.   20 But Peter said
unto him, Thy money perish with thee, because
thou hast thought that the gift of God may be
purchased with money.   21 Thou hast neither
part nor lot in this matter: for thy heart is not
right in the sight of God.   22 Repent therefore
of this thy wickedness, and pray God, if perhaps
the thought of thine heart may be forgiven thee.

Acts 10:   44 While Peter yet spake . . ., the
Holy Ghost fell on all them which heard the word.
45 And they of the circumcision which believed
were astonished, as many as came with Peter, because that on the Gentiles also was poured out the
gift of the Holy Ghost.   46 For they heard them
speak with tongues, and magnify God.   Then answered Peter,   47 Can any man forbid water,
that these should not be baptized, which have received the Holy Ghost as well as we?

Acts 11:   15 . . . As I began to speak, the Holy
Ghost fell on them, as on us at the beginning.
16 Then remembered I the word of the Lord, how
that he said, John indeed baptized with water; but
ye shall be baptized with the Holy Ghost.

Acts 19:   2 He said unto them, Have ye received the Holy Ghost since ye believed?   And
they said unto him, We have not so much as heard
whether there be any Holy Ghost.   3 And he said
unto them, Unto what then were ye baptized?
And they said, Unto John's baptism.   4 Then
said Paul, John verily baptized with the baptism

of repentance, saying unto the people, that they should believe on him which should come after him, that is, on Christ Jesus. 5 When they heard *this*, they were baptized in the name of the Lord Jesus. 6 And when Paul had laid *his* hands upon them, the Holy Ghost came on them; and they spake with tongues, and prophesied.

Rom. 5: 5 . . . Hope maketh not ashamed; because the love of God is shed abroad in our hearts by the Holy Ghost which is given unto us.

Rom. 8: 1 *There is* . . . now no condemnation to them which are in Christ Jesus, who walk not after the flesh, but after the Spirit. 2 For the law of the Spirit of life in Christ Jesus hath made me free from the law of sin and death. 3 For what the law could not do, in that it was weak through the flesh, God sending his own Son in the likeness of sinful flesh, and for sin, condemned sin in the flesh: 4 That the righteousness of the law might be fulfilled in us, who walk not after the flesh, but after the Spirit. 5 For they that are after the flesh do mind the things of the flesh; but they that are after the Spirit, the things of the Spirit. 9 But ye are not in the flesh, but in the Spirit, if so be that the Spirit of God dwell in you. Now if any man have not the Spirit of Christ, he is none of his. 10 And if Christ *be* in you, the body *is* dead because of sin; but the Spirit *is* life because of righteousness. 11 But if the Spirit of him that raised up Jesus from the dead dwell in you, he that raised up Christ from the dead shall also quicken your mortal bodies by his Spirit that dwelleth in you. 12 Therefore, brethren, we are debtors, not to the flesh, to live after the flesh. 13 For if ye live after the flesh, ye shall die: but if ye through the Spirit do mortify the deeds of the body, ye shall live. 14 For as many as are led by the Spirit of God, they are the Sons of God. 15 For ye have not received the spirit of bondage again to fear; but ye have received the Spirit of adoption, whereby we cry, Abba, Father. 16 The Spirit itself beareth witness with our spirit, that we are the children of God: 26 Likewise the Spirit also helpeth our infirmities: for we know not what we should pray for as we ought: but the Spirit itself maketh intercession for us with groanings which cannot be uttered. 27 And he that searcheth the hearts knoweth what *is* the mind of the Spirit, because he maketh intercession for the saints according to *the will of* God.

Rom. 14: 17 . . . The kingdom of God is not meat and drink; but righteousness, and peace, and joy in the Holy Ghost.

Rom. 15: 13 Now the God of hope fill you with all joy and peace in believing, that ye may abound in hope, through the power of the Holy Ghost.

I. Cor. 2: 9 . . . It is written, Eye hath not seen, nor ear heard, neither have entered into the heart of man, the things which God hath prepared for them that love him. 10 But God hath revealed *them* unto us by his Spirit: for the Spirit searcheth all things, yea, the deep things of God. 11 For what man knoweth the things of a man, save the spirit of man which is in him? even so the things of God knoweth no man, but the Spirit of God. 12 Now we have received, not the spirit of the world, but the Spirit which is of God; that we might know the things that are freely given to us of God. 13 Which things also we speak, not in the words which man's wisdom teacheth, but

195

which the Holy Ghost teacheth; comparing spiritual things with spiritual. 14 But the natural man receiveth not the things of the Spirit of God: for they are foolishness unto him: neither can he know *them*, because they are spiritually discerned.

I. Cor. 6:   19 What! know ye not that your body is the temple of the Holy Ghost *which is* in you, which ye have of God, and ye are not your own?

I. Cor. 12:   3 . . . No man speaking by the Spirit of God calleth Jesus accursed: and . . . no man can say that Jesus is the Lord, but by the Holy Ghost.   4 Now there are diversities of gifts, but the same Spirit.   7 But the manifestation of the Spirit is given to every man to profit withal. 8 For to one is given by the Spirit the word of wisdom; to another the word of knowledge by the same Spirit;   9 To another faith by the same Spirit; to another the gifts of healing by the same Spirit;   10 To another the working of miracles; to another prophecy; to another discerning of spirits; to another *divers* kinds of tongues; to another the interpretation of tongues: 11 But all these worketh that one and the selfsame Spirit, dividing to every man severally as he will.   13 For by one Spirit are we all baptized into one body, whether *we be* Jews or Gentiles, whether *we be* bond or free; and have been all made to drink into one Spirit.

II. Cor. 3:   17 Now the Lord is that Spirit: and where the Spirit of the Lord *is*, there *is* liberty.   18 But we all, with open face beholding as in a glass the glory of the Lord, are changed into the same image from glory to glory, *even* as by the Spirit of the Lord.

Gal. 3:   2 This only would I learn of you, Received ye the Spirit by the works of the law, or by the hearing of faith? 13 Christ hath redeemed us from the curse of the law, being made a curse for us: for it is written, Cursed *is* every one that hangeth on a tree: 14 That the blessing of Abraham might come on the Gentiles through Jesus Christ; that we might receive the promise of the Spirit through faith.

Gal. 5: 5 . . . We through the Spirit wait for the hope of righteousness by faith. 16 *This* I say then, Walk in the Spirit, and ye shall not fulfil the lust of the flesh. 17 For the flesh lusteth against the Spirit, and the Spirit against the flesh: and these are contrary the one to the other; so that ye cannot do the things that ye would. 18 But if ye be led of the Spirit, ye are not under the law. 22 . . . The fruit of the Spirit is love, joy, peace, longsuffering, gentleness, goodness, faith, 23 Meekness, temperance: against such there is no law. 25 If we live in the Spirit, let us also walk in the Spirit.

Gal. 6: 8 . . . He that soweth to his flesh shall of the flesh reap corruption; but he that soweth to the Spirit shall of the Spirit reap life everlasting.

Eph. 2: 13 . . . Now, in Christ Jesus, ye who sometime were far off are made nigh by the blood of Christ. 18 For through him we both have access by one Spirit unto the Father. 22 In whom ye also are builded together for a habitation of God through the Spirit.

Eph. 4: 4 *There is* one body, and one Spirit, even as ye are called in one hope of your calling; 30 . . . Grieve not the Holy Spirit of God, whereby ye are sealed unto the day of redemption.

Eph. 5: 9 (. . . The fruit of the Spirit *is* in

all goodness and righteousness and truth;) 18
. . . Be not drunk with wine, wherein is excess;
but be filled with the Spirit;

Eph. 6: 17 . . . Take the helmet of salvation,
and the sword of the Spirit, which is the word of
God: 18 Praying always with all prayer and
supplication in the Spirit, and watching thereunto
with all perseverance and supplication for all
saints;

I. Thess. 5: 19 Quench not the Spirit.

I. Tim. 4: 1 Now the Spirit speaketh expressly, that in the latter times some shall depart from
the faith, giving heed to seducing spirits, and doctrines of devils;

II. Tim. 1: 7 . . . God hath not given us the
spirit of fear; but of power, and of love, and of
a sound mind. 14 That good thing which was
committed unto thee keep by the Holy Ghost
which dwelleth in us.

Tit. 3: 5 Not by works of righteousness which
we have done, but according to his mercy he saved
us, by the washing of regeneration, and renewing
of the Holy Ghost; 6 Which he shed on us
abundantly through Jesus Christ our Saviour;

Heb. 3: 7 . . . The Holy Ghost saith, To day
if ye will hear his voice, 8 Harden not your
hearts, . . .

Heb. 6: 4 . . . *It is* impossible for those who
were once enlightened, and have tasted of the
heavenly gift, and were made partakers of the
Holy Ghost, 5 And have tasted the good word
of God, and the powers of the world to come, 6
If they shall fall away, to renew them again unto
repentance; seeing they crucify to themselves the
Son of God afresh, and put *him* to an open shame.

Heb. 10: 28 He that despised Moses' law died

without mercy under two or three witnesses: 29 Of how much sorer punishment, suppose ye, shall he be thought worthy, who hath trodden under foot the Son of God, and hath counted the blood of the covenant, wherewith he was sanctified, an unholy thing, and hath done despite unto the Spirit of grace?

I. Pet. 3: 18 . . . Christ . . . once suffered for sins, the just for the unjust, that he might bring us to God, being put to death in the flesh, but quickened by the Spirit:

I. Pet. 4: 14 If ye be reproached for the name of Christ, happy *are ye;* for the Spirit of glory and of God resteth upon you: on their part he is evil spoken of, but on your part he is glorified.

II. Pet. 1: 21 . . . The prophecy came not in old time by the will of man: but holy men of God spake *as they were* moved by the Holy Ghost.

I. John 2: 1 My little children, these things write I unto you, that ye sin not. And if any man sin, we have an advocate with the Father, Jesus Christ the righteous:

I. John 4: 2 Hereby know ye the Spirit of God: Every spirit that confesseth that Jesus Christ is come in the flesh is of God: 13 Hereby know we that we dwell in him, and he in us, because he hath given us of his Spirit.

I. John 5: 6 This is he that came by water and blood, *even* Jesus Christ; not by water only, but by water and blood. And it is the Spirit that beareth witness, because the Spirit is truth. 7 For there are three that bear record in heaven, the Father, the Word, and the Holy Ghost: and these three are one. 8 And there are three that bear witness in earth, the spirit, and the water, and the blood: and these three agree in one.

Rev. 22: 17 . . . The Spirit and the bride say, Come. And let him that heareth say, Come. And let him that is athirst come. And whosoever will, let him take the water of life freely.

See FELLOWSHIP; GOD; JESUS; SPIRIT.

HONESTY

Lev. 19: 35 Ye shall do no unrighteousness in judgment, in meteyard, in weight, or in measure.

Psa. 24: 3 Who shall ascend into the hill of the Lord? or who shall stand in his holy place? 4 He that hath clean hands, and a pure heart; who hath not lifted up his soul unto vanity, nor sworn deceitfully.

Prov. 11: 1 A false balance is abomination to the Lord: but a just weight is his delight.

Prov. 12: 22 Lying lips are abomination to the Lord: but they that deal truly are his delight.

Prov. 20: 10 Divers weights, and divers measures, both of them are alike abomination to the Lord.

Isa. 33: 15 He that walketh righteously, and speaketh uprightly; he that despiseth the gain of oppressions, that shaketh his hands from holding of bribes, that stoppeth his ears from hearing of blood, and shutteth his eyes from seeing evil; 16 He shall dwell on high; his place of defence shall be the munitions of rocks: bread shall be given him; his waters shall be sure.

Mark 10: 19 . . . Do not commit adultery, Do not kill, Do not steal, Do not bear false witness, Defraud not, Honour thy father and mother.

Luke 3: 13 . . . Exact no more than that which is appointed you.

Luke 6: 31 . . . As ye would that men should do to you, do ye also to them likewise.

Acts 24: 16 . . . Herein do I exercise myself,

to have always a conscience void of offence toward God, and *toward* men.

II. Cor. 4: 1 . . . Seeing we have this ministry, as we have received mercy, we faint not; 2 But have renounced the hidden things of dishonesty, not walking in craftiness, nor handling the word of God deceitfully; but, by manifestation of the truth, commending ourselves to every man's conscience in the sight of God.

II. Cor. 8: 21 Providing for honest things, not only in the sight of the Lord, but also in the sight of men.

Philip. 4: 8 . . . Whatsoever things are true, whatsoever things *are* honest, whatsoever things *are* just, whatsoever things *are* pure, whatsoever things *are* lovely, whatsoever things *are* of good report; if *there be* any virtue, and if *there be* any praise, think on these things.

Col. 3: 22 Servants, obey in all things *your* masters according to the flesh; not with eyeservice, as menpleasers; but in singleness of heart, fearing God:

I. Pet. 2: 11 . . . Abstain from fleshly lusts, which war against the soul; 12 Having your conversation honest among the Gentiles: that, whereas they speak against you as evil doers, they may by *your* good works, which they shall behold, glorify God in the day of visitation.

See CHARACTER; INTEGRITY; also DISHONESTY.

HOPE

Job 27: 8 . . . What *is* the hope of the hypocrite, though he hath gained, when God taketh away his soul?

Job 31: 24 If I have made gold my hope, or have said to the fine gold, *Thou art* my confidence; 28 This also *were* an iniquity *to be punished by* the judge: for I should have denied the God *that is* above.

Psa. 9: .18 . . . The needy shall not always be forgotten: the expectation of the poor shall *not* perish for ever.

Psa. 31: 24 Be of good courage, and he shall strengthen your heart, all ye that hope in the Lord.

Psa. 33: 18 Behold,·the eye of the Lord *is* upon them that fear him, upon them that hope in his mercy; 22 Let thy mercy, O Lord, be upon us, according as we hope in thee.

Psa. 43: 5 Why art thou cast down, O my soul? and why art thou disquieted within me? hope in God: for I shall yet praise him, *who is* the health of my countenance, and my God.

Psa. 146: 5 Happy *is he* that *hath* the God of Jacob for his help, whose hope *is* in the Lord his God:

Prov. 10: 28 The hope of the righteous *shall be* gladness: but the expectation of the wicked shall perish.

Prov. 13: 12 Hope deferred maketh the heart sick: but *when* the desire cometh, *it is* a tree of life.

Prov. 14: 32 The wicked is driven away in his wickedness: but the righteous hath hope in his death.

Lam. 3: 26 *It is* good that *a man* should both hope and quietly wait for the salvation of the Lord.

Acts 24: 14 . . . This I confess unto thee, that after the way which they call heresy, so worship I the God of my fathers, believing all things which are written in the law and in the prophets: 15 And have hope toward God, . . . that there shall be a resurrection of the dead, both of the just and unjust.

Rom. 5: 1 . . . Being justified by faith, we have peace with God through our Lord Jesus Christ: 2 By whom also we have access by faith into this grace wherein we stand, and rejoice in hope of the glory of God. 3 And not only *so*, but we glory in tribulations also; knowing that tribulation worketh patience; 4 And patience, experience; and experience, hope; 5 And hope maketh not ashamed; because the love of God is shed abroad in our hearts by the Holy Ghost which is given unto us.

Rom. 8: 24 . . . We are saved by hope: but hope that is seen is not hope: for what a man seeth, why doth he yet hope for? 25 But if we hope for that we see not, *then* do we with patience wait for *it*.

Rom. 15: 4 . . . Whatsoever things were written aforetime were written for our learning, that we through patience and comfort of the Scriptures might have hope. 13 Now the God of hope fill you with all joy and peace in believing, that ye may abound in hope, through the power of the Holy Ghost.

I. Cor. 13: 13 . . . Now abideth faith, hope, charity, these three; but the greatest of these *is* charity.

I. Cor. 15: 19 If in this life only we have hope in Christ, we are of all men most miserable.

Gal. 5: 5 . . . We through the Spirit wait for the hope of righteousness by faith.

Eph. 2: 12 . . . At that time ye were with-out Christ, being aliens from the commonwealth of Israel, and strangers from the covenants of promise, having no hope, and without God in the world: 13 But now, in Christ Jesus, ye who sometime were far off are made nigh by the blood of Christ.

Philip. 1: 20 According to my earnest expectation and *my* hope, that in nothing I shall be ashamed, but *that* with all boldness, as always, *so* now also Christ shall be magnified in my body, whether *it be* by life, or by death.

Col. 1: 3 We give thanks to God and the Father of our Lord Jesus Christ, . . . 5 For the hope which is laid up for you in heaven, whereof ye heard before in the word of the truth of the gospel; 21 And you, that were sometime alienated and enemies in *your* mind by wicked works, yet now hath he reconciled 22 In the body of his flesh through death, to present you holy and unblameable and unreproveable in his sight: 23 If ye continue in the faith grounded and settled, and *be* not moved away from the hope of the gospel, which ye have heard, *and* which was preached to every creature which is under heaven; whereof I Paul am made a minister;

I. Thess. 5: 8 . . . Let us, who are of the day, be sober, putting on the breastplate of faith and love; and for a helmet, the hope of salvation.

II. Thess. 2: 16 Now our Lord Jesus Christ himself, and God, even our Father, which hath loved us, and hath given *us* everlasting consolation and good hope through grace, 17 Comfort your hearts, and stablish you in every good word and work.

Tit. 1: 2 . . . Hope of eternal life, which God, that cannot lie, promised before the world began;

Tit. 3: 7 . . . Being justified by his grace, we

204

should be made heirs according to the hope of eternal life.

Heb. 3: 6 . . . Christ as a son over his own house; whose house are we, if we hold fast the confidence and the rejoicing of the hope firm unto the end.

Heb. 6: 17 . . . God, willing more abundantly to shew unto the heirs of promise the immutability of his counsel, confirmed *it* by an oath: 18 That by two immutable things, in which *it was* impossible for God to lie, we might have a strong consolation, who have fled for refuge to lay hold upon the hope set before us: 19 Which *hope* we have as an anchor of the soul, both sure and steadfast, and which entereth into that within the vail;

Heb. 11: 1 . . . Faith is the substance of things hoped for, the evidence of things not seen.

I. Pet. 1: 3 Blessed *be* the God and Father of our Lord Jesus Christ, which according to his abundant mercy hath begotten us again unto a lively hope by the resurrection of Jesus Christ from the dead, 13 Wherefore gird up the loins of your mind, be sober, and hope to the end for the grace that is to be brought unto you at the revelation of Jesus Christ; 21 . . . God . . . raised him up from the dead, and gave him glory; that your faith and hope might be in God.

I. Pet. 3: 15 . . . Sanctify the Lord God in your hearts: and *be* ready always to *give* an answer to every man that asketh you a reason of the hope that is in you, with meekness and fear:

I. John 3: 2 Beloved, now are we the sons of God, and it doth not yet appear what we shall be: but we know that, when he shall appear, we shall be like him; for we shall see him as he is.

205

3 And every man that hath this hope in him purifieth himself, even as he is pure.
See FAITH; SALVATION.

HOSPITALITY

Prov. 23: 6 Eat thou not the bread of *him that hath* an evil eye, neither desire thou his dainty meats: 7 For as he thinketh in his heart, so *is* he: Eat and drink, saith he to thee; but his heart *is* not with thee.

Isa. 58: 6 *Is* not this the fast that I have chosen? . . . 7 *Is it* not to deal thy bread to the hungry, and that thou bring the poor that are cast out to thy house? when thou seest the naked, that thou cover him; and that thou hide not thyself from thine own flesh?

Matt. 25: 31 When the Son of man shall come in his glory, and all the holy angels with him, then shall he sit upon the throne of his glory: 34 Then shall the King say unto them on his right hand, Come, ye blessed of my Father, inherit the kingdom prepared for you from the foundation of the world: 35 For I was a hungered, and ye gave me meat: I was thirsty, and ye gave me drink: I was a stranger, and ye took me in: 36 Naked, and ye clothed me: I was sick, and ye visited me: I was in prison, and ye came unto me. 40 . . . Verily I say unto you, Inasmuch as ye have done *it* unto one of the least of these my brethren, ye have done *it* unto me. 41 Then shall he say also unto them on the left hand, Depart from me, ye cursed, into everlasting fire, prepared for the devil and his angels: 42 For I was a hungered, and ye gave me no meat: I was thirsty, and ye gave me no drink: 43 I was a stranger, and ye took me not in: naked, and ye clothed me not: sick, and in prison, and ye visited me not. 45 . . . Verily I say unto you, Inasmuch as ye did *it* not to one of the least of these, ye did *it* not to me. 46 And these shall go away into everlasting punishment: but the righteous into life eternal.

Mark 9: 41 . . . Whosoever shall give you a cup of water to drink in my name, because ye belong to Christ, verily I say unto you, he shall not lose his reward.

Luke 14: 12 . . . When thou makest a dinner or a supper, call not thy friends, nor thy brethren, neither thy kinsmen, nor *thy* rich neighbours; lest they also bid thee again, and a recompense be made thee. 13 But when thou makest a feast, call the poor, the maimed, the lame, the blind: 14 And thou shalt be blessed; for they cannot recompense thee: for thou shalt be recompensed at the resurrection of the just.

Rom. 12: 10 *Be* kindly affectioned one to another with brotherly love; in honour preferring one another; 13 Distributing to the necessity of saints; given to hospitality.

Heb. 13: 2 Be not forgetful to entertain strangers: for thereby some have entertained angels unawares.

Jas. 2: 15 If a brother or sister be naked, and destitute of daily food, 16 And one of you say unto them, Depart in peace, be *ye* warmed and filled; notwithstanding ye give them not those things which are needful to the body; what *doth it* profit? 17 Even so faith, if it hath not works, is dead, being alone.

I. Pet. 4: 9 Use hospitality one to another without grudging. 10 As every man hath received the gift, *even so* minister the same one to another, as good stewards of the manifold grace of God.

I. John 3: 17 . . . Whoso hath this world's good, and seeth his brother have need, and shutteth up his bowels *of compassion* from him, how dwelleth the love of God in him?

III. John: 5 Beloved, thou doest faithfully whatsoever thou doest to the brethren, and to strangers; 6 Which have borne witness of thy charity before the church: whom if thou bring forward on their journey after a godly sort, thou shalt do well: 7 Because that for his name's sake they went forth, taking nothing of the Gentiles. 8 We therefore ought to receive such, that we might be fellow helpers to the truth.

HUMILITY

Psa. 9: 11 Sing praises to the Lord, . . . 12 . . . he forgetteth not the cry of the humble.

Prov. 3: 34 Surely he scorneth the scorners: but he giveth grace unto the lowly.

Prov. 11: 2 *When* pride cometh, then cometh shame: but with the lowly *is* wisdom.

Prov. 15: 33 The fear of the Lord *is* the instruction of wisdom; and before honour *is* humility.

Prov. 16: 19 Better *it is to be* of an humble spirit with the lowly, than to divide the spoil with the proud.

Prov. 22: 4 By humility *and* the fear of the Lord *are* riches, and honour, and life.

Prov. 27: 2 Let another man praise thee, and not thine own mouth; a stranger, and not thine own lips.

Prov. 29: 23 A man's pride shall bring him low: but honour shall uphold the humble in spirit.

Isa. 57: 15 . . . Thus saith the high and lofty

One that inhabiteth eternity, whose name *is* Holy;
I dwell in the high and holy *place,* with him also
that is of a contrite and humble spirit, to revive
the spirit of the humble, and to revive the heart
of the contrite ones.

Jer. 45: 5 . . . Seekest thou great things for
thyself? seek *them* not: for, behold, I will bring
evil upon all flesh, saith the Lord: . . .

Mic. 6: 8 He hath shewed thee, O man, what
is good; and what doth the Lord require of thee,
but to do justly, and to love mercy, and to walk
humbly with thy God?

Matt. 5: 3 Blessed *are* the poor in spirit: for
theirs is the kingdom of heaven.

Matt. 10: 24 The disciple is not above *his*
master, nor the servant above his lord.

Matt. 18: 2 . . . Jesus called a little child
unto him, and set him in the midst of them, 3
And said, Verily I say unto you, Except ye be
converted, and become as little children, ye shall
not enter into the kingdom of heaven. 4 Whosoever therefore shall humble himself as this little
child, the same is greatest in the kingdom of
heaven.

Matt. 20: 26 . . . Whosoever will be great
among you, let him be your minister; 27 And
whosoever will be chief among you, let him be
your servant: 28 Even as the Son of man came
not to be ministered unto, but to minister, and to
give his life a ransom for many.

Luke 1: 52 He hath put down the mighty from
their seats, and exalted them of low degree.

Luke 14: 8 When thou art bidden of any *man*
to a wedding, sit not down in the highest room;
lest a more honourable man than thou be bidden
of him; 9 And he that bade thee and him come

and say to thee, Give this man place; and thou
begin with shame to take the lowest room. 10
But when thou art bidden, go and sit down in the
lowest room; that when he that bade thee cometh,
he may say unto thee, Friend, go up higher: then
shalt thou have worship in the presence of them
that sit at meat with thee. 11 For whosoever
exalteth himself shall be abased; and he that humbleth himself shall be exalted.

Luke 17: 10 . . . When ye shall have done all
those things which are commanded you, say, We
are unprofitable servants: we have done that
which was our duty to do.

Luke 18: 10 Two men went up into the temple to pray; the one a Pharisee, and the other a
publican. 11 The Pharisee stood and prayed thus
with himself, God, I thank thee, that I am not
as other men *are*, extortioners, unjust, adulterers,
or even as this publican. 12 I fast twice in the
week, I give tithes of all that I possess. 13 And
the publican, standing afar off, would not lift up
so much as *his* eyes unto heaven, but smote upon
his breast, saying, God be merciful to me a sinner.
14 I tell you, this man went down to his house
justified *rather* than the other: for every one that
exalteth himself shall be abased; and he that
humbleth himself shall be exalted.

John 13: 14 If I . . . , *your* Lord and Master,
have washed your feet; ye also ought to wash one
another's feet. 15 For I have given you an example, that ye should do as I have done to you.
16 Verily, verily, I say unto you, The servant is
not greater than his lord; neither he that is sent
greater than he that sent him.

John 21: 15 . . . Jesus saith to Simon Peter,
Simon, *son* of Jonas, lovest thou me more than

210

these? He saith unto him, Yea, Lord; thou knowest that I love thee. He saith unto him, Feed my lambs.

Rom. 11:   20 . . . Be not highminded, but fear:

Rom. 12:   3 . . . I say, through the grace given unto me, to every man that is among you, not to think *of himself* more highly than he ought to think; but to think soberly, according as God hath dealt to every man the measure of faith. 10 *Be* kindly affectioned one to another with brotherly love; in honour preferring one another; 16 *Be* of the same mind one toward another. Mind not high things, but condescend to men of low estate. Be not wise in your own conceits.

I. Cor. 1:   28 . . . Base things of the world, and things which are despised, hath God chosen, *yea*, and things which are not, to bring to nought things that are: 29 That no flesh should glory in his presence.

, I. Cor. 10:   12 . . . Let him that thinketh he standeth take heed lest he fall.

I. Cor. 15:   10 . . . By the grace of God I am what I am: . . .

II. Cor. 3: 5 Not that we are sufficient of ourselves to think any thing as of ourselves; but our sufficiency *is* of God;

II. Cor. 12:   5 . . . Of myself I will not glory, but in mine infirmities.   10 . . . I take pleasure in infirmities, in reproaches, in necessities, in persecutions, in distresses for Christ's sake: for when I am weak, then am I strong.

Gal. 5:   26 Let us not be desirous of vainglory, provoking one another, envying one another.

Philip. 2:   3 *Let* nothing *be done* through strife or vainglory; but in lowliness of mind let each esteem other better than themselves.   4 Look not

211

every man on his own things, but every man also on the things of others. 5 Let this mind be in you, which was also in Christ Jesus: 6 Who, being in the form of God, thought it not robbery to be equal with God: 7 But made himself of no reputation, and took upon him the form of a servant, and was made in the likeness of men: 8 And being found in fashion as a man, he humbled himself, and became obedient unto death. even the death of the cross.

Col. 3: 12 Put on . . ., as the elect of God, holy and beloved, bowels of mercies, kindness, humbleness of mind, meekness, longsuffering;

Jas. 1: 9 Let the brother of low degree rejoice in that he is exalted: 10 But the rich, in that he is made low: because as the flower of the grass he shall pass away.

Jas. 4: 10 Humble yourselves in the sight of the Lord, and he shall lift you up.

I. Pet. 5: 5 . . . Ye younger, submit yourselves unto the elder. Yea, all *of you* be subject one to another, and be clothed with humility: for God resisteth the proud, and giveth grace to the humble. 6 Humble yourselves therefore under the mighty hand of God, that he may exalt you in due time:

See JESUS, Humility of; MEEKNESS; also CONCEIT; PRIDE; SELF-EXALTATION.

HUSBAND—WIFE

Gen. 2: 18 . . . The Lord said, *It is* not good that the man should be alone; I will make him a help meet for him. 23 And Adam said, This *is* now bone of my bones, and flesh of my flesh: she shall be called Woman, because she was taken out of man. 24 Therefore shall a man leave his father and his mother, and shall cleave unto his wife: and they shall be one flesh.

Prov. 5: 18 . . . Rejoice with the wife of thy youth.

Prov. 12: 4 A virtuous woman *is* a crown to her husband: but she that maketh ashamed *is* as rottenness in his bones.

Prov. 18: 22 *Whoso* findeth a wife findeth a good *thing,* and obtaineth favour of the Lord.

Prov. 19: 14 . . . A prudent wife *is* from the Lord.

Prov. 21: 9 *It is* better to dwell in a corner of the housetop, than with a brawling woman in a wide house. 19 *It is* better to dwell in the wilderness, than with a contentious and an angry woman.

Prov. 30: 21 For three *things* the earth is disquieted, and for four *which* it cannot bear: 22 For a servant when he reigneth; and a fool when he is filled with meat; 23 For an odious *woman* when she is married; and a handmaid that is heir to her mistress.

Prov. 31: 10 Who can find a virtuous woman? for her price *is* far above rubies. 11 The heart of her husband doth safely trust in her, so that he shall have no need of spoil. 12 She will do him good and not evil all the days of her life. 26 She openeth her mouth with wisdom; and in her tongue *is* the law of kindness. 27 She looketh well to the ways of her household, and eateth not the bread of idleness. 28 Her children arise up, and call her blessed; her husband *also,* and he praiseth her. 30 Favour *is* deceitful, and beauty *is* vain: *but* a woman *that* feareth the Lord, she shall be praised. 31 Give her of the fruit of her hands; and let her own works praise her in the gates.

Ecc. 9: 9 Live joyfully with the wife whom thou lovest all the days of the life of thy vanity, . . . for that *is* thy portion in *this* life, and in thy labour which thou takest under the sun.

I. Cor. 7: 2 . . . Let every man have his own wife, and let every woman have her own husband. 3 Let the husband render unto the wife due benevolence: and likewise also the wife unto the husband. 4 The wife hath not power of her own body but the husband: and likewise also the husband hath not power of his own body, but the wife. 6 But I speak this by permission, *and* not of commandment. 12 . . . To the rest speak I, not the Lord: If any brother hath a wife that believeth not, and she be pleased to dwell with him, let him not put her away. 13 And the woman which hath a husband that believeth not, and if he be pleased to dwell with her, let her not leave him. 14 For the unbelieving husband is sanctified by the wife, and the unbelieving wife is sanctified by the husband: else were your children unclean; but now are they holy. 15 But if the unbelieving depart, let him depart. A brother or a sister is not under bondage in such *cases:* but God hath called us to peace. 16 For what knowest thou, O wife, whether thou shalt save *thy* husband? or how knowest thou, O man, whether thou shalt save *thy* wife? 39 The wife is bound by the law as long as her husband liveth; but if her husband be dead, she is at liberty to be married to whom she will; only in the Lord.

Eph. 5: 25 Husbands, love your wives, even as Christ also loved the church, and gave himself for it; 26 That he might sanctify and cleanse it with the washing of water by the word, 27 That he might present it to himself a glorious church, not having spot, or wrinkle, or any such thing; but that it should be holy and without blemish. 28 So ought men to love their wives as their own bodies. He that loveth his wife loveth himself. 29 For no man ever yet hated his own flesh; but nourisheth and cherisheth it, even as the Lord the church: 30 For we are members of his body, of his flesh, and of his bones. 31 For this cause shall a man leave his father and mother, and shall be joined unto his wife, and they two shall be one flesh. 32 This is a great mystery: but I speak concerning Christ and the church. 33 Nevertheless, let every one of you in particular so love his wife even as himself; and the wife *see* that she reverence *her* husband.

Col. 3: 18 Wives, submit yourselves unto your own husbands, as it is fit in the Lord. 19 Husbands, love *your* wives, and be not bitter against them.

I. Tim. 5: 14 I will . . . that the younger women marry, bear children, guide the house, give none occasion to the adversary to speak reproachfully.

Tit. 2: 4 . . . Teach the young women to be sober, to love their husbands, to love their children, 5 *To be* discreet, chaste, keepers at home, good, obedient to their own husbands, that the word of God be not blasphemed.

I. Pet. 3: 7 . . . Ye husbands, dwell with *them* according to knowledge, giving honour unto the wife, as unto the weaker vessel, and as being heirs together of the grace of life; that your prayers be not hindered.

See CHILDREN; DIVORCE; MARRIAGE; PARENTS.

HYPOCRISY

Prov. 11: 9 A hypocrite with *his* mouth destroyeth his neighbour: but through knowledge shall the just be delivered.

Prov. 20: 14 *It is* naught, *it is* naught, saith the buyer: but when he is gone his way, then he boasteth.

Prov. 23: 6 Eat thou not the bread of *him that hath* an evil eye, neither desire thou his dainty meats: 7 For as he thinketh in his heart, so *is* he: Eat and drink, saith he to thee; but his heart *is* not with thee.

Prov. 25: 19 Confidence in an unfaithful man in time of trouble *is like* a broken tooth, and a foot out of joint.

Matt. 6: 1 Take heed that ye do not your alms before men, to be seen of them: otherwise ye have no reward of your Father which is in heaven. 5 And when thou prayest, thou shalt not be as the hypocrites *are:* for they love to pray standing in the synagogues and in corners of the streets, that they may be seen of men. Verily I say unto you, They have their reward.

Matt. 7: 4 . . . How wilt thou say to thy brother, Let me pull out the mote out of thine eye; and, behold, a beam *is* in thine own eye? 5 Thou hypocrite, first cast out the beam out of thine own eye; and then shalt thou see clearly to cast out the mote out of thy brother's eye. 15 Beware of false prophets, which come to you in sheep's clothing, but inwardly they are ravening wolves. 21 Not every one that saith unto me, Lord, Lord, shall enter into the kingdom of heaven; but he that doeth the will of my Father which is in heaven. 22 Many will say to me in that day, Lord, Lord, have we not prophesied in thy name? and in thy name have cast out devils? and in thy name done many wonderful works? 23 And then will I profess unto them, I never knew you: depart from me, ye that work iniquity.

Matt. 21: 28 . . . A *certain* man had two sons; and he came to the first, and said, Son, go work to day in my vineyard. 29 He answered and said, I will not; but afterward he repented, and went. 30 And he came to the second, and said likewise. And he answered and said, I *go*, sir; and went not. 31 Whether of them twain did the will of *his* father? They say unto him, The first. . . .

Matt. 23: 23 Woe unto you, scribes and Pharisees, hypocrites! for ye pay tithe of mint and anise and cummin, and have omitted the weightier *matters* of the law, judgment, mercy, and faith: these ought ye to have done, and not to leave the other undone. 24 *Ye* blind guides, which strain at a gnat, and swallow a camel. 25 Woe unto you, scribes and Pharisees, hypocrites! for ye make clean the outside of the cup and of the platter, but within they are full of extortion and excess. 26 *Thou* blind Pharisee, cleanse first that *which is* within the cup and platter, that the outside of them may be clean also. 27 Woe unto you, scribes and Pharisees, hypocrites! for ye are like unto whited sepulchres, which indeed appear beautiful outward, but are within full of dead *men's* bones, and of all uncleanness. 28 Even so ye also outwardly appear righteous unto men, but within ye are full of hypocrisy and ininquity. 33 *Ye* serpents, *ye* generation of vipers, how can ye escape the damnation of hell?

Mark 7: 6 . . . Well hath Esaias prophesied of you hypocrites, as it is written, This people honoureth me with *their* lips, but their heart is far from me. 7 Howbeit in vain do they worship me, teaching *for* doctrines the commandments of men.

Mark 12: 38 . . . He said unto them in his doctrine, Beware of the scribes, which love to go in long clothing and *love* salutations in the marketplaces, 39 And the chief seats in the synagogues, and the uppermost rooms at feasts: 40 Which devour widows' houses, and for a pretense make long prayers: these shall receive greater damnation.

Luke 6: 46 . . . Why call ye me, Lord, Lord, and do not the things which I say?

Luke 12: 1 . . . He began to say unto his disciples first of all, Beware ye of the leaven of the Pharisees, which is hypocrisy. 2 For there is nothing covered, that shall not be revealed; neither hid, that shall not be known.

Luke 16: 13 No servant can serve two masters: for either he will hate the one, and love the other; or else he will hold to the one, and despise the other. Ye cannot serve God and mammon. 15 . . . Ye are they which justify yourselves before men; but God knoweth your hearts: for that which is highly esteemed among men is abomination in the sight of God.

Luke 18: 10 Two men went up into the temple to pray; the one a Pharisee, and the other a publican. 11 The Pharisee stood and prayed thus with himself, God, I thank thee, that I am not as other men *are*, extortioners, unjust, adulterers, or even as this publican. 12 I fast twice in the week, I give tithes of all that I possess. 13 And the publican, standing afar off, would not lift up so much as *his* eyes unto heaven, but smote upon his breast, saying, God be merciful to me a sinner. 14 I tell you, this man went down to his house justified *rather* than the other: . . .

Rom. 2: 1 . . . Thou art inexcusable, O man, whosoever thou art that judgest: for wherein thou judgest another, thou condemnest thyself; for thou that judgest doest the same things. 3 And thinkest thou this, O man, that judgest them which do such things, and doest the same, that thou shalt escape the judgment of God? 21 Thou therefore which teachest another, teachest thou not thyself? thou that preachest a man should not steal, dost thou steal? 22 Thou that sayest a man should not commit adultery, dost thou commit adultery? thou that abhorrest idols, dost thou commit sacrilege? 23 Thou that makest thy boast of the law, through breaking the law dishonourest thou God? 28 For he is not a Jew, which is one outwardly; neither *is that* circumcision, which is outward in the flesh: 29 But he *is* a Jew, which is one inwardly; and circumcision *is that* of the heart, in the spirit, *and* not in the letter; whose praise *is* not of men, but of God.

Rom. 16: 17 . . . Mark them which cause divisions and offences contrary to the doctrine which ye have learned; and avoid them. 18 For they that are such serve not our Lord Jesus Christ, but their own belly; and by good words and fair speeches deceive the hearts of the simple.

I. Cor. 13: 1 Though I speak with the tongues of men and of angels, and have not charity, I am become *as* sounding brass, or a tinkling cymbal.

I. Tim. 4: 1 Now the Spirit speaketh expressly, that in the latter times some shall depart from the faith, giving heed to seducing spirits, and doctrines of devils; 2 Speaking lies in hypocrisy; having their conscience seared with a hot iron; 6 If thou put the brethren in remembrance of these things, thou shalt be a good minister of Jesus Christ, . . .

II. Tim. 3: 2 . . . Men shall be lovers of their own selves, . . . 5 Having a form of godliness, but denying the power thereof: from such turn away.

Tit. 1: 15 Unto the pure all things *are* pure: but unto them that are defiled and unbelieving *is* nothing pure; but even their mind and conscience is defiled. 16 They profess that they know God; but in works they deny *him*, being abnominable, and disobedient, and unto every good work reprobate.

Jas. 1: 22 . . . Be ye doers of the word, and not hearers only, deceiving your own selves. 26 If any man among you seem to be religious, and bridleth not his tongue, but deceiveth his own heart, this man's religion *is* vain.

Jas. 2: 15 If a brother or sister be naked, and destitute of daily food, 16 And one of you say unto them, Depart in peace, be *ye* warmed and filled; notwithstanding ye give them not those things which are needful to the body; what *doth it* profit?

Jas. 3: 17 . . . The wisdom that is from above is first pure, then peaceable, gentle, *and* easy to be entreated, full of mercy and good fruits, without partiality, and without hypocrisy.

Jas. 4: 8 Draw nigh to God, and he will draw nigh to you. Cleanse *your* hands, *ye* sinners; and purify *your* hearts, *ye* doubleminded.

I. John 1: 6 If we say that we have fellowship with him, and walk in darkness, we lie, and do not the truth: 10 If we say that we have not sinned, we make him a liar, and his word is not in us.

I. John 2:   4 He that saith, I know him, and keepeth not his commandments, is a liar, and the truth is not in him.   9 He that saith he is in the light, and hateth his brother, is in darkness even until now.

See FALSEHOOD; DECEIT; SELF-RIGHTEOUSNESS.

IDLENESS—SLOTHFULNESS

Prov. 6:   6 Go to the ant, thou sluggard; consider her ways, and be wise: 7 Which having no guide, overseer, or ruler,   8 Provideth her meat in the summer, *and* gathereth her food in the harvest.

Prov. 10:   4 He becometh poor that dealeth *with* a slack hand: but the hand of the diligent maketh rich.   5 He that gathereth in summer *is* a wise son: *but* he that sleepeth in harvest *is* a son that causeth shame.   26 As vinegar to the teeth, and as smoke to the eyes, so *is* the sluggard to them that send him.

Prov. 12:   9 *He that is* despised, and hath a servant, *is* better than he that honoureth himself, and lacketh bread.   24 The hand of the diligent shall bear rule: but the slothful shall be under tribute.

Prov. 13:   4 The soul of the sluggard desireth, and *hath* nothing: but the soul of the diligent shall be made fat.

Prov. 14:   23 In all labour there is profit: but the talk of the lips *tendeth* only to penury.

Prov. 18:   9 He . . . that is slothful in his work is brother to him that is a great waster.

Prov. 19:   15 Slothfulness casteth into a deep sleep; and an idle soul shall suffer hunger.

Prov. 20:   4 The sluggard will not plough by

reason of the cold; *therefore* shall he beg in harvest, and *have* nothing. 13 Love not sleep, lest thou come to poverty: open thine eyes, *and* thou shalt be satisfied with bread.

Prov. 23: 21 . . . The drunkard and the glutton shall come to poverty: and drowsiness shall clothe *a man* with rags.

Prov. 24: 30 I went by the field of the slothful, and by the vineyard of the man void of understanding; 31 And, lo, it was all grown over with thorns, *and* nettles had covered the face thereof, and the stone wall thereof was broken down. 32 Then I saw, *and* considered *it* well: I looked upon *it, and* received instruction. 33 *Yet* a little sleep, a little slumber, a little folding of the hands to sleep: 34 So shall thy poverty come *as* one that travelleth; and thy want as an armed man.

Prov. 26: 16 The sluggard *is* wiser in his own conceit than seven men that can render a reason.

Ecc. 4: 5 The fool foldeth his hands together, and eateth his own flesh.

Ecc. 10: 18 By much slothfulness the building decayeth; and through idleness of the hands the house droppeth through.

Rom. 12: 10 *Be* . . . 11 Not slothful in business; . . .

II. Thess. 3: 10 . . . This we commanded you, that if any would not work, neither should he eat.

Heb. 6: 12 . . . Be not slothful, but followers of them who through faith and patience inherit the promises.

See PROCRASTINATION; also DILIGENCE; INDUSTRY.

IGNORANCE

Job 8: 9 (. . . We *are but of* yesterday, and know nothing, because our days upon earth *are* a shadow:)

Prov. 7: 7 . . . I discerned among the youths, a young man void of understanding, 10 And, behold, there met him a woman *with* the attire of a harlot, and subtile of heart. 21 With her much fair speech she caused him to yield, with the flattering of her lips she forced him. 22 He goeth after her straightway, as an ox goeth to the slaughter, or as a fool to the correction of the stocks; 23 Till a dart strike through his liver; as a bird hasteth to the snare, and knoweth not that it *is* for his life.

Prov. 22: 3 A prudent *man* foreseeth the evil, and hideth himself: but the simple pass on, and are punished.

Prov. 27: 1 Boast not thyself of to morrow; for thou knowest not what a day may bring forth.

Ecc. 9: 12 . . . Man . . . knoweth not his time: as the fishes that are taken in an evil net, and as the birds that are caught in the snare; so *are* the sons of men snared in an evil time, when it falleth suddenly upon them.

Luke 12: 48 . . . He that knew not, and did commit things worthy of stripes, shall be beaten with few *stripes*. For unto whomsoever much is given, of him shall be much required; and to whom men have committed much, of him they will ask the more.

Luke 23: 34 Then said Jesus, Father, forgive them; for they know not what they do. . . .

Acts 1: 7 . . . It is not for you to know the times or the seasons, which the Father hath put in his own power.

Acts 4: 13 . . . When they saw the boldness of Peter and John, and perceived that they were unlearned and ignorant men, they marvelled; and they took knowledge of them, that they had been with Jesus.

Acts 17: 23 . . . As I passed by, and beheld your devotions, I found an altar with this inscription, TO THE UNKNOWN GOD. Whom therefore ye ignorantly worship, him declare I unto you. 30 And the times of this ignorance God winked at; but now commandeth all men every where to repent:

Rom. 8: 24 . . . We are saved by hope: but hope that is seen is not hope: for what a man seeth, why doth he yet hope for? 25 But if we hope for that we see not, *then* do we with patience wait for *it*. 26 Likewise the Spirit also helpeth our infirmities: for we know not what we should pray for as we ought: but the Spirit itself maketh intercession for us with groanings which cannot be uttered.

I. Cor. 2: 7 . . . We speak the wisdom of God in a mystery, *even* the hidden *wisdom*, which God ordained before the world unto our glory; 8 Which none of the princes of this world knew: for had they known *it*, they would not have crucified the Lord of glory. 9 But as it is written, Eye hath not seen, nor ear heard, neither have entered into the heart of man, the things which God hath prepared for them that love him.

I. Cor. 3: 19 . . . The wisdom of this world is foolishness with God: for it is written, He taketh the wise in their own craftiness. 20 And again, The Lord knoweth the thoughts of the wise, that they are vain.

I. Cor. 13: 9 . . . We know in part, and we

prophesy in part. 10 But when that which is perfect is come, then that which is in part shall be done away. 11 When I was a child, I spake as a child, I understood as a child, I thought as a child: but when I became a man, I put away child-ish things. 12 For now we see through a glass, darkly; but then face to face: now I know in part; but then shall I know even as also I am known.

Eph. 4: 17 .. . . . Walk not as other Gentiles walk, in the vanity of their mind, 18 Having the understanding darkened, being alienated from the life of God through the ignorance that is in them, because of the blindness of their heart: 19 Who being past feeling have given themselves over unto lasciviousness, to work all uncleanness with greed-iness.

I. Tim. 1: 12 . . . I thank Christ Jesus our Lord, who hath enabled me, for that he counted me faithful, putting me into the ministry; 13 Who was before a blasphemer, and a persecutor, and injurious: but I obtained mercy, because I did *it* ignorantly in unbelief.

Jas. 1: 5 If any of you lack wisdom, let him ask of God, that giveth to all *men* liberally, and upbraideth not; and it shall be given him. 6 But let him ask in faith, nothing wavering: for he that wavereth is like a wave of the sea driven with the wind and tossed.

See KNOWLEDGE; WISDOM.

IMMORTALITY

Psa. 23: 6 Surely goodness and mercy shall follow me all the days of my life: and I will dwell in the house of the Lord for ever.

Psa. 49: 15 . . . God will redeem my soul from the power of the grave: for he shall receive me. . . .

Prov. 14: 32 The wicked is driven away in his wickedness: but the righteous hath hope in his death.

Ecc. 12: 7 Then shall the dust return to the earth as it was: and the spirit shall return unto God who gave it.

Dan. 12: 2 . . . Many of them that sleep in the dust of the earth shall awake, some to everlasting life, and some to shame *and* everlasting contempt.

Matt. 10: 28 . . . Fear not them which kill the body, but are not able to kill the soul: but rather fear him which is able to destroy both soul and body in hell.

Matt. 16: 26 . . . What is a man profited, if he shall gain the whole world, and lose his own soul? or what shall a man give in exchange for his soul? 27 For the Son of man shall come in the glory of his Father with his angels; and then he shall reward every man according to his works.

Matt. 19: 16 . . . One came and said unto him, Good Master, what good thing shall I do, that I may have eternal life? 17 And he said unto him, . . . If thou wilt enter into life, keep the commandments.

Matt. 25: 46 . . . These shall go away into everlasting punishment: but the righteous into life eternal.

Mark 10: 29 . . . Jesus . . . said, Verily I say unto you, There is no man that hath left house, or brethren, or sisters, or father, or mother, or wife, or children, or lands, for my sake, and the gospel's, 30 But he shall receive a hundredfold now in this time, houses, and brethren, and sisters, and mothers, and children, and lands, with persecutions; and in the world to come eternal life.

Mark 12: 25 . . . When they shall rise from the dead, they neither marry, nor are given in marriage; but are as the angels which are in heaven. 26 And as touching the dead, that they rise; have ye not read in the book of Moses, how in the bush God spake unto him, saying, I *am* the God of Abraham, and the God of Isaac, and the God of Jacob? 27 He is not the God of the dead, but the God of the living: . . .

John 3: 14 . . . As Moses lifted up the serpent in the wilderness, even so must the Son of man be lifted up: 15 That whosoever believeth in him should not perish, but have eternal life. 16 For God so loved the world, that he gave his only begotten Son, that whosoever believeth in him should not perish, but have everlasting life.

John 6: 40 . . . This is the will of him that sent me, that every one which seeth the Son, and believeth on him, may have everlasting life: and I will raise him up at the last day. 50 This is the bread which cometh down from heaven, that a man may eat thereof, and not die. 51 I am the living bread which came down from heaven: if any man eat of this bread, he shall live for ever: and the bread that I will give is my flesh, which I will give for the life of the world. 53 . . . Jesus said unto them, Verily, verily, I say unto you, Except ye eat the flesh of the Son of man, and drink his blood, ye have no life in you. 54 Whoso eateth my flesh, and drinketh my blood, hath eternal life; and I will raise him up at the last day. 58 This is that bread which came down from heaven: not as your fathers did eat manna, and are dead: he that eateth of this bread shall live for ever.

John 10: 27 My sheep hear my voice, and I

know them, and they follow me: 28 And I give
unto them eternal life; and they shall never perish, neither shall any *man* pluck them out of my
hand.

John 11: 25 Jesus said unto her, I am the
resurrection, and the life: he that believeth in
me, though he were dead, yet shall he live: 26
And whosoever liveth and believeth in me shall
never die. . . .

John 14: 19 Yet a little while, and the world
seeth me no more; but ye see me: because I live,
ye shall live also.

Acts 26: 8 Why should it be thought a thing
incredible with you, that God should raise the
dead?

Rom. 2: 6 Who will render to every man according to his deeds: 7 To them who by patient
continuance in well doing seek for glory and honour and immortality, eternal life:

Rom. 6: 22 . . . Being made free from sin,
and become servants to God, ye have your fruit
unto holiness, and the end everlasting life. 23
For the wages of sin *is* death; but the gift of God
is eternal life through Jesus Christ our Lord.

I. Cor. 15: 12 Now if Christ be preached that
he rose from the dead, how say some among you
that there is no resurrection of the dead? 16 For
if the dead rise not, then is not Christ raised:
17 And if Christ be not raised, your faith *is*
vain; ye are yet in your sins. 18 Then they also
which are fallen asleep in Christ are perished.
19 If in this life only we have hope in Christ, we
are of all men most miserable. 20 But now is
Christ risen from the dead, *and* become the firstfruits of them that slept. 21 For since by man
came death, by man *came* also the resurrection of

the dead.   22 For as in Adam all die, even so in Christ shall all be made alive.   26 The last enemy *that* shall be destroyed *is* death.   35 But some *man* will say, How are the dead raised up? and with what body do they come?   36 *Thou* fool, that which thou sowest is not quickened, except it die: 37 And that which thou sowest, thou sowest not that body that shall be, but bare grain, it may chance of wheat, or of some other *grain:* 38 But God giveth it a body as it hath pleased him, and to every seed his own body.   42 So also *is* the resurrection of the dead.   It is sown in corruption, it is raised in incorruption: 43 It is sown in dishonour, it is raised in glory: it is sown in weakness, it is raised in power: 44 It is sown a natural body, it is raised a spiritual body. There is a natural body, and there is a spiritual body. 51 Behold, I shew you a mystery; We shall not all sleep, but we shall all be changed,   52 In a moment, in the twinkling of an eye, at the last trump: for the trumpet shall sound, and the dead shall be raised incorruptible, and we shall be changed.   53 For this corruptible must put on incorruption, and this mortal *must* put on immortality.   54 So when this corruptible shall have put on incorruption, and this mortal shall have put on immortality, then shall be brought to pass the saying that is written, Death is swallowed up in victory.   55 O death, where *is* thy sting? O grave, where *is* thy victory?

Gal. 6:   8 . . . He that soweth to his flesh shall of the flesh reap corruption; but he that soweth to the Spirit shall of the Spirit reap life everlasting.

I. Thess. 4:   16 . . . The Lord himself shall descend from heaven with a shout, with the voice of the archangel, and with the trump of God: and the dead in Christ shall rise first: 17 Then we which are alive *and* remain shall be caught up together with them in the clouds, to meet the Lord in the air: and so shall we ever be with the Lord.

I. Tim. 4: 8 . . . Bodily exercise profiteth little: but godliness is profitable unto all things, having promise of the life that now is, and of that which is to come.

II. Tim. 1: 10 . . . Our Saviour Jesus Christ, who hath abolished death, and hath brought life and immortality to light through the gospel:

I. Pet. 1: 3 Blessed *be* the God and Father of our Lord Jesus Christ, which according to his abundant mercy hath begotten us again unto a lively hope by the resurrection of Jesus Christ from the dead, 4 To an inheritance incorruptible, and undefiled, and that fadeth not away, reserved in heaven for you, 5 Who are kept by the power of God through faith unto salvation ready to be revealed in the last time.

I. John 2: 17 . . . The world passeth away, and the lust thereof: but he that doeth the will of God abideth for ever. 25 And this is the promise that he hath promised us, *even* eternal life.

Rev. 22: 5 . . . There shall be no night there; and they need no candle, neither light of the sun; for the Lord God giveth them light: and they shall reign for ever and ever.

See DEATH; HEAVEN; HELL; SALVATION.

IMPENITENCE

Psa. 52: 1 Why boastest thou thyself in mischief, O mighty man? the goodness of God *endureth* continually.

Prov. 1: 24 Because I have called, and ye refused; I have stretched out my hand, and no man regarded; 25 But ye have set at nought all my counsel, and would none of my reproof: 26 I also will laugh at your calamity; I will mock when your fear cometh; 27 When your fear cometh as desolation, and your destruction cometh as a whirlwind; when distress and anguish cometh upon you. 28 Then shall they call upon me, but I will not answer; they shall seek me early, but they shall not find me: 29 For that they hated knowledge, and did not choose the fear of the Lord: 30 They would none of my counsel: they despised all my reproof. 31 Therefore shall they eat of the fruit of their own way, and be filled with their own devices.

Prov. 15: 32 He that refuseth instruction despiseth his own soul: . . .

Prov. 28: 13 He that covereth his sins shall not prosper: but whoso confesseth and forsaketh *them* shall have mercy. 14 Happy *is* the man that feareth always: but he that hardeneth his heart shall fall into mischief.

Prov. 29: 1 He, that being often reproved hardeneth *his* neck, shall suddenly be destroyed, and that without remedy.

Ecc. 8: 11 Because sentence against an evil work is not executed speedily, therefore the heart of the sons of men is fully set in them to do evil. 13 But it shall not be well with the wicked, neither shall he prolong *his* days, *which are* as a shadow; because he feareth not before God.

Matt. 24: 48 . . . If that evil servant shall say in his heart, My lord delayeth his coming; 49 And shall begin to smite *his* fellow servants, and to eat and drink with the drunken; 50 The lord of that servant shall come in a day when he looketh not for *him*, and in an hour that he is not aware of, 51 And shall cut him asunder, and appoint *him* his portion with the hypocrites: there shall be weeping and gnashing of teeth.

Matt. 25: 30 . . . Cast ye the unprofitable servant into outer darkness: there shall be weeping and gnashing of teeth. 45 Then shall he answer them, saying, Verily I say unto you, Inasmuch as ye did *it* not to one of the least of these, ye did *it* not to me. 46 And these shall go away into everlasting punishment: but the righteous into life eternal.

Mark 10: 22 . . . He was sad at that saying, and 'went away grieved: for he had great possessions.

Luke 13: 3 . . . Except ye repent, ye shall all likewise perish.

Rom. 2: 4 . . . Despisest thou the riches of his goodness and forbearance and longsuffering; not knowing that the goodness of God leadeth thee to repentance? 5 But, after thy hardness and impenitent heart, treasurest up unto thyself wrath against he day of wrath and revelation of the righteous judgment of God; 6 Who will render to every man according to his deeds:

Heb. 3: 7 . . . The Holy Ghost saith, To day if ye will hear his voice, 8 Harden not your hearts, . . .

See REPENTANCE.

INCONSISTENCY

Matt. 7: 3 . . . Why beholdest thou the mote that is in thy brother's eye, but considerest not the beam that is in thine own eye? 4 Or how wilt thou say to thy brother, Let me pull out the mote out of thine eye; and, behold, a beam *is* in thine own eye? 5 Thou hypocrite, first cast out the

beam out of thine own eye; and then shalt thou
see clearly to cast out the mote out of thy brother's eye.

Luke 11: 39 . . . The Lord said unto him,
Now do ye Pharisees make clean the outside of the
cup and the platter; but your inward part is full
of ravening and wickedness.

Rom. 2: 1 . . . Thou art inexcusable, O man,
·whosoever thou art that judgest: for wherein thou
judgest another, thou condemnest thyself; for
thou that judgest doest the same things. 21 Thou
therefore which teachest another, teachest thou
not thyself? thou that preachest a man should not
steal, dost thou steal? 22 Thou that sayest a
man should not commit adultery, dost thou commit adultery? thou that abhorrest idols, dost thou
commit sacrilege? 23 Thou that makest thy
boast of the law, through breaking the law dishonourest thou God?

Tit. 1: 16 They profess that they know God;
but in works they deny *him*, being abominable,
and disobedient, and unto every good work reprobate.

I. John 1: 6 If we say that we have fellowship with him, and walk in darkness, we lie, and
do not the truth:

I. John 2: 4 He that saith, I know him, and
keepeth not his commandments, is a liar, and the
truth is not in him. 9 He that saith he is in the
light, and hateth his brother, is in darkness even
until now.

I. John 4: 20 If a man say, I love God, and
hateth his brother, he is a liar: for he that loveth
not his brother whom he hath seen, how can he
love God whom he hath not seen?

See CONSISTENCY.

INDECISION

Matt. 6: 24 No man can serve two masters: for either he will hate the one, and love the other; or else he will hold to the one, and despise the other. Ye cannot serve God and mammon.

Matt. 26: 41 Watch and pray, that ye enter not into temptation: the spirit indeed *is* willing, but the flesh *is* weak.

Heb. 4: 12 . . . The word of God *is* quick, and powerful, and sharper than any twoedged sword, piercing even to the dividing asunder of soul and spirit, and of the joints and marrow, and *is* a discerner of the thoughts and intents of the heart. 13 Neither is there any creature that is not manifest in his sight: but all things *are* naked and opened unto the eyes of him with whom we have to do.

Jas. 1: 8 A doubleminded man *is* unstable in all his ways.

Jas. 4: 17 . . . To him that knoweth to do good, and doeth *it* not, to him it is sin.

See DECISION.

INDUSTRY

Prov. 6: 6 Go to the ant, thou sluggard; consider her ways, and be wise: 7 Which having no guide, overseer, or ruler, 8 Provideth her meat in the summer, *and* gathereth her food in the harvest.

Prov. 10: 4 He becometh poor that dealeth *with* a slack hand: but the hand of the diligent maketh rich. 5 He that gathereth in summer *is* a wise son: *but* he that sleepeth in harvest *is* a son that causeth shame.

Prov. 12: 11 He that tilleth his land shall be satisfied with bread: but he that followeth vain *persons is* void of understanding. 24 The hand of the diligent shall bear rule: but the slothful shall be under tribute.

Prov. 13: 4 The soul of the sluggard desireth, and *hath* nothing: but the soul of the diligent shall be made fat. 11 Wealth *gotten* by vanity shall be diminished: but he that gathereth by labour shall increase.

Prov. 14: 23 In all labour there is profit: but the talk of the lips *tendeth* only to penury.

Prov. 20: 13 Love not sleep, lest thou come to poverty: open thine eyes, *and* thou shalt be satisfied with bread.

Prov. 21: 5 The thoughts of the diligent *tend* only to plenteousness; but of every one *that is* hasty only to want.

Prov. 22: 29 Seest thou a man diligent in his business? he shall stand before kings; he shall not stand before mean. *men.*

Prov. 30: 25 The ants *are* a people not strong, yet they prepare their meat in the summer; 26 The conies *are but* a feeble folk, yet make they their houses in the rocks; 28 The spider taketh hold with her hands, and is in kings' palaces.

Ecc. 5: 12 The sleep of a labouring man *is* sweet, whether he eat little or much: but the abundance of the rich will not suffer him to sleep.

Ecc. 9: 10 Whatsoever thy hand findeth to do, do *it* with thy might; for *there is* no work, nor device, nor knowledge, nor wisdom, in the grave, whither thou goest.

Ecc. 11: 4 He that observeth the wind shall not sow; and he that regardeth the clouds shall not reap. 6 In the morning sow thy seed, and in the evening withhold not thine hand: for thou knowest not whether shall prosper, either this or that, or whether they both *shall be* alike good.

235

Rom. 12: 10 *Be* . . . 11 Not slothful in business; . . .

Eph. 4: 28 Let him that stole steal no more: but rather let him labour, working with *his* hands the thing which is good, that he may have to give to him that needeth.

I. Thess. 4: 11 . . . Study to be quiet, and to do your own business, and to work with your own hands, as we commanded you; 12 That ye may walk honestly toward them that are without, and *that* ye may have lack of nothing.

II. Thess. 3: 10 . . . This we commanded you, that if any would not work, neither should he eat.

I. Tim. 5: 8 . . . If any provide not for his own, and specially for those of his own house, he hath denied the faith, and is worse than an infidel.

See EMPLOYER—EMPLOYEE; SERVICE; also IDLENESS—SLOTHFULNESS.

INFLUENCE

Evil: Prov. 22: 24 Make no friendship with an angry man; and with a furious man thou shalt not go; 25 Lest thou learn his ways, and get a snare to thy soul.

Luke 12: 1 . . . Beware ye of the leaven of the Pharisees, which is hypocrisy.

Rom. 14: 21 *It is* good neither to eat flesh, nor to drink wine, nor *any thing* whereby thy brother stumbleth, or is offended, or is made weak.

I. Cor. 5: 6 . . . Know ye not that a little leaven leaveneth the whole lump? 7 Purge out therefore the old leaven, that ye may be a new lump, as ye are unleavened. For even Christ our passover is sacrificed for us: 8 Therefore let us keep the feast, not with old leaven, neither with the leaven of malice and wickedness; but with the unleavened *bread* of sincerity and truth.

I. Cor. 8: 13 . . . If meat make my brother to offend, I will eat no flesh while the world standeth, lest I make my brother to offend.

I. Thess. 1: 8 . . . From you sounded out the word of the Lord not only in Macedonia and Achaia, but also in every place your faith to Godward is spread abroad; so that we need not to speak any thing.

I. Thess. 5: 22 Abstain from all appearance of evil.

II. Tim. 2: 14 . . . Strive not about words to no profit, *but* to the subverting of the hearers.

Heb. 12: 14 Follow peace with all *men,* and holiness, without which no man shall see the Lord: 15 Looking diligently lest any man fail of the grace of God; lest any root of bitterness springing up trouble *you,* and thereby many be defiled;

Heb. 13: 7 Remember them which have the rule over you, who have spoken unto you the word of God: whose faith follow, considering the end of *their* conversation.

See EVIL COMPANY.

Good: Matt. 5: 16 Let your light so shine before men, that they may see yours good works, and glorify your Father which is in heaven.

I. Cor. 7: 12 . . . If any brother hath a wife that believeth not, and she be pleased to dwell with him, let him not put her away. 13 And the woman which hath a husband that believeth not, and if he be pleased to dwell with her, let her not leave him. 14 For the unbelieving husband is sanctified by the wife, and the unbelieving wife is sanctified by the husband: else were your children unclean; but now are they holy. 16 For

what knowest thou, O wife, whether thou shalt
save *thy* husband? or how knowest thou, O man,
whether thou shalt save *thy* wife?

Philip. 2: 14 Do all things without murmur-
ings and disputings: 15 That ye may be blameless and harmless, the sons of God, without
rebuke, in the midst of a crooked and perverse nation, among whom ye shine as lights in the world:

I. Pet. 2: 11 . . . Abstain from fleshly lusts,
which war against the soul; 12 Having your
conversation honest among the Gentiles: that,
whereas they speak against you as evil doers, they
may by *your* good works, which they shall behold,
glorify God in the day of visitation.

I. Pet. 3: 15 . . . Sanctify the Lord God in
your hearts: and *be* ready always to *give* an
answer to every man that asketh you a reason of
the hope that is in you, with meekness and fear:
16 Having a good conscience; that, whereas they
speak evil of you, as of evil doers, they may be
ashamed that falsely accuse your good conversation in Christ.

See EXAMPLE.

INGRATITUDE

Prov. 17: 13 Whoso rewardeth evil for good,
evil shall not depart from his house.

John 1: 11 He came unto his own, and his
own received him not.

Rom. 1: 18 . . . The wrath of God is revealed from heaven against all ungodliness and
unrighteousness of men, who hold the truth in
unrighteousness; 21 Because that, when they
knew God, they glorified *him* not as God, neither
were thankful; but became vain in their imaginations, and their foolish heart was darkened.

II. Tim. 3: 2 . . . Men shall be lovers of their

own selves, covetous, boasters, proud, blasphemers, disobedient to parents, unthankful, unholy,
5 Having a form of godliness, but denying the
power thereof: from such turn away.
See THANKFULNESS.

INJUSTICE

Exod. 20: 16 Thou shalt not bear false witness against thy neighbour.

Job 31: 13 If I did despise the cause of my
manservant or of my maidservant, when they
contended with me; 14 What then shall I do
when God riseth up? and when he visiteth, what
shall I answer him? 15 Did not he that made me
in the womb make him? and did not one fashion
us in the womb?

Prov. 11: 7 When a wicked man dieth, *his* expectation shall perish: and the hope of unjust *men*
perisheth.

Prov. 17: 15 He that justifieth the wicked,
and he that condemneth the just, even they both
are abomination to the Lord.

Prov. 28: 8 He that by usury and unjust gain
increaseth his substance, he shall gather it for him
that will pity the poor.

Prov. 31: 4 . . . *It is* not for kings to drink
wine; nor for princes strong drink: 5 Lest they
drink, and forget the law, and pervert the judgment of any of the afflicted.

Ecc. 5: 8 If thou seest the oppression of the
poor, and violent perverting of judgment and justice in a province, marvel not at the matter: for
he that is higher than the highest regardeth; and
there be higher than they.

Lam. 3: 34 To crush under his feet all the
prisoners of the earth, 35 To turn aside the
right of a man before the face of the Most High,

36 To subvert a man in his cause, the Lord approveth not.

Luke 3: 14 . . . The soldiers likewise demanded of him, saying, And what shall we do? And he said unto them, Do violence to no man, neither accuse *any* falsely; . . .

Luke 16: 10 He that is faithful in that which is least is faithful also in much: and he that is unjust in the least is unjust also in much.

I. Thess. 4: 3 . . . This is the will of God, . . . 6 That no *man* go beyond and defraud his brother in *any* matter: because that the Lord *is* the avenger of all such, . . .

See DISHONESTY; OPPRESSION; also JUSTICE.

INSTRUCTION

Prov. 1: 5 A wise *man* will hear, and will increase learning; and a man of understanding shall attain unto wise counsels: 6 To understand a proverb, and the interpretation; the words of the wise, and their dark sayings. 7 . . . Fools despise wisdom and instruction. 8 My son, hear the instruction of thy father, and forsake not the law of thy mother: 24 Because I have called, and ye refused; I have stretched out my hand, and no man regarded; 25 But ye have set at nought all my counsel, and would none of my reproof: 26 I also will laugh at your calamity; I will mock when your fear cometh; 27 When your fear cometh as desolation, and your destruction cometh as a whirlwind; when distress and anguish cometh upon you. 28 Then shall they call upon me, but I will not answer; they shall seek me early, but they shall not find me: 29 For that they hated knowledge, and did not choose the fear of the Lord:

Prov. 4: 13 Take fast hold of instruction; let *her* not go: keep her; for she *is* thy life.

Prov. 8: 33 Hear instruction, and be wise, and refuse it not.

Prov. 12: 1 Whoso loveth instruction loveth knowledge: but he that hateth reproof *is* brutish.

Prov. 22: 6 Train up a child in the way he should go: and when he is old, he will not depart from it.

Prov. 23: 12 Apply thine heart unto instruction, and thine ears to the words of knowledge. 23 Buy the truth, and sell *it* not; *also* wisdom, and instruction, and understanding.

Prov. 24: 30 I went by the field of the slothful, and by the vineyard of the man void of understanding; 31 And, lo, it was all grown over with thorns, *and* nettles had covered the face thereof, and the stone wall thereof was broken down. 32 Then I saw, *and* considered *it* well: I looked upon *it, and* received instruction. 33 *Yet* a little sleep, a little slumber, a little folding of the hands to sleep: 34 So shall thy poverty come *as* one that travelleth; and thy want as an armed man.

Eph. 6: 4 . . . Provoke not your children to wrath: but bring them up in the nurture and admonition of the Lord.

II. Tim. 3: 14 . . . Continue thou in the things which thou hast learned and hast been assured of, knowing of whom thou hast learned *them;* 15 And that from a child thou hast known the holy Scriptures, which are able to make thee wise unto salvation through faith which is in Christ Jesus. 16 All Scripture *is* given by inspiration of God, and *is* profitable for doctrine, for reproof, for correction, for instruction in righteousness:

241

17 That the man of God may be perfect, thoroughly furnished unto all good works.

See KNOWLEDGE; STUDENT; TEACHER; WISDOM.

INTEGRITY

Psa. 15: 1 Lord, who shall abide in thy tabernacle? who shall dwell in thy holy hill? 2 He that walketh uprightly, and worketh righteousness, and speaketh the truth in his heart. 3 *He that* backbiteth not with his tongue, nor doeth evil to his neighbour, nor taketh up a reproach against his neighbour. 4 In whose eyes a vile person is contemned; but he honoureth them that fear the Lord. *He that* sweareth to *his own* hurt, and changeth not. 5 *He that* putteth not out his money to usury, nor taketh reward against the innocent. He that doeth these *things* shall never be moved.

Psa. 24: 3 Who shall ascend into the hill of the Lord? or who shall stand in his holy place? 4 He that hath clean hands, and a pure heart; who hath not lifted up his soul unto vanity, nor sworn deceitfully. 5 He shall receive the blessing from the Lord, and righteousness from the God of his salvation.

Prov. 2: 1 My son, if thou wilt receive my words, and hide my commandments with thee; 2 So that thou incline thine ear unto wisdom, *and* apply thine heart to understanding; 9 Then shalt thou understand righteousness, and judgment, and equity; *yea,* every good path.

Prov. 3: 3 Let not mercy and truth forsake thee: bind them about thy neck; write them upon the table of thine heart: 4 So shalt thou find favour and good understanding in the sight of God and man.

Prov. 4: 23 Keep thy heart with all diligence;

for out of it *are* the issues of life. 25 Let thine eyes look right on, and let thine eyelids look straight before thee. 26 Ponder the path of thy feet, and let all thy ways be established. 27 Turn not to the right hand nor to the left: remove thy foot from evil.

Prov. 10: 9 He that walketh uprightly walketh surely: but he that perverteth his ways shall be known.

Prov. 11: 3 The integrity of the upright shall guide them: but the perverseness of transgressors shall destroy them. 5 The righteousness of the perfect shall direct his way: but the wicked shall fall by his own wickedness. 6 The righteousness of the upright shall deliver them: but transgressors shall be taken in *their own* naughtiness.

Prov. 12: 22 Lying lips *are* abomination to the Lord: but they that deal truly *are* his delight.

Prov. 14: 30 A sound heart *is* the life of the flesh: but envy the rottenness of the bones.

Prov. 15: 21 Folly *is* joy to *him that is* destitute of wisdom: but a man of understanding walketh uprightly.

Prov. 16: 11 A just weight and balance *are* the Lord's: all the weights of the bag *are* his work.

Prov. 19: 1 Better *is* the poor that walketh in his integrity, than *he that is* perverse in his lips, and is a fool.

Prov. 20: 7 The just *man* walketh in his integrity: his children *are* blessed after him.

Prov. 21: 3 To do justice and judgment *is* more acceptable to the Lord than sacrifice.

Isa. 33: 15 He that walketh righteously, and speaketh uprightly; he that despiseth the gain of oppressions, that shaketh his hands from holding of bribes, that stoppeth his ears from hearing of blood, and shutteth his eyes from seeing evil; 16 He shall dwell on high; his place of defence *shall be* the munitions of rocks: bread shall be given him; his waters *shall be* sure.

Ezek. 18: 5 . . . If a man be just, and do that which is lawful and right, 7 And hath not oppressed any, *but* hath restored to the debtor his pledge, hath spoiled none by violence, hath given his bread to the hungry, and hath covered the naked with a garment; 8 He *that* hath not given forth upon usury, neither hath taken any increase, *that* hath withdrawn his hand from iniquity, hath executed true judgment between man and man, 9 Hath walked in my statutes, and hath kept my judgments, to deal truly; he *is* just, he shall surely live, saith the Lord God.

Mic. 6: 8 He hath shewed thee, O man, what *is* good; and what doth the Lord require of thee, but to do justly, and to love mercy, and to walk humbly with thy God?

Luke 3: 13 . . . He said unto them, Exact no more than that which is appointed you. 14 . . . Do violence to no man, neither accuse *any* falsely; and be content with your wages.

Luke 6: 31 . '. . As ye would that men should do to you, do ye also to them likewise.

Luke 16: 10 He that is faithful in that which is least is faithful also in much: and he that is unjust in the least is unjust also in much.

Acts 24: 16 . . . Herein do I exercise myself, to have always a conscience void of offence toward God, and *toward* men.

Rom. 13: 1 Let every soul be subject unto the higher powers. For there is no power but of God:

the powers that be are ordained of God. 5 Wherefore *ye* must needs be subject, not only for wrath, but also for conscience' sake.

II. Cor. 4: 1 . . . Seeing we have this ministry, as we have received mercy, we faint not; 2 But have renounced the hidden things of dishonesty, not walking in craftiness, nor handling the word of God deceitfully; but, by manifestation of the truth, commending ourselves to every man's conscience in the sight of God.

Philip. 4: 8 . . . Brethren, whatsoever things are true, whatsoever things *are* honest, whatsoever things *are* just, whatsoever things *are* pure, whatsoever things *are* lovely, whatsoever things *are* of good report; if *there be* any virtue, and if *there be* any praise, think on these things.

Col. 3: 22 Servants, obey in all things *your* masters according to the flesh; not with eyeservice, as menpleasers; but in singleness of heart, fearing God: 23 And whatsoever ye do, do *it* heartily, as to the Lord, and not unto men;

I. Tim. 1: 5 . . . The end of the commandment is charity out of a pure heart, and *of* a good conscience, and *of* faith unfeigned:

Tit. 1: 7 . . . A bishop must be blameless, as the steward of God; not selfwilled, not soon angry, not given to wine, no striker, not given to filthy lucre; 8 But a lover of hospitality, a lover of good men, sober, just, holy, temperate; 9 Holding fast the faithful word as he hath been taught, that he may be able by sound doctrine both to exhort and to convince the gainsayers.

I. Pet. 2: 11 . . . Abstain from fleshly lusts, which war against the soul; 12 Having your conversation honest among the Gentiles: that, whereas they speak against you as evil doers, they

245

may by *your* good works, which they shall behold, glorify God in the day of visitation.

See CHARACTER; HONESTY; REPUTATION; STEADFASTNESS.

INTOXICATION

Prov. 20: 1 Wine *is* a mocker, strong drink *is* raging: and whosoever is deceived thereby is not wise.

Prov. 23: 20 Be not among winebibbers; among riotous eaters of flesh: 21 For the drunkard and the glutton shall come to poverty: and drowsiness shall clothe *a man* with rags. 29 Who hath woe? who hath sorrow? who hath contentions? who hath babbling? who hath wounds without cause? who hath redness of eyes? 30 They that tarry long at the wine; they that go to seek mixed wine. 31 Look not thou upon the wine when it is red, when it giveth his colour in the cup, *when* it moveth itself aright. 32 At the last it biteth like a serpent, and stingeth like an adder.

Prov. 31: 4 *It is* not for kings, O Lemuel, *it is* not for kings to drink wine; nor for princes strong drink: 5 Lest they drink, and forget the law, and pervert the judgment of any of the afflicted. 6 Give strong drink unto him that is ready to perish, and wine unto those that be of heavy hearts. 7 Let him drink, and forget his poverty, and remember his misery no more.

Isa. 5: 11 Woe unto them that rise up early in the morning, *that* they may follow strong drink; that continue until night, *till* wine inflame them! 22 Woe unto *them that are* mighty to drink wine, and men of strength to mingle strong drink:

Luke 21: 34 . . . Take heed to yourselves,

lest at any time your hearts be overcharged with surfeiting, and drunkenness, and cares of this life, and so that day come upon you unawares.

Rom. 13: 13 Let us walk honestly, as in the day; not in rioting and drunkenness, not in chambering and wantonness, not in strife and envying:

I. Cor. 5: 11 . . . I have written unto you not to keep company, if any man that is called a brother be a fornicator, or covetous, or an idolater, or a railer, or a drunkard, or an extortioner; with such a one no not to eat.

I. Cor. 6: 9 Know ye not that the unrighteous shall not inherit the kingdom of God? Be not deceived: neither fornicators, . . . 10 . . . nor drunkards, . . . shall inherit the kingdom of God.

I. Cor. 11: 21 . . . In eating every one taketh before other his own supper: and one is hungry, and another is drunken.

Gal. 5: 19 Now the works of the flesh are manifest, which are these, Adultery, fornication, uncleanness, lasciviousness, 20 Idolatry, witchcraft, hatred, variance, emulations, wrath, strife, seditions, heresies, 21 Envyings, murders, drunkenness, revellings, and such like: of the which I tell you before, as I have also told you in time past, that they which do such things shall not inherit the kingdom of God.

Eph. 5: 18 . . . Be not drunk with wine, wherein is excess; but be filled with the spirit;

I. Thess. 5: 6 . . . Let us not sleep, as do others; but let us watch and be sober. 7 For they that sleep sleep in the night; and they that be drunken are drunken in the night. 8 But let us, who are of the day, be sober, putting on the breastplate of faith and love; and for a helmet, the hope of salvation.

See TEMPERANCE.

JEALOUSY

Prov. 6: 34 . . . Jealously *is* the rage of a man: therefore he will not spare in the day of vengeance. 35 He will not regard any ransom; neither will he rest content, though thou givest many gifts.

Song 8: 6 . . . Love *is* strong as death; jealously *is* cruel as the grave: the coals thereof *are* coals of fire, *which hath* a most vehement flame.

See ENVY.

JESUS, THE CHRIST (MESSIAH)

See also GOD; HOLY GHOST.

SON OF GOD (Deity of): Matt. 1: 23 Behold, a virgin shall be with child, and shall bring forth a son, and they shall call his name Emmanuel, which being interpreted is, God with us.

Matt. 11: 27 All things are delivered unto me of my Father: and no man knoweth the Son, but the Father; neither knoweth any man the Father, save the Son, and *he* to whomsoever the Son will reveal *him*.

Matt. 16: 16 . . . Simon Peter . . . said, Thou art the Christ, the Son of the living God.

Matt. 28: 19 Go ye . . . , and teach all nations, baptizing them in the name of the Father, and of the Son, and of the Holy Ghost:

Mark 1: 11 . . . There came a voice from heaven, *saying,* Thou art my beloved Son, in whom I am well pleased.

Mark 3: 11 . . . Unclean spirits, when they

saw him, fell down before him, and cried, saying, Thou art the Son of God.

Mark 14: 61 . . . The high priest asked him, and said unto him, Art thou the Christ, the Son of the Blessed? 62 And Jesus said, I am: and ye shall see the Son of man sitting on the right hand of power, and coming in the clouds of heaven.

Luke 1: 35 . . . The angel . . . said unto her, The Holy Ghost shall come upon thee, and the power of the Highest shall overshadow thee: therefore also that holy thing which shall be born of thee shall be called the Son of God.

Luke 2: 49 . . . He said unto them, How is it that ye sought me? wist ye not that I must be about my Father's business? 50 And they understood not the saying which he spake unto them.

John 1: 1 In the beginning was the Word, and the Word was with God, and the Word was God. 14 And the Word was made flesh, and dwelt among us, (and we beheld his glory, the glory as of the only begotton of the Father,) full of grace and truth. 18 No man hath seen God at any time; the only begotten Son, which is in the bosom of the Father, he hath declared *him*. 34 And I saw, and bare record that this is the Son of God. 49 Nathanael . . . saith unto him, Rabbi, thou art the Son of God; thou art the King of Israel.

John 5: 18 . . . The Jews sought the more to kill him, because he not only had broken the sabbath, but said also that God was his Father, making himself equal with God.

John 11: 4 . . . Jesus . . . said, This sickness is not unto death, but for the glory of God, that the Son of God might be glorified thereby. 27 She saith unto him, Yea, Lord: I believe that

thou art the Christ, the Son of God, which should
come into the world.

John 17: 5 . . . O Father, glorify thou me
with thine own self with the glory which I had
with thee before the world was.

John 20: 28 . . . Thomas . . . said unto him,
My Lord and my God. 30 . . . Many other signs
truly did Jesus in the presence of his disciples,
which are not written in this book: 31 But
these are written, that ye might believe that
Jesus is the Christ, the Son of God; and that believing ye might have life through his name.

Acts 20: 28 Take heed . . . unto yourselves,
and to all the flock, over the which the Holy Ghost
hath made you overseers, to feed the church of
God, which he hath purchased with his own blood.

Rom. 9: 4 . . . Israelites . . . 5 Whose *are*
the fathers, and of whom as concerning the flesh
Christ *came*, who is over all, God blessed for ever.
Amen.

Col. 2: 9 . . . In him dwelleth all the fulness
of the Godhead bodily.

Tit. 2: 13 Looking for that blessed hope, and
the glorious appearing of the great God and our
Saviour Jesus Christ;

Heb. 1: 1 God . . . 2 Hath in these last days
.spoken unto us by *his* Son, whom he hath appointed heir of all things, by whom also he made
the worlds;

II. Pet. 1: 1 Simon Peter, a servant and an
apostle of Jesus Christ, to them that have obtained
like precious faith with us through the righteousness of God and our Saviour Jesus Christ:

Rev. 5: 8 . . . When he had taken the book,
the four beasts and four *and* twenty elders fell
down before the Lamb, having every one of them

harps, and golden vials full of odours, which are
the prayers of saints. 9 And they sung a new
song, saying, Thou art worthy to take the book,
and to open the seals thereof: for thou wast slain,
and hast redeemed us to God by thy blood out of
every kindred, and tongue, and people, and nation;
See Holiness of.

SON OF MAN (Representative Humanity of
Christ Jesus as the Messiah): Matt. 8: 20 . . .
Jesus saith unto him, The foxes have holes, and
the birds of the air *have* nests; but the Son of man
hath not where to lay *his* head.

Matt. 10: 23 . . . When they persecute you
in this city, flee ye into another: for verily I say
unto you, Ye shall not have gone over the cities
of Israel, till the Son of man be come.

Matt. 11: 19 The Son of man came eating and
drinking, and they say, Behold a man gluttonous,
and a winebibber, a friend of publicans and sinners. But wisdom is justified of her children.

Matt. 13: 37 He . . . said unto them, He that
soweth the good seed is the Son of man; 41 The
Son of man shall send forth his angels, and they
shall gather out of his kingdom all things that offend, and them which do iniquity;

Matt. 16: 13 When Jesus came into the coasts
of Cesarea Philippi, he asked his disciples, saying,
Whom do men say that I, the Son of man, am?
27 . . . The Son of man shall come in the glory
of his Father with his angels; and then he shall
reward every man according to his works.

Matt. 17: 9 . . . As they came down from the
mountain, Jesus charged them, saying, Tell the
vision to no man, until the Son of man be risen
again from the dead. 12 . . . I say unto you,

251

That Elias is come already, and they knew him not, but have done unto him whatsoever they listed. Likewise shall also the Son of man suffer of them. 22 And while they abode in Galilee, Jesus said unto them, The Son of man shall be betrayed into the hands of men:

Matt. 24: 30 . . . Then shall appear the sign of the Son of man in heaven: and then shall all the tribes of the earth mourn, and they shall see the Son of man coming in the clouds of heaven with power and great glory.

Matt. 26: 2 Ye know that after two days is *the feast of* the passover, and the Son of man is betrayed to be crucified. 24 The Son of man goeth as it is written of him: but woe unto that man by whom the Son of man is betrayed! it had been good for that man if he had not been born. 45 Then cometh he to his disciples, and saith unto them, Sleep on now, and take *your* rest: behold, the hour is at hand, and the Son of man is betrayed into the hands of sinners. 64 Jesus saith unto him, . . . Hereafter shall ye see the Son of man sitting on the right hand of power, and coming in the clouds of heaven.

Mark 2: 10 . . . That ye may know that the Son of man hath power on earth to forgive sins, (he saith to the sick of the palsy,) 11 I say unto thee, Arise, and take up thy bed, and go thy way into thine house. 28 . . . The Son of man is Lord also of the sabbath.

Mark 10: 33 . . . Behold, we go up to Jerusalem; and the Son of man shall be delivered unto the chief priests, and unto the scribes; and they shall condemn him to death, and shall deliver him to the Gentiles:

Mark 13: 26 . . . Then shall they see the Son

of man coming in the clouds with great power and glory.

Luke 17: 22 . . . He said unto the disciples, The days will come, when ye shall desire to see one of the days of the Son of man, and ye shall not see *it.*

John 12: 32 . . . I, if I be lifted up from the earth, will draw all *men* unto me. 33 This he said, signifying what death he should die. 34 The people answered him, We have heard out of the law that Christ abideth for ever: and how sayest thou, The Son of man must be lifted up? who is this Son of man?

John 13: 31 . . . Jesus said, Now is the Son of man glorified, and God is glorified in him.

As an Example: Matt. 11: 29 Take my yoke upon you, and learn of me; for I am meek and lowly in heart: and ye shall find rest unto your souls.

Mark 10: 43 . . . Whosoever will be great among you, shall be your minister: 44 And whosoever of you will be the chiefest, shall be servant of all. 45 For even the Son of man came not to be ministered unto, but to minister, and to give his life a ransom for many.

John 10: 11 I am the good shepherd: the good shepherd giveth his life for the sheep.

John 13: 13 Ye call me Master and Lord: and ye say well; for *so* I am. 14 If I then, *your* Lord and Master, have washed your feet; ye also ought to wash one another's feet. 15 For I have given you an example, that ye should do as I have done to you. 34 A new commandment I give unto you, That ye love one another; as I have loved you, that ye also love one another. 35 By this shall all *men* know that ye are my disciples, if ye have love one to another.

Rom. 15: 2 Let every one of us please *his* neighbour for *his* good to edification. 3 For even Christ pleased not himself; but, as it is written, The reproaches of them that reproached thee fell on me. 5 Now the God of patience and consolation grant you to be likeminded one toward another according to Christ Jesus: 6 That ye may with one mind *and* one mouth glorify God, even the Father of our Lord Jesus Christ. 7 Wherefore receive ye one another, as Christ also received us, to the glory of God.

II. Cor. 8: 9 . . . Ye know the grace of our Lord Jesus Christ, that, though he was rich, yet for your sakes he became poor, that ye through his poverty might be rich.

Eph. 5: 2 . . . Walk in love, as Christ also hath loved us, and hath given himself for us an offering and a sacrifice to God for a sweetsmelling savour.

Philip. 2: 5 Let this mind be in you, which was also in Christ Jesus: 6 Who, being in the form of God, thought it not robbery to be equal with God: 7 But made himself of no reputation, and took upon him the form of a servant, and was made in the likeness of men: 8 And being found in fashion as a man, he humbled himself, and became obedient unto death, even the death of the cross.

Col. 3: 12 Put on . . . , as the elect of God, holy and beloved, bowels of mercies, kindness, humbleness of mind, meekness, longsuffering; 13 Forbearing one another, and forgiving one another, if any man have a quarrel against any: even as Christ forgave you, so also *do* ye.

Heb. 3: 1 . . . Holy brethren, partakers of the heavenly calling, consider the Apostle and High Priest of our profession, Christ Jesus; 2 Who was faithful to him that appointed him, as also Moses *was faithful* in all his house.

Heb. 12: 1 . . . Let us lay aside every weight, and the sin which doth so easily beset *us*, and let us run with patience the race that is set before us, 2 Looking unto Jesus the author and finisher of *our* faith; who for the joy that was set before him endured the cross, despising the shame, and is set down at the right hand of the throne of God. 3 For consider him that endured such contradiction of sinners against himself, lest ye be wearied and faint in your minds. 4 Ye have not yet resisted unto blood, striving against sin.

I. Pet. 1: 15 . . . As he which hath called you is holy, so be ye holy in all manner of conversation;

I. Pet. 2: 21 . . . Christ . . . suffered for us, leaving us an example, that ye should follow his steps: 22 Who did no sin, neither was guile found in his mouth: 23 Who, when he was reviled, reviled not again; when he suffered, he threatened not; but committed *himself* to him that judgeth righteously: 24 Who his own self bare our sins in his own body on the tree, that we, being dead to sins, should live unto righteousness: by whose stripes ye were healed.

I. Pet. 3: 17 . . . *It is* better, if the will of God be so, that ye suffer for well doing, than for evil doing. 18 For Christ also hath once suffered for sins, the just for the unjust, that he might bring us to God, being put to death in the flesh, but quickened by the Spirit:

I. Pet. 4: 1 Forasmuch then as Christ hath suffered for us in the flesh, arm yourselves likewise with the same mind: for he that hath suffered in the flesh hath ceased from sin; 2 That he no longer should live the rest of *his* time in the flesh to the lusts of men, but to the will of God.

I. John 2: 6 He that saith he abideth in him ought himself also so to walk, even as he walked.

I. John 3: 2 . . . We know that, when he shall appear, we shall be like him; for we shall see him as he is. 3 And every man that hath this hope in him purifieth himself, even as he is pure. 16 Hereby perceive we the love *of God,* because he laid down his life for us: and we ought to lay down *our* lives for the brethren.

Rev. 3: 21 To him that overcometh will I grant to sit with me in my throne, even as I also overcame, and am set down with my Father in his throne.

See EXAMPLE.

As Judge: Isa. 11: 1 . . . There shall come forth a rod out of the stem of Jesse, and a Branch shall grow out of his roots: 2 And the Spirit of the Lord shall rest upon him, the spirit of wisdom and understanding, the spirit of counsel and might, the spirit of knowledge and of the fear of the Lord; 3 And shall make him of quick understanding in the fear of the Lord: and he shall not judge after the sight of his eyes, neither reprove after the hearing of his ears: 4 But with righteousness shall he judge the poor, and reprove with equity for the meek of the earth: and he shall smite the earth with the rod of his mouth, and with the breath of his lips shall he slay the wicked.

Matt. 16: 27 . . . The Son of man shall come

256

in the glory of his Father with his angels; and then he shall reward every man according to his works.

Matt. 25: 31 When the Son of man shall come in his glory, and all the holy angels with him, then shall he sit upon the throne of his glory: 32 And before him shall be gathered all nations: and he shall separate them one from another, as a shepherd divideth *his* sheep from the goats: 33 And he shall set the sheep on his right hand, but the goats on the left. 34 Then shall the King say unto them on his right hand, Come, ye blessed of my Father, inherit the kingdom prepared for you from the foundation of the world: 35 For I was a hungered, and ye gave me meat: I was thirsty, and ye gave me drink: I was a stranger, and ye took me in:. 36 Naked, and ye clothed me: I was sick, and ye visited me: I was in prison, and ye came unto me. 37 Then shall the righteous answer him, saying, Lord, when saw we thee a hungered, and fed *thee?* or thirsty, and gave *thee* drink? 38 When saw we thee a stranger, and took *thee* in? or naked, and clothed *thee?* 39 Or when saw we thee sick, or in prison, and came unto thee? 40 And the King shall answer and say unto them, Verily I say unto you, Inasmuch as ye have done *it* unto one of the least of these my brethren, ye have done *it* unto me. 41 Then shall he say also unto them on the left hand, Depart from me, ye cursed, into everlasting fire, prepared for the devil and his angels: 42 For I was a hungered, and ye gave me no meat: I was thirsty, and ye gave me no drink: 43 I was a stranger, and ye took me not in: naked, and ye clothed me not: sick, and in prison, and ye visited me not. 44 Then shall they also answer him, saying, Lord, when saw we thee a hungered, or athrist, or a stranger, or naked, or sick, or in prison, and did not minister unto thee? 45 Then shall he answer them, saying, Verily I say unto you, Inasmuch as ye did *it* not to one of the least of these, ye did *it* not to me. 46 And these shall go away into everlasting punishment: but the righteous into life eternal.

Rom. 14: 10 . . . Why dost thou judge thy brother? or why dost thou set at nought thy brother? for we shall all stand before the judgment seat of Christ.

I. Cor. 4: 4 . . . He that judgeth me is the Lord. 5 Therefore judge nothing before the time, until the Lord come, who both will bring to light the hidden things of darkness, and will make manifest the counsels of the hearts: and then shall every man have praise of God.

II. Cor. 5: 10 . . . We must all appear before the judgment seat of Christ; that every one may receive the things *done* in *his* body, according to that he hath done, whether *it be* good or bad.

II. Tim. 4: 1 I charge *thee* . . . before God, and the Lord Jesus Christ, who shall judge the quick and the dead at his appearing and his kingdom; 2 Preach the word; be instant in season, out of season; reprove, rebuke, exhort with all longsuffering and doctrine. 8 Henceforth there is laid up for me a crown of righteousness, which the Lord, the righteous judge, shall give me at that day: and not to me only, but unto all them also that love his appearing.

As Savior: Mal. 4: 2 . . . Unto you that fear my name shall the Sun of righteousness arise with healing in his wings; and ye shall go forth, and grow up as calves of the stall.

Matt. 1: 21 . . . Thou shalt call his name JESUS: for he shall save his people from their sins.

Luke 1: 68 Blessed *be* the Lord God of Israel; for he hath visited and redeemed his people, 69 And hath raised up a horn of salvation for us in the house of his servant David;

Luke 2: 11 . . . Unto you is born this day in the city of David a Saviour, which is Christ the Lord.

Luke 19: 10 . . . The Son of man is come to seek and to save that which was lost.

ᵇ John 1: 29 . . . John seeth Jesus coming unto him, and saith, Behold the Lamb of God, which taketh away the sin of the world!

John 3: 16 . . . God so loved the world, that he gave his only begotten Son, that whosoever believeth in him should not perish, but have everlasting life. 17 For God sent not his Son into the world to condemn the world; but that the world through him might be saved.

John 4: 14 . . . Whosoever drinketh of the water that I shall give him shall never thrist; but the water that I shall give him shall be in him a well of water springing up into everlasting life.

John 6: 27 Labor not for the meat which perisheth, but for that meat which endureth unto everlasting life, which the Son of man shall give unto you: for him hath God the Father sealed. 35 And Jesus said unto them, I am the bread of life: he that cometh to me shall never hunger; and he that believeth on me shall never thirst. 37 All that the Father giveth me shall come to me; and him that cometh to me I will in no wise cast out. 51 I am the living bread which came down from heaven: if any man eat of this bread, he shall live for ever: and the bread that I will give is my flesh, which I will give for the life of the world. 57 As the living Father hath sent me, and I live by the Father; so he that eateth me, even he shall live by me. 63 It is the Spirit that quickeneth; the flesh profiteth nothing: the words that I speak unto you, *they* are spirit, and *they* are life.

John 8: 12 Then spake Jesus . . . unto them, saying, I am the light of the world: he that followeth me shall not walk in darkness, but shall have the light of life.

John 10: 9 I am the door: by me if any man enter in, he shall be saved; and shall go in and out, and find pasture. 11 I am the good shepherd: the good shepherd giveth his life for the sheep. 16 And other sheep I have, which are not of this fold: them also I must bring, and they shall hear my voice; and there shall be one fold, *and* one shepherd. 28 And I give unto them eternal life; and they shall never perish, neither shall any *man* pluck them out of my hand.

John 11: 25 Jesus said unto her, I am the resurrection, and the life: he that believeth in me, though he were dead, yet shall he live: 26 And whosoever liveth and believeth in me shall never die. . . .

John 12: 47 . . . I came not to judge the world, but to save the world.

John 14: 6 Jesus saith unto him, I am the way, the truth, and the life: no man cometh unto the Father, but by me.

Acts 4: 12 Neither is there salvation in any other: for there is none other name under heaven given among men, whereby we must be saved.

Acts 13: 38 Be it known unto you . . . , men *and* brethren, that through this man is preached unto you the forgiveness of sins: 39 And by him all that believe are justified from all things, from which ye could not be justified by the law of Moses.

Rom. 5: 1 . . . Being justified by faith, we have peace with God through our Lord Jesus Christ: 2 By whom also we have access by faith into this grace wherein we stand, and rejoice in hope of the glory of God. 8 . . . God commendeth his love toward us, in that, while we were yet sinners, Christ died for us. 9 Much more then, being now justified by his blood, we shall be saved from wrath through him. 10 For if, when we were enemies, we were reconciled to God by the death of his Son; much more, being reconciled, we shall be saved by his life. 20 . . . Where sin abounded, grace did much more abound: 21 That as sin hath reigned unto death, even so might grace reign through righteousness unto eternal life by Jesus Christ our Lord.

Rom. 6: 23 . . . The wages of sin *is* death; but the gift of God *is* eternal life through Jesus Christ our Lord.

Rom. 8: 2 . . . The law of the Spirit of life in Christ Jesus hath made me free from the law of sin and death.

Rom. 10: 9 . . . If thou shalt confess with thy mouth the Lord Jesus, and shalt believe in thine heart that God hath raised him from the dead, thou shalt be saved.

Gal. 1: 3 Grace *be* to you, and peace, from God the Father, and *from* our Lord Jesus Christ, 4 Who gave himself for our sins, that he might deliver us from this present evil world, according to the will of God and our Father:

Col. 1: 14 In whom we have redemption through his blood, *even* the forgiveness of sins:

I. Thess. 5: 9 . . . God hath not appointed us to wrath, but to obtain salvation by our Lord Jesus Christ, 10 Who died for us, that, whether we wake or sleep, we should live together with him.

I. Tim. 1: 15 This *is* a faithful saying, and worthy of all acceptation, that Christ Jesus came into the world to save sinners; . . .

Heb. 5: 9 . . . Being made perfect, he became the author of eternal salvation unto all them that obey him;

Heb. 7: 25 . . . He is able . . . to save them to the uttermost that come unto God by him, seeing he ever liveth to make intercession for them.

I. Pet. 1: 18 . . . Ye were not redeemed with corruptible things, *as* silver and gold, from your vain conversation *received* by tradition from your fathers; 19 But with the precious blood of Christ, as of a lamb without blemish and without spot:

I. Pet. 3: 18 . . . Christ . . . hath once suffered for sins, the just for the unjust, that he might bring us to God, being put to death in the flesh, but quickened by the Spirit:

I. John 4: 9 In this was manifested the love of God toward us, because that God sent his only begotten Son into the world, that we might live through him. 10 Herein is love, not that we loved God, but that he loved us, and sent his Son *to be* the propitiation for our sins. 14 And we have seen and do testify that the Father sent the Son *to be* the Saviour of the world.

See SALVATION.

As Teacher: Matt. 7: 29 . . . He taught them as *one* having authority, and not as the scribes.

Matt. 22: 16 . . . They sent out unto him their disciples with the Herodians, saying, Master, we know that thou art true, and teachest the way of God in truth, neither carest thou for any *man:* for thou regardest not the person of men.

Matt. 23: 8 . . . Be not ye called Rabbi: for one is your Master, *even* Christ; and all ye are brethren.

John 3: 1 There was a man of the Pharisees, named Nicodemus, a ruler of the Jews: 2 The same came to Jesus by night, and said unto him, Rabbi, we know that thou art a teacher come from God: for no man can do these miracles that thou doest, except God be with him.

See TEACHER.

Compassion of: Matt. 20: 28 . . . The Son of man came not to be ministered unto, but to minister, and to give his life a ransom for many. 30 . . . Two blind men sitting by the way side, when they heard that Jesus passed by, cried out, saying, Have mercy on us, O Lord, *thou* Son of David. 34 So Jesus had compassion *on them,* and touched their eyes: and immediately their eyes received sight, and they followed him.

Matt. 23: 37 O Jerusalem, Jerusalem, *thou* that killest the prophets, and stonest them which are sent unto thee, how often would I have gathered thy children together, even as a hen gathereth her chickens under *her* wings, and ye would not!

Mark 8: 2 I have compassion on the multitude, because they have now been with me three days, and have nothing to eat: 3 And if I send

263

them away fasting to their own houses, they will
faint by the way: for divers of them came from
far.   6 And he commanded the people to sit down
on the ground: and he took the seven loaves, and
gave thanks, and brake, and gave to his disciples
to set before *them;* and they did set *them* before
the people.   7 And they had a few small fishes:
and he blessed, and commanded to set them also
before *them.*   8 So they did eat, and were filled:
. . .

John 11: 33 When Jesus . . . saw her weeping, and the Jews also weeping which came with
her, he groaned in the spirit, and was troubled,
34 And said, Where have ye laid him? They say
unto him, Lord, come and see. 35 Jesus wept.
36 Then said the Jews, Behold how he loved him!

II. Cor. 8: 9 . . . Ye know the grace of our
Lord Jesus Christ, that, though he was rich, yet
for your sakes he became poor, that ye through
his poverty might be rich.

See Love of.

Holiness of: Luke 1: 35 . . . The angel . . .
said unto her, The Holy Ghost shall come upon
thee, and the power of the Highest shall overshadow thee: therefore also that holy thing which
shall be born of thee shall be called the Son of
God.

John 7: 16 Jesus . . . said, My doctrine is
not mine, but his that sent me. 18 He that
speaketh of himself seeketh his own glory: but he
that seeketh his glory that sent him, the same is
true, and no unrighteousness is in him.

John 14: 30 . . . The prince of this world
cometh, and hath nothing in me.

II. Cor. 4: 3 . . . If our gospel be hid, it is
hid to them that are lost: 4 In whom the god

of this world hath blinded the minds of them which believe not, lest the light of the glorious gospel of Christ, who is the image of God, should shine unto them.

Heb. 4: 15 . . . We have not a high priest which cannot be touched with the feeling of our infirmities; but was in all points tempted like as *we are, yet* without sin.

Heb. 7: 26 . . . Such a high priest became us, *who is* holy, harmless, undefiled, separate from sinners, and made higher than the heavens;

Heb. 9: 13 . . . If the blood of bulls and of goats, and the ashes of a heifer sprinkling the unclean, sanctifieth to the purifying of the flesh; 14 How much more shall the blood of Christ, who through the Eternal Spirit offered himself without spot to God, purge your conscience from dead works to serve the living God?

I. Pet. 1: 15 . . . As he which hath called you is holy, so be ye holy in all manner of conversation;

I. Pet. 2: 21 . . . Christ . . . suffered for us, leaving us an example, that ye should follow his steps: 22 Who did no sin, neither was guile in his mouth:

I. John 2: 29 If ye know that he is righteous, ye know that every one that doeth righteousness is born of him.

See JESUS, Son of God.

Humility of: Matt. 9: 10 . . . As Jesus sat at meat in the house, behold, many publicans and sinners came and sat down with him and his disciples. 11 And when the Pharisees saw *it,* they said unto his disciples, Why eateth your master with publicans and sinners?

Luke 22: 27 . . . Whether *is* greater, he that

265

sitteth at meat, or he that serveth? *is* not he that sitteth at meat? but I am among you as he that serveth.

John 13: 5 . . . He poureth water into a basin, and began to wash the disciples' feet, and to wipe *them* with the towel wherewith he was girded. 12 . . . After he had washed their feet, and had taken his garments, and was set down again, he said unto them, Know ye what I have done to you? 13 Ye call me Master and Lord: and ye say well; for *so* I am. 14 If I then, *your* Lord and Master, have washed your feet; ye also ought to wash one another's feet.

Acts 8: 32 . . . He was led as a sheep to the slaughter; and like a lamb dumb before his shearer, so opened he not his mouth: 33 In his humiliation his judgment was taken away: and who shall declare his generation? for his life is taken from the earth.

II. Cor. 8: 9 . . . Ye know the grace of our Lord Jesus Christ, that, though he was rich, yet for your sakes be became poor, that ye through his poverty might be rich.

Philip. 2: 5 . . . Christ Jesus: 7 . . . made himself of no reputation, and took upon him the form of a servant, and was made in the likeness of men: 8 And being found in fashion as a man, he humbled himself, and became obedient unto death, even the death of the cross.

See Meekness of; also Humility.

Love of: Mark 3: 34 . . . He looked round about on them which sat about him, and said, Behold my mother and my brethren! 35 For whosoever shall do the will of God, the same is my brother, and my sister, and mother.

Mark 9: 36 . . . He took a child, and set

him in the midst of them: and when he had taken him in his arms, he said unto them, 37 Whosoever shall receive one of such children in my name, receiveth me; and whosoever shall receive me, receiveth not me, but him that sent me.

Mark 10: 13 . . . They brought young children to him, that he should touch them; and *his* disciples rebuked those that brought *them*. 14 But when Jesus saw *it*, he was much displeased, and said unto them, Suffer the little children to come unto me, and forbid them not; for of such is the kingdom of God. 16 And he took them up in his arms, put *his* hands upon them, and blessed them.

John 10: 11 I am the good shepherd: the good shepherd giveth his life for the sheep.

John 13: 1 . . . When Jesus knew that his hour was come that he should depart out of this world unto the Father, having loved his own which were in the world, he loved them unto the end. 34 A new commandment I give unto you, That ye love one another; as I have loved you, that ye also love one another.

John 14: 21 He that hath my commandments, and keepeth them, he it is that loveth me: and he that loveth me shall be loved of my Father, and I will love him, and will manifest myself to him.

John 15: 9 As the Father hath loved me, so have I loved you: continue ye in my love. 10 If ye keep my commandments, ye shall abide in my love; even as I have kept my Father's commandments, and abide in his love. 13 Greater love hath no man that this, that a man lay down his life for his friends. 15 Henceforth I call you not servants; for the servant knoweth not what his lord doeth: but I have called you friends; for

all things that I have heard of my Father I have
made known unto you.

John 19: 26 When Jesus . . . saw his mother,
and the disciple standing by, whom he loved, he
saith unto his mother, Woman, behold thy son!
27 Then saith he to the disciple, Behold thy
mother! . . .

Rom. 8: 35 Who shall separate us from the
love of Christ? *shall* tribulation, or distress, or
persecution, or famine, or nakedness, or peril, or
sword? 37 Nay, in all these things we are more
than conquerors through him that loved us. 38
For I am persuaded, that neither death, nor life,
nor angels, nor principalities, nor powers, nor
things present, nor things to come, 39 Nor
height, nor depth, nor any other creature, shall
be able to separate us from the love of God,
which is in Christ Jesus our Lord.

Gal. 2: 20 . . . Christ liveth in me: and the
life which I now live in the flesh I live by the
faith of the Son of God, who loved me, and gave
himself for me.

Eph. 3: 14 For this cause I bow my knees
unto the Father of our Lord Jesus Christ, 16
That he would grant you, according to the riches
of his glory, to be strengthened with might by
his Spirit in the inner man; 17 That Christ
may dwell in your hearts by faith; that ye, being rooted and grounded in love, 18 May be able
to comprehend with all saints what *is* the breadth,
and length, and depth, and height; 19 And to
know the love of Christ, which passeth knowledge, that ye might be filled with all the fulness
of God.

Eph. 5: 2 . . . Walk in love, as Christ also
hath loved us, and hath given himself for us an

offering and a sacrifice to God for a sweetsmelling savour. 25 Husbands, love your wives, even as Christ also loved the church, and gave himself for it; 29 . . . No man ever yet hated his own flesh; but nourisheth and cherisheth it, even as the Lord the church: 30 For we are members of his body, of his flesh, and of his bones.

I. John 3: 16 Hereby perceive we the love *of God*, because he laid down his life for us: . . .

Rev. 3: 19 As many as I love, I rebuke and chasten: be zealous therefore, and repent.

See Compassion of; also LOVE.

Meekness of: Isa. 53: 7 He was oppressed, and he was afflicted, yet he opened not his mouth: he is brought as a lamb to the slaughter, and as a sheep before her shearers is dumb, so he openeth not his mouth.

Matt. 11: 29 Take my yoke upon you, and learn of me; for I am meek and lowly in heart: and ye shall find rest unto your souls.

Matt. 12: 19 He shall not strive, nor cry; neither shall any man hear his voice in the streets. 20 A bruised reed shall he not break, and smoking flax shall he not quench, till he send forth judgment unto victory.

Matt. 21: 5 . . . Behold, thy King cometh unto thee, meek, and sitting upon an ass, and a colt the foal of an ass.

Matt. 26: 51 . . . One of them which were with Jesus stretched out *his* hand, and drew his sword, and struck a servant of the high priest, and smote off his ear. 52 Then said Jesus unto him, Put up again thy sword into his place: for all they that take the sword shall perish with the sword. 53 Thinkest thou that I cannot now pray to my Father, and he shall presently give me

more than twelve legions of angels? 54 But
how then shall the Scriptures be fulfilled, that
thus it must be? 59 Now the chief priests, and
elders, and all the council, sought false witness
against Jesus, to put him to death; 60 . . . At
the last came two false witnesses, 61 And said,
This *fellow* said, I am able to destroy the temple
of God, and to build it in three days. 62 And
the high priest arose, and said unto him, An-
swerest thou nothing? what *is it which* these
witness against thee? 63 But Jesus held his
peace. . . .

Matt. 27: 12 And when he was accused of the
chief priests and elders, he answered nothing.
13 Then said Pilate unto him, Hearest thou not
how many things they witness against thee?
14 And he answered him to never a word; insomuch that the governor marveled greatly.

Luke 23: 34 Then said Jesus, Father, forgive
them; for they know not what they do. . . .

Heb. 12: 1 . . . Let us run with patience the
race that is set before us, 2 Looking unto
Jesus the author and finisher of *our* faith; who
for the joy that was set before him endured the
cross, despising the shame, and is set down at
the right hand of the throne of God. 3 For consider him that endured such contradiction of
sinners against himself, lest ye be wearied and
faint in your minds.   '

I. Pet. 2: 21 . . . Christ . . . suffered for us,
leaving us an example, that ye should follow his
steps: 23 Who, when he was reviled, reviled
not again; when he suffered, he threatened not;
but committed *himself* to him that judgeth
righteously:

See Humility of; also MEEKNESS.

Obedience of: Matt. 3: 13 Then cometh Jesus from Galilee to Jordan unto John, to be baptized of him. 14 But John forbade him, saying, I have need to be baptized of thee, and comest thou to me? 15 And Jesus answering said unto him, Suffer *it to be so* now: for thus it becometh us to fulfil all righteousness. Then he suffered him.

Matt. 26: 39 . . . He went a little further, and fell on his face, and prayed, saying, O my Father, if it be possible, let this cup pass from me: nevertheless, not as I will, but as thou *wilt.* 42 He went away again the second time, and prayed, saying, O my Father, if this cup may not pass away from me, except I drink it, thy will be done.

John 5: 30 I can of mine own self do nothing: as I hear, I judge: and my judgment is just; because I seek not mine own will, but the will of the Father which hath sent me.

John 6: 38 . . . I came down from heaven, not to do mine own will, but the will of him that sent me.

John 9: 4 I must work the works of him that sent me, while it is day: the night cometh, when no man can work.

John 14: 31 . . . That the world may know that I love the Father; and as the Father gave me commandment, even so I do. . . .

John 17: 1 These words spake Jesus, and lifted up his eyes to heaven, and said, Father, the hour is come; glorify thy Son, that thy Son also may glorify thee: 4 I have glorified thee on the earth: I have finished the work which thou gavest me to do. 6 I have manifested thy name unto the men which thou gavest me out of the world:

271

thine they were, and thou gavest them me; and
they have kept ,thy word. 8 For I have given
unto them the words which thou gavest me; . . .

John 19: 28 . . . Jesus knowing that all
things were now accomplished, that the Scripture
might be fulfilled, saith, I thirst. 30 When Jesus
therefore had received the vinegar, he said, It is
finished: and he bowed his head, and gave up the
ghost.

Philip. 2: 8 . . . Being found in fashion as
a man, he humbled himself, and became obedient
unto death, even the death of the cross.

Heb. 5: 8 Though he were a son, yet learned
he obedience by the things which he suffered;

See OBEDIENCE.

Zeal of: Matt. 4: 23 . . . Jesus went about
all Galilee, teaching in their synagogues, and
preaching the gospel of the kingdom, and healing
all manner of sickness and all manner of disease
among the people.

Luke 2: 49 . . . He said unto them, How is it
that ye sought me? wist ye not that I must be
about my Father's business?

Luke 8: 1 . . . He went throughout every
city and village, preaching and shewing the glad
tidings of the kingdom of God: and the twelve
were with him,

Luke 13: 31 . . . There came certain of the
Pharisees, saying unto him, Get thee out, and depart hence; for Herod will kill thee. 32 And he
said unto them, Go ye, and tell that fox, Behold,
I cast out devils, and I do cures to day and to morrow, and the third *day* I shall be perfected. 33
Nevertheless I must walk to day and to morrow,
and the *day* following: for it cannot be that a
prophet perish out of Jerusalem.

John 4: 34 Jesus saith unto them, My meat is to do the will of him that sent me, and to finish his work.

John 9: 4 I must work the works of him that sent me, while it is day: the night cometh, when no man can work.

JUSTICE

Prov. 18: 5 *It is* not good to accept the person of the wicked, to overthrow the righteous in judgment.

Prov. 28: 21 To have respect of persons *is* not good: for, for a piece of bread *that* man will transgress.

Ecc. 5: 8 If thou seest the oppression of the poor, and violent perverting of judgment and justice in a province, marvel not at the matter: for *he that is* higher than the highest regardeth; and *there be* higher than they.

Isa. 1: 17 Learn to do well; seek judgment, relieve the oppressed, judge the fatherless, plead for the widow.

Isa. 56: 1 Thus saith the Lord, Keep ye judgment, and do justice: . . .

Zech. 8: 16 These *are* the things that ye shall do; Speak ye every man the truth to his neighbour; execute the judgment of truth and peace in your gates:

Matt. 12: 7 . . . If ye had known what *this* meaneth, I will have mercy, and not sacrifice, ye would not have condemned the guiltless.

John 7: 24 Judge not according to the appearance, but judge righteous judgment. 51 Doth our law judge *any* man, before it hear him, and know what he doeth?

See JESUS as Judge; also INJUSTICE.

KINDNESS

Prov. 14: 21 He that despiseth his neighbour sinneth: but he that hath mercy on the poor, happy *is* he.

Matt. 5: 42 Give to him that asketh thee, and from him that would borrow of thee turn not thou away.

Matt. 25: 34 Then shall the King say unto them on his right hand, Come, ye blessed of my Father, inherit the kingdom prepared for you from the foundation of the world: 35 For I was a hungered, and ye gave me meat: I was thirsty, and ye gave me drink: I was a stranger, and ye took me in: 36 Naked, and ye clothed me: I was sick, and ye visited me: I was in prison, and ye come unto me. 40 . . . Verily I say unto you, Inasmuch as ye have done *it* unto one of the least of these my brethren, ye have done *it* unto me.

Luke 6: 34 . . . If ye lend *to them* of whom ye hope to receive, what thank have ye? for sinners also lend to sinners, to receive as much again. 35 But love ye your enemies, and do good, and lend, hoping for nothing again; and your reward shall be great, and ye shall be the children of the Highest: for he is kind unto the unthankful and *to* the evil.

Acts 20: 35 . . . Ye ought to support the weak, and to remember the words of the Lord Jesus, how he said, It is more blessed to give than to receive.

Rom. 12: 10 *Be* kindly affectioned one to another with brotherly love; in honour preferring one another; 13 Distributing to the necessity of saints; given to hospitality. 15 Rejoice with them that do rejoice, and weep with them that weep.

Rom. 15: 1 We . . . that are strong ought to bear the infirmities of the weak, and not to please ourselves. 2 Let every one of us please *his* neighbour for *his* good to edification. 3 For even Christ pleased not himself; . . . 5 Now the God of patience and consolation grant you to be likeminded one toward another according to Christ Jesus:

I. Cor. 13: 4 Charity suffereth long, *and* is kind; charity envieth not; charity vaunteth not itself, is not puffed up. 5 Doth not behave itself unseemly, seeketh not her own, is not easily provoked, thinketh no evil;

Gal. 6: 1 Brethren, if a man be overtaken in a fault, ye which are spiritual, restore such a one in the spirit of meekness; considering thyself, lest thou also be tempted. 2 Bear ye one another's burdens, and so fulfil the law of Christ. 10 As we have therefore opportunity, let us do good unto all *men*, especially unto them who are of the household of faith.

Eph. 4: 32 . . . Be ye kind one to another, tenderhearted, forgiving one another, even as God for Christ's sake hath forgiven you.

Col. 3: 12 Put on . . . , as the elect of God, holy and beloved, bowels of mercies, kindness, humbleness of mind, meekness, longsuffering; 13 Forbearing one another, and forgiving one another, if any man have a quarrel against any: even as Christ forgave you, so also *do* ye.

I. Pet. 3: 8 . . . *Be ye* all of one mind, having compassion one of another; love as brethren, *be* pitiful, *be* courteous: 9 Not rendering evil for evil, or railing for railing: but contrariwise blessing; knowing that ye are thereunto called, that ye should inherit a blessing.

275

II. Pet. 1: 5 . . . Giving all diligence, add to your . . . 7 . . . godliness, brotherly kindness; and to brotherly kindness, charity.

I. John 3: 17 . . . Whoso hath this world's good, and seeth his brother have need, and shutteth up his bowels *of compassion* from him, how dwelleth the love of God in him? 18 My little children, let us not love in word, neither in tongue; but in deed and in truth.

See BENEFICENCE; CHARITABLENESS; MERCY.

KNOWLEDGE

Prov. 1: 7 The fear of the Lord *is* the beginning of knowledge: *but* fools despise wisdom and instruction. 22 How long, ye simple ones, will ye love simplicity? and the scorners delight in their scorning, and fools hate knowledge?

Prov. 2: 6 . . . The Lord giveth wisdom: out of his mouth *cometh* knowledge and understanding.

Prov. 8: 10 Receive my instruction, and not silver; and knowledge rather than choice gold.

Prov. 13: 16 Every prudent *man* dealeth with knowledge: but a fool layeth open *his* folly.

Prov. 15: 14 The heart of him that hath understanding seeketh knowledge: but the mouth of fools feedeth on foolishness.

Prov. 18: 15 The heart of the prudent getteth knowledge; and the ear of the wise seeketh knowledge.

Prov. 24: 5 A wise man *is* strong; yea, a man of knowledge increaseth strength.

I. Cor. 2: 9 . . . Eye hath not seen, nor ear heard, neither have entered into the heart of man, the things which God hath prepared for them that love him. 10 But God hath revealed *them* unto us by his Spirit: for the Spirit searcheth all things, yea, the deep things of God. 11 For what man knoweth the things of a man, save the spirit of man which is in him? even so the things of God knoweth no man, but the Spirit of God.

I. Cor. 13: 12 . . . Now we see through a glass, darkly; but then face to face: now I know in part; but then shall I know even as also I am known.

Philip. 3: 8 . . . I count all things *but* loss for the excellency of the knowledge of Christ Jesus my Lord: . . . 10 That I may know him, and the power of his resurrection, and the fellowship of his sufferings, being made conformable unto his death;

See INSTRUCTION; STUDENT; TEACHER; WISDOM.

LASCIVIOUSNESS—ADULTERY—FORNICATION

Exod. 20: 14 Thou shalt not commit adultery.

Prov. 2: 11 Discretion shall preserve thee, understanding shall keep thee: 16 To deliver thee from the strange woman, *even* from the stranger *which* flattereth with her words; 17 Which forsaketh the guide of her youth, and forgetteth the covenant of her God. 18 For her house inclineth unto death, and her paths unto the dead. 19 None that go unto her return again, neither take they hold of the paths of life.

Prov. 5: 3 . . . The lips of a strange woman drop *as* a honeycomb, and her mouth *is* smoother than oil: 4 But her end is bitter as wormwood, sharp as a twoedged sword. 5 Her feet go down to death; her steps take hold on hell. 8 Remove thy way far from her, and come not nigh the door of her house: 9 Lest thou give thine honour

277

unto others, and thy years unto the cruel: 10 Lest strangers be filled with thy wealth; and thy labours *be* in the house of a stranger; 11 And thou mourn at the last, when thy flesh and thy body are consumed, 12 And say, How have I hated instruction, and my heart despised reproof; 13 And have not obeyed the voice of my teachers, nor inclined mine ear to them that instructed me!

Prov. 6: 23 . . . The commandment *is* a lamp; and the law *is* light; and reproofs of instruction *are* the way of life: 24 To keep thee from the evil woman, from the flattery of the tongue of a strange woman. 25 Lust not after her beauty in thine heart; neither let her take thee with her eyelids. 26 For by means of a whorish woman *a man is brought* to a piece of bread: and the adulteress will hunt for the precious life. 27 Can a man take fire in his bosom, and his clothes not be burned? 28 Can one go upon hot coals, and his feet not be burned? 29 So he that goeth in to his neighbour's wife; whosoever toucheth her shall not be innocent. 32 . . . Whoso committeth adultery with a woman lacketh understanding: he *that* doeth it destroyeth his own soul. 33 A wound and dishonour shall he get; and his reproach shall not be wiped away. 34 For jealousy *is* the rage of a man: therefore he will not spare in the day of vengeance. 35 He will not regard any ransom; neither will he rest content, though thou givest many gifts.

Prov. 9: 13 A foolish woman *is* clamorous: *she is* simple, and knoweth nothing. 14 For she sitteth at the door of her house, on a seat in the high places of the city, 15 To call passengers who go right on their ways: 16 Whoso *is* simple, let him turn in hither: and *as for* him that wanteth understanding, she saith to him, 17 Stolen waters are sweet, and bread *eaten* in secret is pleasant. 18 But he knoweth not that the dead *are* there; *and that* her guests *are* in the depths of hell.

Prov. 22: 14 The mouth of strange women *is* a deep pit: he that is abhorred of the Lord shall fall therein.

Prov. 29: 3 Whoso loveth wisdom rejoiceth his father: but he that keepeth company with harlots spendeth *his* substance.

Prov. 31: 3 Give not thy strength unto women, nor thy ways to that which destroyeth kings.

Mal. 3: 5 . . . I will be a swift witness against the sorcerers, and against the adulterers, . . . saith the Lord of hosts.

Matt. 5: 27 Ye have heard that it was said by them of old time, Thou shalt not commit adultery: 28 But I say unto you, That whosoever looketh on a woman to lust after her hath committed adultery with her already in his heart. 31 It hath been said, Whosoever shall put away his wife, let him give her a writing of divorcement: 32 But I say unto you, That whosoever shall put away his wife, saving for the cause of fornication, causeth her to commit adultery: and whosoever shall marry her that is divorced committeth adultery.

Matt. 19: 18 . . . Jesus said, . . . Thou shalt not commit adultery, . . .

Mark 7: 21 . . . From within, out of the heart of men, proceed evil thoughts, adulteries, fornications, murders, 22 Thefts, covetousness, wickedness, deceit, lasciviousness, an evil eye, blasphemy, pride, foolishness: 23 All these evil things come from within, and defile the man.

Mark 10: 11 . . . He saith unto them, Whosoever shall put away his wife, and marry another, committeth adultery against her. 12 And if a woman shall put away her husband, and be married to another, she committeth adultery.

John 8: 3 . . . The scribes and Pharisees brought unto him a woman taken in adultery; and when they had set her in the midst, 4 They say unto him, Master, this woman was taken in adultery, in the very act. 5 Now Moses in the law commanded us, that such should be stoned: but what sayest thou? 7 . . . When they continued asking him, he lifted up himself, and said unto them, He that is without sin among you, let him first cast a stone at her. 9 And they which heard *it*, being convicted by *their own* conscience, went out one by one, beginning at the eldest, *even* unto the last: and Jesus was left alone, and the woman standing in the midst. 10 When Jesus . . . saw none but the woman, he said unto her, Woman, where are those thine accusers? hath no man condemned thee? 11 She said, No man, Lord. And Jesus said unto her, Neither do I condemn thee: go, and sin no more.

Rom. 1: 28 . . . As they did not like to retain God in *their* knowledge, God gave them over to a reprobate mind, to do those things which are not convenient; 29 Being filled with all unrighteousness, fornication, wickedness, . . . 32 Who, knowing the judgment of God, that they which commit such things are worthy of death, not only do the same, but have pleasure in them that do them.

Rom. 7: 3 . . . If, while *her* husband liveth, she be married to another man, she shall be called an adulteress: but if her husband be dead, she is free from that law; so that she is no adulteress, though she be married to another man.

Rom. 13: 13 Let us walk honestly, as in the day; not in rioting and drunkenness, not in chambering and wantonness, not in strife and envying: 14 But put ye on the Lord Jesus Christ, and make not provision for the flesh, to *fulfil* the lusts *thereof.*

I. Cor. 5: 9 I wrote unto you in an epistle not to company with fornicators: 10 Yet not altogether with the fornicators of this world, or with the covetous, or extortioners, or with idolaters; for then must ye needs go out of the world. 11 But now I have written unto you not to keep company, if any man that is called a brother be a fornicator, or covetous, or an idolater, or a railer, or a drunkard, or an extortioner; with such a one no not to eat.

I. Cor. 6: 9 Know ye not that the unrighteous shall not inherit the kingdom of God? Be not deceived: neither fornicators, nor idolaters, nor adulterers, nor effeminate, nor abusers of themselves with mankind, 10 Nor thieves, not covetous, nor drunkards, nor revilers, nor extortioners, shall inherit the kingdom of God. 13 . . . Now the body *is* not for fornication, but for the Lord; and the Lord for the body. 15 Know ye not that your bodies are the members of Christ? shall I then take the members of Christ, and make *them* the members of a harlot? God forbid. 16 What! know ye not that he which is joined to a harlot is one body? for two, saith he, shall be one flesh. 18 Flee fornication. Every sin that a

281

man doeth is without the body; but he that committeth fornication sinneth against his own body. 19 What! know ye not that your body is the temple of the, Holy Ghost *which is* in you, which ye have of God, and ye are not your own? 20 For ye are bought with a price: therefore glorify God in your body, and in your spirit, which are God's.

Gal. 5: 19 Now the works of the flesh are manifest, which are *these*, Adultery, fornication, uncleanness, lasciviousness, 21 . . . revellings, and such like: of the which I tell you before, as I have also told *you* in time past, that they which do such things shall not inherit the kingdom of God. 24 And they that are Christ's have crucified the flesh with the affections and lusts.

Eph. 4: 17 This I say . . . , and testify in the Lord, that ye henceforth walk not as other Gentiles walk, in the vanity of their mind, 19 Who being past feeling have given themselves over unto lasciviousness, to work all uncleanness with greediness.

Eph. 5: 3 . . . Fornication, and all uncleanness, or covetousness, let it not be once named among you, as becometh saints; 4 Neither filthiness, nor foolish talking, nor jesting, which are not convenient: but rather giving of thanks. 5 For this ye know, that no whoremonger, nor unclean person, nor covetous man, who is an idolater, hath any inheritance in the kingdom of Christ and of God. 6 Let no man deceive you with vain words: for because of these things cometh the wrath of God upon the children of disobedience. 7 Be not ye therefore partakers with them. 11 And have no fellowship with the unfruitful works of darkness, but rather reprove *them*. 12 For it is a shame even to speak of those things which are done of them in secret.

Col. 3: 5 Mortify . . . your members which are upon the earth; fornication, uncleanness, inordinate affection, evil concupiscence, and covetousness, which is idolatry: 6 For which things' sake the wrath of God cometh on the children of disobedience:

I. Thess. 4: 3 . . . This is the will of God, *even* your sanctification, that ye should abstain from fornication: 4 That every one of you should know how to possess his vessel in sanctification and honour; 5 Not in the lust of concupiscence, even as the Gentiles which know not God: 7 For God hath not called us unto uncleanness, but unto holiness.

I. Tim. 1: 9 . . . The law is not made for a righteous man, but for the lawless and disobedient, for the ungodly and for sinners, for unholy and profane, . . . 10 For whoremongers, for them that defile themselves with mankind, . . . and if there be any other thing that is contrary to sound doctrine;

II. Tim. 3: 2 . . . Men shall be lovers of their own selves, . . . unholy, 3 Without natural affection, . . . incontinent, . . . 4 . . . lovers of pleasures more than lovers of God; 5 Having a form of godliness, but denying the power thereof: from such turn away. 6 For of this sort are they which creep into houses, and lead captive silly women laden with sins, led away with divers lusts,

Heb. 13: 4 Marriage *is* honourable in all, and the bed undefiled: but whoremongers and adulterers God will judge.

Jas. 2: 10 . . . Whosoever shall keep the whole law, and yet offend in one *point*, he is guilty of all. 11 For he that said, Do not commit adultery, said also, Do not kill. Now if thou commit no adultery, yet if thou kill, thou are become a transgressor of the law.

II. Pet. 2: 9 The Lord knoweth how to deliver the godly out of temptation, and to reserve the unjust unto the day of judgment to be punished: 10 But chiefly them that walk after the flesh in the lust of uncleanness, and despise government. . . . 12 . . . These, as natural brute beasts made to be taken and destroyed, speak evil of the things that they understand not; and shall utterly perish in their own corruption; 13 And shall receive the reward of unrighteousness, as they that count it pleasure to riot in the daytime. Spots *they are* and blemishes, sporting themselves with their own deceivings while they feast with you; 14 Having eyes full of adultery, and that cannot cease from sin; beguiling unstable souls: a heart they have exercised with covetous practices; cursed children:

Jude: 7 . . . Sodom and Gomorrah, and the cities about them in like manner, giving themselves over to fornication, and going after strange flesh, are set forth for an example, suffering the vengeance of eternal fire. 8 Likewise also these *filthy* dreamers defile the flesh, despise dominion, and speak evil of dignities.

Rev. 21: 8 . . . The fearful, and unbelieving, and the abominable, and murderers, and whoremongers, and sorcerers, and idolaters, and all liars, shall have their part in the lake which burneth with fire and brimstone: which is the second death.

Rev. 22: 14 Blessed *are* they that do his commandments, that they may have right to the tree

284

of life, and may enter in through the gates into
the city.   15 For without *are* dogs, and sorcerers,
and whoremongers, and murderers, and idolaters,
and whosoever loveth and maketh a lie.
See FOLLY; "SOWING WILD OATS"; WICKED.

LIBERALITY

Prov. 11:   24 There is that scattereth, and yet
increaseth; and *there is* that withholdeth more
than is meet, but *it tendeth* to poverty.   25 The
liberal soul shall be made fat: and he that water-
eth shall be watered also himself.   26 He that
withholdeth corn, the people shall curse him: but
blessing *shall be* upon the head of him that selleth
it.

Prov. 13:   7 There is that maketh himself
rich, yet *hath* nothing: *there is* that maketh himself poor, yet *hath* great riches.

Prov. 21:   26 . . . The righteous giveth and
spareth not.

Acts 20:   35 . . . Ye ought to support the
weak, and to remember the words of the Lord
Jesus, how he said, It is more blessed to give than
to receive.

Rom. 12:   8 . . . He that giveth, *let him do it*
with simplicity; . . .   13 Distributing to the necessity of saints; given to hospitality.

II. Cor. 8:   2 . . . In a great trial of affliction,
the abundance of their joy and their deep poverty
abounded unto the riches of their liberality.   7
. . . As ye abound in every *thing, in* faith, and
utterance, and knowledge, and *in* all diligence,
and *in* your love to us, *see* that ye abound in this
grace also.

I. Tim. 6:   17 Charge them that are rich in
this world, that they be not highminded, nor trust

in uncertain riches, but in the living God, who giveth us richly all things to enjoy; 18 That they do good, that they be rich in good works, ready to distribute, willing to communicate; 19 Laying up in store for themselves a good foundation against the time to come, that they may lay hold on eternal life.

See ALMS; BENEFICENCE; CHURCH Support; GIVING; POOR.

LONGEVITY

Exod. 20: 12 Honour thy father and thy mother: that thy days may be long upon the land which the Lord thy God giveth thee.

Prov. 3: 1 My son, forget not my law; but let thine heart keep my commandments: 2 For length of days, and long life, and peace, shall they add to thee.

Prov. 10: 27 The fear of the Lord prolongeth days: but the years of the wicked shall be shortened.

I. Pet. 3: 10 . . . He that will love life, and see good days, let him refrain his tongue from evil, and his lips that they speak no guile: 11 Let him eschew evil, and do good; let him seek peace, and ensue it. 12 For the eyes of the Lord *are* over the righteous, and his ears *are open* unto their prayers: but the face of the Lord *is* against them that do evil.

See OLD AGE.

LOVE

Prov. 15: 17 Better *is* a dinner of herbs where love is, than a stalled ox and hatred therewith.

Matt. 10: 37 He that loveth father or mother more than me is not worthy of me: and he that loveth son or daughter more than me is not worthy of me.

Mark 12: 30 . . . Thou shalt love the Lord thy God with all thy heart, and will all thy soul, and with all thy mind, and with all thy strength: this *is* the first commandment. 31 And the second *is* like, *namely* this, Thou shalt love thy neighbour as thyself. There is none other commandment greater than these.

Luke 6: 31 . . . As ye would that men should do to you, do ye also to them likewise. 32 For if ye love them which love you, what thank have ye? for sinners also love those that love them. 35 But love ye your enemies, and do good, and lend, hoping for nothing again; and your reward shall be great, and ye shall be the children of the Highest: for he is kind unto the unthankful and *to* the evil.

John 3: 16 . . . God so loved the world, that he gave his only begotten Son, that whosoever believeth in him should not perish, but have everlasting life.

John 13: 34 A new commandment I give unto you, That ye love one another; as I have loved you, that ye also love one another. 35 By this shall all *men* know that ye are my disciples, if ye have love one to another.

John 14: 15 If ye love me, keep my commandments. 21 He that hath my commandments, and keepeth them, he it is that loveth me: and he that loveth me shall be loved of my Father, and I will love him, and will manifest myself to him. 23 Jesus . . . said unto him, If a man love me, he will keep my words: and my Father will love him, and we will come unto him, and make our abode with him. 24 He that loveth me not keepeth not my sayings: and the word which ye hear is not mine, but the Father's which sent me.

287

John 15: 13 Greater love hath no man than this, that a man lay down his life for his friends.

Rom. 5: 8 . . . God commendeth his love toward us, in that, while we were yet sinners, Christ died for us.

Rom. 8: 28 . . . We know that all things work together for good to them that love God, to them who are the called according to *his* purpose.

Rom. 12: 9 *Let* love be without dissimulàtion. . . . 10 *Be* kindly affectioned one to another with brotherly love; in honour preferring one another;

Rom. 13: 8 Owe no man any thing, but to love one another: for he that loveth another hath fulfilled the law. 9 For this, Thou shalt not commit adultery, Thou shalt not kill, Thou shalt not steal, Thou shalt not bear false witness, Thou shalt not covet; and if *there be* any other commandment, it is briefly comprehended in this saying, namely, Thou shalt love thy neighbour as thyself. 10 Love worketh no ill to his neighbour: therefore love *is* the fulfilling of the law.

I. Cor. 13: 1 Though I speak with the tongues of men and of angels, and have not charity, I am become *as* sounding brass, or a tinkling cymbal. 2 And though I have *the gift* of prophecy, and understand all mysteries, and all knowledge; and though I have all faith, so that I could remove mountains, and have not charity, I am nothing. 3 And though I bestow all my goods to feed *the poor*, and though I give my body to be burned, and have not charity, it profiteth me nothing. 4 Charity suffereth long, *and* is kind; charity envieth not; charity vaunteth not itself, is not puffed up, 5 Doth not behave itself unseemly, seeketh not her own, is not easily provoked, thinketh

no evil: 6 Rejoiceth not in iniquity, but rejoiceth in the truth;   7 Beareth all things, believeth
all things, hopeth all things, endureth all things.
8 Charity never faileth: but whether *there be*
prophecies, they shall fail; whether *there be*
tongues, they shall cease; whether *there be* knowledge, it shall vanish away.   13 And now abideth
faith, hope, charity, these three; but the greatest
of these *is* charity.

Gal. 5:   22 . . . The fruit of the Spirit is love,
joy, peace, longsuffering, gentleness, goodness,
faith,   23 Meekness, temperance: against such
there is no law.

I. Tim. 6:   10 . . . The love of money is the
root of all evil: which while some coveted after,
they have erred from the faith, and pierced themselves through with many sorrows.   11 But thou,
O man of God, flee these things; and follow after
righteousness, godliness, faith, love, patience,
meekness.

Heb. 6:   10 . . . God *is* not unrighteous to forget your work and labour of love, which ye have
shewed toward his name, in that ye have ministered to the saints, and do minister.

Heb. 13:   1 Let brotherly love continue.

I. John 2:   5 . . . Whoso keepeth his word,
in him verily is the love of God perfected: hereby
know we that we are in him.   15 Love not the
world, neither the things *that are* in the world.
If any man love the world, the love of the Father
is not in him.

I. John 3:   18 My little children, let us not
love in word, neither in tongue; but in deed and
in truth.

I. John 4:   7 Beloved, let us love one another:
for love is of God; and every one that loveth is

born of God, and knoweth God. 8 He that loveth not, knoweth not God; for God is love. 9 In this was manifested the love of God toward us, because that God sent his only begotten Son into the world, that we might live through him. 10 Herein is love, not that we loved God, but that he loved us, and sent his Son *to be* the propitiation for our sins. 11 Beloved, if God so loved us, we ought also to love one another. 12 No man hath seen God at any time. If we love one another, God dwelleth in us, and his love is perfected in us. 16 And we have known and believed the love that God hath to us. God is love; and he that dwelleth in love dwelleth in God, and God in him. 17 Herein is our love made perfect, that we may have boldness in the day of judgment: because as he is, so are we in this world. 18 There is no fear in love; but perfect love casteth out fear: because fear hath torment. He that feareth is not made perfect in love. 19 We love him, because he first loved us. 20 If a man say, I love God, and hateth his brother, he is a liar: for he that loveth not his brother whom he hath seen, how can he love God whom he hath not seen? 21 And this commandment have we from him, That he who loveth God love his brother also.

See FAMILY LOVE; JESUS, Love of; also FELLOWSHIP; FRIENDSHIP.

LOYALTY

II. Sam. 10: 12 Be of good courage, and let us play the men for our people, and for the cities of our God: and the Lord do that which seemeth him good.

Ecc. 8: 2 I *counsel thee* to keep the king's commandment, and *that* in regard of the oath of God.

John 15: 13 Greater love hath no man than this, that a man lay down his life for his friends. 14 Ye are my friends, if ye do whatsoever I command you.

Rom. 13: 1 Let every soul be subject unto the higher powers. For there is no power but of God: the powers that be are ordained of God.

See FAMILY Loyalty; OBEDIENCE; STEADFAST-NESS.

MALICE

Prov. 11: 17 The merciful man doeth good to his own soul: but *he that is* cruel troubleth his own flesh.

Prov. 17: 5 Whoso mocketh the poor reproacheth his Maker: *and* he that is glad at calamities shall not be unpunished.

Prov. 24: 17 Rejoice not when thine enemy falleth, and let not thine heart be glad when he stumbleth: 29 Say not, I will do so to him as he hath done to me: I will render to the man according to his work.

Matt. 6: 15 . . . If ye forgive not men their trespasses, neither will your Father forgive your trespasses.

Matt. 26: 51 . . . Behold, one of them which were with Jesus stretched out *his* hand, and drew his sword, and struck a servant of the high priest, and smote off his ear. 52 Then said Jesus unto him, Put up again thy sword into his place: for all they that take the sword shall perish with the sword.

Rom. 12: 19 Dearly beloved, avenge not yourselves, but *rather* give place unto wrath: for it is written, Vengeance *is* mine; I will repay, saith the Lord.

I. Cor. 5: 8 . . . Let us keep the feast, not

with old leaven, neither with the leaven of malice
and wickedness; but with the unleavened *bread*
of sincerity and truth.

Eph. 4: 31 Let all bitterness, and wrath, and
anger, and clamour, and evil speaking, be put
away from you, with all malice:

Jas. 2: 13 . . . He shall have judgment without mercy, that hath shewed no mercy; and mercy
rejoiceth against judgment.

See ANGER; ENEMY; HATRED; RETALIATION;
also CHARITABLENESS.

MANHOOD

Luke 6: 45 A good man out of the good treasure of his heart bringeth forth that which is good;
and an evil man out of the evil treasure of his
heart bringeth forth that which is evil: for of the
abundance of the heart his mouth speaketh.

Rom. 12: 1 I beseech you . . . , brethren, by
the mercies of God, that ye present your bodies a
living sacrifice, holy, acceptable unto God, *which
is* your reasonable service.

I. Cor. 9: 25 . . . Every man that striveth
for the mastery is temperate in all things. . . .

I. Cor. 15: 58 . . . My beloved brethren, be
ye steadfast, unmovable, always abounding in the
work of the Lord, forasmuch as ye know that your
labour is not in vain in the Lord.

I. Cor. 16: 13 Watch ye, stand fast in the
faith, quit you like men, be strong.

I. Thess. 4: 3 . . . This is the will of God,
even your sanctification, that ye should abstain
from fornication:

Tit. 2: 1 . . . Speak thou the things which
become sound doctrine: 2 That the aged men be
sober, grave, temperate, sound in faith, in charity,

in patience. 6 Young men likewise exhort to be soberminded.

See CHARACTER; GRACES, Christian; WOMAN-HOOD.

MARRIAGE

Prov. 18: 22 *Whoso* findeth a wife findeth a good *thing*, and obtaineth favour of the Lord.

Mark 10: 6 . . . From the beginning of the creation God made them male and female. 7 For this cause shall a man leave his father and mother, and cleave to his wife; 8 And they twain shall be one flesh: so then they are no more twain, but one flesh. 9 What therefore God hath joined together, let not man put asunder.

Rom. 7: 2 . . . The woman which hath a husband is bound by the law to *her* husband so long as he liveth; but if the husband be dead, she is loosed from the law of *her* husband. 3 So then if, while *her* husband liveth, she be married to another man, she shall be called an adulteress: but if her husband be dead, she is free from that law; so that she is no adulteress, though she be married to another man.

I. Tim. 4: 1 Now the Spirit speaketh expressly, that in the latter times some shall depart from the faith, giving heed to seducing spirits, and doctrines of devils; 3 Forbidding to marry, . . .

I. Tim. 5: 14 I will . . . that the younger women marry, bear children, guide the house, give none occasion to the adversary to speak reproachfully.

Heb. 13: 4 Marriage *is* honourable in all, and the bed undefiled: . . .

See HUSBAND—WIFE; also DIVORCE.

293

MEDITATION

Psa. 1: 1 Blessed *is* the man that walketh not in the counsel of the ungodly, nor standeth in the way of sinners, nor sitteth in the seat of the scornful. 2 But his delight *is* in the law of the Lord; and in his law doth he meditate day and night.

Psa. 4: 4 Stand in awe, and sin not: commune with your own heart upon your bed, and be still. . . .

Psa. 19: 14 Let the words of my mouth, and the meditation of my heart, be acceptable in thy sight, O Lord, my strength, and my redeemer.

See MIND; also HEART.

MEEKNESS

Psa. 25: 9 The meek will he guide in judgment: and the meek will he teach his way.

Psa. 37: 11 . . . The meek shall inherit the earth; and shall delight themselves in the abundance of peace.

Psa. 147: 6 The Lord lifteth up the meek: . . .

Psa. 149: 4 . . . The Lord taketh pleasure in his people: he will beautify the meek with salvation.

Prov. 15: 1 A soft answer turneth away wrath: but grievous words stir up anger. 18 A wrathful man stirreth up strife: but *he that is* slow to anger appeaseth strife.

Prov. 19: 11 The discretion of a man deferreth his anger; and *it is* his glory to pass over a transgression.

Matt. 5: 5 Blessed *are* the meek: for they shall inherit the earth.

Rom. 12: 14 Bless them which persecute you: bless, and curse not. 17 Recompense to no man

evil for evil. . . . 18 If it be possible, as much
as lieth in you, live peaceably with all men. 19
Dearly beloved, avenge not yourselves, but *rather*
give place unto wrath: for it is written, Vengeance
is mine; I will repay, saith the Lord.

I. Cor. 13: 4 Charity suffereth long, *and* is
kind; charity envieth not; charity vaunteth not
itself, is not puffed up. 5 Doth not behave itself unseemly, seeketh not her own, is not easily
provoked, thinketh no evil; 7 Beareth all things,
believeth all things, hopeth all things, endureth
all things.

Gal. 5: 22 . . . The fruit of the Spirit is love,
joy, peace, longsuffering, gentleness, goodness,
faith, 23 Meekness, temperance: against such
there is no law.

Gal. 6: 1 Brethren, if a man be overtaken in
a fault, ye which are spiritual, restore such a one
in the spirit of meekness; considering thyself,
lest thou also be tempted.

Eph. 4: 1 I . . . beseech you that ye walk
worthy of the vocation wherewith ye are called,
2 With all lowliness and meekness, with longsuffering, forbearing one another in love;

I. Tim. 6: 11 . . . Follow after righteousness,
godliness, faith, love, patience, meekness.

II. Tim. 2: 24 . . . The servant of the Lord
must not strive; but be gentle unto all *men*, apt
to teach, patient; 25 In meekness instructing
those that oppose themselves; . . .

Jas. 1: 19 . . . My beloved brethren, let every
man be swift to hear, slow to speak, slow to wrath:
21 . . . Lay apart all filthiness and superfluity
of naughtiness, and receive with meekness the engrafted word, which is able to save your souls.

I. Pet. 3: 4 . . . *The ornament* of a meek and

quiet spirit, which is in the sight of God of great price.

See HUMILITY; JESUS, Meekness of.

MERCY

Prov. 3: 3 Let not mercy and truth forsake thee: bind them about thy neck; write them upon the table of thine heart: 4 So shalt thou find favour and good understanding in the sight of God and man.

Prov. 11: 17 The merciful man doeth good to his own soul: but *he that is* cruel troubleth his own flesh.

Prov. 12: 10 A righteous *man* regardeth the life of his beast: but the tender mercies of the wicked *are* cruel.

Matt. 5: 7 Blessed *are* the merciful: for they shall obtain mercy.

Luke 6: 36 Be ye . . . merciful, as your Father also is merciful.

Luke 10: 30 . . . Jesus . . . said, A certain *man* went down from Jerusalem to Jericho, and fell among thieves, which stripped him of his raiment, and wounded *him*, and departed, leaving *him* half dead. 31 And by chance there came down a certain priest that way; and when he saw him, he passed by on the other side. 32 And likewise a Levite, when he was at the place, came and looked *on him*, and passed by on the other side. 33 But a certain Samaritan, as he journeyed, came where he was; and when he saw him, he had compassion *on him*, 34 And went to *him*, and bound up his wounds, pouring in oil and wine, and set him on his own beast, and brought him to an inn, and took care of him. 35 And on the morrow when he departed, he took out two pence, and gave *them* to the host, and said unto him,

Take care of him: and whatsoever thou spendest more, when I come again, I will repay thee. 36 Which now of these three, thinkest thou, was neighbour unto him that fell among the thieves? 37 And he said, He that shewed mercy on him. Then said Jesus unto him, Go, and do thou likewise.

Jas. 2: 13 . . . He shall have judgment without mercy, that hath shewed no mercy; and mercy rejoiceth against judgment.

See ALMS; CHARITABLENESS; JESUS, Compassion of; KINDNESS.

MIND—THOUGHTS

I. Chr. 28: 9 . . . Thou, Solomon my son, know thou the God of thy father, and serve him with a perfect heart and with a willing mind: for the Lord searcheth all hearts, and understandeth all the imaginations of the thoughts: if thou seek him, he will be found of thee; but if thou forsake him, he will cast thee off for ever.

Psa. 94: 11 The Lord knoweth the thoughts of man, that they *are* vanity.

Prov. 16: 3 Commit thy works unto the Lord, and thy thoughts shall be established.

Prov. 23: 7 . . . As he thinketh in his heart, so *is he:* . . .

Prov. 29: 11 A fool uttereth all his mind: but a wise *man* keepeth it in till afterwards.

Isa. 26: 3 Thou wilt keep *him* in perfect peace, *whose* mind *is* stayed *on thee:* because he trusteth in thee.

Luke 10: 27 . . . Thou shalt love the Lord thy God with all thy heart, and with all thy soul, and with all thy strength, and with all thy mind; and thy neighbour as thyself.

Rom. 1: 28 . . . As they did not like to retain God in *their* knowledge, God gave them over to a reprobate mind, to do those things which are not convenient; 29 Being filled with all unrighteousness, fornication, wickedness, covetousness, maliciousness; full of envy, murder, debate, deceit, malignity; whisperers, 30 Backbiters, haters of God, despiteful, proud, boasters, inventors of evil things, disobedient to parents, 31 Without understanding, covenant-breakers, without natural affection, implacable, unmerciful: 32 Who, knowing the judgment of God, that they which commit such things are worthy of death, not only do the same, but have pleasure in them that do them.

Rom. 8: 6 . . . To be carnally minded *is* death; but to be spiritually minded *is* life and peace. 7 Because the carnal mind *is* enmity against God: for it is not subject to the law of God, neither indeed can be.

I. Cor. 2: 16 . . . Who hath known the mind of the Lord, that he may instruct him? But we have the mind of Christ.

II. Cor. 8: 12 . . . If there be first a willing mind, *it is* accepted according to that a man hath, *and* not according to that he hath not.

II. Cor. 10: 3 . . . Though we walk in the flesh, we do not war after the flesh: 5 Casting down imaginations, and every high thing that exalteth itself against the knowledge of God, and bringing into captivity every thought to the obedience of Christ;

II. Cor. 13: 11 . . . Be perfect, be of good comfort, be of one mind, live in peace; and the God of love and peace shall be with you.

Philip. 2: 5 Let this mind be in you, which was also in Christ Jesus: 6 Who, being in the form of God, thought it not robbery to be equal with God: 7 But made himself of no reputation, and took upon him the form of a servant, and was made in the likeness of men: 8 And being found in fashion as a man, he humbled himself, and became obedient unto death, even the death of the cross.

Philip. 4: 8 . . . Whatsoever things are true, whatsoever things *are* honest, whatsoever things *are* just, whatsoever things *are* pure, whatsoever things *are* lovely, whatsoever things *are* of good report; if *there be* any virtue, and if *there be* any praise, think on these things.

Heb. 4: 12 . . . The word of God *is* quick, and powerful, and sharper than any twoedged sword, piercing even to the dividing asunder of soul and spirit, and of the joints and marrow, and *is* a discerner of the thoughts and intents of the heart.

I. Pet. 4: 1 . . . As Christ hath suffered for us in the flesh, arm yourselves likewise with the same mind: for he that hath suffered in the flesh hath ceased from sin; 2 That he no longer should live the rest of *his* time in the flesh to the lusts of men, but to the will of God.

See HEART; MEDITATION.

MINISTER

Duties of: I. Thess. 1: 7 . . . Ye were ensamples to all that believe in Macedonia and Achaia.

I. Thess. 2: 2 . . . Even after that we had suffered before, and were shamefully entreated, as ye know, at Philippi, we were bold in our God to speak unto you the gospel of God with much contention. 3 For our exhortation *was* not of deceit, nor of uncleanness, nor in guile: 4 But as we were allowed of God to be put in trust with the gospel, even so we speak; not as pleasing

men, but God, which trieth our hearts. · 5 For
neither at any time used we flattering words, as
ye know, nor a cloak of covetousness; God *is* witness: 6 Nor of men sought we glory, neither of
you, nor *yet* of others, when we might have been
burdensome, as the apostles of Christ.   7 But we
were gentle among you, even as a nurse cherisheth
her children: 8 So being affectionately desirous
of you, we were willing to have imparted unto you,
not the gospel of God only, but also our own souls,
because ye were dear unto us.   9 For ye remember, brethren, our labour and travail: for labouring night and day, because we would not be
chargeable unto any of you, we preached unto you
the gospel of God.   10 Ye *are* witnesses, and God
also, how holily and justly and unblameably we
behaved ourselves among you that believe: 11
As ye know how we exhorted and comforted and
charged every one of you, as a father *doth* his
children,

I. Tim. 1:   12 . . . I thank Christ Jesus our
Lord, who hath enabled me, for that he counted
me faithful, putting me into the ministry;

I. Tim. 3:   1 This *is* a true saying, If a man
desire the office of a bishop, he desireth a good
work.   2 A bishop then must be blameless, the
husband of one wife, vigilant, sober, of good behaviour, given to hospitality, apt to teach;   3 Not
given to wine, no striker, not greedy of filthy
lucre; but patient, not a brawler, not covetous;
4 One that ruleth well his own house, having his
children in subjection with all gravity;   5 (For
if a man know not how to rule his own house,
how shall he take care of the church of God?)
6 Not a novice, lest being lifted up with pride he
fall into the condemnation of the devil.   7 More-

over he must have a good report of them which
are without; lest he fall into reproach and the
snare of the devil.   8 Likewise *must* the deacons
be grave, not double-tongued, not given to much
wine, not greedy of filthy lucre;   9 Holding the
mystery of the faith in a pure conscience.   10
And let these also first be proved; then let them
use the office of a deacon, being *found* blameless.
11 Even so *must their* wives *be* grave, not slan-
derers, sober, faithful in all things.   12 Let the
deacons be the husbands of one wife, ruling their
children and their own houses well.

II. Tim. 4:   2 Preach the word; be instant in
season, out of season; reprove, rebuke, exhort with
all longsuffering and doctrine.   5 . . . Watch
thou in all things, endure afflictions, do the work
of an evangelist, make full proof of thy ministry.
6 For I am now ready to be offered, and the time
of my departure is at hand.   7 I have fought a
good fight, I have finished *my* course, I have kept
the faith: 8 Henceforth there is laid up for me
a crown of righteousness, which the Lord, the
righteous judge, shall give me at that day: and
not to me only, but unto all them also that love his
appearing.

Tit. 1:   5 For this cause left I thee in Crete,
that thou shouldest set in order the things
that are wanting, and ordain elders in every
city, as I had appointed thee: 6 If any be blameless, the husband of one wife, having faithful
children not accused of riot or unruly.   7 For a
bishop must be blameless, as the steward of God;
not self-willed, not soon angry, not given to wine,
no striker, not given to filthy lucre;   8 But a lover
of hospitality, a lover of good men, sober, just,
holy, temperate;   9 Holding fast the faithful

301

word as he hath been taught, that he may be able by sound doctrine both to exhort and to convince the gainsayers.

Duties to: I. Cor. 11: 1 Be ye followers of me, even as I also *am* of Christ.

Philip. 2: 29 Receive him . . . in the Lord with all gladness; and hold such in reputation:

I. Thess. 5: 12 . . . We beseech you, brethren, to know them which labour among you, and are over you in the Lord, and admonish you; 13 And to esteem them very highly in love for their work's sake. . . .

I. Tim. 5: 17 Let the elders that rule well be counted worthy of double honour, especially they who labour in the word and doctrine. 18 For the Scripture saith, Thou shalt not muzzle the ox that treadeth out the corn. And, The labourer *is* worthy of his reward. 19 Against an elder receive not an accusation, but before two or three witnesses.

Heb. 13: 7 Remember them which have the rule over you, who have spoken unto you the word of God: whose faith follow, considering the end of *their* conversation. 17 Obey them that have the rule over you, and submit yourselves: for they watch for your souls, as they that must give account, that they may do it with joy, and not with grief: for that *is* unprofitable for you. 18 Pray for us: . . .

See CHURCH.

MISSIONS

Psa. 96: 2 Sing unto the Lord, bless his name; shew forth his salvation from day to day. 3 Declare his glory among the heathen, his wonders among all people.

Matt. 24: 14 . . . This gospel of the kingdom

shall be preached in all the world for a witness unto all nations; and then shall the end come.

Matt. 28: 19 Go ye . . . , and teach all nations, baptizing them in the name of the Father, and of the Son, and of the Holy Ghost: 20 Teaching them to observe all things whatsoever I have commanded you: and, lo, I am with you alway, *even* unto the end of the world. Amen.

Mark 16: 15 . . . He said unto them, Go ye into all the world, and preach the gospel to every creature.

Luke 24: 46 . . . Thus it is written, and thus it behooved Christ to suffer, and to rise from the dead the third day: 47 And that repentance and remission of sins should be preached in his name among all nations, beginning at Jerusalem.

John 10: 16 . . . Other sheep I have, which are not of this fold: them also I must bring, and they shall hear my voice; and there shall be one fold, *and* one shepherd.

Acts 10: 42 . . . He commanded us to preach unto the people, and to testify that it is he which was ordained of God *to be* the Judge of quick and dead.

See ALMS; CHURCH Activity, Support; PERSONAL CHRISTIAN WORK.

MURDER

Exod. 20: 13 Thou shalt not kill.

Psa. 5: 6 . . . The Lord will abhor the bloody and deceitful man.

Matt. 15: 19 . . . Out of the heart proceed evil thoughts, murders, adulteries, fornications, thefts, false witness, blasphemies: 20 These are *the things* which defile a man: . . .

Matt. 19: 18 . . . Jesus said, Thou shalt do no murder, . . .

303

Jas. 2: 11 . . . He that said, Do not commit
adultery, said also, Do not kill. Now if thou commit no adultery, yet if thou kill, thou art become
a transgressor of the law.

I. John 3: 15 Whosoever hateth his brother is
a murderer: and ye know that no murderer hath
eternal life abiding in him.

Rev. 21: 8 . . . Murderers . . . shall have
their part in the lake which burneth with fire and
brimstone: which is the second death.

See CRIMINAL OFFENSES.

MUSIC—SONG

Psa. 98: 4 Make a joyful noise unto the Lord,
all the earth: make a loud noise, and rejoice, and
sing praise. 5 Sing unto the Lord with the harp;
with the harp, and the voice of a psalm. 6 With
trumpets and sound of cornet make a joyful noise
before the Lord, the King.

Psa. 150: 1 Praise ye the Lord. Praise God
in his sanctuary: praise him in the firmament of
his power. 2 Praise him for his mighty acts:
praise him according to his excellent greatness.
3 Praise him with the sound of the trumpet:
praise him with the psaltery and harp. 4 Praise
him with the timbrel and dance: praise him with
stringed instruments and organs. 5 Praise him
upon the loud cymbals: praise him upon the high
sounding cymbals. 6 Let every thing that hath
breath praise the Lord. Praise ye the Lord.

Mark 14: 26 . . . When they had sung a
hymn, they went out into the mount of Olives.

I. Cor. 14: 15 . . . I will pray with the spirit,
and I will pray with the understanding also: I
will sing with the spirit, and I will sing with the
understanding also.

Eph. 5: 18 . . . Be filled with the Spirit; 19

Speaking to yourselves in psalms and hymns and
spiritual songs, singing and making melody in
your heart to the Lord;

Col. 3: 16 Let the word of Christ dwell in
you richly in all wisdom; teaching and admonishing one another in psalms and hymns and spiritual songs, singing with grace in your hearts to
the Lord.

NEIGHBOURS

Exod. 20: 16 Thou shalt not bear false witness against thy neighbour.

Prov. 3: 28 Say not unto thy neighbour, Go,
and come again, and to morrow I will give; when
thou hast it by thee. 29 Devise not evil against
thy neighbour, seeing he dwelleth securely by
thee.

Prov. 14: 21 He that despiseth his neighbour
sinneth: but he that hath mercy on the poor,
happy *is* he.

Prov. 16: 28 A froward man soweth strife:
and a whisperer separateth chief friends. 29 A
violent man enticeth his neighbour, and leadeth
him into the way *that is* not good.

Mark 12: 31 . . . Thou shalt love thy neighbour as thyself. . . .

Rom. 13: 10 Love worketh no ill to his neighbour: therefore love *is* the fulfilling of the law.

Rom. 15: 2 Let every one of us please *his*
neighbour for *his* good to edification. 3 For even
Christ pleased not himself; . . .

Jas. 2: 8 If ye fulfil the royal law according
to the Scripture, Thou shalt love thy neighbour
as thyself, ye do well: 9 But if ye have respect
to persons, ye commit sin, and are convinced of
the law as transgressors.

OBEDIENCE

Ecc. 12: 13 Let us hear the conclusion of the whole matter: Fear God, and keep his commandments: for this *is* the whole *duty* of man.

Matt. 19: 17 . . . He said unto him, Why callest thou me good? *there is* none good but one, *that is*, God: but if thou wilt enter into life, keep the commandments. 29 ʌ. . . Every one that hath forsaken houses, or brethren, or sisters, or father, or mother, or wife, or children, or lands, for my name's sake, shall receive a hundredfold, and shall inherit everlasting life.

John 13: 17 If ye know these things, happy are ye if ye do them.

John 14: 15 If ye love me, keep my commandments. 21 He that hath my commandments, and keepeth them, he it is that loveth me: and he that loveth me shall be loved of my Father, and I will love him, and will manifest myself to him. 23 Jesus . . . said unto him, If a man love me, he will keep my words: and my Father will love him, and we will come unto him, and make our abode with him.

Acts 5: 29 . . . Peter and the *other* apostles . . . said, We ought to obey God rather than men.

Eph. 6: 1 Children, obey your parents in the Lord: for this is right. 5 Servants, be obedient to them that are *your* masters according to the flesh, with fear and trembling, in singleness of your heart, as unto Christ; 6 Not with eyeservice, as menpleasers; but as the servants of Christ, doing the will of God from the heart;

Tit. 3: 1 Put them in mind to be subject to principalities and powers, to obey magistrates, to be ready to every good work,

Jas. 1: 22 . . . Be ye doers of the word, and

306

not hearers only, deceiving your own selves. 25
. . . Whoso looketh into the perfect law of liberty,
and continueth *therein*, he being not a forgetful
hearer, but a doer of the work, this man shall be
blessed in his deed.

I. Pet. 2: 13 Submit yourselves to every ordinance of man for the Lord's sake: whether it
be to the king, as supreme; 14 Or unto governors, as unto them that are sent by him for the
punishment of evil doers, and for the praise of
them that do well.

See JESUS, Obedience of.

OLD AGE

Lev. 19: 32 Thou shalt rise up before the
hoary head, and honour the face of the old man,
and fear thy God: I *am* the Lord.

Job 12: 12 With the ancient *is* wisdom; and
in length of days understanding.

Prov. 16: 31 The hoary head *is* a crown of
glory, *if* it be found in the way of righteousness.

Tit. 2: 1 . . . Speak thou the things which
become sound doctrine: 2 That the aged men be
sober, grave, temperate, sound in faith, in charity,
in patience. 3 The aged women likewise, that
they be in behaviour as becometh holiness, not
false accusers, not given to much wine, teachers
of good things; 4 That they may teach the young
women to be sober, to love their husbands, to love
their children, 5 *To be* discreet, chaste, keepers
at home, good, obedient to their own husbands,
that the word of God be not blasphemed.

See LONGEVITY.

OPPORTUNITY

Prov. 1: 24 Because I have called, and ye refused; I have stretched out my hand, and no man

regarded;   25 But ye have set at nought all my
counsel, and would none of my reproof: 26 I also
will laugh at your calamity; I will mock when your
fear cometh;   33 But whoso hearkeneth unto me
shall dwell safely, and shall be quiet from fear of
evil.

Ezek. 3:   18 When I say unto the wicked, Thou
shalt surely die; and thou givest him not warning,
nor speakest to warn the wicked from his wicked
way, to save his life; the same wicked *man* shall
die in his iniquity; but his blood will I require at
thine hand.   19 Yet if thou warn the wicked, and
he turn not from his wickedness, nor from his
wicked way, he shall die in his iniquity; but thou
hast delivered thy soul.

Matt. 25:   34 Then shall the King say unto
them on his right hand, Come, ye blessed of my
Father, inherit the kingdom prepared for you
from the foundation of the world: 35 For I was
a hungered, and ye gave me meat: I was thirsty,
and ye gave me drink: I was a stranger, and ye
took me in: 36 Naked, and ye clothed me: I
was sick, and ye visited me: I was in prison, and
ye came unto me.   40 . . . Verily I say unto you,
Inasmuch as ye have done *it* unto one of the least
of these my brethren, ye have done *it* unto me.
41 Then shall he say also unto them on the left
hand, Depart from me, ye cursed, into everlasting
fire, prepared for the devil and his angels: 42
For I was a hungered, and ye gave me no meat:
I was thirsty, and ye gave me no drink: 43 I
was a stranger, and ye took me not in: naked, and
ye clothed me not: sick, and in prison, and ye
visited me not.   45 . . . Verily I say unto you,
Inasmuch as ye did *it* not to one of the least of
these, ye did *it* not to me.   46 And these shall

go away into everlasting punishment: but the
righteous into life eternal.

John 12: 48 He that rejecteth me, and receiveth not my words, hath one that judgeth him:
the word that I have spoken, the same shall judge
him in the last day.

Gal. 6: 7 Be not deceived; God is not mocked:
for whatsoever a man soweth, that shall he also
reap. 8 For he that soweth to his flesh shall of
the flesh reap corruption; but he that soweth to
the Spirit shall of the Spirit reap life everlasting.
9 And let us not be weary in well doing: for in
due season we shall reap, if we faint not. 10 As
we have therefore opportunity, let us do good unto
all *men*, especially unto them who are of the
household of faith.

Heb. 2: 3 How shall we escape, if we neglect
so great salvation; which at the first began to be
spoken by the Lord, and was confirmed unto us
by them that heard *him;* 4 God also bearing
them witness, both with signs and wonders, and
with divers miracles, and gifts of the Holy Ghost,
according to his own will?

See RESPONSIBILITY, Individual.

OPPRESSION

Psa. 9: 9 The Lord . . . will be a refuge for
the oppressed, a refuge in times of trouble.

Psa. 62: 10 Trust not in oppression, and become not vain in robbery: if riches increase, set
not your heart *upon them.* 11 God hath spoken
once; twice have I heard this; that power *belongeth* unto God.

Prov. 14: 31 He that oppresseth the poor reproacheth his Maker: but he that honoureth him
hath mercy on the poor.

Prov. 28: 3 A poor man that oppresseth the

poor *is like* a sweeping rain which leaveth no food.

Ecc. 5: 8 If thou seest the oppression of the poor, and violent perverting of judgment and justice in a province, marvel not at the matter: for *he that is* higher than the highest regardeth; and *there be* higher than they.

Zech. 7: 10 . . . Oppress not the widow, nor the fatherless, the stranger, nor the poor; and let none of you imagine evil against his brother in your heart.

See EXTORTION; INJUSTICE; UNJUST GAIN.

PARENTS

Psa. 103: 13 Like as a father pitieth *his* children, *so* the Lord pitieth them that fear him.

Prov. 3: 12 . . . Whom the Lord loveth he correcteth; even as a father the son *in whom* he delighteth.

Prov. 13: 22 A good *man* leaveth an inheritance to his children's children: and the wealth of the sinner *is* laid up for the just.

Matt. 10: 37 He that loveth father or mother more than me is not worthy of me: and he that loveth son or daughter more than me is not worthy of me.

Luke 11: 11 If a son shall ask bread of any of you that is a father, will he give him a stone? or if *he ask* a fish, will he for a fish give him a serpent? 12 Or if he shall ask an egg, will he offer him a scorpion? 13 If ye then, being evil, know how to give good gifts unto your children; how much more shall *your* heavenly Father give the Holy Spirit to them that ask him?

See CHILDREN, Duties of; FAMILY.

Duties of: Prov. 22: 6 Train up a child in

the way he should go: and when he is old, he
will not depart from it.

Prov. 29: 15 The rod and reproof give wisdom: but a child left *to himself* bringeth his
mother to shame. 17 Correct thy son, and he
shall give thee rest; yea, he shall give delight
unto thy soul.

Isa. 38: 19 The living, the living, he shall
praise thee, as I *do* this day: the father to the
children shall make known thy truth.

Eph. 6: 4 . . . Ye fathers, provoke not your
children to wrath: but bring them up in the nurture and admonition of the Lord.

Col. 3: 21 Fathers, provoke not your children
to anger, lest they be discouraged.

I. Tim. 3: 2 A bishop . . . must be blameless,
. . . 4 One that ruleth well his own house, having his children in subjection with all gravity;
5 (For if a man know not how to rule his own
house, how shall he take care of the church of
God?)

I. Tim. 5: 8 . . . If any provide not for his
own, and specially for those of his own house,
he hath denied the faith, and is worse than an
infidel.

See CHILDREN.

PARTIALITY

Prov. 24: 23 These *things* also *belong* to the
wise. *It is* not good to have respect of persons
in judgment.

I. Tim. 5: 21 I charge *thee* before God, and
the Lord Jesus Christ, and the elect angels, that
thou observe these things without preferring one
before another, doing nothing by partiality.

Jas. 2: 1 My brethren, have not the faith of
our Lord Jesus Christ, *the Lord* of glory, with

respect of persons. 2 For if there come unto your assembly a man with a gold ring, in goodly apparel, and there come in also a poor man in vile raiment; 3 And ye have respect to him that weareth the gay clothing, and say unto him, Sit thou here in a good place; and say to the poor, Stand thou there, or sit here under my footstool: 4 Are ye not then partial in yourselves, and are become judges of evil thoughts? 8 If ye fulfil the royal law according to the Scripture, Thou shalt love thy neighbour as thyself, ye do well: 9 But if ye have respect to persons, ye commit sin, and are convinced of the law as transgressors.

Jas. 3: 17 . . . The wisdom that is from above is first pure, then peaceable, gentle, *and* easy to be entreated, full of mercy and good fruits, without partiality, and without hypocrisy.

See EQUALITY OF PERSONS.

PATIENCE

Psa. 37: 7 Rest in the Lord, and wait patiently for him: fret not thyself because of him who prospereth in his way, because of the man who bringeth wicked devices to pass. 8 Cease from anger, and forsake wrath: fret not thyself in any wise to do evil. 9 For evil doers shall be cut off: but those that wait upon the Lord, they shall inherit the earth.

Ecc. 7: 8 Better *is* the end of a thing than the beginning thereof: *and* the patient in spirit *is* better than the proud in spirit.

Lam. 3: 25 The Lord *is* good unto them that wait for him, to the soul *that* seeketh him. 26 *It is* good that *a man* should both hope and quietly wait for the salvation of the Lord.

Rom. 2: 7 To them who by patient continuance in well doing seek for glory and honour and immortality, eternal life:

Rom. 5: 3 . . . We glory in tribulations also; knowing that tribulation worketh patience; 4 And patience, experience; and experience, hope:

Rom. 15: 4 . . . Whatsoever things were written aforetime were written for our learning, that we through patience and comfort of the Scriptures might have hope. 5 Now the God of patience and consolation grant you to be like-minded one toward another according to Christ Jesus:

Gal. 6: 9 . . . Let us not be weary in well doing: for in due season we shall reap, if we faint not.

Col. 1: 9 . . . We . . . do not cease to pray for you, and to desire that ye might be filled with the knowledge of his will in all wisdom and spiritual understanding; 10 That ye might walk worthy of the Lord unto all pleasing, being fruitful in every good work, and increasing in the knowledge of God; 11 Strengthened with all might, according to his glorious power, unto all patience and longsuffering with joyfulness;

I. Thess. 5: 14 Now we exhort you, brethren, warn them that are unruly, comfort the feebleminded, support the weak, be patient toward all *men.*

II. Thess. 3: 5 . . . The Lord direct your hearts into the love of God, and into the patient waiting for Christ.

II. Tim. 2: 24 . . . The servant of the Lord must not strive; but be gentle unto all *men,* apt to teach, patient;

Heb. 10: 36 . . . Ye have need of patience, that, after ye have done the will of God, ye might receive the promise. 37 For yet a little while, and he that shall come will come, and will not tarry.

Heb. 12: 1 . . . Let us lay aside every weight, and the sin which doth so easily beset *us*, and let us run with patience the race that is set before us, 2 Looking unto Jesus the author and finisher of *our* faith; who for the joy that was set before him endured the cross, despising the shame, and is set down at the right hand of the throne of God. 7 If ye endure chastening, God dealeth with you as with sons; for what son is he whom the father chasteneth not?

Jas. 1: 2 My brethren, count it all joy when ye fall into divers temptations; 3 Knowing *this*, that the trying of your faith worketh patience. 4 But let patience have *her* perfect work, that ye may be perfect and entire, wanting nothing.

See STEADFASTNESS.

PEACE

Psa. 133: 1 Behold, how good and how pleasant *it is* for brethren to dwell together in unity!

Prov. 16: 7 When a man's ways please the Lord, he maketh even his enemies to be at peace with him.

Prov. 17: 1 Better *is* a dry morsel, and quietness therewith, than a house full of sacrifices *with* strife.

Prov. 20: 3 *It is* an honour for a man to cease from strife: but every fool will be meddling.

Ecc. 4: 6 Better *is* a handful *with* quietness, than both the hands full *with* travail and vexation of spirit.

Matt. 5: 9 Blessed *are* the peacemakers: for they shall be called the children of God.

Luke 2:   14 Glory to God in the highest, and on earth peace, good will toward men.

John 14:   27 Peace I leave with you, my peace I give unto you: not as the world giveth, give I unto you. Let not your heart be troubled, neither let it be afraid.

John 16:   33 These things I have spoken unto you, that in me ye might have peace. In the world ye shall have tribulation: but be of good cheer; I have overcome the world.

Rom. 5:   1 . . . . Being justified by faith, we have peace with God through our Lord Jesus Christ:

Rom. 8:   6 . . . To be carnally minded *is* death: but to be spiritually minded *is* life and peace.

· Rom. 12:   18 If it be possible, as much as lieth in you, live peaceably with all men.

Rom. 14:   17 . . . The kingdom of God is not meat and drink; but righteousness, and peace, and joy in the Holy Ghost.

II. Cor. 13:   11 . . . Be perfect, be of good comfort, be of one mind, live in peace; and the God of love and peace shall be with you.

Gal. 5:   22 . . . The fruit of the Spirit is love, joy, peace, longsuffering, gentleness, goodness, faith,   23 Meekness, temperance: against such there is no law.

Philip. 4:   7 . . . The peace of God, which passeth all understanding, shall keep your hearts and minds through Christ Jesus.

II. Tim. 2:   22 Flee . . . youthful lusts: but follow righteousness, faith, charity, peace, with them that call on the Lord out of a pure heart.

Heb. 12:   14 Follow peace with all *men*, and holiness, without which no man shall see the Lord:

Jas. 3: 17 . . . The wisdom that is from
above is first pure, then peaceable, gentle, *and*
easy to be entreated, full of mercy and good
fruits, without partiality, and without hypocrisy.
18 And the fruit of righteousness is sown in
peace of them that make peace.

I. Pet. 3: 10 . . . He that will love life, and
see good days, let him refrain his tongue from
evil, and his lips that they speak no guile: 11
Let him eschew evil, and do good; let him seek
peace, and ensue it.

See CHARITABLENESS; CONTENTMENT; HAPPI-
NESS.

PERSONAL CHRISTIAN WORK

Psa. 37: 3 Trust in the Lord, and do good; *so*
shalt thou dwell in the land, and verily thou shalt
be fed.

Psa. 96: 2 Sing unto the Lord, bless his
name; shew forth his salvation from day to day.
3 Declare his glory among the heathen, his wonders among all people.

Psa. 126: 5 They that sow in tears shall reap
in joy. 6 He that goeth forth and weepeth, bearing precious seed, shall doubtless come again
with rejoicing, bringing his sheaves *with him*.

Prov. 11: 30 The fruit of the righteous *is* a
tree of life; and he that winneth souls *is* wise.

Ezek. 33: 8 When I say unto the wicked, O
wicked *man,* thou shalt surely die; if thou dost
not speak to warn the wicked from his way, that
wicked *man* shall die in his iniquity; but his
blood will I require at thine hand. 9 Nevertheless, if thou warn the wicked of his way to turn
from it; if he do not turn from his way, he shall
die in his iniquity; but thou hast delivered thy
soul.

Matt. 5: 16 Let your light so shine before men, that they may see your good works, and glorify your Father which is in heaven.

Matt. 25: 34 Then shall the King say unto them on his right hand, Come, ye blessed of my Father, inherit the kingdom prepared for you from the foundation of the world: 35 For I was a hungered, and ye gave me meat: I was thirsty, and ye gave me drink: I was a stranger, and ye took me in: 36 Naked, and ye clothed me: I was sick, and ye visited me: I was in prison, and ye came unto me. 40 . . . Verily I say unto you, Inasmuch as ye have done *it* unto one of the least of these my brethren, ye have done *it* unto me. 41 Then shall he say also unto them on the left hand, Depart from me, ye cursed, into everlasting fire, prepared for the devil and his angels: 42 For I was a hungered, and ye gave me no meat: I was thirsty, and ye gave me no drink: 43 I was a stranger, and ye took me not in: naked, and ye clothed me not: sick, and in prison, and ye visited me not. 45 . . . Verily I say unto you, Inasmuch as ye did *it* not to one of the least of these, ye did *it* not to me. 46 And these shall go away into everlasting punishment: but the righteous into life eternal.

John 15: 1 I am the true vine; and my Father is the husbandman. 2 Every branch in me that beareth not fruit he taketh away: and every *branch* that beareth fruit, he purgeth it, that it may bring forth more fruit. 5 I am the vine, ye *are* the branches. He that abideth in me, and I in him, the same bringeth forth much fruit; for without me ye can do nothing. 8 Herein is my Father glorified, that ye bear much fruit; so shall ye be my disciples.

317

II. Cor. 9 : 6 . . . He which soweth sparingly
shall reap also sparingly; and he which soweth
bountifully shall reap also bountifully.

Jas. 1 : 22 . . . Be ye doers of the word, and
not hears only, deceiving your own selves.

Jas. 5 : 20 . . . He which converteth the sinner from the error of his way shall save a soul
from death, and shall hide a multitude of sins.

See AFFLICTED, Duty to; ALMS; CHURCH Activity, Support; MISSIONS; SERVICE; STEWARDSHIP.

PLEASURE

Prov. 15 : 21 Folly *is* joy to *him that is* destitute of wisdom: but a man of understanding
walketh uprightly.

Prov. 21 : 17 He that loveth pleasure *shall be*
a poor man: he that loveth wine and oil shall not
be rich.

Ecc. 2 : 1 I said in mine heart, Go to now, I
will prove thee with mirth; therefore enjoy pleasure: and, behold, this also *is* vanity. 10 And
whatsoever mine eyes desired I kept not from
them, I withheld not my heart from any joy; for
my heart rejoiced in all my labour: and this was
my portion of all my labour. 11 Then I looked
on all the works that my hands had wrought, and
on the labour that I had laboured to do: and,
behold, all *was* vanity and vexation of spirit, and
there was no profit under the sun.

Isa. 5 : 11 Woe unto them that rise up early
in the morning, *that* they may follow strong
drink; that continue until night, *till* wine inflame
them! 12 And the harp and the viol, the tabret
and pipe, and wine, are in their feasts: but they
regard not the work of the Lord, neither consider the operation of his hands.

Luke 8: 11 Now the parable is this: The seed is the word of God. 14 And that which fell among thorns are they, which, when they have heard, go forth, and are choked with cares and riches and pleasures of *this* life, and bring no fruit to perfection.

Luke 12: 19 . . . I will say to my soul, Soul, thou hast much goods laid up for many years; take thine ease, eat, drink, *and* be merry. 20 But God said unto him, *Thou* fool, this night thy soul shall be required of thee: then whose shall those things be, which thou hast provided?

I. Tim. 5: 6 . . . She that liveth in pleasure is dead while she liveth.

II. Tim. 3: 4 Traitors, heady, highminded, lovers of pleasures more than lovers of God; 5 Having a form of godliness, but denying the power thereof: from such turn away.

Heb. 11: 24 By faith Moses, when he was come to years, refused to be called the son of Pharaoh's daughter; 25 Choosing rather to suffer affliction with the people of God, than to enjoy the pleasures of sin for a season; 26 Esteeming the reproach of Christ greater riches than the treasures in Egypt: for he had respect unto the recompense of the reward.

See CONTENTMENT; HAPPINESS; WORLDLINESS.

POOR

Psa. 9: 18 . . . The needy shall not always be forgotten: the expectation of the poor shall *not* perish for ever.

Psa. 41: 1 Blessed *is* he that considereth the poor: the Lord will deliver him in time of trouble.

Psa. 82: 3 Defend the poor and fatherless: do justice to the afflicted and needy. 4 Deliver the poor and needy: rid *them* out of the hand of the wicked.

Psa. 102: 17 He will regard the prayer of the destitute, and not despise their prayer.

Prov. 13: 7 There is that maketh himself rich, yet *hath* nothing: *there is* that maketh himself poor, yet *hath* great riches. 23 Much food *is in* the tillage of the poor: but there is *that is* destroyed for want of judgment.

Prov. 14: 31 He that oppresseth the poor reproacheth his Maker: but he that honoureth him hath mercy on the poor.

Prov. 19: 1 Better *is* the poor that walketh in his integrity, than *he that is* perverse in his lips, and is a fool. 17 He that hath pity upon the poor lendeth unto the Lord; and that which he hath given will he pay him again.

Prov. 22: 2 The rich and poor meet together: the Lord *is* maker of them all. 22 Rob not the poor, because he *is* poor: neither oppress the afflicted in the gate: 23 For the Lord will plead their cause, and spoil the soul of those that spoiled them.

Prov. 23: 21 . . . The drunkard and the glutton shall come to poverty: and drowsiness shall clothe *a man* with rags.

Prov. 28: 8 He that by usury and unjust gain increaseth his substance, he shall gather it for him that will pity the poor. 11 The rich man *is* wise in his own conceit; but the poor that hath understanding searcheth him out.

Prov. 31: 9 Open thy mouth, judge righteously, and plead the cause of the poor and needy.

Ecc. 4: 6 Better *is* a handful *with* quietness, than both the hands full *with* travail and vexation of spirit.

Mark 12: 43 . . . He called *unto him* his disciples, and saith unto them, Verily I say unto you, That this poor widow hath cast more in, than all they which have cast into the treasury: 44 For all *they* did cast in of their abundance; but she of her want did cast in all that she had, *even* all her living.

Luke 14: 12 . . . When thou makest a dinner or a supper, call not thy friends, nor thy brethren, neither thy kinsmen, nor *thy* rich neighbours; lest they also bid thee again, and a recompense be made thee. 13 But when thou makest a feast, call the poor, the maimed, the lame, the blind: 14 And thou shalt be blessed; for they cannot recompense thee: for thou shalt be recompensed at the resurrection of the just.

Jas. 2: 2 . . . If there come unto your assembly a man with a gold ring, in goodly apparel, and there come in also a poor man in vile raiment; 3 And ye have respect to him that weareth the gay clothing, and say unto him, Sit thou here in a good place; and say to the poor, Stand thou there, or sit here under my footstool: 4 Are ye not then partial in yourselves, and are become judges of evil thoughts? 5 Hearken, my beloved brethren, Hath not God chosen the poor of this world rich in faith, and heirs of the kingdom which he hath promised to them that love him? 8 If ye fulfil the royal law according to the Scripture, Thou shalt love thy neighbour as thyself, ye do well: 9 But if ye have respect to persons, ye commit sin, and are convinced of the law as transgressors.

See ALMS.

321

PRAYER

II. Chron. 7: 13 If I shut up heaven that there be no rain, or if I command the locusts to devour the land, or if I send pestilence among my people; 14 If my people, which are called by my name, shall humble themselves, and pray, and seek my face, and turn from their wicked ways; then will I hear from heaven, and will forgive their sin, and will heal their land.

Psa. 66: 18 If I regard iniquity in my heart, the Lord will not hear *me:*

Psa. 145: 18 The Lord *is* nigh unto all them that call upon him, to all that call upon him in truth.

Prov. 15: 8 The sacrifice of the wicked *is* an abomination to the Lord: but the prayer of the upright *is* his delight.

Ecc. 5: 2 Be not rash with thy mouth, and let not thine heart be hasty to utter *any* thing before God: for God *is* in heaven, and thou upon earth: therefore let thy words be few.

Lam. 3: 41 Let us lift up our heart with *our* hands unto God in the heavens.

Matt. 6: 5 . . . When thou prayest, thou shalt not be as the hypocrites *are:* for they love to pray standing in the synagogues and in the corners of the streets, that they may be seen of men. Verily I say unto you, They have their reward. 6 But thou, when thou prayest, enter into thy closet, and when thou hast shut thy door, pray to thy Father which is in secret; and thy Father which seeth in secret shall reward thee openly. 7 But when ye pray, use not vain repetitions, as the heathen *do:* for they think that they shall be heard for their much speaking. 8 Be not ye therefore like unto them: for your

Father knoweth what things ye have need of, before ye ask him.   9 After this manner therefore pray ye: Our Father which art in heaven, Hallowed be thy name.   10 Thy kingdom come. Thy will be done in earth, as *it is* in heaven.   11 Give us this day our daily bread.   12 And forgive us our debts, as we forgive our debtors.   13 And lead us not into temptation, but deliver us from evil: For thine is the kingdom, and the power, and the glory, for ever. Amen.

Matt. 7:   7 Ask, and it shall be given you; seek, and ye shall find; knock, and it shall be opened unto you: 8 For every one that asketh receiveth; and he that seeketh findeth; and to him that knocketh it shall be opened.   11 If ye . . . , being evil, know how to give good gifts unto your children, how much more shall your Father which is in heaven give good things to them that ask him?

Matt. 18:   19 . . . I say unto you, That if two of you shall agree on earth as touching any thing that they shall ask, it shall be done for them of my Father which is in heaven.   20 For where two or three are gathered together in my name, there am I in the midst of them.

Mark 11:   24 . . . I say unto you, What things soever ye desire, when ye pray, believe that ye receive *them*, and ye shall have *them*.   25 And when ye stand praying, forgive, if ye have aught against any; that your Father also which is in heaven may forgive you your trespasses.

Luke 18:   1 . . . He spake a parable unto them *to this end*, that men ought always to pray, and not to faint;   11 The Pharisee stood and prayed thus with himself, God, I thank thee, that I am not as other men *are*, extortioners, unjust, adulterers, or

323

even as this publican. 13 And the publican,
standing afar off, would not lift up so much as *his*
eyes unto heaven, but smote upon his breast, saying, God be merciful to me a sinner. 14 I tell
you, this man went down to his house justified
rather than the other: for every one that exalteth
himself shall be abased; and he that humbleth himself shall be exalted.

John 9: 31 Now we know that God heareth
not sinners: but if any man be a worshipper of
God, and doeth his will, him he heareth.

John 15: 7 If ye abide in me, and my words
abide in you, ye shall ask what ye will, and it
shall be done unto you.

Rom. 8: 26 . . . The Spirit . . . helpeth our
infirmities: for we know not what we should
pray for as we ought: but the Spirit itself maketh
intercession for us with groanings which cannot
be uttered. 27 And he that searcheth the hearts
knoweth what *is* the mind of the Spirit, because
he maketh intercession for the saints according to
the will of God.

Rom. 10: 12 . . . There is no difference between the Jew and the Greek: for the same Lord
over all is rich unto all that call upon him. 13
For whosoever shall call upon the name of the
Lord shall be saved.

Philip. 4: 6 Be careful for nothing; but in
every thing by prayer and supplication with
thanksgiving let your requests be made known
unto God. 7 And the peace of God, which passeth all understanding, shall keep your hearts and
minds through Christ Jesus.

I. Thess. 5: 17 Pray without ceasing. 18 In
every thing give thanks: for this is the will of
God in Christ Jesus concerning you.

Jas. 1: 5 If any of you lack wisdom, let him

ask of God, that giveth to all *men* liberally, and
upbraideth not; and it shall be given him.   6 But
let him ask in faith, nothing wavering: for he
that wavereth is like a wave of the sea driven
with the wind and tossed.   7 For let not that
man think that he shall receive any thing of the
Lord.

Jas. 4:   2 Ye lust, and have not: ye kill, and
desire to have, and cannot obtain: ye fight and
war, yet ye have not, because ye ask not.   3 Ye
ask, and receive not, because ye ask amiss, that
ye may consume *it* upon your lusts.

Jas. 5:   13 Is any among you afflicted? let him
pray. Is any merry? let him sing psalms.   14 Is
any sick among you? let him call for the elders
of the church; and let them pray over him, anointing him with oil in the name of the Lord: 15
And the prayer of faith shall save the sick, and
the Lord shall raise him up; and if he have committed sins, they shall be forgiven him.   16 Confess *your* faults one to another, and pray one for
another, that ye may be healed.   The effectual
fervent prayer of a righteous man availeth much.

See FAITH.

PRESUMPTION

Prov. 18:   12 Before destruction the heart of
man is haughty; and before honour *is* humility.
13 He that answereth a matter before he heareth
it, it *is* folly and shame unto him.

Rom. 9:   20 . . . O man, who art thou that
repliest against God? Shall the thing formed say
to him that formed *it*, Why hast thou made me
thus?

Jas. 4:   13 Go to now, ye that say, To day
or to morrow we will go into such a city, and
continue there a year, and buy and sell, and get

gain: 14 Whereas ye know not what *shall be* on the morrow. For what *is* your life? It is even a vapour, that appeareth for a little time, and then vanisheth away. 15 For that ye *ought* to say, If the Lord will, we shall live, and do this, or that. 16 But now ye rejoice in your boastings: all such rejoicing is evil.

II. Pet. 2: 9 The Lord knoweth how to deliver the godly out of temptation, and to reserve the unjust unto the day of judgment to be punished: 10 But chiefly them that walk after the flesh in the lust of uncleanness, and despise government. Presumptuous *are they*, selfwilled, they are not afraid to speak evil of dignities.

See CONCEIT; SELF-EXALTATION; also HUMILITY; MEEKNESS.

PRIDE

I. Sam. 2: 3 Talk no more so exceeding proudly; let *not* arrogancy come out of your mouth: for the Lord *is* a God of knowledge, and by him actions are weighed.

Psa. 9: 20 Put them in fear, O Lord: *that* the nations may know themselves *to be but* men. . . .

Psa. 10: 2 The wicked in *his* pride doth persecute the poor: let them be taken in the devices that they have imagined. 4 The wicked, through the pride of his countenance, will not seek *after God:* God *is* not in all his thoughts.

Psa. 138: 6 Though the Lord *be* high, yet hath he respect unto the lowly: but the proud he knoweth afar off.

Prov. 10: 17 He *is in* the way of life that keepeth instruction: but he that refuseth reproof erreth.

Prov. 12: 9 *He that is* despised, and hath a servant, *is* better than he that honoureth himself, and lacketh bread.

Prov. 13 :   10 Only by pride cometh contention: but with the well advised *is* wisdom.

Prov. 15 :   25 The Lord will destroy the house
of the proud: but he will establish the border of
the widow.

Prov. 16 :   18 Pride *goeth* before destruction,
and a haughty spirit before a fall.   19 Better *it
is to be* of an humble spirit with the lowly, than
to divide the spoil with the proud.

Prov. 18 :   12 Before destruction the heart of
man is haughty; and before honour *is* humility.

Prov. 21 :   4 A high look, and a proud heart,
and the ploughing of the wicked, *is* sin.

Prov. 25 :   27 *It is* not good to eat much ฀
honey: so *for men* to search their own glory
is not glory.

Isa. 2 :   11 The lofty looks of man shall be
humbled, and the haughtiness of men shall be
bowed down; and the Lord alone shall be exalted
in that day.   12 For the day of the Lord of
hosts *shall be* upon every *one that is* proud and
lofty, and upon every *one that is* lifted up; and he
shall be brought low:

Isa. 13 :   11 . . . I will punish the world for
their evil, and the wicked for their iniquity; and
I will cause the arrogancy of the proud to cease,
and will lay low the haughtiness of the terrible.

Mark 7 :   21 . . . From within, out of the
heart of men, proceed evil thoughts, adulteries,
fornications, murders,   22 Thefts, covetousness,
wickedness, deceit, lasciviousness, an evil eye,
blasphemy, pride, foolishness: 23 All these evil
things come from within, and defile the man.

I. Cor. 4 :   7 . . . Who maketh thee to differ
from another? and what hast thou that thou didst
not receive? now if thou didst receive *it*, why dost

327

thou glory, as if thou hadst not received *it?*

I. Cor. 8: 1 . . . Knowledge puffeth up, but charity edifieth. 2 And if any man think that he knoweth any thing, he knoweth nothing yet as he ought to know.

II. Cor. 10: 18 . . . Not he that commendeth himself is approved, but whom the Lord commendeth.

Rev. 3: 17 Because thou sayest, I am rich, and increased with goods, and have need of nothing; and knowest not that thou art wretched, and miserable, and poor, and blind, and naked: 18 I counsel thee to buy of me gold tried in the fire, that thou mayest be rich; and white raiment, that thou mayest be clothed, and *that* the shame of thy nakedness do not appear; and anoint thine eyes with eyesalve, that thou mayest see.

See CONCEIT; SELF-EXALTATION; also HUMILITY; MEEKNESS.

PROCRASTINATION

Matt. 24: 42 Watch . . . ; for ye know not what hour your Lord doth come. 48 But and if that evil servant shall say in his heart, My lord delayeth his coming; 49 And shall begin to smite *his* fellow servants, and to eat and drink with the drunken; 50 The lord of that servant shall come in a day when he looketh not for *him,* and in an hour that he is not aware of, 51 And shall cut him asunder, and appoint *him* his portion with the hypocrites: there shall be weeping and gnashing of teeth.

Luke 9: 62 . . . Jesus said unto him, No man, having put his hand to the plough, and looking back, is fit for the kingdom of God.

I. Thess. 5: 2 . . . Yourselves know perfectly that the day of the Lord so cometh as a thief in the night. 3 For when they shall say, Peace and safety; then sudden destruction cometh upon them, as travail upon a woman with child; and they shall not escape.

Heb. 3: 7 . . . As the Holy Ghost saith, To day if ye will hear his voice, 8 Harden not your hearts, as in the provocation, in the day of temptation in the wilderness: 13 But exhort one another daily, while it is called To day; lest any of you be hardened through the deceitfulness of sin.

See EXCUSE; IDLENESS.

PRUDENCE

Job 34: 3 . . . The ear trieth words, as the mouth tasteth meat. 4 Let us choose to us judgment: let us know among ourselves what *is* good.

Prov. 11: 15 He that is surety for a stranger shall smart *for it:* and he that hateth suretiship is sure.

Prov. 12: 16 A fool's wrath is presently known: but a prudent *man* covereth shame.

Prov. 13: 16 Every prudent *man* dealeth with knowledge: but a fool layeth open *his* folly.

Prov. 14: 15 The simple believeth every word: but the prudent *man* looketh well to his going.

Prov. 15: 5 A fool despiseth his father's instruction: but he that regardeth reproof is prudent. 22 Without counsel purposes are disappointed: but in the multitude of counsellors they are established.

Prov. 21: 23 Whoso keepeth his mouth and his tongue, keepeth his soul from troubles.

Prov. 23: 9 Speak not in the ears of a fool: for he will despise the wisdom of thy words.

Prov. 24: 27 Prepare thy work without, and

make it fit for thyself in the field; and afterwards
build thine house.

Prov. 25:   8 Go not forth hastily to strive, lest
thou know not what to do in the end thereof, when
thy neighbour hath put thee to shame.   9 Debate
thy cause with thy neighbour *himself;* and dis-
cover not a secret to another: 10 Lest he that
heareth *it* put thee to shame, and thine infamy
turn not away.

Prov. 29:   11 A fool uttereth all his mind: but
a wise *man* keepeth it in till afterwards.

Matt. 7:   1 Judge not, that ye be not judged.
2 For with what judgment ye judge, ye shall be
judged: and with what measure ye mete, it shall
be measured to you again.   6 Give not that which
is holy unto the dogs, neither cast ye your pearls
before swine, lest they trample them under their
feet, and turn again and rend you.

Luke 14:   28 . . . Which of you, intending to
build a tower, sitteth not down first, and counteth
the cost, whether he have *sufficient* to finish *it?*
29 Lest haply, after he hath laid the foundation,
and is not able to finish *it,* all that behold *it* begin
to mock him,   30 Saying, This man began to
build, and was not able to finish.

Jas. 1:   19 . . . My beloved brethren, let
every man be swift to hear, slow to speak, slow
to wrath:

See COUNSEL; DIPLOMACY; TACT.

PURITY

Psa. 24:   3 Who shall ascend into the hill of
the Lord? or who shall stand in his holy place?
4 He that hath clean hands, and a pure heart;
who hath not lifted up his soul unto vanity, nor
sworn deceitfully.   5 He shall receive the blessing from the Lord, and righteousness from the

God of his salvation.

Prov. 15: 26 The thoughts of the wicked *are* an abomination to the Lord: but *the words* of the pure *are* pleasant words.

Prov. 21: 8 The way of man *is* froward and strange: but *as for* the pure, his work *is* right.

Mic. 6: 11 Shall I count *them* pure with the wicked balances, and with the bag of deceitful weights?

Matt. 5: 8 Blessed *are* the pure in heart: for they shall see God.

Philip. 4: 8 . . . Whatsoever things are true, whatsoever things *are* honest, whatsoever things *are* just, whatsoever things *are* pure, whatsoever things *are* lovely, whatsoever things *are* of good report: if *there be* any virtue, and if *there be* any praise, think on these things.

I. Tim. 1: 5 Now the end of the commandment is charity out of a pure heart, and *of* a good conscience, and *of* faith unfeigned:

I. Tim. 5: 22 Lay hands suddenly on no man, neither be partaker of other men's sins: keep thyself pure.

II. Tim. 2: 22 Flee . . . youthful lusts: but follow righteousness, faith, charity, peace, with them that call on the Lord out of a pure heart.

Tit. 1: 15 Unto the pure all things *are* pure: but unto them that are defiled and unbelieving *is* nothing pure; but even their mind and conscience is defiled.

Heb. 9: 13 . . . If the blood of bulls and of goats, and the ashes of a heifer sprinkling the unclean, sanctifieth to the purifying of the flesh; 14 How much more shall the blood of Christ, who through the eternal Spirit offered himself without spot to God, purge your conscience from dead works to serve the living God?

Jas. 4: 8 Draw nigh to God, and he will draw nigh to you. Cleanse *your* hands, *ye* sinners; and purify *your* hearts, *ye* doubleminded.

See GRACES, Christian; HEART; RIGHTEOUS; VIRTUE.

RECONCILIATION

Matt. 5: 23 . . . If thou bring thy gift to the altar, and there rememberest that thy brother hath aught against thee; 24 Leave there thy gift before the altar, and go thy way; first be reconciled to thy brother, and then come and offer thy gift. 25 Agree with thine adversary quickly, while thou art in the way with him; lest at any time the adversary deliver thee to the judge, and the judge deliver thee to the officer, and thou be cast into prison.

Rom. 5: 1 . . . Being justified by faith, we have peace with God through our Lord Jesus Christ: 10 For if, when we were enemies, we were reconciled to God by the death of his son; much more, being reconciled, we shall be saved by his life.

Rom. 11: 1 . . . Hath God cast away his people? God forbid. For I also am an Israelite, of the seed of Abraham, *of* the tribe of Benjamin. 11 I say then, Have they stumbled that they should fall? God forbid: but *rather* through their fall salvation *is come* unto the Gentiles, for to provoke them to jealousy. 15 For if the casting away of them *be* the reconciling of the world, what *shall* the receiving *of them be*, but life from the dead?

I. Cor. 7: 10 . . . Unto the married I command, *yet* not I, but the Lord, Let not the wife depart from *her* husband: 11 But and if she depart, let her remain unmarried, or be reconciled

to *her* husband: and let not the husband put away
his wife.

II. Cor. 5: 18 . . . All things *are* of God, who
hath reconciled us to himself by Jesus Christ, and
hath given to us the ministry of reconciliation;
19 To wit, that God was in Christ, reconciling the
world unto himself, not imputing their trespasses
unto them; and hath committed unto us the word
of reconciliation. 20 Now then we are ambas-
sadors for Christ, as though God did beseech *you*
by us: we pray *you* in Christ's stead, be ye reconciled to God. 21 For he hath made him *to be*
sin for us, who knew no sin; that we might be
made the righteousness of God in him.

See CHARITABLENESS; UNSELFISHNESS.

REGENERATION

Matt. 18: 3 . . . Verily I say unto you, Except ye be converted, and become as little children,
ye shall not enter into the kingdom of heaven.

John 3: 3 Jesus . . . said unto him, Verily,
verily, I say unto thee, Except a man be born
again, he cannot see the kingdom of God. 5 . . .
Except a man be born of water and *of* the Spirit,
he cannot enter into the kingdom of God. 6 That
which is born of the flesh is flesh; and that which
is born of the Spirit is spirit. 8 The wind bloweth where it listeth, and thou hearest the sound
thereof, but canst not tell whence it cometh, and
whither it goeth: so is every one that is born of
the Spirit.

John 5: 24 Verily, verily, I say unto you, He
that heareth my word, and believeth on him that
sent me, hath everlasting life, and shall not come
into condemnation; but is passed from death unto
life.

John 8: 12 Then spake Jesus . . . unto them,

333

saying, I am the light of the world: he that followeth me shall not walk in darkness, but shall have the light of life.

Rom. 2: 28 . . . He is not a Jew, which is one outwardly; neither *is that* circumcision, which is outward in the flesh: 29 But he *is* a Jew, which is one inwardly; and circumcision *is that* of the heart, in the spirit, *and* not in the letter; whose praise *is* not of men, but of God.

Rom. 6: 3 Know ye not, that so many of us as were baptized into Jesus Christ were baptized into his death? 4 Therefore we are buried with him by baptism into death: that like as Christ was raised up from the dead by the glory of the Father, even so we also should walk in newness of life. 5 For if we have been planted together in the likeness of his death, we shall be also *in the likeness* of *his* resurrection: 6 Knowing this, that our old man is crucified with *him*, that the body of sin might be destroyed, that henceforth we should not serve sin.

Rom. 7: 6 . . . Now we are delivered from the law, that being dead wherein we were held; that we should serve in newness of spirit, and not *in* the oldness of the letter.

Rom. 12: 2 . . . Be not conformed to this world: but be ye transformed by the renewing of your mind, that ye may prove what *is* that good, and acceptable, and perfect will of God.

I. Cor. 2: 12 Now we have received, not the spirit of the world, but the Spirit which is of God; that we might know the things that are freely given to us of God. 14 But the natural man receiveth not the things of the Spirit of God: for they are foolishness unto him: neither can he know *them*, because they are spiritually discerned.

334

I. Cor. 12: 13 . . . By one Spirit are we all baptized into one body, whether *we be* Jews or Gentiles, whether *we be* bond or free; and have been all made to drink into one Spirit.

II. Cor. 3: 18 . . . We all, with open face beholding as in a glass the glory of the Lord, are changed into the same image from glory to glory, *even* as by the Spirit of the Lord.

Gal. 2: 20 I am crucified with Christ: nevertheless I live; yet not I, but Christ liveth in me: and the life which I now live in the flesh I live by the faith of the Son of God, who loved me, and gave himself for me.

Gal. 6: 15 . . . In Christ Jesus neither circumcision availeth any thing, nor uncircumcision, but a new creature.

Eph. 4: 21 If so be that ye have heard him, and have been taught by him, as the truth is in Jesus: 22 That ye put off concerning the former conversation the old man, which is corrupt according to the deceitful lusts; 23 And be renewed in the spirit of your mind; 24 And that ye put on the new man, which after God is created in righteousness and true holiness.

Col. 2: 11 In whom . . . ye are circumcised with the circumcision made without hands, in putting off the body of the sins of the flesh by the circumcision of Christ: 12 Buried with him in baptism, wherein also ye are risen with *him* through the faith of the operation of God, who hath raised him from the dead. 13 And you, being dead in your sins and the uncircumcision of your flesh, hath he quickened together with him, having forgiven you all trespasses;

Tit. 3: 5 Not by works of righteousness which we have done, but according to his mercy he

saved us, by the washing of regeneration, and renewing of the Holy Ghost; 6 Which he shed on
us abundantly through Jesus Christ our Saviour;
7 That being justified by his grace, we should be
made heirs according to the hope of eternal life.

Heb. 10: 22 Let us draw near with a true
heart in full assurance of faith, having our hearts
sprinkled from an evil conscience, and our bodies
washed with pure water.

I. Pet. 1: 3 Blessed *be* the God and Father of
our Lord Jesus Christ, which according to his
abundant mercy hath begotten us again unto a
lively hope by the resurrection of Jesus Christ
from the dead, 22 Seeing ye have purified your
souls in obeying the truth through the Spirit unto
unfeigned love of the brethren, *see that ye* love
one another with a pure heart fervently: 23 Being born again, not of corruptible seed, but of
incorruptible, by the word of God, which liveth
and abideth for ever.

II. Pet. 1: 3 According as his divine power
hath given unto us all things that *pertain* unto life
and godliness, through the knowledge of him that
hath called us to glory and virtue: 4 Whereby
are given unto us exceeding great and precious
promises; that by these ye might be partakers of
the divine nature, having escaped the corruption
that is in the world through lust.

I. John 3: 9 Whosoever is born of God doth
not commit sin; for his seed remaineth in him:
and he cannot sin, because he is born of God.

I. John 4: 7 Beloved, let us love one another:
for love is of God; and every one that loveth is
born of God, and knoweth God.

See SALVATION.

REMORSE

Prov. 28: 1 The wicked flee when no man pursueth: but the righteous are bold as a lion.

Isa. 57: 20 . . . The wicked *are* like the troubled sea, when it cannot rest, whose waters cast up mire and dirt. 21 *There is* no peace, saith my God, to the wicked.

Matt. 27: 3 . . . Judas, which had betrayed him, when he saw that he was condemned, repented himself, and brought again the thirty pieces of silver to the chief priests and elders, 4 Saying, I have sinned in that I have betrayed the innocent blood. And they said, What *is that* to us? see thou *to that.* 5 And he cast down the pieces of silver in the temple, and departed, and went and hanged himself.

Luke 13: 28 There shall be weeping and gnashing of teeth, when ye shall see Abraham, and Isaac, and Jacob, and all the prophets, in the kingdom of God, and you *yourselves* thrust out.

I. John 3: 20 . . . If our heart condemn us, God is greater than our heart, and knoweth all things.

See REPENTANCE; also CONSCIENCE.

REPENTANCE

II. Chron. 7: 13 If I shut up heaven that there be no rain, or if I command the locusts to devour the land, or if I send pestilence among my people; 14 If my people, which are called by my name, shall humble themselves, and pray, and seek my face, and turn from their wicked ways; then will I hear from heaven, and will forgive their sin, and will heal their land.

Psa. 34: 14 Depart from evil, and do good; seek peace, and pursue it. 18 The Lord *is* nigh unto them that are of a broken heart; and saveth such as be of a contrite spirit.

Prov. 28: 13 He that covereth his sins shall not prosper: but whoso confesseth and forsaketh *them* shall have mercy.

Isa. 55: 7 Let the wicked forsake his way, and the unrighteous man his thoughts: and let him return unto the Lord, and he will have mercy upon him; and to our God, for he will abundantly pardon.

Matt. 3: 2 . . . Repent ye: for the kingdom of heaven is at hand.

Matt. 21: 28 . . . A *certain* man had two sons; and he came to the first, and said, Son, go work to day in my vineyard. 29 He answered and said, I will not; but afterward he repented, and went. 30 And he came to the second, and said likewise. And he answered and said, I *go*, sir; and went not. 31 Whether of them twain did the will of *his* father? They say unto him, The first. Jesus saith unto them, Verily I say unto you, That the publicans and the harlots go into the kingdom of God before you. 32 For John came unto you in the way of righteousness, and ye believed him not; but the publicans and the harlots believed him: and ye, when ye had seen *it*, repented not afterward, that ye might believe him.

Luke 5: 32 I came not to call the righteous, but sinners to repentance.

Luke 13: 3 . . . Except ye repent, ye shall all . . . perish.

Luke 17: 3 Take heed to yourselves: If thy brother trespass against thee, rebuke him; and if he repent, forgive him. 4 And if he trespass against thee seven times in a day, and seven times in a day turn again to thee, saying, I repent; thou shalt forgive him.

Acts 2: 38 . . . Peter said unto them, Repent, and be baptized every one of you in the name of Jesus Christ for the remission of sins, and ye shall receive the gift of the Holy Ghost. 39 For the promise is unto you, and to your children, and to all that are afar off, *even* as many as the Lord our God shall call.

Acts 3: 19 Repent ye . . . , and be converted, that your sins may be blotted out, when the times of refreshing shall come from the presence of the Lord;

II. Cor. 7: 8 . . . Though I made you sorry with a letter, I do not repent, though I did repent: for I perceive that the same epistle hath made you sorry, though *it were* but for a season. 9 Now I rejoice, not that ye were made sorry, but that ye sorrowed to repentance: for ye were made sorry after a godly manner, that ye might receive damage by us in nothing. 10 For godly sorrow worketh repentance to salvation not to be repented of: but the sorrow of the world worketh death. 11 For behold this selfsame thing, that ye sorrowed after a godly sort, what carefulness it wrought in you, yea, *what* clearing of yourselves, yea, *what* indignation, yea, *what* fear, yea, *what* vehement desire, yea, *what* zeal, yea, *what* revenge! In all *things* ye have approved yourselves to be clear in this matter.

Heb. 3: 7 . . . As the Holy Ghost saith, To day if ye will hear his voice, 8 Harden not your hearts, as in the provocation, in the day of temptation in the wilderness:

Jas. 4: 8 Draw nigh to God, and he will draw nigh to you. Cleanse *your* hands, *ye* sinners; and purify *your* hearts, *ye* doubleminded. 9 Be afflicted, and mourn, and weep: let your laughter be turned to mourning, and *your* joy to heaviness.

339

10 Humble yourselves in the sight of the Lord, and he shall lift you up.

Rev. 3: 19 As many as I love, I rebuke and chasten: be zealous therefore, and repent.

See REMORSE; SALVATION; SIN, Forgiveness of.

REPROOF

Prov. 9: 8 Reprove not a scorner, lest he hate thee: rebuke a wise man, and he will love thee.

Prov. 13: 18 Poverty and shame *shall be to* him that refuseth instruction: but he that regardeth reproof shall be honoured.

Prov. 15: 5 A fool despiseth his father's instruction: but he that regardeth reproof is prudent. 31 The ear that heareth the reproof of life abideth among the wise. 32 He that refuseth instruction despiseth his own soul: but he that heareth reproof getteth understanding.

Prov. 17: 10 A reproof entereth more into a wise man than a hundred stripes into a fool.

Prov. 25: 12 *As* an earring of gold, and an ornament of fine gold, *so is* a wise reprover upon an obedient ear.

Prov. 28: 23 He that rebuketh a man, afterwards shall find more favour than he that flattereth with the tongue.

Matt. 18: 15 . . . If thy brother shall trespass against thee, go and tell him his fault between thee and him alone: if he shall hear thee, thou hast gained thy brother.

Luke 17: 3 Take heed to yourselves: If thy brother trespass against thee, rebuke him; and if he repent, forgive him.

Eph. 5: 11 . . . Have no fellowship with the unfruitful works of darkness, but rather reprove *them.*

I. Tim. 5: 1 Rebuke not an elder, but entreat

him as a father; *and* the younger men as brethren; 2 The elder women as mothers; the younger as sisters, with all purity.
See COUNSEL.

REPUTATION

Prov. 22: 1 A *good* name *is* rather to be chosen than great riches, *and* loving favour rather than silver and gold.

Ecc. 7: 1 A good name *is* better than precious ointment; and the day of death than the day of one's birth.

Ecc. 10: 1 Dead flies cause the ointment of the apothecary to send forth a stinking savour: *so doth* a little folly him that is in reputation for wisdom *and* honour.

Tit. 2: 1 . . . Speak thou the things which become sound doctrine: 7 In all things shewing thyself a pattern of good works: in doctrine *shewing* uncorruptness, gravity, sincerity, 8 Sound speech, that cannot be condemned; that he that is of the contrary part may be ashamed, having no evil thing to say of you.
See CHARACTER; INTEGRITY.

RESPONSIBILITY, Individual

Ezek. 18: 20 The soul that sinneth, it shall die. The son shall not bear the iniquity of the father, neither shall the father bear the iniquity of the son: the righteousness of the righteous shall be upon him, and the wickedness of the wicked shall be upon him.

Ezek. 33: 8 When I say unto the wicked, O wicked *man*, thou shalt surely die; if thou dost not speak to warn the wicked from his way, that wicked *man* shall die in his iniquity; but his blood will I require at thine hand. 9 Nevertheless, if

thou warn the wicked of his way to turn from it;
if he do not turn from his way, he shall die in his
iniquity; but thou hast delivered thy soul.

Matt. 12: 36 . . . I say unto you, That every
idle word that men shall speak, they shall give account thereof in the day of judgment.   37 For by
thy words thou shalt be justified, and by thy words
thou shalt be condemned.

John 12: 48 He that rejecteth me, and receiveth not my words, hath one that judgeth him:
the word that I have spoken, the same shall judge
him in the last day.

John 15: 22 If I had not come and spoken
unto them, they had not had sin; but now they
have no cloak for their sin.

Rev. 2: 23 . . . All the churches shall know
that I am he which searcheth the reins and hearts:
and I will give unto every one of you according to
your works.

See OPPORTUNITY; STEWARDSHIP.

RETALIATION

Prov. 20: 22 Say not thou, I will recompense
evil; *but* wait on the Lord, and he shall save thee.

Prov. 26: 27 Whoso diggeth a pit shall fall
therein: and he that rolleth a stone, it will return
upon him.

Matt. 5: 38 Ye have heard that it hath been
said, An eye for an eye, and a tooth for a tooth:
39 But I say unto you, That ye resist not evil:
but whosoever shall smite thee on thy right cheek,
turn to him the other also. 40 And if any
man will sue thee at the law, and take away thy
coat, let him have *thy* cloak also.   41 And whosoever shall compel thee to go a mile, go with him
twain.   42 Give to him that asketh thee, and
from him that would borrow of thee turn not

thou away. 43 Ye have heard that it hath been said, Thou shalt love thy neighbour, and hate thine enemy. 44 But I say unto you, Love your enemies, bless them that curse you, do good to them that hate you, and pray for them which despitefully use you, and persecute you; 45 That ye may be the children of your Father which is in heaven: for he maketh his sun to rise on the evil and on the good, and sendeth rain on the just and on the unjust.

Rom. 12: 17 Recompense to no man evil for evil. Provide things honest in the sight of all men. 18 If it be possible, as much as lieth in you, live peaceably with all men. 19 Dearly beloved, avenge not yourselves, but *rather* give place unto wrath: for it is written, Vengeance *is* mine; I will repay, saith the Lord.

I. Thess. 5: 15 See that none render evil for evil unto any *man;* but ever follow that which is good, both among yourselves, and to all *men.*

I. Pet. 3: 8 . . . *Be ye* all of one mind, having compassion one of another; love as brethren, *be* pitiful, *be* courteous: 9 Not rendering evil for evil, or railing for railing: but contrariwise blessing; knowing that ye are thereunto called, that ye should inherit a blessing.

See ANGER; ENEMY; HATRED; MALICE.

REVERENCE

Exod. 20: 12 Honour thy father and thy mother: that thy days may be long upon the land which the Lord thy God giveth thee.

Psa. 34: 7 The angel of the Lord encampeth round about them that fear him, and delivereth them.

Psa. 103: 13 Like as a father pitieth *his* children, *so* the Lord pitieth them that fear him. 17

. . . The mercy of the Lord *is* from everlasting to everlasting upon them that fear him, and his righteousness unto children's children;

Prov. 1: 7 The fear of the Lord *is* the beginning of knowledge: *but* fools despise wisdom and instruction.

Prov. 8: 13 The fear of the Lord *is* to hate evil: pride, and arrogancy, and the evil way, and the froward mouth, do I hate.

Prov. 15: 16 Better *is* little with the fear of the Lord, than great treasure and trouble therewith.

Ecc. 12: 13 Let us hear the conclusion of the whole matter: Fear God, and keep his commandments: for this *is* the whole *duty* of man.

Matt. 10: 28 . . . Fear not them which kill the body, but are not able to kill the soul: but rather fear him which is able to destroy both soul and body in hell.

II. Cor. 7: 1 . . . Let us cleanse ourselves from all filthiness of the flesh and spirit, perfecting holiness in the fear of God.

I. Thess. 5: 12 . . . We beseech you, brethren, to know them which labour among you, and are over you in the Lord, and admonish you; 13 And to esteem them very highly in love for their work's sake. *And* be at peace among yourselves.

Heb. 12: 28 . . . We receiving a kingdom which cannot be moved, let us have grace, whereby we may serve God acceptably with reverence and godly fear:

RIGHTEOUS, RIGHTEOUSNESS

Psa. 37: 3 Trust in the Lord, and do good: *so* shalt thou dwell in the land, and verily thou shalt be fed. 25 I have been young, and *now* am old; yet have I not seen the righteous for-

᠎saken, nor his seed begging bread.

Psa. 55: 22 Cast thy burden upon the Lord, and he shall sustain thee: he shall never suffer the righteous to be moved.

Prov. 10: 2 Treasures of wickedness profit nothing: but righteousness delivereth from death. 3 The Lord will not suffer the soul of the righteous to famish: but he casteth away the substance of the wicked.

Prov. 21: 3 To do justice and judgment *is* more acceptable to the Lord than sacrifice.

Matt. 7: 17 . . . Every good tree bringeth forth good fruit; but a corrupt tree bringeth forth evil fruit. 18 A good tree cannot bring forth evil fruit, neither *can* a corrupt tree bring forth' good fruit. 20 Wherefore by their fruits ye shall know them.

Matt. 12: 50 . . . Whosoever shall do the will of my Father which is in heaven, the same is my brother, and sister, and mother.

Luke 6: 45 A good man out of the good treasure of his heart bringeth forth that which is good; and an evil man out of the evil treasure of his heart bringeth forth that which is evil: for of the abundance of the heart his mouth speaketh.

Luke 18: 29 . . . He said unto them, Verily I say unto you, There is no man that hath left house, or parents, or brethren, or wife, or children, for the kingdom of God's sake, 30 Who shall not receive manifold more in this present time, and in the world to come life everlasting.

John 13: 35 By this shall all *men* know that ye are my disciples, if ye have love one to another.

Rom. 1: 16 . . . I am not ashamed of the gospel of Christ: for it is the power of God unto salvation to every one that believeth; to the Jew first, and also to the Greek. 17 For therein is the

righteousness of God revealed from faith to faith:
as it is written, The just shall live by faith.

Rom. 3: 21 . . . The righteousness of God
without the law is manifested, being witnessed
by the law and the prophets; 22 Even the righteousness of God *which is* by faith of Jesus Christ
unto all and upon all them that believe; for there
is no difference: 23 For all have sinned, and
come short of the glory of God; 24 Being justified freely by his grace through the redemption
that is in Christ Jesus: 25 Whom God hath set
forth *to be* a propitiation through faith in his
blood, to declare his righteousness for the remission of sins that are past, through the forbearance
of God; 26 To declare, *I say*, at this time his
righteousness: that he might be just, and the justifier of him which believeth in Jesus.

Rom. 4: 3 . . . What saith the Scripture?
Abraham believed God, and it was counted unto
him for righteousness.

Rom. 6: 13 Neither yield ye your members *as*
instruments of unrighteousness unto sin: but yield
yourselves unto God, as those that are alive from
the dead, and your members *as* instruments of
righteousness unto God. 18 Being then made
free from sin, ye became the servants of righteousness.

Rom. 8: 1 *There is* . . . now no condemnation to them which are in Christ Jesus, who walk
not after the flesh, but after the Spirit. 10 And
if Christ *be* in you, the body *is* dead because of
sin; but the Spirit *is* life because of righteousness. 11 But if the Spirit of him that raised up
Jesus from the dead dwell in you, he that raised
up Christ from the dead shall also quicken your
mortal bodies by his Spirit that dwelleth in you.
14 . . . As many as are led by the Spirit of God,

they are the sons of God. 17 And if children, then heirs; heirs of God, and joint heirs with Christ; if so be that we suffer with *him*, that we may be also glorified together. 28 And we know that all things work together for good to them that love God, to them who are the called according to *his* purpose.

Rom. 14: 17 . . . The kingdom of God is not meat and drink; but righteousness, and peace, and joy in the Holy Ghost. 18 For he that in these things serveth Christ *is* acceptable to God, and approved of men.

I. Cor. 2: 9 . . . It is written, Eye hath not seen, nor ear heard, neither have entered into the heart of man, the things which God hath prepared for them that love him.

Gal. 6: 8 . . . He that soweth to his flesh shall of the flesh reap corruption; but he that soweth to the Spirit shall of the Spirit reap life everlasting. 9 And let us not be weary in well doing: for in due season we shall reap, if we faint not.

Philip. 1: 29 . . . Unto you it is given in the behalf of Christ, not only to believe on him, but also to suffer for his sake;

Philip. 3: 3 . . . . We are the circumcision, which worship God in the spirit, and rejoice in Christ Jesus, and have no confidence in the flesh.

Philip. 4: 8 . . . Whatsoever things are true, whatsoever things *are* honest, whatsoever things *are* just, whatsoever things *are* pure, whatsoever things *are* lovely, whatsoever things *are* of good report; if *there be* any virtue, and if *there be* any praise, think on these things.

I. Tim. 4: 8 . . . Bodily exercise profiteth little: but godliness is profitable unto all things,

347

having promise of the life that now is, and of that which is to come.

II. Tim. 2: 19 . . . The foundation of God standeth sure, having this seal, The Lord knoweth them that are his. And, Let every one that nameth the name of Christ depart from iniquity. 22 Flee . . . youthful lusts: but follow righteousness, faith, charity, peace, with them that call on the Lord out of a pure heart. 23 But foolish and unlearned questions avoid, knowing that they do gender strifes. 24 And the servant of the Lord must not strive; but be gentle unto all *men*, apt to teach, patient; 25 In meekness instructing those that oppose themselves; if God peradventure will give them repentance to the acknowledging of the truth;

Tit. 2: 11 . . . The grace of God that bringeth salvation hath appeared to all men, 12 Teaching us that, denying ungodliness and worldly lusts, we should live soberly, righteously, and godly, in this present world; 13 Looking for that blessed hope, and the glorious appearing of the great God and our Saviour Jesus Christ; 14 Who gave himself for us, that he might redeem us from all iniquity, and purify unto himself a peculiar people, zealous of good works.

Jas. 1: 12 Blessed *is* the man that endureth temptation: for when he is tried, he shall receive the crown of life, which the Lord hath promised to them that love him. 27 Pure religion and undefiled before God and the Father is this, To visit the fatherless and widows in their affliction, *and* to keep himself unspotted from the world.

Jas. 4: 7 Submit yourselves . . . to God. Resist the devil, and he will flee from you. 8 Draw nigh to God, and he will draw nigh to you.

. . . 10 Humble yourselves in the sight of the Lord, and he shall lift you up.

I. Pet. 2: 5 Ye . . . , as lively stones, are built up a spiritual house, a holy priesthood, to offer up spiritual sacrifices, acceptable to God by Jesus Christ.

I. Pet. 3: 8 . . . *Be ye* all of one mind, having compassion one of another; love as brethren, *be* pitiful, *be* courteous: 9 Not rendering evil for evil, or railing for railing: but contrariwise blessing; knowing that ye are thereunto called, that ye should inherit a blessing. 10 For he that will love life, and see good days, let him refrain his tongue from evil, and his lips that they speak no guile: 11 Let him eschew evil, and do good; let him seek peace, and ensue it. 12 For the eyes of the Lord *are* over the righteous, and his ears *are open* unto their prayers: but the face of the Lord *is* against them that do evil.

I. John 2: 3 . . . Hereby we do know that we know him, if we keep his commandments. 5 . . . Whoso keepeth his word, in him verily is the love of God perfected: hereby know we that we are in him. 6 He that saith he abideth in him ought himself also so to walk, even as he walked. 10 He that loveth his brother abideth in the light, and there is none occasion of stumbling in him.

Rev. 3: 21 To him that overcometh will I grant to sit with me in my throne, even as I also overcame, and am set down with my Father in his throne.

See FAITH; FAITHFULNESS; GRACES, Christian; HEAVEN; SALVATION.

SABBATH

Jewish: Exod. 20: 8 Remember the sabbath

day, to keep it holy. 9 Six days shalt thou labour, and do all thy work: 10 But the seventh
day *is* the sabbath of the Lord thy God: *in it*
thou shalt not do any work, thou,. nor thy son,
nor thy daughter, thy manservant, nor thy maidservant, nor thy cattle, nor thy stranger that *is*
within thy gates: 11 For *in* six days the Lord
made heaven and earth, the sea, and all that in
them *is*, and rested the seventh day: wherefore
the Lord blessed the sabbath day, and hallowed it.

Mark 2: 27 . . . He said unto them, The sabbath was made for man, and not man for the
sabbath: 28 Therefore the Son of man is Lord
also of the sabbath.

John 5: 16 . . . Therefore did the Jews persecute Jesus, and sought to slay him, because he
had done these things on the sabbath day. 17
But Jesus answered them, My Father worketh
hitherto, and I work. 18 Therefore the Jews
sought the more to kill him, because he not only
had broken the sabbath, but said also that God
was his Father, making himself equal with God.

Col. 2: 16 Let no man . . . judge you in
meat, or in drink, or in respect of a holyday, or
of the new moon, or of the sabbath *days:* 17
Which are a shadow of things to come; but the
body *is* of Christ.

Christian—Sunday: The Lord's Day: Mark 16:
9 . . . When *Jesus* was risen early the first *day*
of the week, he appeared first to Mary Magda-
lene, out of whom he had cast seven devils.

Acts 20: 7 . . . Upon the first *day* of the
week, when the disciples came together to break
bread, Paul preached unto them, ready to depart
on the morrow; and continued his speech until
midnight.

Rom. 14: 5 One man esteemeth one day above another: another esteemeth every day *alike.* Let every man be fully persuaded in his own mind.

I. Cor. 16: 2 Upon the first *day* of the week let every one of you lay by him in store, as *God* hath prospered him, that there be no gatherings when I come.

Col. 2: 16 Let no man . . . judge you in meat, or in drink, or in respect of a holyday, or of the new moon, or of the sabbath *days:*

Rev. 1: 10 I was in the Spirit on the Lord's day, and heard behind me a great voice, as of a trumpet, 11 Saying, I am Alpha and Omega, the first and the last: . . .

SALVATION

Isa. 55: 6 Seek ye the Lord while he may be found, call ye upon him while he is near: 7 Let the wicked forsake his way, and the unrighteous man his thoughts: and let him return unto the Lord, and he will have mercy upon him; and to our God, for he will abundantly pardon.

Matt. 11: 28 Come unto me, all *ye* that labour and are heavy laden, and I will give you rest. 29 Take my yoke upon you, and learn of me; for I am meek and lowly in heart: and ye shall find rest unto your souls.

Matt. 18: 3 . . . Verily I say unto you, Except ye be converted, and become as little children, ye shall not enter into the kingdom of heaven.

Matt. 19: 16 . . . Behold, one came and said unto him, Good Master, what good thing shall I do, that I may have eternal life? 17 And he said unto him, Why callest thou me good? *there is* none good but one, *that is,* God: but if thou wilt

enter into life, keep the commandments. 18 He
saith unto him, Which? Jesus said, Thou shalt
do no murder, Thou shalt not commit adultery,
Thou shalt not steal, Thou shalt not bear false
witness, 19 Honour thy father and *thy* mother:
and, Thou shalt love thy neighbour as thyself.

Matt. 24: 12 . . . Because iniquity shall
abound, the love of many shall wax cold. 13 But
he that shall endure unto the end, the same shall
be saved.

Mark 16: 16 He that believeth and is baptized shall be saved; but he that believeth not
shall be damned.

Luke 3: 6 . . . All flesh shall see the salvation of God.

John 3: 3 Jesus . . . said unto him, Verily,
verily, I say unto thee, Except a man be born
again, he cannot see the kingdom ·of God. 4
Nicodemus saith unto him, How can a man be
born when he is old? can he enter the second
time into his mother's womb, and be born? 5
Jesus answered, Verily, verily, I say unto thee,
Except a man be born of water and *of* the Spirit,
he cannot enter into the kingdom of God. 6 That
which is born of flesh is flesh; and that which
is born of the Spirit is spirit. 7 Marvel not that
I said unto thee, Ye must be born again. 8 The
wind bloweth where it listeth, and thou hearest
the sound thereof, but canst not tell whence it
cometh, and whither it goeth: so is every one that
is born of the Spirit. 14 . . . As Moses lifted
up the serpent in the wilderness, even so must the
Son of man be lifted up: 15 That whosoever
believeth in him should not perish, but have eternal life. 16 For God so loved the world, that
he gave his only begotten Son, that whosoever

believeth in him should not perish, but have everlasting life.   17 For God sent not his Son into
the world to condemn the world; but that the
world through him might be saved.

John 5:   24 Verily, verily, I say unto you, He
that heareth my word, and believeth on him that
sent me, hath everlasting life, and shall not come
into condemnation; but is passed from death unto
life.

John 20:   30 . . . Many other signs truly did
Jesus in the presence of his disciples, which are
not written in this book: 31 But these are written, that ye might believe that Jesus is the Christ,
the Son of God; and that believing ye might have
life through his name.

Acts 11:   18 When they heard these things,
they held their peace, and glorified God, saying,
Then hath God also to the Gentiles granted repentance unto life.

Acts 13:   26 Men *and* brethren, children of the
stock of Abraham, and whosoever among you
feareth God, to you is the word of this salvation
sent.   38 Be it known unto you therefore, men
and brethren, that through this man is preached
unto you the forgiveness of sins: 39 And by
him all that believe are justified from all things,
from which ye could not be justified by the law
of Moses.

Acts 15:   7 . . . Peter rose up, and said unto
them, Men *and* brethren, ye know how that a good
while ago God made choice among us, that the
Gentiles by my mouth should hear the word of
the gospel, and believe.   8 And God, which knoweth the hearts, bare them witness, giving them
the Holy Ghost, even as *he did* unto us; 9 And
put no difference between us and them, purifying

their hearts by faith. 11 But we believe that through the grace of the Lord Jesus Christ we shall be saved, even as they.

Rom. 1: 16 . . . I am not ashamed of the gospel of Christ: for it is the power of God unto salvation to every one that believeth; to the Jew first, and also to the Greek. 17 For therein is the righteousness of God revealed from faith to faith: as it is written, The just shall live by faith.

Rom. 3: 23 . . . All have sinned, and come short of the glory of God; 24 Being justified freely by his grace through the redemption that is in Christ Jesus: 25 Whom God hath set forth *to be* a propitiation through faith in his blood, to declare his righteousness for the remission of sins that are past, through the forbearance of God;

Rom. 10: 4 . . . Christ *is* the end of the law for righteousness to everyone that believeth. 9 . . . If thou shalt confess with thy mouth the Lord Jesus, and shalt believe in thine heart that God hath raised him from the dead, thou shalt be saved. 10 For with the heart man believeth unto righteousness; and with the mouth confession is made unto salvation. 11 For the Scripture saith, Whosoever believeth on him shall not be ashamed. 12 For there is no difference between the Jew and the Greek: for the same Lord over all is rich unto all that call upon him. 13 For whosoever shall call upon the name of the Lord shall be saved.

II. Cor. 6: 17 . . . Come out from among them, and be ye separate, saith the Lord, and touch not the unclean *thing;* and I will receive you, 18 And will be a Father unto you, and ye shall be my sons and daughters, saith the Lord Almighty.

II. Cor. 7: 10 . . . Godly sorrow worketh repentance to salvation not to be repented of: but the sorrow of the world worketh death.

Gal. 2: 16 Knowing that a man is not justified by the works of the law, but by the faith of Jesus Christ, even we have believed in Jesus Christ, that we might be justified by the faith of Christ, and not by the works of the law: for by the works of the law shall no flesh be justified.

Gal. 3: 8 . . . The Scripture, foreseeing that God would justify the heathen through faith, preached before the gospel unto Abraham, *saying*, In thee shall all nations be blessed. 13 Christ hath redeemed us from the curse of the law, being made a curse for us: for it is written, Cursed *is* every one that hangeth on a tree: 14 That the blessing of Abraham might come on the Gentiles through Jesus Christ; that we might receive the promise of the Spirit through faith. 26 For ye are all the children of God by faith in Christ Jesus. 27 For as many of you as have been baptized into Christ have put on Christ. 28 There is neither Jew nor Greek, there is neither bond nor free, there is neither male nor female: for ye are all one in Christ Jesus. 29 And if ye *be* Christ's, then are ye Abraham's seed, and heirs according to the promise.

Eph. 1: 3 Blessed *be* the God and Father of our Lord Jesus Christ, who hath blessed us with all spiritual blessings in heavenly *places* in Christ: 7 In whom we have redemption through his blood, the forgiveness of sins, according to the riches of his grace;

Eph. 2: 8 . . . By grace are ye saved through

355

Salvation (Cont.)   THE BIBLE IN MY EVERYDAY LIFE

faith; and that not of yourselves: *it is* the gift of God:

Eph. 5: 14 . . . Awake thou that sleepest, and arise from the dead, and Christ shall give thee light.

I. Thess. 5: 8 . . . Let us, who are of the day, be sober, putting on the breastplate of faith and love; and for a helmet, the hope of salvation. 9 For God hath not appointed us to wrath, but to obtain salvation by our Lord Jesus Christ, 10 Who died for us, that, whether we wake or sleep, we should live together with him.

II. Thess. 2: 13 . . . We are bound to give thanks always to God for you, brethren beloved of the Lord, because God hath from the beginning chosen you to salvation through sanctification of the Spirit and belief of the truth:

I. Tim. 1: 15 This *is* a faithful saying, and worthy of all acceptation, that Christ Jesus came into the world to save sinners; of whom I am chief. 16 Howbeit for this cause I obtained mercy, that in me first Jesus Christ might shew forth all longsuffering, for a pattern to them which should hereafter believe on him to life everlasting.

II. Tim. 3: 15 . . . From a child thou hast known the holy Scriptures, which are able to make thee wise unto salvation through faith which is in Christ Jesus.

Tit. 3: 5 Not by works of righteousness which we have done, but according to his mercy he saved us, by the washing of regeneration, and renewing of the Holy Ghost; 6 Which he shed on us abundantly through Jesus Christ our Saviour; 7 That being justified by his grace, we should be made heirs according to the hope of

356

eternal life.

Heb. 2 : 3 How shall we escape, if we neglect so great salvation; which at the first began to be spoken by the Lord, and was confirmed unto us by them that heard *him;* 9 . . . We see Jesus, who was made a little lower than the angels for the suffering of death, crowned with glory and honour; that he by the grace of God should taste death for every man. 10 For it became him, for whom *are* all things, and by whom *are* all things, in bringing many sons unto glory, to make the captain of their salvation perfect through sufferings.

Heb. 7 : 25 . . . He is able . . . to save them to the uttermost that come unto God by him, seeing he ever liveth to make intercession for them.

Jas. 1 : 21 . . . Lay apart all filthiness and superfluity of naughtiness, and receive with meekness the engrafted word, which is able to save your souls.

II. Pet. 3 : 9 The Lord is not slack concerning his promise, as some men count slackness; but is longsuffering to us-ward, not willing that any should perish, but that all should come to repentance.

I. John 2 : 25 . . . This is the promise that he hath promised us, *even* eternal life.

Rev. 3 : 20 Behold, I stand at the door, and knock: if any man hear my voice, and open the door, I will come in to him, and will sup with him, and he with me. 21 To him that overcometh will I grant to sit with me in my throne, even as I also overcame, and am set down with my Father in his throne.

Rev. 21 : 6 . . . I am Alpha and Omĕga, the

357

beginning and the end. I will give unto him that
is athirst of the fountain of the water of life
freely. 7 He that overcometh shall inherit all
things; and I will be his God, and he shall be my
son.

Rev. 22: 17 . . . The Spirit and the bride
say, Come. And let him that heareth say, Come.
And let him that is athirst come. And whosoever
will, let him take the water of life freely.

See FAITH; JESUS as Saviour; REGENERATION;
REPENTANCE; also HEAVEN; RIGHTEOUS.

SELF-DELUSION

Psa. 10: 4 The wicked, through the pride of
his countenance, will not seek *after God:* God *is*
not in all his thoughts. 6 He hath said in his
heart, I shall not be moved: for *I shall* never *be*
in adversity.

Prov. 14: 12 There is a way which seemeth
right unto a man; but the end thereof *are* the
ways of death.

Prov. 30: 12 *There is* a generation *that are*
pure in their own eyes, and *yet* is not washed from
their filthiness.

Matt. 7: 21 Not every one that saith unto me,
Lord, Lord, shall enter into the kingdom of
heaven; but he that doeth the will of my Father
which is in heaven. 22 Many will say to me in
that day, Lord, Lord, have we not prophesied in
thy name? and in thy name have cast out devils?
and in thy name done many wonderful works?
23 And then will I profess unto them, I never
knew you: depart from me, ye that work iniquity.

Matt. 24: 44 . . . Be ye . . . ready: for in
such an hour as ye think not the Son of man
cometh. 48 But and if that evil servant shall
say in his heart, My lord delayeth his coming;

49 And shall begin to smite *his* fellow servants, and to eat and drink with the drunken; 50 The lord of that servant shall come in a day when he looketh not for *him*, and in an hour that he is not aware of, 51 And shall cut him asunder, and appoint *him* his portion with the hypocrites: there shall be weeping and gnashing of teeth.

Luke 12: 19 . . . I will say to my soul, Soul, thou hast much goods laid up for many years; take thine ease, eat, drink, *and* be merry. 20 But God said unto him, *Thou* fool, this night thy soul shall be required of thee: then whose shall those things be, which thou hast provided? 21 So *is* he that layeth up treasure for himself, and is not rich toward God.

Luke 18: 10 Two men went up into the temple to pray; the one a Pharisee, and the other a publican. 11 The Pharisee stood and prayed thus with himself, God, I thank thee, that I am not as other men *are*, extortioners, unjust, adulterers, or even as this publican. 12 I fast twice in the week, I give tithes of all that I possess. 13 And the publican, standing afar off, would not lift up so much as *his* eyes unto heaven, but smote upon his breast, saying, God be merciful to me a sinner. 14 I tell you, this man went down to his house justified *rather* than the other: for every one that exalteth himself shall be abased; and he that humbleth himself shall be exalted.

I. Thess. 5: 2 . . . Yourselves know perfectly that the day of the Lord so cometh as a thief in the night. 3 For when they shall say, Peace and safety; then sudden destruction cometh upon them, as travail upon a woman with child; and they shall not escape.

Jas. 4: 13 Go to now, ye that say, To day or

to morrow we will go into such a city, and continue there a year, and buy and sell, and get gain: 14 Whereas ye know not what *shall be* on the morrow. For what *is* your life? It is even a vapour, that appeareth for a little time, and then vanisheth away. 15 For that ye *ought* to say, If the Lord will, we shall live, and do this, or that.

Rev. 3: 17 Because thou sayest, I am rich, and increased with goods, and have need of nothing; and knowest not that thou are wretched, and miserable, and poor, and blind, and naked: 18 I counsel thee to buy of me gold tried in the fire, that thou mayest be rich; and white raiment, that thou mayest be clothed, and *that* the shame of thy nakedness do not appear; and anoint thine eyes with eyesalve, that thou mayest see.

SELF-DENIAL

Prov. 16: 32 *He that is* slow to anger *is* better than the mighty; and he that ruleth his spirit than he that taketh a city.

Matt. 8: 19 . . . A certain scribe came, and said unto him, Master, I will follow thee whithersoever thou goest. 20 And Jesus saith unto him, The foxes have holes, and the birds of the air *have* nests; but the Son of man hath not where to lay *his* head. 21 And another of his disciples said unto him, Lord, suffer me first to go and bury my father. 22 But Jesus said unto him, Follow me; and let the dead bury their dead.

Matt. 10: 37 He that loveth father or mother more than me is not worthy of me: and he that loveth son or daughter more than me is not worthy of me. 38 And he that taketh not his cross, and followeth after me, is not worthy of me. 39 He that findeth his life shall lose it: and he that loseth his life for my sake shall find it.

Matt. 13: 44 . . . The kingdom of heaven is like unto treasure hid in a field; the which when a man hath found, he hideth, and for joy thereof goeth and selleth all that he hath, and buyeth that field. 45 Again, the kingdom of heaven is like unto a merchantman, seeking goodly pearls: 46 Who, when he had found one pearl of great price, went and sold all that he had, and bought it.

Matt. 18: 8 . . . If thy hand or thy foot offend thee, cut them off, and cast *them* from thee: it is better for thee to enter into life halt or maimed, rather than having two hands or two feet to be cast into everlasting fire.

Matt. 19: 21 Jesus said unto him, If thou wilt be perfect, go *and* sell that thou hast, and give to the poor, and thou shalt have treasure in heaven: and come *and* follow me.

Luke 18: 29 . . . He said unto them, Verily I say unto you, There is no man that hath left house, or parents, or brethren, or wife, or children, for the kingdom of God's sake, 30 Who shall not receive manifold more in this present time, and in the world to come life everlasting.

Luke 21: 1 . . . He looked up, and saw the rich men casting their gifts into the treasury. 2 And he saw also a certain poor widow casting in thither two mites. 3 And he said, Of a truth I say unto you, that this poor widow hath cast in more than they all: 4 For all these have of their abundance cast in unto the offerings of God: but she of her penury hath cast in all the living that she had.

Acts 21: 13 . . . Paul answered, What mean ye to weep and to break mine heart? for I am ready not to be bound only, but also to die at Jerusalem for the name of the Lord Jesus.

Rom. 8: 13 . . . If ye live after the flesh, ye shall die: but if ye through the Spirit do mortify the deeds of the body, ye shall live. 35 Who shall separate us from the love of Christ? *shall* tribulation, or distress, or persecution, or famine, or nakedness, or peril, or sword? 36 As it is written, For thy sake we are killed all the day long; we are accounted as sheep for the slaughter. 37 Nay, in all these things we are more than conquerors through him that loved us.

Rom. 13: 14 . . . Put ye on the Lord Jesus Christ, and make not provision for the flesh, to *fulfil* the lusts *thereof.*

Rom. 14: 21 *It is* good neither to eat flesh, nor to drink wine, nor *any thing* whereby thy brother stumbleth, or is offended, or is made weak.

Rom. 15: 1 We . . . that are strong ought to bear the infirmities of the weak, and not to please ourselves. 2 Let every one of us please *his* neighbour for *his* good to edification. 3 For even Christ pleased not himself; but, as it is written, The reproaches of them that reproached thee fell on me. 5 Now the God of patience and consolation grant you to be likeminded one toward another according to Christ Jesus:

I. Cor. 8: 13 . . . If meat make my brother to offend, I will eat no flesh while the world standeth, lest I make my brother to offend.

I. Cor. 9: 19 . . . Though I be free from all *men,* yet have I made myself servant unto all, that I might gain the more. 27 . . . I keep under my body, and bring *it* into subjection: lest that by any means, when I have preached to others, I myself should be a castaway.

I. Cor. 10: 24 Let no man seek his own, but every man another's *wealth.*

Gal. 5: 16 *This* I say then, Walk in the Spirit, and ye shall not fulfil the lust of the flesh. 17 For the flesh lusteth against the Spirit, and the Spirit against the flesh: and these are contrary the one to the other; so that ye cannot do the things that ye would.

Gal. 6: 14 . . . God forbid that I should glory, save in the cross of our Lord Jesus Christ, by whom the world is crucified unto me, and I unto the world.

Philip. 2: 4 Look not every man on his own things, but every man also on the things of others.

Philip. 3: 7 . . . What things were gain to me, those I counted loss for Christ. 8 Yea doubtless, and I count all things *but* loss for the excellency of the knowledge of Christ Jesus my Lord: for whom I have suffered the loss of all things, and do count them *but* dung, that I may win Christ,

Col. 3: 5 Mortify . . . your members which are upon the earth; fornication, uncleanness, inordinate affection, evil concupiscence, and covetousness, which is idolatry: 6 For which things' sake the wrath of God cometh on the children of disobedience:

Tit. 2: 11 . . . The grace of God that bringeth salvation hath appeared to all men, 12 Teaching us that, denying ungodliness and worldly lusts, we should live soberly, righteously, and godly, in this present world;

I. Pet. 2: 11 Dearly beloved, I beseech *you* as strangers and pilgrims, abstain from fleshly lusts, which war against the soul; 13 Submit yourselves to every ordinance of man for the Lord's sake: whether it be to the king, as supreme; 14 Or unto governors, as unto them that are sent by him for the punishment of evil doers, and for the praise of them that do well.

I. Pet. 4: 1 Forasmuch . . . as Christ hath suffered for us in the flesh, arm yourselves likewise with the same mind: for he that hath suffered in the flesh hath ceased from sin; 2 That he no longer should live the rest of *his* time in the flesh to the lusts of men, but to the will of God.

See TEMPERANCE.

SELF-EXALTATION

Prov. 25: 14 Whoso boasteth himself of a false gift *is like* clouds and wind without rain. 27 *It is* not good to eat much honey: so *for men* to search their own glory *is not* glory.

Prov. 26: 12 Seest thou a man wise in his own conceit? *there is* more hope of a fool than of him.

Prov. 27: 2 Let another man praise thee, and not thine own mouth; a stranger, and not thine own lips.

Luke 14: 8 When thou art bidden of any *man* to a wedding, sit not down in the highest room; lest a more honourable man than thou be bidden of him; 9 And he that bade thee and him come and say to thee, Give this man place; and thou begin with shame to take the lowest room. 10 But when thou art bidden, go and sit down in the lowest room; that when he that bade thee cometh, he may say unto thee, Friend, go up higher: then shalt thou have worship in the presence of them that sit at meat with thee. 11 For whosoever exalteth himself shall be abased; and he that humbleth himself shall be exalted.

II. Cor. 10: 17 . . . He that glorieth, let him glory in the Lord. 18 For not he that commendeth himself is approved, but whom the Lord commendeth.

Gal. 6: 3 . . . If a man think himself to be something, when he is nothing, he deceiveth himself.

II. Thess. 2: 3 Let no man deceive you by any means: for *that day shall not come*, except there come a falling away first, and that man of sin be revealed, the son of perdition; 4 Who opposeth and exalteth himself above all that is called God, or that is worshipped; so that he as God sitteth in the temple of God, shewing himself that he is God.

See BOASTING; CONCEIT; PRESUMPTION; PRIDE; SELF-RIGHTEOUSNESS; also HUMILITY.

SELF-EXAMINATION

Psa. 4: 4 Stand in awe, and sin not: commune with your own heart upon your bed, and be still. . . .

Jer. 17: 9 The heart *is* deceitful above all *things*, and desperately wicked: who can know it?

Lam. 3: 40 Let us search and try our ways, and turn again to the Lord.

I. Cor. 11: 27 . . . Whosoever shall eat this bread, and drink *this* cup of the Lord, unworthily, shall be guilty of the body and blood of the Lord. 28 But let a man examine himself, and so let him eat of *that* bread, and drink of *that* cup. 31 For if we would judge ourselves, we should not be judged.

II. Cor. 13: 5 Examine yourselves, whether

ye be in the faith; prove your own selves. Know
ye not your own selves, how that Jesus Christ
is in you, except ye be reprobates?

Gal. 6: 3 . . . If a man think himself to be
something, when he is nothing, he deceiveth himself. 4 But let every man prove his own work,
and then shall he have rejoicing in himself alone,
and not in another.

See MEDITATION.

SELFISHNESS

Prov. 11: 26 He that withholdeth corn, the
people shall curse him: but blessing *shall be* upon
the head of him that selleth *it*.

Prov. 28: 27 He that giveth unto the poor
shall not lack: but he that hideth his eyes shall
have many a curse.

Matt. 19: 21 Jesus said unto him, If thou wilt
be perfect, go *and* sell that thou hast, and give
to the poor, and thou shalt have treasure in
heaven: and come *and* follow me. 22 But when
the young man heard that saying, he went away
sorrowful: for he had great possessions. 23
Then said Jesus unto his disciples, Verily I say
unto you, That a rich man shall hardly enter into
the kingdom of heaven. 24 And again I say unto
you, It is easier for a camel to go through the eye
of a needle, than for a rich man to enter into the
kingdom of God. 25 When his disciples heard *it*,
they were exceedingly amazed, saying, Who then
can be saved? 26 But Jesus beheld *them*, and
said unto them, With men this is impossible; but
with God all things are possible.

Luke 6: 32 . . . If ye love them which love
you, what thank have ye? for sinners also love
those that love them. 33 And if ye do good to

them which do good to you, what thank have ye? for sinners also do even the same. 34 And if ye lend *to them* of whom ye hope to receive, what thank have ye? for sinners also lend to sinners, to receive as much again.

Rom. 14: 21 *It is* good neither to eat flesh, nor to drink wine, nor *any thing* whereby thy brother stumbleth, or is offended, or is made weak.

I. Cor. 10: 24 Let no man seek his own, but every man another's *wealth.*

II. Tim. 3: 2 . . . Men shall be lovers of their own selves, covetous, boasters, proud, blasphemers, disobedient to parents, unthankful, unholy, 3 Without natural affection, trucebreakers, false accusers, incontinent, fierce, despisers of those that are good, 4 Traitors, heady, highminded, lovers of pleasures more than lovers of God; 5 Having a form of godliness, but denying the power thereof: from such turn away.

Jas. 2: 15 If a brother or sister be naked, and destitute of daily food, 16 And one of you say unto them, Depart in peace, be *ye* warmed and filled; notwithstanding ye give them not those things which are needful to the body; what *doth it* profit?

I. John 3: 17 . . . Whoso hath this world's good, and seeth his brother have need, and shutteth up his bowels *of compassion* from him, how dwelleth the love of God in him?

See COVETOUSNESS; also UNSELFISHNESS.

SELF-RIGHTEOUSNESS

Prov. 12: 15 The way of a fool *is* right in his own eyes: but he that hearkeneth unto counsel *is* wise.

Prov. 14: 12 There is a way which seemeth

right unto a man; but the end thereof *are* the ways of death.

Prov. 20: 6 Most men will proclaim every one his own goodness: but a faithful man who can find?

Prov. 21: 2 Every way of a man *is* right in his own eyes: but the Lord pondereth the hearts.

Prov. 28: 13 He that covereth his sins shall not prosper: but whoso confesseth and forsaketh *them* shall have mercy. 26 He that trusteth in his own heart is a fool: but whoso walketh wisely, he shall be delivered.

Prov. 30: 12 *There is* a generation *that are* pure in their own eyes, and *yet* is not washed from their filthiness.

Matt. 7: 22 Many will say to me in that day, Lord, Lord, have we not prophesied in thy name? and in thy name cast out devils? and in thy name done many wonderful works? 23 And then will I profess unto them, I never knew you: depart from me, ye that work iniquity.

Luke 7: 36 . . . One of the Pharisees desired him that he would eat with him. And he went into the Pharisee's house, and sat down to meat. 37 And, behold, a woman in the city, which was a sinner, when she knew that *Jesus* sat at meat in the Pharisee's house, brought an alabaster box of ointment, 38 And stood at his feet behind *him* weeping, and began to wash his feet with tears, and did wipe *them* with the hairs of her head, and kissed his feet, and anointed *them* with the ointment. 39 Now when the Pharisee which had bidden him saw *it,* he spake within himself, saying, This man, if he were a prophet, would have known who and what manner of woman *this is* that toucheth him; for she is a sinner. 40

And Jesus answering said unto him, Simon, I have somewhat to say unto thee. And he saith, Master, say on. 41 There was a certain creditor which had two debtors: the one owed five hundred pence, and the other fifty. 42 And when they had nothing to pay, he frankly forgave them both. Tell me therefore, which of them will love him most? 43 Simon answered and said, I suppose that *he*, to whom he forgave most. And he said unto him, Thou hast rightly judged. 44 And he turned to the woman, and said unto Simon, Seest thou this woman? I entered into thine house, thou gavest me no water for my feet: but she hath washed my feet with tears, and wiped *them* with the hairs of her head. 45 Thou gavest me no kiss: but this woman, since the time I came in, hath not ceased to kiss my feet. 46 My head with oil thou didst not anoint: but this woman hath anointed my feet with ointment. 47 Wherefore I say unto thee, Her sins, which are many, are forgiven; for she loved much: but to whom little is forgiven, *the same* loveth little.

Luke 18: 9 . . . He spake this parable unto certain which trusted in themselves that they were righteous, and despised others: 10 Two men went up into the temple to pray; the one a Pharisee, and the other a publican. 11 The Pharisee stood and prayed thus with himself, God, I thank thee, that I am not as other men *are*, extortioners, unjust, adulterers, or even as this publican. 12 I fast twice in the week, I give tithes of all that I possess. 13 And the publican, standing afar off, would not lift up so much as *his* eyes unto heaven, but smote upon his breast, saying, God be merciful to me a sinner. 14 I tell you, this man went down to his house justified *rather* than the other: for every one that exalteth himself shall be abased; and he that humbleth himself shall be exalted.

John 9: 40 . . . *Some* of the Pharisees which were with him heard these words, and said unto him, Are we blind also? 41 Jesus said unto them, If ye were blind, ye should have no sin: but now ye say, We see; therefore your sin remaineth.

Rom. 2: 21 Thou . . . which teachest another, teachest thou not thyself? thou that preachest a man should not steal, dost thou steal? 22. Thou that sayest a man should not commit adultery, dost thou commit adultery? thou that abhorrest idols, dost thou commit sacrilege? 23 Thou that makest thy boast of the law, through breaking the law dishonourest thou God?

Rom. 10: 3 . . . They, being ignorant of God's righteousness, and going about to establish their own righteousness, have not submitted themselves unto the righteousness of God.

II. Cor. 10: 17 . . . He that glorieth, let him glory in the Lord. 18 For not he that commendeth himself is approved, but whom the Lord commendeth.

Gal. 6: 3 . . . If a man think himself to be something, when he is nothing, he deceiveth himself.

Rev. 3: 17 Because thou sayest, I am rich, and increased with goods, and have need of nothing; and knowest not that thou art wretched, and miserable, and poor, and blind, and naked: 18 I counsel thee to buy of me gold tried in the fire, that thou mayest be rich; and white raiment, that thou mayest be clothed, and *that* the shame of thy nakedness do not appear; and anoint thine eyes with eyesalve, that thou mayest see.

See CONCEIT; HYPOCRISY; PRIDE; SELF-EXALTA-
TION; also HUMILITY.

SERVICE

Mark 9: 35 . . . He sat down, and called the
twelve, and saith unto them, If any man desire to
be first, *the same* shall be last of all, and servant
of all.

Mark 10: 43 . . . Whosoever will be great
among you, shall be your minister: 44 And
Whosoever of you will be the chiefest, shall be
servant of all. 45 For even the Son of man
came not to be ministered unto, but to minister,
and to give his life a ransom for many.

John 13: 12 . . . After he had washed their
feet, and had taken his garments, and was set
down again, he said unto them, Know ye what I
have done to you? 13 Ye call me Master and
Lord: and ye say well; for *so* I am. 14 If I
then, *your* Lord and Master, have washed your
feet; ye also ought to wash one another's feet.
15 For I have given you an example, that ye
should do as I have done to you.

Rom. 15: 1 We . . . that are strong ought
to bear the infirmities of the weak, and not to
please ourselves. 2 Let every one of us please
his neighbour for *his* good to edification. 3 For
even Christ pleased not himself; but, as it is written, The reproaches of them that reproached thee
fell on me.

I. Cor. 9: 19 . . . Though I be free from all
men, yet have I made myself servant unto all,
that I might gain the more. 20 And unto the
Jews I became as a Jew, that I might gain the
Jews; to them that are under the law, as under
the law, that I might gain them that are under

the law; 21 To them that are without law, as without law, (being not without law to God, but under the law to Christ,) that I might gain them that are without law. 22 To the weak became I as weak, that I might gain the weak: I am made all things to all *men*, that I might by all means save some.

I. Cor. 10: 24 Let no man seek his own, but every man another's *wealth*. 31 Whether . . . ye eat, or drink, or whatsoever ye do, do all to the glory of God. 32 Give none offence, neither to the Jews, nor to the Gentiles, nor to the church of God: 33 Even as I please all *men* in all *things*, not seeking mine own profit, but the *profit* of many, that they may be saved.

II. Cor. 8: 9 . . . Ye know the grace of our Lord Jesus Christ, that, though he was rich, yet for your sakes he became poor, that ye through his poverty might be rich.

Gal. 6: 9 . . . Let us not be weary in well doing: for in due season we shall reap, if we faint not. 10 As we have therefore opportunity, let us do good unto all *men*, especially unto them who are of the household of faith.

Eph. 6: 5 Servants, be obedient to them that are *your* masters according to the flesh, with fear and trembling, in singleness of your heart, as unto Christ; 6 Not with eyeservice, as mènpleasers; but as the servants of Christ, doing the will of God from the heart; 7 With good will doing service, as to the Lord, and not to men: 8 Knowing that whatsoever good thing any man doeth, the same shall he receive of the Lord, whether *he be* bond or free.

Philip. 2: 3 *Let* nothing *be done* through strife or vainglory; but in lowliness of mind let each· esteem other better than themselves. 4 Look not every man on his own things, but every man also on the things of others.

See CHURCH Activity, Support; EMPLOYER—EMPLOYEE; INDUSTRY; PERSONAL CHRISTIAN WORK; STEWARDSHIP.

SIN, Forgiveness of

Isa. 55: 6 Seek ye the Lord while he may be found, call ye upon him while he is near: 7 Let the wicked forsake his way, and the unrighteous man his thoughts: and let him return unto the Lord, and he will have mercy upon him; and to our God, for he will abundantly pardon.

Ezek. 33: 14 . . . When I say unto the wicked, Thou shalt surely die; if he turn from his sin, and do that which is lawful and right; 15 *If* the wicked restore the pledge, give again that he had robbed, walk in the statutes of life, without committing iniquity; he shall surely live, he shall not die. 16 None of his sins that he hath committed shall be mentioned unto him: he hath done that which is lawful and right; he shall surely live.

Matt. 1: 21 . . . Thou shalt call his name JESUS: for he shall save his people from their sins.

Matt. 6: 14 . . . If ye forgive men their trespasses, your heavenly Father will also forgive you: 15 But if ye forgive not men their trespasses, neither will your Father forgive your trespasses.

Matt. 12: 31 . . . I say unto you, All manner of sin and blasphemy shall be forgiven unto men: but the blasphemy *against* the *Holy* Ghost shall not be forgiven unto men. 32 And whosoever speaketh a word against the Son of man, it shall be forgiven him: but whosoever speaketh against the Holy Ghost, it shall not be forgiven him, neither in this world, neither in the *world* to come.

Matt. 18: 23 Therefore is the kingdom of heaven likened unto a certain king, which would take account of his servants. 24 And when he had begun to reckon, one was brought unto him, which owed him ten thousand talents. 25 But forasmuch as he had not to pay, his Lord commanded him to be sold, and his wife, and children, and all that he had, and payment to be made. 26 The servant therefore fell down, and worshipped him, saying, Lord, have patience with me, and I will pay thee all. 27 Then the lord of that servant was moved with compassion, and loosed him, and forgave him the debt. 28 But the same servant went out, and found one of his fellow servants, which owed him a hundred pence: and he laid hands on him, and took *him* by the throat, saying, Pay me that thou owest. 29 And his fellow servant fell down at his feet, and besought him, saying, Have patience with me, and I will pay thee all. 30 And he would not: but went and cast him into prison, till he should pay the debt. 31 So when his fellow servants saw what was done, they were very sorry, and came and told unto their lord all that was done. 32 Then his lord, after that he had called him, said unto him, O thou wicked servant, I forgave thee all that debt, because thou desiredst me: 33 Shouldest not thou also have had compassion on thy fellow servant, even as I had pity on thee? 34 And his lord was wroth, and delivered him to the tormentors, till he should pay all that was due unto him. 35 So likewise shall my heavenly Father do also unto you, if ye from your hearts forgive not every one his brother their trespasses.

Matt. 26: 27 . . . He took the cup, and gave thanks, and gave *it* to them, saying, Drink ye all of it; 28 For this is my blood of the new testament, which is shed for many for the remission of sins.

Acts 2: 38 . . . Peter said unto them, Repent, and be baptized every one of you in the name of Jesus Christ for the remission of sins, and ye shall receive the gift of the Holy Ghost. 39 For the promise is unto you, and to your children, and to all that are afar off, *even* as many as the Lord our God shall call.

Acts 10: 43 To him give all the prophets witness, that through his name whosoever believeth in him shall receive remission of sins.

Acts 13: 38 Be it known unto you . . . , men *and* brethren, that through this man is preached unto you the forgiveness of sins: 39 And by him all that believe are justified from all things, from which ye could not be justified by the law of Moses.

Rom. 4: 7 . . . Blessed *are* they whose iniquities are forgiven, and whose sins are covered. 8 Blessed *is* the man to whom the Lord will not impute sin.

Eph. 4: 32 . . . Be ye kind one to another, tenderhearted, forgiving one another, even as God for Christ's sake hath forgiven you.

Heb. 9: 22 . . . Almost all things are by the law purged with blood; and without shedding of blood is no remission. 28 So Christ was once offered to bear the sins of many; and unto them

375

that look for him shall he appear the second time
without sin unto salvation.

Jas. 5: 15 . . . The prayer of faith shall
save the sick, and the Lord shall raise him up;
and if he have committed sins, they shall be forgiven him. 19 Brethren, if any of you do err
from the truth, and one convert him; 20 Let
him know, that he which converteth the sinner
from the error of his way shall save a soul from
death, and shall hide a multitude of sins.

I. John 1: 7 . . . If we walk in the light, as
he is in the light, we have fellowship one with
another, and the blood of Jesus Christ his Son
cleanseth us from all sin. 9 If we confess our
sins, he is faithful and just to forgive us *our*
sins, and to cleanse us from all unrighteousness.

I. John 2: 1 My little children, these things
write I unto you, that ye sin not. And if any
man sin, we have an advocate with the Father,
Jesus Christ the righteous: 2 And he is the
propitiation for our sins: and not for ours only,
but also for *the sins of* the whole world.

Rev. 1: 5 . . . Jesus Christ, *who is* the faithful witness, *and* the firstbegotten of the dead,
and the prince of the kings of the earth. Unto
him that loved us, and washed us from our sins
in his own blood, 6 And hath made us kings and
priests unto God and his Father; to him *be* glory
and dominion for ever and ever. Amen.

See JESUS as Saviour; REGENERATION; RE-
PENTANCE; SALVATION.

SINCERITY

Psa. 32: 2 Blessed *is* the man unto whom the
Lord imputeth not iniquity, and in whose spirit
there is no guile.

Matt. 18: 34 . . . His lord was wroth, and delivered him to the tormentors, till he should pay all that was due unto him. 35 So likewise shall my heavenly Father do also unto you, if ye from your hearts forgive not every one his brother their trespasses.

Rom. 12: 9 *Let* love be without dissimulation. Abhor that which is evil; cleave to that which is good.

I. Cor. 5: 8 . . . Let us keep the feast, not with old leaven, neither with the leaven of malice and wickedness; but with the unleavened *bread* of sincerity and truth.

II. Cor. 1: 12 . . . Our rejoicing is this, the testimony of our conscience, that in simplicity and godly sincerity, not with fleshly wisdom, but by the grace of God, we have had our conversation in the world, and more abundantly to youward.

II. Cor. 2: 17 . . . We are not as many, which corrupt the word of God: but as of sincerity, but as of God, in the sight of God speak we in Christ.

Eph. 6: 5 Servants, be obedient to them that are *your* masters according to the flesh, with fear and trembling, in singleness of your heart, as unto Christ; 6 Not with eyeservice, as menpleasers; but as the servants of Christ, doing the will of God from the heart; 24 Grace *be* with all them that love our Lord Jesus Christ in sincerity. Amen.

Philip. 1: 9 . . . This I pray, that your love may abound yet more and more in knowledge and *in* all judgment; 10 That ye may approve things that are excellent; that ye may be sincere and without offence till the day of Christ;

I. Thess. 2: 3 . . . Our exhortation *was* not of deceit, nor of uncleanness, nor in guile: 4 But as we were allowed of God to be put in trust with the gospel, even so we speak; not as pleasing men, but God, which trieth our hearts.

I. Tim. 1: 5 Now the end of the commandment is charity out of a pure heart, and *of* a good conscience, and *of* faith unfeigned:

I. Pet. 1: 22 Seeing ye have purified your souls in obeying the truth through the Spirit unto unfeigned love of the brethren, *see that ye* love one another with a pure heart fervently:

I. Pet. 2: 1 . . . Laying aside all malice, and all guile, and hypocrisies, and envies, and all evil speakings, 2 As newborn babes, desire the sincere milk of the word, that ye may grow thereby: 21 . . . Even hereunto were ye called: because Christ also suffered for us, leaving us an example, that ye should follow his steps: 22 Who did no sin, neither was guile found in his mouth:

I. John 3: 18 My little children, let us not love in word, neither in tongue; but in deed and in truth.

See TRUTH.

SKEPTICISM

Psa. 14: 1 The fool hath said in his heart, *There is* no God. They are corrupt, they have done abominable works, *there is* none that doeth good.

John 20: 24 . . . Thomas, one of the twelve, called Didymus, was not with them when Jesus came. 25 The other disciples therefore said unto him, We have seen the Lord. But he said unto them, Except I shall see in his hands the print of the nails, and put my finger into the print of the nails, and thrust my hand into his side, I will not believe. 26 And after eight days again his disciples were within, and Thomas with them: *then* came Jesus, the doors being shut, and stood in the midst, and said, Peace *be* unto you. 27 Then saith he to Thomas, Reach hither thy finger, and behold my hands; and reach hither thy hand, and thrust *it* into my side; and be not faithless, but believing. 28 And Thomas answered and said unto him, My Lord and my God. 29 Jesus saith unto him, Thomas, because thou hast seen me, thou hast believed: blessed *are* they that have not seen, and *yet* have believed.

See ATHEISM; UNBELIEF.

SLANDER

Psa. 101: 5 Whoso privily slandereth his neighbour, him will I cut off: him that hath a high look and a proud heart will not I suffer.

Prov. 10: 18 He that hideth hatred *with* lying lips, and he that uttereth a slander, *is* a fool.

Prov. 11: 9 A hypocrite with *his* mouth destroyeth his neighbour: but through knowledge shall the just be delivered.

I. Cor. 6: 9 Know ye not that the unrighteous shall not inherit the kingdom of God? Be not deceived: neither fornicators, . . . 10 Nor thieves, nor covetous, nor drunkards, nor revilers, nor extortioners, shall inherit the kingdom of God.

Jas. 4: 11 Speak not evil one of another, brethren. He that speaketh evil of *his* brother, and judgeth his brother, speaketh evil of the law, and judgeth the law: but if thou judge the law, thou art not a doer of the law, but a judge. 12

There is one lawgiver, who is able to save and to destroy: who art thou that judgest another?

I. Pet. 2: 1 . . . Laying aside all malice, and all guile, and hypocrisies, and envies, and all evil speakings, 2 As newborn babes, desire the sincere milk of the word, that ye may grow thereby:

See ACCUSATION, False; BACKBITING; FALSEHOOD.

"SOWING WILD OATS"

Job 4: 8 Even as I have seen, they that plough iniquity, and sow wickedness, reap the same.

Prov. 6: 12 A naughty person, a wicked man, walketh with a froward mouth. 13 He winketh with his eyes, he speaketh with his feet, he teacheth with his fingers; 14 Frowardness is in his heart, he deviseth mischief continually; he soweth discord. 15 Therefore shall his calamity come suddenly; suddenly shall he be broken without remedy.

Prov. 19: 13 A foolish son is the calamity of his father: . . .

Prov. 22: 8 He that soweth iniquity shall reap vanity: and the rod of his anger shall fail.

Gal. 6: 7 Be not deceived; God is not mocked; for whatsoever a man soweth, that shall he also reap. 8 For he that soweth to his flesh shall of the flesh reap corruption; but he that soweth to the Spirit shall of the Spirit reap life everlasting.

See FOLLY; LASCIVIOUSNESS; WICKED.

SPIRIT—SOUL

Job 32: 8 . . . There is a spirit in man: and the inspiration of the Almighty giveth them understanding.

Prov. 20: 27 The spirit of man *is* the candle of the Lord, searching all the inward parts of the belly.

Ecc. 3: 21 Who knoweth the spirit of man that goeth upward, and the spirit of the beast that goeth downward to the earth?

Ecc. 12: 7 Then shall the dust return to the earth as it was: and the spirit shall return unto God who gave it.

Matt. 10: 28 . . . Fear not them which kill the body, but are not able to kill the soul: but rather fear him which is able to destroy both soul and body in hell.

Matt. 16: 26 . . . What is a man profited, if he shall gain the whole world, and lose his own soul? or what shall a man give in exchange for his soul?

Matt. 26: 41 Watch and pray, that ye enter not into temptation: the spirit indeed *is* willing, but the flesh *is* weak.

Luke 23: 46 . . . When Jesus had cried with a loud voice, he said, Father, into thy hands I commend my spirit: and having said thus, he gave up the ghost.

Luke 24: 39 Behold my hands and my feet, that it is I myself: handle me, and see; for a spirit hath not flesh and bones, as ye see me have.

John 3: 5 Jesus answered, Verily, verily, I say unto thee, Except a man be born of water and *of* the Spirit, he cannot enter into the kingdom of God. 6 That which is born of the flesh is flesh; and that which is born of the Spirit is spirit. 7 Marvel not that I said unto thee, Ye must be born again. 8 The wind bloweth where it listeth, and thou hearest the sound thereof, but canst not tell whence it cometh, and whither it goeth: so is every one that is born of the Spirit.

John 4: 24 God *is* a Spirit: and they that worship him must worship *him* in spirit and in truth.

Rom. 2: 29 . . . He *is* a Jew, which is one inwardly; and circumcision *is that* of the heart, in the spirit, *and* not in the letter; whose praise *is* not of men, but of God.

Rom. 7: 14 . . . We know that the law is spiritual: but I am carnal, sold under sin. 18 For I know that in me (that is, in my flesh,) dwelleth no good thing: for to will is present with me; but *how* to perform that which is good I find not. 22 For I delight in the law of God after the inward man: 23 But I see another law in my members, warring against the law of my mind, and bringing me into captivity to the law of sin which is in my members. 24 O wretched man that I am! who shall deliver me from the body of this death? 25 I thank God through Jesus Christ our Lord. So then with the mind I myself serve the law of God; but with the flesh the law of sin.

I. Cor. 2: 11 . . . What man knoweth the things of a man, save the spirit of man which is in him? even so the things of God knoweth no man, but the Spirit of God.

I. Cor. 14: 14 . . . If I pray in an *unknown* tongue, my spirit prayeth, but my understanding is unfruitful. 15 What is it then? I will pray with the spirit, and I will pray with the understanding also: I will sing with the spirit, and I will sing with the understanding also.

Eph. 3: 14 For this cause I bow my knees unto the Father of our Lord Jesus Christ, 16 That he would grant you, according to the riches of his glory, to be strengthened with might by his Spirit in the inner man;

Jas. 2: 26 . . . As the body without the spirit is dead, so faith without works is dead also.

See HEART; HOLY GHOST; also SALVATION.

SPIRITUAL—SPIRITUALITY

Psa. 1: 1 Blessed *is* the man that walketh not in the counsel of the ungodly, nor standeth in the way of sinners, nor sitteth in the seat of the scornful. 2 But his delight *is* in the law of the Lord; and in his law doth he meditate day and night.

Isa. 26: 3 Thou wilt keep *him* in perfect peace, *whose* mind *is* stayed *on thee:* because he trusteth in thee.

Matt. 5: 6 Blessed *are* they which do hunger and thirst after righteousness: for they shall be filled.

John 6: 27 Labour not for the meat which perisheth, but for that meat which endureth unto everlasting life, which the Son of man shall give unto you: for him hath God the Father sealed.

John 14: 16 . . . I will pray the Father, and he shall give you another Comforter, that he may abide with you for ever; 17 *Even* the Spirit of truth; whom the world cannot receive, because it seeth him not, neither knoweth him: but ye know him; for he dwelleth with you, and shall be in you.

Rom. 8: 6 . . . To be carnally minded *is* death; but to be spiritually minded *is* life and peace.

Rom. 14: 17 . . . The kingdom of God is not meat and drink; but righteousness, and peace, and joy in the Holy Ghost. 18 For he that in these things serveth Christ *is* acceptable to God, and approved of men.

I. Cor. 2: 14 . . . The natural man receiveth not the things of the Spirit of God: for they are foolishness unto him: neither can he know *them*, because they are spiritually discerned. 15 But he that is spiritual judgeth all things, yet he himself is judged of no man. 16 For who hath known the mind of the Lord, that he may instruct him? But we have the mind of Christ.

Col. 3: 1 If ye . . . be risen with Christ, seek those things which are above, where Christ sitteth on the right hand of God. 2 Set your affection on things above, not on things on the earth. 3 For ye are dead, and your life is hid with Christ in God. 4 When Christ, *who is* our life, shall appear, then shall ye also appear with him in glory.

See CONSECRATION; RIGHTEOUS; also HOLY GHOST; SPIRIT.

STEADFASTNESS

John 15: 7 If ye abide in me, and my words abide in you, ye shall ask what ye will, and it shall be done unto you.

Rom. 8: 38 . . . I am persuaded, that neither death, nor life, nor angels, nor principalities, nor powers, nor things present, nor things to come, 39 Nor height, nor depth, nor any other creature, shall be able to separate us from the love of God, which is in Christ Jesus our Lord.

I. Cor. 15: 58 . . . My beloved brethren, be ye steadfast, unmovable, always abounding in the work of the Lord, forasmuch as ye know that your labour is not in vain in the Lord.

I. Cor. 16: 13 Watch ye, stand fast in the faith, quit you like men, be strong.

Gal. 5: 1 Stand fast . . . in the liberty wherewith Christ hath made us free, and be not entangled again with the yoke of bondage.

Eph. 6: 13 . . . Take unto you the whole armour of God, that ye may be able to withstand in the evil day, and having done all, to stand.

I. Thess. 5: 21 Prove all things; hold fast that which is good.

II. Thess. 2: 15 . . . Brethren, stand fast, and hold the traditions which ye have been taught, whether by word, or our epistle.

II. Tim. 3: 14 . . . Continue thou in the things which thou hast learned and hast been assured of, knowing of whom thou hast learned *them;*

Heb. 10: 23 Let us hold fast the profession of *our* faith without wavering; for he *is* faithful that promised;

Heb. 12: 7 If ye endure chastening, God dealeth with you as with sons; for what son is he whom the father chasteneth not?

Jas. 1: 12 Blessed *is* the man that endureth temptation: for when he is tried, he shall receive the crown of life, which the Lord hath promised to them that love him.

I. Pet. 1: 13 . . . Gird up the loins of your mind, be sober, and hope to the end for the grace that is to be brought unto you at the revelation of Jesus Christ;

I. Pet. 2: 19 . . . This *is* thankworthy, if a man for conscience toward God endure grief, suffering wrongfully.

I. Pet. 5: 8 Be sober, be vigilant; because your adversary the devil, as a roaring lion, walketh about, seeking whom he may devour: 9 Whom resist steadfast in the faith, knowing that the same afflictions are accomplished in your brethren that are in the world.

II. Pet. 3: 17 . . . Beware lest ye also, being

led away with the error of the wicked, fall from
your own steadfastness.

Rev. 3: 11 Behold, I come quickly: hold that
fast which thou hast, that no man take thy crown.

See PATIENCE; also INTEGRITY.

STEWARDSHIP

Luke 12: 47 . . . That servant, which knew
his lord's will, and prepared not *himself*, neither
did according to his will, shall be beaten with
many *stripes*. 48 But he that knew not, and did
commit things worthy of stripes, shall be beaten
with few *stripes*. For unto whomsoever much is
given, of him shall be much required; and to whom
men have committed much, of him they will ask
the more. ·

Luke 16: 11 If . . . ye have not been faithful in the unrighteous mammon, who will commit
to your trust the true *riches?* 12 And if ye have
not been faithful in that which is another man's,
who shall give you that which is your own?

I. Cor. 4: 1 Let a man so account of us, as of
the ministers of Christ, and stewards of the mysteries of God. 2 Moreover it is required in stewards, that a man be found faithful.

I. Cor. 6: 20 . . . Ye are bought with a price:
therefore glorify God in your body, and in your
spirit, which are God's.

I. Pet. 4: 10 As every man hath received the
gift, *even so* minister the same one to another, as
good stewards of the manifold grace of God.

See FAITHFULNESS; OPPORTUNITY; PERSONAL
CHRISTIAN WORK; SERVICE.

STRANGERS

Deut. 27: 19 Cursed *be* he that perverteth the
judgment of the stranger, fatherless, and wid-

ow: and all the people shall say, Amen.

Ecc. 11: 1 Cast thy bread upon the waters: for thou shalt find it after many days.

Matt. 25: 34 Then shall the King say unto them on his right hand, Come, ye blessed of my Father, inherit the kingdom prepared for you from the foundation of the world: 35 For I was a hungered, and ye gave me meat: I was thirsty, and ye gave me drink: I was a stranger, and ye took me in: 40 . . . Verily I say unto you, Inasmuch as ye have done it unto one of the least of these my brethren, ye have done it unto me.

Heb. 13: 2 Be not forgetful to entertain strangers: for thereby some have entertained angels unawares.

STUBBORNNESS

Prov. 1: 24 Because I have called, and ye refused; I have stretched out my hand, and no man regarded; 25 But ye have set at nought all my counsel, and would none of my reproof: 26 I also will laugh at your calamity; I will mock when your fear cometh; 27 When your fear cometh as desolation, and your destruction cometh as a whirlwind; when distress and anguish cometh upon you. 28 Then shall they call upon me, but I will not answer; they shall seek me early, but they shall not find me: 29 For that they hated knowledge, and did not choose the fear of the Lord: 30 They would none of my counsel: they despised all my reproof. 31 Therefore shall they eat of the fruit of their own way, and be filled with their own devices.

Prov. 29: 1 He, that being often reproved hardeneth his neck, shall suddenly be destroyed, and that without remedy.

Rom. 2: 4 . . . Despisest thou the riches of

his goodneses and forbearance and longsuffering;
not knowing that the goodness of God leadeth thee
to repentance? 5 But, after thy hardness and
impenitent heart, treasurest up unto thyself
wrath against the day of wrath and revelation of
the righteous judgment of God;

STUDENT

Psa. 119: 12 Blessed *art* thou, O Lord:
teach me thy statutes. 18 Open thou mine eyes,
that I may behold wondrous things out of thy
law.

I. Cor. 14: 20 Brethren, be not children in understanding: howbeit in malice be ye children, but
in understanding be men.

II. Tim. 2: 15 Study to shew thyself approved
unto God, a workman that needeth not to be
ashamed, rightly dividing the word of truth.

See INSTRUCTION; KNOWLEDGE; TEACHER; WIS-
DOM.

SURETYSHIP

Prov. 6: 1 My son, if thou be surety for thy
friend, *if* thou hast stricken thy hand with a
stranger, 2 Thou art snared with the words of
thy mouth, thou art taken with the words of thy
mouth.

Prov. 11: 15 He that is surety for a stranger
shall smart *for it:* and he that hateth suretiship
is sure.

Prov. 17: 18 A man void of understanding
striketh hands, *and* becometh surety in the presence of his friend.

Prov. 22: 26 Be not thou *one* of them that
strike hands, *or* of them that are sureties for
debts. 27 If thou hast nothing to pay, why
should he take away thy bed from under thee?

See CONTRACTS.

SYMPATHY

Ecc. 7: 2 *It is* better to go to the house of mourning, than to go to the house of feasting: for that *is* the end of all men; and the living will lay *it* to his heart.

Philip. 2: 1 If *there be* . . . any consolation in Christ, if any comfort of love, if any fellowship of the Spirit, if any bowels and mercies, 2 Fulfil ye my joy, that ye be likeminded, having the same love, *being* of one accord, of one mind.

I. Pet. 3: 8 . . . *Be ye* all of one mind, having compassion one of another; love as brethren, *be* pitiful, *be* courteous:

See AFFLICTED, Duty to; BEREAVEMENT; JESUS, Compassion of; KINDNESS; MERCY.

TACT

Prov. 15: 1 A soft answer turneth away wrath: but grievous words stir up anger. .

Prov. 25: 11 A word fitly spoken *is like* apples of gold in pictures of silver. 15 By long forbearing is a prince persuaded, and a soft tongue breaketh the bone.

II. Cor. 12: 6 . . . Though I would desire to glory, I shall not be a fool; for I will say the truth: but *now* I forbear, lest any man should think of me above that which he seeth me *to be*, or *that* he heareth of me.

See COURTESY; DIPLOMACY; EXPEDIENCY; PRUDENCE.

TEACHER

Matt. 5: 19 Whosoever . . . shall break one of these least commandments, and shall teach men so, he shall be called the least in the kingdom of heaven: but whosoever shall do and teach *them*, the same shall be called great in the kingdom of heaven.

Luke 6: 39 . . . He spake a parable unto them; Can the blind lead the blind? shall they not both fall into the ditch? 40 The disciple is not above his master: but every one that is perfect shall be as his master.

John 13: 14 If I . . . , *your* Lord and Master, have washed your feet; ye also ought to wash one another's feet.

John 14: 26 . . . The Comforter, *which is* the Holy Ghost, whom the Father will send in my name, he shall teach you all things, and bring all things to your remembrance, whatsoever I have said unto you.

John 16: 13 . . . When he, the Spirit of truth, is come, he will guide you into all truth: for he shall not speak of himself; but whatsoever he shall hear, *that* shall he speak: and he will shew you things to come. 14 He shall glorify me: for he shall receive of mine, and shall shew *it* unto you. 15 All things that the Father hath are mine: therefore said I, that he shall take of mine, and shall shew *it* unto you.

Rom. 2: 21 Thou . . . which teachest another, teachest thou not thyself? . . .

I. Cor. 12: 4 . . . There are diversities of gifts, but the same Spirit. 6 And there are diversities of operations, but it is the same God which worketh all in all. 28 And God hath set some in the church, first apostles, secondarily prophets, thirdly teachers, after that miracles, then gifts of healings, helps, governments, diversities of tongues.

Eph. 4: 11 . . . He gave some, apostles; and some, prophets; and some, evangelists; and some,

pastors and teachers; 12 For the perfecting of
the saints, for the work of the ministry, for the
edifying of the body of Christ:

Tit. 2: 1 . . . Speak thou the things which
become sound doctrine: 2 That the aged men be
sober, grave, temperate, sound in faith, in charity,
in patience. 3 The aged women likewise, that
they be in behaviour as becometh holiness, not
false accusers, not given to much wine, teachers
of good things; 4 That they may teach the
young women to be sober, to love their husbands,
to love their children, 5 *To be* discreet, chaste,
keepers at home, good, obedient to their own husbands, that the word of God be not blasphemed.
6 Young men likewise exhort to be soberminded.

See INSTRUCTION; JESUS as Teacher; KNOWL-
EDGE; STUDENT; WISDOM.

TEMPERANCE

Prov. 23: 20 Be not among winebibbers;
among riotous eaters of flesh: 21 For the drunkard and the glutton shall come to poverty: and
drowsiness shall clothe *a man* with rags. 31
Look not thou upon the wine when it is red, when
it giveth his colour in the cup, *when* it moveth itself aright. 32 At the last it biteth like a serpent,
and stingeth like an adder.

Prov. 25: 16 Hast thou found honey? eat so
much as is sufficient for thee, lest thou be filled
therewith, and vomit it.

Rom. 13: 14 . . . Put ye on the Lord Jesus
Christ, and make not provision for the flesh, to
fulfil the lusts *thereof.*

I. Cor. 9: 25 . . . Every man that striveth
for the mastery is temperate in all things. . . .
27 . . . I keep under my body, and bring *it* into

subjection: lest that by any means, when I have preached to others, I myself should be a castaway.

Philip. 4: 5 Let your moderation be known unto all men. The Lord *is* at hand.

I. Thess. 5: 6 . . . Let us not sleep, as *do* others; but let us watch and be sober. 7 For they that sleep sleep in the night; and they that be drunken are drunken in the night. 8 But let us, who are of the day, be sober, putting on the breastplate of faith and love; and for a helmet, the hope of salvation.

I. Tim. 3: 2 A bishop . . . must be blameless, the husband of one wife, vigilant, sober, of good behaviour, given to hospitality, apt to teach; 3 Not given to wine, no striker, not greedy of filthy lucre; but patient, not a brawler, not covetous; 8 Likewise *must* the deacons *be* grave, not double-tongued, not given to much wine, not greedy of filthy lucre;

Tit. 2: 1 . . . Speak thou the things which become sound doctrine: 2 That the aged men be sober, grave, temperate, sound in faith, in charity, in patience. 3 The aged women likewise, that *they be* in behaviour as becometh holiness, not false accusers, not given to much wine, teachers of good things; 4 That they may teach the young women to be sober, to love their husbands, to love their children, 6 Young men likewise exhort to be soberminded.

II. Pet. 1: 5 . . . Giving all diligence, add to your faith virtue; and to virtue, knowledge; 6 And to knowledge, temperance; and to temperance, patience; and to patience, godliness;

See SELF-DENIAL; also EXTRAVAGANCE; GLUTTONY; INTOXICATION.

TEMPTATION

Prov. 1: 10 My son, if sinners entice thee, consent thou not.

Prov. 6: 27 Can a man take fire in his bosom, and his clothes not be burned? 28 Can one go upon hot coals, and his feet not be burned?

Prov. 28: 10 Whoso causeth the righteous to go astray in an evil way, he shall fall himself into his own pit: but the upright shall have good *things* in possession.

Matt. 4: 1 Then was Jesus led up of the Spirit into the wilderness to be tempted of the devil. 2 And when he had fasted forty days and forty nights, he was afterward a hungered. 3 And when the tempter came to him, he said, If thou be the Son of God, command that these stones be made bread. 4 But he answered and said, It is written, Man shall not live by bread alone, but by every word that proceedeth out of the mouth of God. 5 Then the devil taketh him up into a holy city, and setteth him on a pinnacle of the temple, 6 And saith unto him, If thou be the Son of God, cast thyself down: for it is written, He shall give his angels charge concerning thee: and in *their* hands they shall bear thee up, lest at any time thou dash thy foot against a stone. 7 Jesus said unto him, It is written again, Thou shalt not tempt the Lord thy God. 8 Again, the devil taketh him up into an exceeding high mountain, and sheweth him all the kingdoms of the world, and the glory of them; 9 And saith unto him, All these things will I give thee, if thou wilt fall down and worship me. 10 Then saith Jesus unto him, Get thee hence, Satan: for it is written, Thou shalt worship the Lord thy God, and him only shalt thou serve. 11 Then the devil leaveth him, and, behold, angels came and ministered unto him.

Mark 14: 38 Watch ye and pray, lest ye enter into temptation. The spirit truly *is* ready, but the flesh *is* weak.

Luke 22: 46 . . . Why sleep ye? rise and pray, lest ye enter into temptation.

Rom. 12: 21 Be not overcome of evil, but overcome evil with good.

Rom. 14: 21 *It is* good neither to eat flesh, nor to drink wine, nor *any thing* whereby thy brother stumbleth, or is offended, or is made weak.

I. Cor. 10: 13 There hath no temptation taken you but such as is common to man: but God *is* faithful, who will not suffer you to be tempted above that ye are able; but will with the temptation also make a way to escape, that ye may be able to bear *it*.

I. Cor. 16: 13 Watch ye, stand fast in the faith, quit you like men, be strong.

Eph. 6: 11 Put on the whole armour of God, that ye may be able to stand against the wiles of the devil. 14 Stand therefore, having your loins girt about with truth, and having on the breastplate of righteousness; 15 And your feet shod with the preparation of the gospel of peace; 16 Above all, taking the shield of faith, wherewith ye shall be able to quench all the fiery darts of the wicked. 17 And take the helmet of salvation, and the sword of the Spirit, which is the word of God: 18 Praying always with all prayer and supplication in the Spirit, and watching thereunto with all perseverance and supplication for all saints;

I. Tim. 6: 9 . . . They that will be rich fall into temptation and a snare, and *into* many foolish and hurtful lusts, which drown men in destruction and perdition. 10 For the love of money is the root of all evil: which while some coveted after, they have erred from the faith, and pierced themselves through with many sorrows.

Jas. 1: 2 My brethren, count it all joy when ye fall into divers temptations; 3 Knowing *this*, that the trying of your faith worketh patience. 4 But let patience have *her* perfect work, that ye may be perfect and entire, wanting nothing. 12 Blessed *is* the man that endureth temptation: for when he is tried, he shall receive the crown of life, which the Lord hath promised to them that love him. 13 Let no man say when he is tempted, I am tempted of God: for God cannot be tempted with evil, neither tempteth he any man: 14 But every man is tempted, when he is drawn away of his own lust, and enticed. 15 Then when lust hath conceived, it bringeth forth sin; and sin, when it is finished, bringeth forth death. 16 Do not err, my beloved brethren.

Jas. 4: 7 Submit yourselves . . . to God. Resist the devil, and he will flee from you.

II. Pet. 2: 9 The Lord knoweth how to deliver the godly out of temptation, and to reserve the unjust unto the day of judgment to be punished:

See EVIL COMPANY; INFLUENCE, Evil.

TESTIMONY

Mark 5: 19 . . . Jesus . . . saith unto him, Go home to thy friends, and tell them how great things the Lord hath done for thee, and hath had compassion on thee.

Luke 12: 8 . . . I say unto you, Whosoever shall confess me before men, him shall the Son of man also confess before the angels of God: 9 But he that denieth me before men shall be denied before the angels of God.

Acts 4: 19 . . . Peter and John . . . said unto them, Whether it be right in the sight of God to hearken unto you more than unto God, judge ye. 20 For we cannot but speak the things which we have seen and heard.

II. Tim. 1: 8 Be not thou . . . ashamed of the testimony of our Lord, nor of me his prisoner: but be thou partaker of the afflictions of the gospel according to the power of God;

I. Pet. 3: 15 . . . Sanctify the Lord God in your hearts: and *be* ready always to *give* an answer to every man that asketh you a reason of the hope that is in you, with meekness and fear:

THANKFULNESS

Psa. 107: 1 O give thanks unto the Lord, for *he is* good: for his mercy *endureth* for ever.

Matt. 26: 27 . . . He took the cup, and gave thanks, and gave *it* to them, saying, Drink ye all of it;

John 11: 41 . . . They took away the stone *from the place* where the dead was laid. And Jesus lifted up *his* eyes, and said, Father, I thank thee that thou hast heard me.

Eph. 5: 18 . . . Be not drunk with wine, wherein is excess; but be filled with the Spirit; 20 Giving thanks always for all things unto God and the Father in the name of our Lord Jesus Christ;

Col. 3: 15 . . . Let the peace of God rule in your hearts, to the which also ye are called in one body; and be ye thankful. 17 And whatsoever ye do in word or deed, *do* all in the name of the Lord Jesus, giving thanks to God and the Father by him.

I. Tim. 4: 4 . . . Every creature of God *is* good, and nothing to be refused, if it be received

with thanksgiving: 5 For it is sanctified by the
word of God and prayer.

Heb. 13: 15 By him . . . let us offer the sacrifice of praise to God continually, that is, the fruit
of *our* lips, giving thanks to his name.

See PRAYER; also INGRATITUDE.

THEFT—THIEF

Exod. 20: 15 Thou shalt not steal.

Psa. 62: 10 Trust not in oppression, and become not vain in robbery: if riches increase, set
not your heart *upon them.*

Matt. 6: 19 Lay not up for yourselves treasures upon earth, where moth and rust doth corrupt, and where thieves break through and steal:
20 But lay up for yourselves treasures in heaven,
where neither moth nor rust doth corrupt, and
where thieves do not break through nor steal:

Matt. 19: 18 . . . Jesus said, Thou shalt do
no murder, Thou shalt not commit adultery, Thou
shalt not steal, Thou shalt not bear false witness,

I. Cor. 6: 9 Know ye not that the unrighteous
shall not inherit the kingdom of God? Be not deceived: neither fornicators, . . . 10 Nor thieves,
nor covetous, nor drunkards, nor revilers, nor extortioners, shall inherit the kingdom of God.

Eph. 4: 28 Let him that stole steal no more:
but rather let him labour, working with *his* hands
the thing which is good, that he may have to give
to him that needeth.

See DISHONESTY.

TITHES

Lev. 27: 30 . . . All the tithe of the land,
whether of the seed of the land, *or* of the fruit of
the tree, *is* the Lord's: *it is* holy unto the Lord.

Mal. 3: 10 Bring ye all the tithes into the

storehouse, that there may be meat in mine house, and prove me now herewith, saith the Lord of hosts, if I will not open you the windows of heaven, and pour you out a blessing, that *there shall* not *be room* enough *to receive it.*

Matt. 23: 23 Woe unto you, scribes and Pharisees, hypocrites! for ye pay tithe of mint and anise and cummin, and have omitted the weightier *matters* of the law, judgment, mercy, and faith: these ought ye to have done, and not to leave the other undone.

See ALMS; CHURCH Support.

TOLERANCE

Luke 9: 49 . . . John . . . said, Master, we saw one casting out devils in thy name; and we forbade him, because he followeth not with us. 50 And Jesus said unto him, Forbid *him* not: for he that is not against us is for us.

Rom. 14: 10 . . . Why dost thou judge thy brother? or why dost thou set at nought thy brother? for we shall all stand before the judgment seat of Christ. 13 Let us not therefore judge one another any more: but judge this rather, that no man put a stumblingblock or an occasion to fall in *his* brother's way.

See CHARITABLENESS; also BIGOTRY.

TRUTH

Psa. 96: 13 . . . He shall judge the world with righteousness, and the people with his truth.

Psa. 100: 5 . . . The Lord *is* good; his mercy *is* everlasting; and his truth *endureth* to all generations.

Prov. 3: 3 Let not mercy and truth forsake thee: bind them about thy neck; write them upon the table of thine heart: 4 So shalt thou find fa-

vour and good understanding in the sight of God
and man.

Prov. 12: 19 The lip of truth shall be established for ever: but a lying tongue *is* but for a
moment.

Prov. 16: 13 Righteous lips *are* the delight of
kings; and they love him that speaketh right.

John 1: 1 In the beginning was the Word,
and the Word was with God, and the Word was
God. 14 And the Word was made flesh, and
dwelt among us, (and we beheld his glory, the
glory as of the only begotten of the Father,) full
of grace and truth.

John 8: 31 Then said Jesus to those Jews
which believed on him, If ye continue in my word,
then are ye my disciples indeed; 32 And ye shall
know the truth, and the truth shall make you free.

John 14: 6 Jesus saith unto him, I am the
way, the truth, and the life: no man cometh unto
the Father, but by me. 16 And I will pray the
Father, and he shall give you another Comforter,
that he may abide with you for ever; 17 *Even*
the Spirit of truth; whom the world cannot receive, because it seeth him not, neither knoweth
him: but ye know him; for he dwelleth with you,
and shall be in you.

John 16: 13 . . . When he, the Spirit of
truth, is come, he will guide you into all truth:
for he shall not speak of himself; but whatsoever
he shall hear, *that* shall he speak: and he will shew
you things to come.

John 17: 17 Sanctify them through thy truth:
thy word is truth. 19 And for their sakes I
sanctify myself, that they also might be sanctified
through the truth. 20 Neither pray I for these
alone, but for them also which shall believe on me
through their word;

John 18: 37 Pilate . . . said unto him, Art thou a king then? Jesus answered, Thou sayest that I am a king. To this end was I born, and for this cause came I into the world, that I should bear witness unto the truth. Every one that is of the truth heareth my voice.

Rom. 2: 2 . . . We are sure that the judgment of God is according to truth against them which commit such things.

See SINCERITY; also FALSEHOOD.

UNBELIEF

Mark 16: 16 He that believeth and is baptized shall be saved; but he that believeth not shall be damned.

John 3: 18 He that believeth on him is not condemned: but he that believeth not is condemned already, because he hath not believed in the name of the only begotten Son of God. 36 He that believeth on the Son hath everlasting life: and he that believeth not the Son shall not see life; but the wrath of God abideth on him.

John 5: 44 How can ye believe, which receive honour one of another, and seek not the honour that *cometh* from God only?

John 12: 47 . . . If any man hear my words, and believe not, I judge him not: for I came not to judge the world, but to save the world. 48 He that rejecteth me, and receiveth not my words, hath one that judgeth him: the word that I have spoken, the same shall judge him in the last day.

Acts 13: 40 Beware . . . , lest that come upon you, which is spoken of in the prophets; 41 Behold, ye despisers, and wonder, and perish: for I work a work in your days, a work which ye shall in no wise believe, though a man declare it unto you.

I. Cor. 2: 14 . . . The natural man receiveth not the things of the Spirit of God: for they are foolishness unto him: neither can he know *them*, because they are spiritually discerned.

II. Cor. 6: 14 Be ye not unequally yoked together with unbelievers: for what fellowship hath righteousness with unrighteousness? and what communion hath light with darkness? 15 And what concord hath Christ with Belial? or what part hath he that believeth with an infidel?

Tit. 1: 15 Unto the pure all things *are* pure: but unto them that are defiled and unbelieving *is* nothing pure; but even their mind and conscience is defiled. 16 They profess that they know God; but in works they deny *him*, being abominable, and disobedient, and unto every good work reprobate.

Heb. 3: 12 Take heed, brethren, lest there be in any of you an evil heart of unbelief, in departing from the living God.

I. John 2: 22 Who is a liar but he that denieth that Jesus is the Christ? He is antichrist, that denieth the Father and the Son. 23 Whosoever denieth the Son, the same hath not the Father: . . .

I. John 5: 10 He that believeth on the Son of God hath the witness in himself: he that believeth not God hath made him a liar; because he believeth not the record that God gave of his Son. 12 He that hath the Son hath life; *and* he that hath not the Son of God hath not life.

Jude: 5 I will . . . put you in remembrance, though ye once knew this, how that the Lord, having saved the people out of the land of Egypt, afterward destroyed them that believed not.

Rev. 21: 8 . . . The fearful, and unbelieving,

and the abominable, and murderers, and whore-mongers, and sorcerers, and idolaters, and all liars, shall have their part in the lake which burn-eth with fire and brimstone: which is the second death.

See ATHEISM; SKEPTICISM.

UNJUST GAIN

Prov. 10: 2 Treasures of wickedness profit nothing: but righteousness delivereth from death.

Prov. 11: 24 There is that scattereth, and yet increaseth; and *there is* that withholdeth more than is meet, but *it tendeth* to poverty. 26 He that withholdeth corn, the people shall curse him: but blessing *shall be* upon the head of him that selleth *it.*

Prov. 13: 7 There is that maketh him-self rich, yet *hath* nothing: *there is* that maketh himself poor, yet *hath* great riches.

Prov. 15: 16 Better *is* little with the fear of the Lord, than great treasure and trouble there-with. 17 Better *is* a dinner of herbs where love is, than a stalled ox and hatred therewith. 27 He that is greedy of gain troubleth his own house; but he that hateth gifts shall live.

Prov. 16: 8 Better *is* a little with righteous-ness, than great revenues without right.

Prov. 21: 6 The getting of treasures by a ly-ing tongue *is* a vanity tossed to and fro of them that seek death. 7 The robbery of the wicked shall destroy them; because they refuse to do judgment.

Prov. 22: 16 He that oppresseth the poor to increase his *riches, and* he that giveth to the rich, *shall* surely *come* to want.

Prov. 28: 8 He that by usury and unjust gain increaseth his substance, he shall gather it for him that will pity the poor. 20 A faithful man shall abound with blessings: but he that maketh haste to be rich shall not be .innocent. 22 He that hasteth to be rich *hath* an evil eye, and considereth not that poverty shall come upon him. 24 Whoso robbeth his father or his mother, and saith, *It is* no transgression; the same *is* the companion of a destroyer.

Jer. 17: 11 *As* the partridge sitteth *on eggs,* and hatcheth *them* not; *so* he that getteth riches, and not by right, shall leave them in the midst of his days, and at the end shall be a fool.

Jas. 5: 1 Go to now, *ye* rich men, weep and howl for your miseries that shall come upon *you.* 2 Your riches are corrupted, and your garments are motheaten. 3 Your gold and silver is cankered; and the rust of them shall be a witness against you, and shall eat your flesh as it were fire. Ye have heaped treasure together for the last days. 4 Behold, the hire of the labourers. who have reaped down your fields, which is of you kept back by fraud, crieth: and the cries of them which have reaped are entered into the ears of the Lord of Sabaoth. 5 Ye have lived in pleasure on the earth, and been wanton; ye have nourished your hearts, as in a day of slaughter. 6 Ye have condemned *and* killed the just; *and* he doth not resist you.

See AVARICE; COVETOUSNESS; DISHONESTY; WEALTH.

UNSELFISHNESS

Matt. 7: 12 . . . All things whatsoever ye would that men should do to you, do ye even so to them: for this is the law and the prophets.

Rom. 12: 10 *Be* kindly affectioned one to an-

other with brotherly love; in honour preferring
one another;

Rom. 15: 1 We . . . that are strong ought to
bear the infirmities of the weak, and not to please
ourselves. 2 Let every one of us please *his* neighbour for *his* good to edification. 3 For even
Christ pleased not himself; but; as it is written,
The reproaches of them that reproached thee fell
on me.

I. Cor. 10: 24 Let no man seek his own, but
every man another's *wealth.* 32 Give none offence, neither to the Jews, nor to the Gentiles, nor
to the church of God: 33 Even as I please all
men in all *things,* not seeking mine own profit, but
the *profit* of many, that they may be saved.

I. Cor. 13: 4 Charity suffereth long, *and* is
kind; charity envieth not; charity vaunteth not
itself, is not puffed up, 5 Doth not behave itself
unseemly, seeketh not her own, is not easily provoked, thinketh no evil;

II. Cor. 5: 15 . . . He died for all, that they
which live should not henceforth live unto themselves, but unto him which died for them, and rose
again.

II. Cor. 8: 9 . . . Ye know the grace of our
Lord Jesus Christ, that, though he was rich, yet
for your sakes he became poor, that ye through his
poverty might be rich.

Gal. 6: 2 Bear ye one another's burdens, and
so fulfil the law of Christ.

Philip. 2: 3 *Let* nothing *be done* through
strife or vainglory; but in lowliness of mind let
each esteem other better than themselves. 4 Look
not every man on his own things, but every man
also on the things of others.

Jas. 2: 8 If ye fulfil the royal law according

404

to the Scripture, Thou shalt love thy neighbour as thyself, ye do well:

See BENEFICENCE; CHARITABLENESS; LIBERALITY; SELF-DENIAL; also SELFISHNESS.

VIRTUE

Philip. 4: 8 . . . Whatsoever things are true, whatsoever things *are* honest, whatsoever things *are* just, whatsoever things *are* pure, whatsoever things *are* lovely, whatsoever things *are* of good report; if *there be* any virtue, and if *there be* any praise, think on these things.

II. Pet. 1: 5 . . . Giving all diligence, add to your faith virtue; and to virtue, knowledge;

See GRACES, Christian; PURITY; RIGHTEOUS.

WAGES

Jer. 22: 13 Woe unto him that buildeth his house by unrighteousness, and his chambers by wrong; *that* useth his neighbour's service without wages, and giveth him not for his work;

Luke 3: 14 . . . The soldiers . . . demanded of him, saying, And what shall we do? And he said unto them, Do violence to no man, neither accuse *any* falsely; and be content with your wages.

Luke 10: 7 . . . The labourer is worthy of his hire. . . .

Rom. 6: 23 . . . The wages of sin *is* death; but the gift of God *is* eternal life through Jesus Christ our Lord.

Col. 4: 1 Masters, give unto *your* servants that which is just and equal; knowing that ye also have a Master in heaven.

Jas. 5: 4 Behold, the hire of the labourers who have reaped down your fields, which is of you kept back by fraud, crieth: and the cries of them which have reaped are entered into the ears of the Lord of Sabaoth.

See EMPLOYER—EMPLOYEE; SERVICE.

WEALTH

Psa. 37: 16 A little that a righteous man hath *is* better than the riches of many wicked.

Prov. 10: 22 The blessing of the Lord, it maketh rich, and he addeth no sorrow with it.

Prov. 11: 4 Riches profit not in the day of wrath: but righteousness delivereth from death. 28 He that trusteth in his riches shall fall: but the righteous shall flourish as a branch.

Prov. 15: 6 In the house of the righteous *is* much treasure: but in the revenues of the wicked is trouble.

Prov. 23: 4 Labour not to be rich: cease from thine own wisdom. 5 Wilt thou set thine eyes upon that which is not? for *riches* certainly make themselves wings; they fly away as an eagle toward heaven.

Prov. 30: 8 Remove far from me vanity and lies; give me neither poverty nor riches; feed me with food convenient for me: 9 Lest I be full, and deny *thee,* and say, Who *is* the Lord? or lest I be poor, and steal, and take the name of my God *in vain.*

Ecc. 5: 10 He that loveth silver shall not be satisfied with silver; nor he that loveth abundance with increase: this *is* also vanity. 11 When goods increase, they are increased that eat them: and what good *is there* to the owners thereof, saving the beholding *of them* with their eyes? 12 The sleep of a labouring man *is* sweet, whether he eat little or much: but the abundance of the rich will not suffer him to sleep. 13 There is a sore evil *which* I have seen under the sun, *namely,* riches kept for the owners thereof to their hurt. 14 But those riches perish by evil travail: and he begetteth a son, and *there is* nothing in his hand. 15 As he came forth of his mother's womb, naked shall he return to go as he came, and shall take nothing of his labour, which he may carry away in his hand. 16 And this also *is* a sore evil, *that* in all points as he came, so shall he go: and what profit hath he that hath laboured for the wind? 18 Behold *that* which I have seen: *it is* good and comely *for one* to eat and to drink, and to enjoy the good of all his labour that he taketh under the sun all the days of his life, which God giveth him: for it *is* his portion. 19 Every man also to whom God hath given riches and wealth, and hath given him power to eat thereof, and to take his portion, and to rejoice in his labour; this *is* the gift of God.

Ecc. 7: 12 . . . Wisdom *is* a defence, *and* money *is* a defence: but the excellency of knowledge *is, that* wisdom giveth life to them that have it. 14 In the day of prosperity be joyful, but in the day of adversity consider: God also hath set the one over against the other, to the end that man should find nothing after him.

Matt. 6: 19 Lay not up for yourselves treasures upon earth, where moth and rust doth corrupt, and where thieves break through and steal: 20 But lay up for yourselves treasures in heaven, where neither moth nor rust doth corrupt, and where thieves do not break through nor steal: 21 For where your treasure is, there will your heart be also.

Matt. 19: 21 Jesus said unto him, If thou wilt be perfect, go *and* sell that thou hast, and give to the poor, and thou shalt have treasure in heaven: and come *and* follow me. 22 But when the young

man heard that saying, he went away sorrowful:
for he had great possessions.   23 Then said Jesus
unto his disciples, Verily I say unto you, That
a rich man shall hardly enter into the kingdom of
heaven.   24 And again I say unto you, It is easier
for a camel to go through the eye of a needle, than
for a rich man to enter into the kingdom of God.
25 When his disciples heard *it*, they were exceedingly amazed, saying, Who then can be saved?
26 But Jesus beheld *them*, and said unto them,
With men this is impossible; but with God all
things are possible.   29 And every one that hath
forsaken houses, or brethren, or sisters, or father,
or mother, or wife, or children, or lands, for my
name's sake, shall receive a hundredfold, and shall
inherit everlasting life.

Mark 4:   19 . . . The cares of this world, and
the deceitfulness of riches, and the lusts of other
things entering in, choke the word, and it becometh unfruitful.

I. Tim. 6:   7 . . . We brought nothing into
this world, *and it is* certain we can carry nothing
out.   8 And having food and raiment, let us be
therewith content.   9 But they that will be rich
fall into temptation and a snare, and *into* many
foolish and hurtful lusts, which drown men in
destruction and perdition.   10 For the love of
money is the root of all evil: which while some
coveted after, they have erred from the faith, and
pierced themselves through with many sorrows.
11 But thou, O man of God, flee these things; and
follow after righteousness, godliness, faith, love,
patience, meekness.   17 Charge them that are
rich in this world, that they be not highminded,
nor trust in uncertain riches, but in the living
God, who giveth us richly all things to enjoy;   18

That they do good, that they be rich in good works, ready to distribute, willing to communicate; 19 Laying up in store for themselves a good foundation against the time to come, that they may lay hold on eternal life.

I. John 3: 17 . . . Whoso hath this world's good, and seeth his brother have need, and shutteth up his bowels *of compassion* from him, how dwelleth the love of God in him? 18 My little children, let us not love in word, neither in tongue; but in deed and in truth.

See COVETOUSNESS; UNJUST GAIN.

WICKED—WICKEDNESS

Psa. 37: 1 Fret not thyself because of evil doers, neither be thou envious against the workers of iniquity. 2 For they shall soon be cut down like the grass, and wither as the green herb.

Psa. 53: 1 The fool hath said in his heart, *There is* no God. Corrupt are they, and have done abominable iniquity: *there is* none that doeth good.

Psa. 107: 17 Fools, because of their transgression, and because of their iniquities, are afflicted.

Prov. 10: 28 The hope of the righteous *shall be* gladness: but the expectation of the wicked shall perish.

Prov. 11: 3 The integrity of the upright shall guide them: but the perverseness of transgressors shall destroy them. 5 The righteousness of the perfect shall direct his way: but the wicked shall fall by his own wickedness. 6 The righteousness of the upright shall deliver them: but transgressors shall be taken in *their own* naughtiness. 8 The righteous is delivered out of trouble, and the wicked cometh in his stead. 10 When it goeth well with the righteous, the city rejoiceth: and when the wicked perish, *there is* shouting. 11 By the blessing of the upright the city is exalted: but it is overthrown by the mouth of the wicked.

Prov. 12: 13 The wicked is snared by the transgression of *his* lips: but the just shall come out of trouble.

Prov. 13: 13 Whoso despiseth the word shall be destroyed: but he that feareth the commandment shall be rewarded. 15 Good understanding giveth favour: but the way of transgressors *is* hard. 21 Evil pursueth sinners: but to the righteous good shall be repaid. 22 A good *man* leaveth an inheritance to his children's children: and the wealth of the sinner *is* laid up for the just.

Prov. 14: 9 Fools make a mock at sin: but among the righteous *there is* favour. 12 There is a way which seemeth right unto a man; but the end thereof *are* the ways of death.

Prov. 15: 6 In the house of the righteous *is* much treasure: but in the revenues of the wicked is trouble.

Prov. 28: 1 The wicked flee when no man pursueth: but the righteous are bold as a lion. 13 He that covereth his sins shall not prosper: but whoso confesseth and forsaketh *them* shall have mercy. 15 *As* a roaring lion, and a ranging bear; *so is* a wicked ruler over the poor people.

Isa. 57: 20 . . . The wicked *are* like the troubled sea, when it cannot rest, whose waters cast up mire and dirt. 21 *There is* no peace, saith my God, to the wicked.

Matt. 3: 10 . . . The axe is laid unto the root of the trees: therefore every tree which bringeth not forth good fruit is hewn down, and cast into the fire. 11 I indeed baptize you with water unto repentance: but he that cometh after me is mightier than I, whose shoes I am not worthy to bear: he shall baptize you with the Holy Ghost, and *with* fire: 12 Whose fan *is* in his hand, and he will thoroughly purge his floor, and gather his wheat into the garner; but he will burn up the chaff with unquenchable fire.

Matt. 7: 13 Enter ye in at the strait gate: for wide *is* the gate, and broad *is* the way, that leadeth to destruction, and many there be which go in thereat:

Matt. 10: 33 . . . Whosoever shall deny me before men, him will I also deny before my Father which is in heaven.

Matt. 13: 30 . . . In the time of harvest I will say to the reapers, Gather ye together first the tares, and bind them in bundles to burn them: but gather the wheat into my barn. 37 . . . He that soweth the good seed is the Son of man; 38 The field is the world; the good seed are the children of the kingdom; but the tares are the children of the wicked one; 39 The enemy that sowed them is the devil; the harvest is the end of the world; and the reapers are the angels. 40 As therefore the tares are gathered and burned in the fire; so shall it be in the end of this world. 41 The Son of man shall send forth his angels, and they shall gather out of his kingdom all things that offend, and them which do iniquity; 42 And ·shall cast them into a furnace of fire: there shall be wailing and gnashing of teeth.

Matt. 25: 31 When the Son of man shall come in his glory, and all the holy angels with him, then shall he sit upon the throne of his glory: 32 And before him shall be gathered all nations: and he shall separate them one from another, as a shepherd divideth *his* sheep from the goats: 33 And he shall set the sheep on his right hand, but the goats on the left. 41 Then shall he say . . . unto them on the left hand, Depart from me, ye cursed, into everlasting fire, prepared for the devil and his angels: 42 For I was a hungered, and ye gave me no meat: I was thirsty, and ye gave me no drink: 43 I was a stranger, and ye took me not in: naked, and ye clothed me not: sick, and in prison, and ye visited me not. 45 . . . Verily I say unto you, Inasmuch as ye did *it* not to one of the least of these, ye did *it* not to me. 46 And these shall go away into everlasting punishment: but the righteous into life eternal.

Luke 9: 25 . . . What is a man advantaged, if he gain the whole world, and lose himself, or be cast away? 26 For whosoever shall be ashamed of me and of my words, of him shall the Son of man be ashamed, when he shall come in his own glory, and *in his* Father's, and of the holy angels.

John 9: 31 Now we know that God heareth not sinners: but if any man be a worshipper of God, and doeth his will, him he heareth.

Rom. 2: 8 . . . Unto them that are contentious, and do not obey the truth, but obey unrighteousness, indignation and wrath, 9 Tribulation and anguish, upon every soul of man that doeth evil; of the Jew first, and also of the Gentile;

I. Cor. 3: 17 If any man defile the temple of God, him shall God destroy; for the temple of God is holy, which *temple* ye are.

I. Cor. 6: 9 Know ye not that the unrighteous shall not inherit the kingdom of God? Be not deceived: neither fornicators, nor idolaters, nor adulterers, nor effeminate, nor abusers of them-

THE BIBLE IN MY EVERYDAY LIFE

selves with mankind,   10 Nor thieves, nor covetous, nor drunkards, nor revilers, nor extortioners,
shall inherit the kingdom of God.

I. Thess. 5: 3 . . . When they shall say,
Peace and safety; then sudden destruction cometh
upon them, as travail upon a woman with child;
and they shall not escape.

II. Thess. 1: 7 . . . To you who are troubled
rest with us, when the Lord Jesus shall be revealed from heaven with his mighty angels, 8
In flaming fire taking vengeance on them that
know not God, and that obey not the gospel of
our Lord Jesus Christ: 9 Who shall be punished with everlasting destruction from the
presence of the Lord, and from the glory of his
power;

Heb. 2: 3 How shall we escape, if we neglect
so great salvation; which at the first began to be
spoken by the Lord, and was confirmed unto us
by them that heard *him;*

Heb. 10: 28 He that despised Moses' law
died without mercy under two or three witnesses:
29 Of how much sorer punishment, suppose ye,
shall he be thought worthy, who hath trodden
under foot the Son of God, and hath counted
the blood of the covenant, wherewith he was
sanctified, an unholy thing, and hath done despite
unto the Spirit of grace? 30 For we know him
that hath said, Vengeance *belongeth* unto me, I
will recompense, saith the Lord. And again, The
Lord shall judge his people. 31 *It is* a fearful
thing to fall into the hands of the living God.

Jas. 1: 14 . . . Every man is tempted, when
he is drawn away of his own lust, and enticed.
15 Then when lust hath conceived, it bringeth
forth sin; and sin, when it is finished, bringeth

413

forth death. 16 Do not err, my beloved brethren.

Jas. 4: 4 . . . Know ye not that the friendship of the world is enmity with God? whosoever therefore will be a friend of the world is the enemy of God.

II. Pet. 2: 9 The Lord knoweth how to deliver the godly out of temptation, and to reserve the unjust unto the day of judgment to be punished: 10 But chiefly them that walk after the flesh in the lust of uncleanness, and despise government. Presumptuous *are they*, selfwilled, they are not afraid to speak evil of dignities.

I. John 1: 6 If we say that we have fellowship with him, and walk in darkness, we lie, and do not the truth:

See DEPRAVITY; EVIL COMPANY; HELL; INFLUENCE, Evil; LASCIVIOUSNESS; UNBELIEF; also REPENTANCE; SIN, Forgiveness of.

WIDOWS—ORPHANS

Exod. 22: 22 Ye shall not afflict any widow, or fatherless child.

Deut. 27: 19 Cursed *be* he that perverteth the judgment of the stranger, fatherless, and widow: and all the people shall say, Amen.

Psa. 68: 5 A father of the fatherless, and a judge of the widows, *is* God in his holy habitation.

Jer. 22: 3 Thus saith the Lord; Execute ye judgment and righteousness, and deliver the spoiled out of the hand of the oppressor: and do no wrong, do no violence to the stranger, the fatherless, nor the widow, neither shed innocent blood in this place.

I. Tim. 5: 3 Honour widows that are widows indeed. 4 But if any widow have children or nephews, let them learn first to shew piety at home, and to requite their parents: for that is good and acceptable before God.   5 Now she that is a widow indeed, and desolate, trusteth in God, and continueth in supplications and prayers night and day.   6 But she that liveth in pleasure is dead while she liveth.   16 If any man or woman that believeth have widows, let them relieve them, and let not the church be charged; that it may relieve them that are widows indeed.

Jas. 1: 27 Pure religion and undefiled before God and the Father is this, To visit the fatherless and widows in their affliction, *and* to keep himself unspotted from the world.

WISDOM

Job 28: 28 . . . Unto man he said, Behold, the fear of the Lord, that *is* wisdom; and to depart from evil *is* understanding.

Prov. 3: 7 Be not wise in thine own eyes: fear the Lord, and depart from evil.

Prov. 15: 21 Folly *is* joy to *him that is* destitute of wisdom: but a man of understanding walketh uprightly.

Prov. 17: 10 A reproof entereth more into a wise man than a hundred stripes into a fool.

Prov. 24: 6 . . . By wise counsel thou shalt make thy war: and in multitude of counsellors *there is* safety.

Ecc. 1: 18 . . . In much wisdom *is* much grief: and he that increaseth knowledge increaseth sorrow.

Ecc. 7: 11 Wisdom *is* good with an inheritance: and *by it there is* profit to them that see the sun.   12 For wisdom *is* a defence, *and* money *is* a defence: but the excellency of knowledge *is*,

415

that wisdom giveth life to them that have it.

Ecc. 8: 16 When I applied mine heart to know wisdom, and to see the business that is done upon the earth: (for also *there is that* neither day nor night seeth sleep with his eyes:) 17 Then I beheld all the work of God, that a man cannot find out the work that is done under the sun: because though a man labour to seek *it* out, yet he shall not find *it;* yea further; though a wise *man* think to know *it,* yet shall he not be able to find *it.*

Jer. 9: 23 Thus saith the Lord, Let not the wise *man* glory in his wisdom, neither let the mighty *man* glory in his might, let not the rich *man* glory in his riches: 24 But let him that glorieth glory in this, that he understandeth and knoweth me, that I *am* the Lord which exercise lovingkindness, judgment, and righteousness, in the earth: for in these *things* I delight, saith the Lord.

Matt. 7: 24 . . . Whosoever heareth these sayings of mine, and doeth them, I will liken him unto a wise man, which built his house upon a rock: 25 And the rain descended, and the floods came, and the winds blew, and beat upon that house; and it fell not: for it was founded upon a rock.

I. Cor. 1: 25 . . . The foolishness of God is wiser than men; and the weakness of God is stronger than men. 26 For ye see your calling, brethren, how that not many wise men after the flesh, not many mighty, not many noble, *are called:* 27 But God hath chosen the foolish things of the world to confound the wise; and God hath chosen the weak things of the world to confound the things which are mighty; 30 But of him are ye in Christ Jesus, who of God is made unto us wisdom, and righteousness, and sanctification, and redemption:

II. Cor. 1: 12 . . . Our rejoicing is this, the testimony of our conscience, that in simplicity and godly sincerity, not with fleshly wisdom, but by the grace of God, we have had our conversation in the world, and more abundantly to youward.

Jas. 1: 5 If any of you lack wisdom, let him ask of God, that giveth to all *men* liberally, and upbraideth not; and it shall be given him. 6 But let him ask in faith, nothing wavering: for he that wavereth is like a wave of the sea driven with the wind and tossed.

See INSTRUCTION; KNOWLEDGE.

WOMANHOOD

Prov. 11: 16 A gracious woman retaineth honour: . . .

Prov. 12: 4 A virtuous woman *is* a crown to her husband: but she that maketh ashamed *is* as rottenness in his bones.

Prov. 14: 1 Every wise woman buildeth her house: but the foolish plucketh it down with her hands.

Prov. 19: 14 . . . A prudent wife *is* from the Lord.

Prov. 31: 10 Who can find a virtuous woman? for her price *is* far above rubies. 11 The heart of her husband doth safely trust in her, so that he shall have no need of spoil. 12 She will do him good and not evil all the days of her life. 20 She stretcheth out her hand to the poor; yea, she reacheth forth her hands to the needy. 26 She openeth her mouth with wisdom; and in her tongue *is* the law of kindness. 27 She looketh well to the ways of her household, and eateth not the bread of idleness. 28 Her children arise up, and call her blessed; her husband *also*, and he praiseth her. 30 Favour *is* deceitful, and beauty *is* vain: *but* a woman *that* feareth the Lord, she shall be praised. 31 Give her of the fruit of her hands; and let her own works praise her in the gates.

I. Tim. 5: 14 I will . . . that the younger women marry, bear children, guide the house, give none occasion to the adversary to speak reproachfully.

Tit. 2: 1 . . . Speak thou the things which become sound doctrine: 3 The aged women . . . , that *they be* in behaviour as becometh holiness, not false accusers, not given to much wine, teachers of good things; 4 That they may teach the young women to be sober, to love their husbands, to love their children, 5 *To be* discreet, chaste, keepers at home, good, obedient to their own husbands, that the word of God be not blasphemed.

See MANHOOD.

WORLDLINESS

Rom. 12: 2 . . . Be not conformed to this world: but be ye transformed by the renewing of your mind, that ye may prove what *is* that good, and acceptable, and perfect will of God.

Col. 3: 2 Set your affection on things above, not on things on the earth.

I. John 2: 15 Love not the world, neither the things *that are* in the world. If any man love the world, the love of the Father is not in him. 16 For all that *is* in the world, the lust of the flesh, and the lust of the eyes, and the pride of

life, is not of the Father, but is of the world.
17 And the world passeth away, and the lust
thereof: but he that doeth the will of God abideth
for ever.

See COVETOUSNESS; FOLLY; LASCIVIOUSNESS;
WICKED; also RIGHTEOUS.

YOUTH

Psa. 119: 9 Wherewithal shall a young man
cleanse his way? by taking heed *thereto* according to thy word.

Psa. 148: 12 Both young men, and maidens;
old men, and children: 13 Let them praise the
name of the Lord: for his name alone is excellent; his glory *is* above the earth and heaven.

Prov. 3: 1 My son, forget not my law; but
let thine heart keep my commandments: 2 For
length of days, and long life, and peace, shall they
add to thee.

Ecc. 11: 9 Rejoice, O young man, in thy
youth; and let thy heart cheer thee in the days
of thy youth, and walk in the ways of thine heart,
and in the sight of thine eyes: but know thou,
that for all these *things* God will bring thee into
judgment. 10 Therefore remove sorrow from
thy heart, and put away evil from thy flesh: for
childhood and youth *are* vanity.

Ecc. 12: 1 Remember now thy Creator in the
days of thy youth, while the evil days come not,
nor the years draw nigh, when thou shalt say,
I have no pleasure in them;

Lam. 3: 27 *It is* good for a man that he bear
the yoke in his youth.

I. Tim. 4: 12 Let no man despise thy youth;
but be thou an example of the believers, in word,
in conversation, in charity, in spirit, in faith, in

purity.

II. Tim. 2: 1 Thou . . . , my son, be strong in the grace that is in Christ Jesus. 22 Flee . . . youthful lusts: but follow righteousness, faith, charity, peace, with them that call on the Lord out of a pure heart.

Tit. 2: 4 . . . Teach the young women to be sober, to love their husbands, to love their children, 5 *To be* discreet, chaste, keepers at home, good, obedient to their own husbands, that the word of God be not blasphemed. 6 Young men likewise exhort to be soberminded.

I. John 2: 13 . . . I write unto you, young men, because ye have overcome the wicked one. I write unto you, little children, because ye have known the Father. 14 . . . I have written unto you, young men, because ye are strong, and the word of God abideth in you, and ye have overcome the wicked one.

See CHILDREN; PARENTS.

MY VERSE FOR TODAY

Selections made by
CHARLES GALLAUDET TRUMBULL

JANUARY

January 1. Being confident of this very thing, that he which hath begun a good work in you will perform *it* until the day of Jesus Christ:—Philip. 1:6.

January 2. Thy word *is* a lamp unto my feet, and a light unto my path.—Psa. 119:105.

January 3. For unto us a child is born, unto us a son is given: and the government shall be upon his shoulder: and his name shall be called Wonderful, Counsellor, The mighty God, The everlasting Father, The Prince of Peace.—Isa. 9:6.

January 4. And Simon Peter answered and said, Thou art the Christ, the Son of the living God.—Matt. 16:16.

January 5. Who his own self bare our sins in his own body on the tree, that we, being dead to sins, should live unto righteousness: by whose stripes ye were healed.—I. Pet. 2:24.

January 6. Neither is there salvation in any other: for there is none other name under heaven given among men, whereby we must be saved.—Acts 4:12.

January 7. That if thou shalt confess with thy mouth the Lord Jesus, and shalt believe in thine heart that God hath raised him from the dead, thou shalt be saved.—Rom. 10:9.

421

January 8. For he hath made him *to be* sin for us, who knew no sin; that we might be made the righteousness of God in him.—II. Cor. 5:21.

January 9. For the law of the Spirit of life in Christ Jesus hath made me free from the law of sin and death.—Rom. 8:2.

January 10. Wherefore, my beloved, as ye have always obeyed, not as in my presence only, but now much more in my absence, work out your own salvation with fear and trembling:—Philip. 2:12.

January 11. For it is God which worketh in you both to will and to do of *his* good pleasure.—Philip. 2:13.

January 12. If any of you lack wisdom, let him ask of God, that giveth to all *men* liberally, and upbraideth not; and it shall be given him.—Jas. 1:5.

January 13. And God said, Let there be light: and there was light.—Gen. 1:3.

January 14. And the bow shall be in the cloud; and I will look upon it, that I may remember the everlasting covenant between God and every living creature of all flesh that *is* upon the earth.—Gen. 9:16.

January 15. If ye shall ask any thing in my name, I will do *it.*—John 14:14.

January 16. Abide in me, and I in you. As the branch cannot bear fruit of itself, except it abide in the vine; no more can ye, except ye abide in me.—John 15:4.

January 17. If ye abide in me, and my words abide in you, ye shall ask what ye will, and it shall be done unto you.—John 15:7.

January 18. Herein is my Father glorified, that ye bear much fruit; so shall ye be my disciples.—John 15:8.

January 19. A *good* name *is* rather to be chosen than great riches, *and* loving favour rather than silver and gold.—Prov. 22:1.

January 20. Beloved, think it not strange concerning the fiery trial which is to try you, as though some strange thing happened unto you:—I. Pet. 4:12.

January 21. But rejoice, inasmuch as ye are partakers of Christ's sufferings; that, when his glory shall be revealed, ye may be glad also with exceeding joy.—I. Pet. 4:13.

January 22. Be sober, be vigilant; because your adversary the devil, as a roaring lion, walketh about, seeking whom he may devour:—I. Pet. 5:8.

January 23. Whom resist steadfast in the faith, knowing that the same afflictions are accomplished in your brethren that are in the world.—I. Pet. 5:9.

January 24. But the God of all grace, who hath called us unto his eternal glory by Christ Jesus, after that ye have suffered a while, make you perfect, stablish, strengthen, settle *you.*—I. Pet. 5:10.

January 25. But seek ye first the kingdom of God, and his righteousness; and all these things shall be added unto you.—Matt. 6:33.

January 26. If ye then, being evil, know how to give good gifts unto your children, how much more shall your Father which is in heaven give good things to them that ask him?—Matt. 7:11.

January 27. No man can serve two masters: for either he will hate the one, and love the other; or else he will hold to the one, and despise the other. Ye cannot serve God and mammon.—Matt. 6:24.

January 28. Knowing *this*, that the trying of your faith worketh patience.—Jas. 1:3.

January 29. But let patience have *her* perfect work, that ye may be perfect and entire, wanting nothing.—Jas. 1:4.

January 30. . . . I *being* in the way, the Lord led me . . .—Gen. 24:27.

January 31. In thee, O Lord, do I put my trust: let me never be put to confusion.—Psa. 71:1.

FEBRUARY

February 1. Save me, O God; for the waters are come in unto *my* soul.—Psa. 69:1.

February 2. For the Lord heareth the poor, and despiseth not his prisoners.—Psa. 69:33.

February 3. I will praise the name of God with a song, and will magnify him with thanksgiving.—Psa. 69:30.

February 4. The Lord *is* my light and my salvation; whom shall I fear? the Lord *is* the strength of my life; of whom shall I be afraid?—Psa. 27:1.

February 5. And they that be wise shall shine as the brightness of the firmament; and they that turn many to righteousness, as the stars for ever and ever.—Dan. 12:3.

February 6. Go ye therefore, and teach all nations, baptizing them in the name of the Father, and of the Son, and of the Holy Ghost:—Matt. 28:19.

February 7. Teaching them to observe all things whatsoever I have commanded you: and, lo, I am with you alway, *even* unto the end of the world. Amen.—Matt. 28:20.

February 8. In my Father's house are many mansions: if *it were* not *so,* I would have told you. I go to prepare a place for you.—John 14:2.

February 9. And if I go and prepare a place for you, I will come again, and receive you unto myself; that where I am, *there* ye may be also.— John 14:3.

February 10. But as it is written, Eye hath not seen, nor ear heard, neither have entered into the heart of man, the things which God hath prepared for them that love him.—I. Cor. 2:9.

February 11. For we know that, if our earthly house of *this* tabernacle were dissolved, we have a building of God, a house not made with hands, eternal in the heavens.—II. Cor. 5:1.

February 12. And as ye would that men should do to you, do ye also to them likewise.— Luke 6:31.

February 13. Let every soul be subject unto the higher powers. For there is no power but of God: the powers that be are ordained of God.— Rom. 13:1.

February 14. But ye *are* a chosen generation, a royal priesthood, a holy nation, a peculiar people; that ye should shew forth the praises of him who hath called you out of darkness into his marvelous light:—I. Pet. 2:9.

February 15. Humble yourselves in the sight of the Lord, and he shall lift you up.—Jas. 4:10.

425

February 16. Lay not up for yourselves treasures upon earth, where moth and rust doth corrupt, and where thieves break through and steal: —Matt. 6:19.

February 17. But lay up for yourselves treasures in heaven, where neither moth nor rust doth corrupt, and where thieves do not break through nor steal:—Matt. 6:20.

February 18. For where your treasure is, there will your heart be also.—Matt. 6:21.

February 19. The Lord *is* my shepherd; I shall not want.—Psa. 23:1.

February 20. And Pharaoh said unto his servants, Can we find *such a one* as this *is*, a man in whom the Spirit of God *is?*—Gen. 41:38.

February 21. What! know ye not that your body is the temple of the Holy Ghost *which is* in you, which ye have of God, and ye are not your own?—I. Cor. 6:19.

February 22. Watch ye, stand fast in the faith, quit you like men, be strong.—I. Cor. 16:13.

February 23. For sin shall not have dominion over you: for ye are not under the law, but under grace.—Rom. 6:14.

February 24. I beseech you therefore, brethren, by the mercies of God, that ye present your bodies a living sacrifice, holy, acceptable unto God, *which is* your reasonable service.—Rom. 12:1.

February 25. And be not conformed to this world: but be ye transformed by the renewing of your mind, that ye may prove what *is* that good, and acceptable, and perfect will of God.—Rom. 12:2.

February 26. Take therefore no thought for the morrow: for the morrow shall take thought for the things of itself. Sufficient unto the day *is* the evil thereof.—Matt. 6:34.

February 27. Therefore if thine enemy hunger, feed him; if he thirst, give him drink: for in so doing thou shalt heap coals of fire on his head. —Rom. 12:20.

February 28. Be not overcome of evil, but overcome evil with good.—Rom. 12:21.

February 29. Beloved, let us love one another: for love is of God; and every one that loveth is born of God, and knoweth God.—I. John 4:7.

MARCH

March 1. For God so loved the world, that he gave his only begotten Son, that whosoever believeth in him should not perish, but have everlasting life.—John 3:16.

March 2. And they said, Believe on the Lord Jesus Christ, and thou shalt be saved, and thy house.—Acts 16:31.

March 3. Open thou mine eyes, that I may behold wondrous things out of thy law.—Psa. 119:18.

March 4. Thy word have I hid in mine heart, that I might not sin against thee.—Psa. 119:11.

March 5. For ever, O Lord, thy word is settled in heaven.—Psa. 119:89.

March 6. Blessed *is* the man that walketh not in the counsel of the ungoldly, nor standeth in the way of sinners, nor sitteth in the seat of the scornful.—Psa. 1:1.

March 7. But his delight *is* in the law of the Lord; and in his law doth he meditate day and night.—Psa. 1:2.

March 8. O our God, wilt thou not judge them? for we have no might against this great company that cometh against us; neither know we what to do: but our eyes *are* upon thee.—II. Chron. 20:12.

March 9. . . . Thus saith the Lord unto you, Be not afraid nor dismayed by reason of this great multitude; for the battle *is* not yours, but God's.—II. Chron. 20:15.

March 10. Ye shall not *need* to fight in this *battle:* set yourselves, stand ye *still,* and see the salvation of the Lord with you, . . .—II. Chron. 20:17.

March 11. Let the words of my mouth, and the meditation of my heart, be acceptable in thy sight, O Lord, my strength, and my redeemer.—Psa. 19:14.

March 12. I *am* the Lord thy God, which brought thee out of the land of Egypt: open thy mouth wide, and I will fill it.—Psa. 81:10.

March 13. The angel of the Lord encampeth round about them that fear him, and delivereth them.—Psa. 34:7.

March 14. . . . And who knoweth whether thou art come to the kingdom for *such* a time as this?—Esther 4:14.

March 15. But my God shall supply all your need according to his riches in glory by Christ Jesus.—Philip. 4:19.

March 16. Be careful for nothing; but in every thing by prayer and supplication with thanksgiving let your requests be made known unto God.—Philip. 4:6.

March 17. And the peace of God, which passeth all understanding, shall keep your hearts and minds through Christ Jesus.—Philip. 4:7.

March 18. Therefore, my beloved brethren, be ye steadfast, unmoveable, always abounding in the work of the Lord, forasmuch as ye know that your labour is not in vain in the Lord.—I. Cor. 15:58.

March 19. Now thanks *be* unto God, which always causeth us to triumph in Christ, and maketh manifest the savour of his knowledge by us in every place.—II. Cor. 2:14.

March 20. . . . Thou shalt call his name JESUS: for he shall save his people from their sins.—Matt. 1:21.

March 21. And thou Bethlehem, *in* the land of Juda, art not the least among the princes of Juda: for out of thee shall come a Governor, that shall rule my people Israel.—Matt. 2:6.

March 22. And lo a voice from heaven, saying, This is my beloved Son, in whom I am well pleased.—Matt. 3:17.

March 23. But he answered and said, It is written, Man shall not live by bread alone, but by every word that proceedeth out of the mouth of God.—Matt. 4:4.

March 24. Then saith Jesus unto him, Get thee hence, Satan: for it is written, Thou shalt worship the Lord thy God, and him only shalt thou serve.—Matt. 4:10.

March 25. And he saith unto them, Follow me, and I will make you fishers of men.—Matt. 4:19.

March 26. Blessed are ye, when *men* shall revile you, and persecute *you*, and shall say all manner of evil against you falsely, for my sake.—Matt. 5:11.

429

March 27. Therefore whosoever heareth these sayings of mine, and doeth them, I will liken him unto a wise man, which built his house upon a rock:—Matt. 7:24.

March 28. And Jesus put forth *his* hand, and touched him, saying, I will; be thou clean. And immediately his leprosy was cleansed.—Matt. 8:3.

March 29. But if we walk in the light, as he is in the light, we have fellowship one with another, and the blood of Jesus Christ his Son cleanseth us from all sin.—I. John 1:7.

March 30. And he saith unto them, Why are ye fearful, O ye of little faith? Then he arose, and rebuked the winds and the sea; and there was a great calm.—Matt. 8:26.

March 31. And he that taketh not his cross, and followeth after me, is not worthy of me.—Matt. 10:38.

APRIL

April 1. And there was a cloud that overshadowed them: and a voice came out of the cloud, saying, This is my beloved Son: hear him. —Mark 9:7.

April 2. And suddenly, when they had looked round about, they saw no man any more, save Jesus only with themselves.—Mark 9:8.

April 3. For he taught his disciples, and said unto them, The Son of man is delivered into the hands of men, and they shall kill him; and after that he is killed, he shall rise the third day.— Mark 9:31.

April 4. For the Son of man is come to seek and to save that which was lost.—Luke 19:10.

April 5. But they cried, saying, Crucify *him,* crucify him.—Luke 23:21.

April 6. And he said unto Jesus, Lord, remember me when thou comest into thy kingdom. —Luke 23:42.

April 7. And when Jesus had cried with a loud voice, he said, Father, into thy hands I commend my spirit: and having said thus, he gave up the ghost.—Luke 23:46.

April 8. Christ hath redeemed us from the curse of the law, being made a curse for us: for it is written, Cursed *is* every one that hangeth on a tree:—Gal. 3:13.

April 9. . . . Behold the Lamb of God, which taketh away the sin of the world!—John 1:29.

April 10. For all have sinned, and come short of the glory of God;—Rom. 3:23.

April 11. For the wages of sin *is* death; but the gift of God *is* eternal life through Jesus Christ our Lord.—Rom. 6:23.

April 12. But to him that worketh not, but believeth on him that justifieth the ungodly, his faith is counted for righteousness.—Rom. 4:5.

April 13. But God commendeth his love toward us, in that, while we were yet sinners, Christ died for us.—Rom. 5:8.

April 14. For if, when we were enemies, we were reconciled to God by the death of his Son; much more, being reconciled, we shall be saved by his life.—Rom. 5:10.

April 15. And said unto them, Thus it is written, and thus it behoved Christ to suffer, and to rise from the dead the third day:—Luke 24:46.

431

April 16. . . . Then were the disciples glad, when they saw the Lord.—John 20:20.

April 17. And after eight days again his disciples were within, and Thomas with them: *then* came Jesus, the doors being shut, and stood in the midst, and said, Peace *be* unto you.—John 20:26.

April 18. Jesus saith unto him, Thomas, because thou hast seen me, thou hast believed: blessed *are* they that have not seen, and *yet* have believed.—John 20:29.

April 19. Jesus said unto her, I am the resurrection, and the life: he that believeth in me, though he were dead, yet shall he live:—John 11:25.

April 20. But now is Christ risen from the dead, *and* become the firstfruits of them that slept.—I. Cor. 15:20.

April 21. For as in Adam all die, even so in Christ shall all be made alive.—I. Cor. 15:22.

April 22. So when this corruptible shall have put on incorruption, and this mortal shall have put on immortality, then shall be brought to pass the saying that is written, Death is swallowed up in victory.—I. Cor. 15:54.

April 23. Be it known unto you all, and to all the people of Israel, that by the name of Jesus Christ of Nazareth, whom ye crucified, whom God raised from the dead, *even* by him doth this man stand here before you whole.—Acts 4:10.

April 24. Because the creature itself also shall be delivered from the bondage of corruption into the glorious liberty of the children of God.—Rom. 8:21.

April 25. But these are written, that ye might believe that Jesus is the Christ, the Son of God; and that believing ye might have life through his name.—John 20:31.

April 26. But thanks *be* to God, which giveth us the victory through our Lord Jesus Christ.— I. Cor. 15:57.

April 27. Therefore if any man *be* in Christ, *he is* a new creature: old things are passed away; behold, all things are become new.—II. Cor. 5:17.

April 28. . . . Behold, I make all things new. . . .—Rev. 21:5.

April 29. To him that overcometh will I grant to sit with me in my throne, even as I also overcame, and am set down with my Father in his throne.—Rev. 3:21.

April 30. Behold, I come quickly: hold that fast which thou hast, that no man take thy crown. —Rev. 3:11.

MAY

May 1. A good tree cannot bring forth evil fruit, neither *can* a corrupt tree bring forth good fruit.—Matt. 7:18.

May 2. Wherefore by their fruits ye shall know them.—Matt. 7:20.

May 3. Fear thou not; for I *am* with thee: be not dismayed; for I *am* thy God: I will strengthen thee; yea, I will help thee; yea, I will uphold thee with the right hand of my righteousness.—Isa. 41:10.

May 4. Then said David to the Philistine, Thou comest to me with a sword, and with a spear, and with a shield: but I come to thee in the name of the Lord of hosts, the God of the armies of Israel, whom thou hast defied.—I. Sam. 17:45.

May 5. And he went down with them, and came to Nazareth, and was subject unto them: but his mother kept all these sayings in her heart. —Luke 2:51.

May 6. Honour thy father and thy mother: that thy days may be long upon the land which the Lord thy God giveth thee.—Exod. 20:12.

May 7. As one whom his mother comforteth, so will I comfort you; . . . —Isa. 66:13.

May 8. My son, hear the instruction of thy father, and forsake not the law of thy mother: —Prov. 1:8.

May 9. The hoary head *is* a crown of glory, *if* it be found in the way of righteousness.— Prov. 16:31.

May 10. Children, obey *your* parents in all things: for this is well pleasing unto the Lord.— Col. 3:20.

May 11. And *even* to *your* old age I *am* he; and *even* to hoar hairs will I carry *you:* I have made, and I will bear; even I will carry, and will deliver *you.*—Isa. 46:4.

May 12. Let not sin therefore reign in your mortal body, that ye should obey it in the lusts thereof.—Rom. 6:12.

May 13. Neither yield ye your members *as* instruments of unrighteousness unto sin: but yield yourselves unto God, as those that are alive from the dead, and your members *as* instruments of righteousness unto God.—Rom. 6:13.

May 14. Likewise reckon ye also yourselves to be dead indeed unto sin, but alive unto God through Jesus Christ our Lord.—Rom. 6:11.

May 15. Being then made free from sin, ye became the servants of righteousness.—Rom. 6:18.

May 16. If ye then be risen with Christ, seek those things which are above, where Christ sitteth on the right hand of God.—Col. 3:1.

May 17. For ye are dead, and your life is hid with Christ in God.—Col. 3:3.

May 18. When Christ, *who is* our life, shall appear, then shall ye also appear with him in glory.—Col. 3:4.

May 19. As ye have therefore received Christ Jesus the Lord, *so* walk ye in him:—Col. 2:6.

May 20. Blessed *be* the God and Father of our Lord Jesus Christ, who hath blessed us with all spiritual blessings in heavenly *places* in Christ: —Eph. 1:3.

May 21. The eyes of your understanding being enlightened; that ye may know what is the hope of his calling, and what the riches of the glory of his inheritance in the saints,—Eph. 1:18.

May 22. And to know the love of Christ, which passeth knowledge, that ye might be filled with all the fulness of God.—Eph. 3:19.

May 23. Now unto him that is able to do exceeding abundantly above all that we ask or think, according to the power that worketh in us,—Eph. 3:20.

May 24. Beloved, believe not every spirit, but try the spirits whether they are of God: because many false prophets are gone out into the world. —I. John 4:1.

May 25. But there were false prophets also among the people, even as there shall be false teachers among you, who privily shall bring in damnable heresies, even denying the Lord that bought them, and bring upon themselves swift destruction.—II. Pet. 2:1.

May 26. Fight the good fight of faith, lay hold on eternal life, whereunto thou art also called, and hast professed a good profession before many witnesses.—I. Tim. 6:12.

May 27. As newborn babes, desire the sincere milk of the word, that ye may grow thereby:—I. Pet. 2:2.

May 28. Wherefore also it is contained in the Scripture, Behold, I lay in Sion a chief corner stone, elect, precious: and he that believeth on him shall not be confounded.—I. Pet. 2:6.

May 29. But the wisdom that is from above is first pure, then peaceable, gentle, *and* easy to be entreated, full of mercy and good fruits, without partiality, and without hypocrisy.—Jas. 3:17.

May 30. Greater love hath no man than this, that a man lay down his life for his friends.—John 15:13.

May 31. Put them in mind to be subject to principalities and powers, to obey magistrates, to be ready to every good work,—Tit. 3:1.

JUNE

June 1. And I will pray the Father, and he shall give you another Comforter, that he may abide with you for ever;—John 14:16.

June 2. *Even* the Spirit of truth; whom the world cannot receive, because it seeth him not, neither knoweth him: but ye know him; for he dwelleth with you, and shall be in you.—John 14:17.

June 3. Let brotherly love continue.—Heb. 13:1.

June 4. Nevertheless I tell you the truth; It is expedient for you that I go away: for if I go not away, the Comforter will not come unto you; but if I depart, I will send him unto you.—John 16:7.

June 5. All Scripture *is* given by inspiration of God, and *is* profitable for doctrine, for reproof, for correction, for instruction in righteousness: —II. Tim. 3:16.

June 6. Study to shew thyself approved unto God, a workman that needeth not to be ashamed, rightly dividing the word of truth.—II. Tim. 2:15.

June 7. Peace I leave with you, my peace I give unto you: not as the world giveth, give I unto you. Let not your heart be troubled, neither let it be afraid.—John 14:27.

June 8. And you *hath he quickened,* who were dead in trespasses and sins;—Eph. 2:1.

June 9. For by grace are ye saved through faith; and that not of yourselves: *It is* the gift of God:—Eph. 2:8.

June 10. For we are his workmanship, created in Christ Jesus unto good works, which God hath before ordained that we should walk in them.— Eph. 2:10.

June 11. Thy right hand, O Lord, is become glorious in power: thy right hand, O Lord, hath dashed in pieces the enemy.—Exod. 15:6.

June 12. Know therefore that the Lord thy God, he *is* God, the faithful God, which keepeth covenant and mercy with them that love him and keep his commandments to a thousand generations;—Deut. 7:9.

June 13. Wherefore he is able also to save them to the uttermost that come unto God by him, seeing he ever liveth to make intercession for them.—Heb. 7:25.

June 14. Thou wilt keep *him* in perfect peace, *whose* mind *is* stayed *on thee:* because he trusteth in thee.—Isa. 26:3.

June 15. Trust ye in the Lord for ever: for in the Lord JEHOVAH *is* everlasting strength.—Isa. 26:4.

June 16. The Lord God *is* my strength, and he will make my feet like hinds' *feet,* and he will make me to walk upon mine high places. . . . —Hab. 3:19.

June 17. Let this mind be in you, which was also in Christ Jesus:—Philip. 2:5.

June 18. For to me to live *is* Christ, and to die *is* gain.—Philip. 1:21.

June 19. For unto you it is given in the behalf of Christ, not only to believe on him, but also to suffer for his sake;—Philip. 1:29.

June 20. I exhort therefore, that, first of all, supplications, prayers, intercessions, *and* giving of thanks, be made for all men;—I. Tim. 2:1.

June 21. And he spake a parable unto them *to this end,* that men ought always to pray, and not to faint;—Luke 18:1.

June 22. For it is easier for a camel to go through a needle's eye, than for a rich man to enter into the kingdom of God.—Luke 18:25.

June 23. And he said, The things which are impossible with men are possible with God.—Luke 18:27.

June 24. For what shall it profit a man, if he shall gain the whole world, and lose his own soul? —Mark 8:36.

June 25. For whosoever will save his life shall lose it; but whosoever shall lose his life for my sake and the gospel's, the same shall save it.— Mark 8:35.

June 26. And he said unto them, This kind can come forth by nothing, but by prayer and fasting.—Mark 9:29.

June 27. And he said unto her, Daughter, thy faith hath made thee whole; go in peace, and be whole of thy plague.—Mark 5:34.

June 28. And Jesus answering saith unto them, Have faith in God.—Mark 11:22.

June 29. For verily I say unto you, That whosoever shall say unto this mountain, Be thou removed, and be thou cast into the sea; and shall not doubt in his heart, but shall believe that those things which he saith shall come to pass; he shall have whatsoever he saith.—Mark 11:23.

June 30. Therefore I say unto you, What things soever ye desire, when ye pray, believe that ye receive *them,* and ye shall have *them.*—Mark. 11:24.

JULY

July 1. And this is the confidence that we have in him, that, if we ask any thing according to his will, he heareth us:—I. John 5:14.

July 2. And if we know that he hear us, whatsoever we ask, we know that we have the petitions that we desired of him.—I. John 5:15.

July 3. Thus saith the Lord the King of Israel, and his Redeemer the Lord of hosts; I *am* the first, and I *am* the last; and besides me *there is* no God. —Isa. 44:6.

July 4. Stand fast therefore in the liberty wherewith Christ hath made us free, and be not entangled again with the yoke of bondage.—Gal. 5:1.

July 5. God *is* a Spirit: and they that worship him must worship *him* in spirit and in truth.— John 4:24.

July 6. He that loveth not, knoweth not God; for God is love.—I. John 4:8.

July 7. There hath no temptation taken you but such as is common to man: but God *is* faithful, who will not suffer you to be tempted above that ye are able; but will with the temptation also make a way to escape, that ye may be able to bear *it.*—I. Cor. 10:13.

July 8. Casting all your care upon him; for he careth for you.—I. Pet. 5:7.

July 9. But one thing is needful; and Mary hath chosen that good part, which shall not be taken away from her.—Luke 10:42.

July 10. Come unto me, all *ye* that labor and are heavy laden, and I will give you rest.—Matt. 11:28.

July 11. Take my yoke upon you, and learn of me; for I am meek and lowly in heart: and ye shall find rest unto your souls.—Matt. 11:29.

July 12. For my yoke *is* easy, and my burden is light.—Matt. 11:30.

July 13. . . . This same Jesus, which is taken up from you into heaven, shall so come in like manner as ye have seen him go into heaven. —Acts 1:11.

July 14. Let not your heart be troubled: ye believe in God, believe also in me.—John 14:1.

July 15. Verily I say unto you, There be some standing here, which shall not taste of death, till they see the Son of man coming in his kingdom. —Matt. 16:28.

July 16. For as the lightning cometh out of the east, and shineth even unto the west; so shall also the coming of the Son of man be.—Matt. 24:27.

July 17. Behold, I shew you a mystery: We shall not all sleep, but we shall all be changed,— I. Cor. 15:51.

July 18. For the Lord himself shall descend from heaven with a shout, with the voice of the archangel, and with the trump of God: and the dead in Christ shall rise first:—I. Thess. 4:16.

July 19. Then we which are alive *and* remain shall be caught up together with them in the clouds, to meet the Lord in the air: and so shall we ever be with the Lord.—I. Thess. 4:17.

July 20. And the very God of peace sanctify you wholly; and *I pray God* your whole spirit and soul and body be preserved blameless unto the coming of our Lord Jesus Christ.—I. Thess. 5:23.

July 21. Ye are the light of the world. A city that is set on a hill cannot be hid.—Matt. 5:14.

July 22. And whosoever shall compel thee to go a mile, go with him twain.—Matt. 5:41.

441

July 23. Give, and it shall be given unto you; good measure, pressed down, and shaken together, and running over, shall men give into your bosom. For with the same measure that ye mete withal it shall be measured to you again.—Luke 6:38.

July 24. And why call ye me, Lord, Lord, and do not the things which I say?—Luke 6:46.

July 25. But love ye your enemies, and do good, and lend, hoping for nothing again; and your reward shall be great, and ye shall be the children of the Highest: for he is kind unto the unthankful and *to* the evil.—Luke 6:35.

July 26. And he said unto them, Come ye yourselves apart into a desert place, and rest awhile: . . . —Mark 6:31.

July 27. And Jesus answering said unto them, They that are whole need not a physician; but they that are sick.—Luke 5:31.

July 28. Praise ye the Lord. Blessed *is* the man *that* feareth the Lord, *that* delighteth greatly in his commandments.—Psa. 112:1.

July 29. Let us therefore fear, lest, a promise being left *us* of entering into his rest, any of you should seem to come short of it.—Heb. 4:1.

July 30. For he that is entered into his rest, he also hath ceased from his own works, as God *did* from his.—Heb. 4:10.

July 31. Return unto thy rest, O my soul; for the Lord hath dealt bountifully with thee.—Psa. 116:7.

AUGUST

August 1. For thou hast delivered my soul from death, mine eyes from tears, *and* my feet from falling.—Psa. 116:8.

August 2. . . . Verily, verily, I say unto you, Hereafter ye shall see heaven open, and the angels of God ascending and descending upon the Son of man.—John 1:51.

August 3. And no man hath ascended up to heaven, but he that came down from heaven, *even* the Son of man which is in heaven.—John 3:13.

August 4. Now we have received, not the spirit of the world, but the Spirit which is of God; that we might know the things that are freely given to us of God.—I. Cor. 2:12.

August 5. Every man's work shall be made manifest: for the day shall declare it, because it shall be revealed by fire; and the fire shall try every man's work of what sort it is.—I. Cor. 3:13.

August 6. If any man's work abide which he hath built thereupon, he shall receive a reward. —I. Cor. 3:14.

August 7. If any man's work shall be burned, he shall suffer loss: but he himself shall be saved; yet so as by fire.—I. Cor. 3:15.

August 8. For we must all appear before the judgment seat of Christ; that every one may receive the things *done* in *his* body, according to that he hath done, whether *it be* good or bad.—II. Cor. 5:10.

August 9. For our conversation is in heaven; from whence also we look for the Saviour, the Lord Jesus Christ:—Philip. 3:20.

August 10. Who shall change our vile body, that it may be fashioned like unto his glorious body, according to the working whereby he is able even to subdue all things unto himself.—Philip. 3:21.

August 11. I will bless the Lord at all times: his praise *shall* continually *be* in my mouth.—Psa. 34:1.

August 12. My soul shall make her boast in the Lord: the humble shall hear *thereof*, and be glad.—Psa. 34:2.

August 13. O magnify the Lord with me, and let us exalt his name together.—Psa. 34:3.

August 14. I sought the Lord, and he heard me, and delivered me from all my fears.—Psa. 34:4.

August 15. They looked unto him, and were lightened: and their faces were not ashamed.—Psa. 34:5.

August 16. This poor man cried, and the Lord heard *him*, and saved him out of all his troubles.—Psa. 34:6.

August 17. O taste and see that the Lord *is* good: blessed *is* the man *that* trusteth in him.—Psa. 34:8.

August 18. The Lord redeemeth the soul of his servants: and none of them that trust in him shall be desolate.—Psa. 34:22.

August 19. But though we, or an angel from heaven, preach any other gospel unto you than that which we have preached unto you, let him be accursed.—Gal. 1:8.

August 20. Knowing that a man is not justified by the works of the law, but by the faith of Jesus Christ, even we have believed in Jesus Christ, that we might be justified by the faith of Christ, and not by the works of the law: for by the works of the law shall no flesh be justified.—Gal. 2:16.

August 21. I am crucified with Christ: nevertheless I live; yet not I, but Christ liveth in me: and the life which I now live in the flesh I live by the faith of the Son of God, who loved me, and gave himself for me.—Gal. 2:20.

August 22. But that no man is justified by the law in the sight of God, *it is* evident: for, The just shall live by faith.—Gal. 3:11.

August 23. There is neither Jew nor Greek, there is neither bond nor free, there is neither male nor female: for ye are all one in Christ Jesus. —Gal. 3:28.

August 24. Wherefore thou art no more a servant, but a son; and if a son, then an heir of God through Christ.—Gal. 4:7.

August 25. Brethren, if a man be overtaken in a fault, ye which are spiritual, restore such a one in the spirit of meekness; considering thyself, lest thou also be tempted.—Gal. 6:1.

August 26. Now the Spirit speaketh expressly, that in the latter times some shall depart from the faith, giving heed to seducing spirits, and doctrines of devils;—I. Tim. 4:1.

August 27. This know also, that in the last days perilous times shall come.—II. Tim. 3:1.

August 28. Having a form of godliness, but denying the power thereof: from such turn away. —II. Tim. 3:5.

August 29. Yea, and all that will live godly in Christ Jesus shall suffer persecution.—II. Tim. 3:12.

August 30. But evil men and seducers shall wax worse and worse, deceiving, and being deceived.—II. Tim. 3:13.

445

August 31. Preach the word; be instant in season, out of season; reprove, rebuke, exhort with all longsuffering and doctrine.—II. Tim. 4:2.

SEPTEMBER

September 1. Whatsoever thy hand findeth to do, do *it* with thy might; . . . —Ecc. 9:10.

September 2. I must work the works of him that sent me, while it is day: the night cometh, when no man can work.—John 9:4.

September 3. Servants, obey in all things *your* masters according to the flesh; not with eyeservice, as menpleasers; but in singleness of heart, fearing God:—Col. 3:22.

September 4. Masters, give unto *your* servants that which is just and equal; knowing that ye also have a Master in heaven.—Col. 4:1.

September 5. Even so faith, if it hath not works, is dead, being alone.—Jas. 2:17.

September 6. For as the body without the spirit is dead, so faith without works is dead also. —Jas. 2:26.

September 7. If any man will do his will, he shall know of the doctrine, whether it be of God, or *whether* I speak of myself.—John 7:17.

September 8. *There is* therefore now no condemnation to them which are in Christ Jesus, who walk not after the flesh, but after the Spirit.— Rom. 8:1.

September 9. For as many as are led by the Spirit of God, they are the sons of God.—Rom. 8:14.

September 10. And we know that all things work together for good to them that love God, to them who are the called according to *his* purpose. —Rom. 8:28.

September 11. Finally, my brethren, be strong in the Lord, and in the power of his might. —Eph. 6:10.

September 12. Put on the whole armour of God, that ye may be able to stand against the wiles of the devil.—Eph. 6:11.

September 13. For we wrestle not against flesh and blood, but against principalities, against powers, against the rulers of the darkness of this world, against spiritual wickedness in high *places.*—Eph. 6:12.

September 14. Wherefore take unto you the whole armour of God, that ye may be able to withstand in the evil day, and having done all, to stand. —Eph. 6:13.

September 15. Stand therefore, having your loins girt about with truth, and having on the breastplate of righteousness;—Eph. 6:14.

September 16. And your feet shod with the preparation of the gospel of peace;—Eph. 6:15.

September 17. Above all, taking the shield of faith, wherewith ye shall be able to quench all the fiery darts of the wicked.—Eph. 6:16.

September 18. And take the helmet of salvation, and the sword of the Spirit, which is the word of God:—Eph. 6:17.

September 19. Praying always with all prayer and supplication in the Spirit, and watching thereunto with all perseverance and supplication for all saints;—Eph. 6:18.

September 20. And be not drunk with wine, wherein is excess; but be filled with the Spirit;— Eph. 5:18.

September 21. He answered and said, Lo, I see four men loose, walking in the midst of the fire, and they have no hurt; and the form of the fourth is like the Son of God.—Dan. 3:25.

September 22. Now when Daniel knew that the writing was signed, he went into his house; and, his windows being open in his chamber toward Jerusalem, he kneeled upon his knees three times a day, and prayed, and gave thanks before his God, as he did aforetime.—Dan. 6:10.

September 23. My God hath sent his angel, and hath shut the lions' mouths, that they have not hurt me: forasmuch as before him innocency was found in me; and also before thee, O king, have I done no hurt.—Dan. 6:22.

September 24. Then said he unto me, Fear not, Daniel: for from the first day that thou didst set thine heart to understand, and to chasten thyself before thy God, thy words were heard, and I am come for thy words.—Dan. 10:12.

September 25. . . . O man greatly beloved, fear not: peace be unto thee; be strong, yea, be strong. And when he had spoken unto me, I was strengthened, . . . —Dan. 10:19.

September 26. Now there are diversities of gifts, but the same Spirit.—I. Cor. 12:4.

September 27. For as the body is one, and hath many members, and all the members of that one body, being many, are one body: so also is Christ.—I. Cor. 12:12.

September 28. Though I speak with the tongues of men and of angels, and have not *charity, I am become as sounding brass, or a tinkling cymbal.—I. Cor. 13:1.

September 29. *Charity suffereth long, *and* is kind; *charity envieth not; *charity vaunteth not itself, is not puffed up.—I. Cor. 13:4.

September 30. *Charity never faileth: . . . —I. Cor. 13:8.

*Revised Version, "love."

OCTOBER

October 1. And he said unto him, If thy presence go not *with me,* carry us not up hence.— Exod. 33:15.

October 2. For wherein shall it be known here that I and thy people have found grace in thy sight? *is it* not in that thou goest with us? So shall we be separated, I and thy people, from all the people that *are* upon the face of the earth.— Exod. 33:16.

October 3. And he said, My presence shall go *with thee,* and I will give thee rest.—Exod. 33:14.

October 4. For my thoughts *are* not your thoughts, neither *are* your ways my ways, saith the Lord.—Isa. 55:8.

October 5. For *as* the heavens are higher than the earth, so are my ways higher than your ways, and my thoughts than your thoughts.—Isa. 55:9.

October 6. So shall my word be that goeth forth out of my mouth: it shall not return unto me void, but it shall accomplish that which I please, and it shall prosper *in the thing* whereto I sent it.—Isa. 55:11.

October 7. He is despised and rejected of men; a man of sorrows, and acquainted with grief: and we hid as it were *our* faces from him; he was despised, and we esteemed him not.—Isa. 53:3.

449

October 8. Surely he hath borne our griefs, and carried our sorrows: yet we did esteem him stricken, smitten of God, and afflicted.—Isa. 53:4.

October 9. But he *was* wounded for our transgressions, *he was* bruised for our iniquities: the chastisement of our peace *was* upon him; and with his stripes we are healed.—Isa. 53:5.

October 10. All we like sheep have gone astray; we have turned every one to his own way; and the Lord hath laid on him the iniquity of us all.—Isa. 53:6.

October 11. And he said unto me, My grace is sufficient for thee: for my strength is made perfect in weakness. Most gladly therefore will I rather glory in my infirmities, that the power of Christ may rest upon me.—II. Cor. 12:9.

October 12. Therefore I take pleasure in infirmities, in reproaches, in necessities, in persecutions, in distresses for Christ's sake: for when I am weak, then am I strong.—II. Cor. 12:10.

October 13. To whom God would make known what *is* the riches of the glory of this mystery among the Gentiles; which is Christ in you, the hope of glory:—Col. 1:27.

October 14. Set your affection on things above, not on things on the earth.—Col. 3:2.

October 15. And whatsoever ye do in word or deed, *do* all in the name of the Lord Jesus, giving thanks to God and the Father by him.—Col. 3:17.

October 16. Looking for that blessed hope, and the glorious appearing of the great God and our Saviour Jesus Christ;—Tit. 2:13.

October 17. So Christ was once offered to bear the sins of many; and unto them that look for him shall he appear the second time without sin unto salvation.—Heb. 9:28.

October 18. Wherefore, seeing we also are compassed about with so great a cloud of witnesses, let us lay aside every weight, and the sin which doth so easily beset *us,* and let us run with patience the race that is set before us,—Heb. 12:1.

October 19. Looking unto Jesus the author and finisher of *our* faith; who for the joy that was set before him endured the cross, despising the shame, and is set down at the right hand of the throne of God.—Heb. 12:2.

October 20. If ye endure chastening, God dealeth with you as with sons; for what son is he whom the father chasteneth not?—Heb. 12:7.

October 21. Now our chastening for the present seemeth to be joyous, but grievous: nevertheless, afterward it yieldeth the peaceable fruit of righteousness unto them which are exercised thereby.—Heb. 12:11.

October 22. Now unto him that is able to keep you from falling, and to present *you* faultless before the presence of his glory with exceeding joy, —Jude 24.

October 23. . . . Earnestly contend for the faith which was once delivered unto the saints. —Jude 3.

October 24. O Lord our Lord, how excellent *is* thy name in all the earth! who hast set thy glory above the heavens.—Psa. 8:1.

October 25. Thou preparest a table before me in the presence of mine enemies: thou anointest my head with oil; my cup runneth over.—Psa. 23:5.

451

October 26. Behold the fowls of the air: for they sow not, neither do they reap, nor gather into barns; yet your heavenly Father feedeth them. Are ye not much better than they?—Matt. 6:26.

October 27. Ask, and it shall be given you; seek, and ye shall find; knock, and it shall be opened unto you:—Matt. 7:7.

October 28. But if any provide not for his own, and specially for those of his own house, he hath denied the faith, and is worse than an infidel. —I. Tim. 5:8.

October 29. The fruit of the righteous *is* a tree of life; and he that winneth souls *is* wise.—Prov. 11:30.

October 30. Let him know, that he which converteth the sinner from the error of his way shall save a soul from death, and shall hide a multitude of sins.—Jas. 5:20.

October 31. In your patience possess ye your souls.—Luke 21:19.

NOVEMBER

November 1. And not only *so*, but we glory in tribulations also; knowing that tribulation worketh patience;—Rom. 5:3.

November 2. Love not the world, neither the things *that are* in the world. If any man love the world, the love of the Father is not in him.—I. John 2:15.

November 3. And the world passeth away, and the lust thereof: but he that doeth the will of God abideth for ever.—I. John 2:17.

November 4. We love him, because he first loved us.—I. John 4:19.

452

November 5. And the Lord spake unto Moses face to face, as a man speaketh unto his friend. . . . —Exod. 33:11.

November 6. Pray ye therefore the Lord of the harvest, that he will send forth labourers into his harvest.—Matt. 9:38.

November 7. I can do all things through Christ which strengtheneth me.—Philip. 4:13.

November 8. . . . Let us go up at once, and possess it; for we are well able to overcome it.—Num. 13:30.

November 9. For the Lord thy God bringeth thee into a good land, a land of brooks of water, of fountains and depths that spring out of valleys and hills;—Deut. 8:7.

November 10. This book of the law shall not depart out of thy mouth; but thou shalt meditate therein day and night, that thou mayest observe to do according to all that is written therein: for then thou shalt make thy way prosperous, and then thou shalt have good success.—Josh. 1:8.

November 11. But now, in Christ Jesus, ye who sometime were far off are made nigh by the blood of Christ.—Eph. 2:13.

November 12. The eternal God *is thy* refuge, and underneath *are* the everlasting arms: . . . —Deut. 33:27.

November 13. Have not I commanded thee? Be strong and of a good courage; be not afraid, neither be thou dismayed: for the Lord thy God *is* with thee whithersoever thou goest.—Josh. 1:9.

November 14. *There is* none holy as the Lord: for *there is* none besides thee: neither *is there* any rock like our God.—I. Sam. 2:2.

November 15. Blessed *be* the Lord, . . . there hath not failed one word of all his good promise, which he promised . . .—I. Kings 8:56.

November 16. And he answered, Fear not: for they that *be* with us *are* more than they that *be* with them.—II. Kings 6:16.

November 17. The Lord *is* my strength and my shield; my heart trusted in him, and I am helped: therefore my heart greatly rejoiceth; and with my song will I praise him.—Psa. 28:7.

November 18. I acknowledged my sin unto thee, and mine iniquity have I not hid. I said, I will confess my transgressions unto the Lord; and thou forgavest the iniquity of my sin. . . . —Psa. 32:5.

November 19. I will instruct thee and teach thee in the way which thou shalt go: I will guide thee with mine eye.—Psa. 32:8.

November 20. O give thanks unto the Lord, for *he is* good: for his mercy *endureth* for ever.— Psa. 107:1.

November 21. Then they cried unto the Lord in their trouble, *and* he delivered them out of their distresses.—Psa. 107:6.

November 22. Cast thy bread upon the waters: for thou shalt find it after many days.— Ecc. 11:1.

November 23. Behold, God *is* my salvation; I will trust, and not be afraid: for the Lord JEHOVAH *is* my strength and *my* song; he also is become my salvation.—Isa. 12:2.

November 24. Oh that *men* would praise the Lord *for* his goodness, and *for* his wonderful works to the children of men!—Psa. 107:8.

November 25. Giving thanks always for all things unto God and the Father in the name of our Lord Jesus Christ;—Eph. 5:20.

November 26. By him therefore let us offer the sacrifice of praise to God continually, that is, the fruit of *our* lips, giving thanks to his name.— Heb. 13:15.

November 27. And he took the cup, and gave thanks, . . . —Matt. 26:27.

November 28. And God *is* able to make all grace abound toward you; that ye, always having all sufficiency in all *things,* may abound to every good work:—II. Cor. 9:8.

November 29. Thanks *be* unto God for his unspeakable gift.—II. Cor. 9:15.

November 30. Giving thanks unto the Father, which hath made us meet to be partakers of the inheritance of the saints in light:—Col. 1:12.

DECEMBER

December 1. Herein is love, not that we loved God, but that he loved us, and sent his Son *to be* the propitiation for our sins.—I. John 4:10.

December 2. And the Word was made flesh, and dwelt among us, (and we beheld his glory, the glory as of the only begotten of the Father,) full of grace and truth.—John 1:14.

December 3. For the law was given by Moses, *but* grace and truth came by Jesus Christ.—John 1:17.

December 4. And Jesus went about all the cities and villages, teaching in their synagogues, and preaching the gospel of the kingdom, and healing every sickness and every disease among the people.—Matt. 9:35.

455

December 5. But when he saw the multitudes, he was moved with compassion on them, because they fainted, and were scattered abroad, as sheep having no shepherd.—Matt. 9:36.

December 6. All things are delivered unto me of my Father: and no man knoweth the Son, but the Father; neither knoweth any man the Father, save the Son, and *he* to whomsoever the Son will reveal *him.*—Matt. 11:27.

December 7. For the Son of man shall come in the glory of his Father with his angels; and then he shall reward every man according to his works. —Matt. 16:27.

December 8. Watch therefore; for ye know not what hour your Lord doth come.—Matt. 24:42.

December 9. But his bow abode in strength, and the arms of his hands were made strong by the hands of the mighty *God* of Jacob; (from thence *is* the shepherd, the stone of Israel;)—Gen. 49:24.

December 10. And I will restore to you the years that the locust hath eaten, . . . —Joel 2:25.

December 11. At that time will I bring you *again*, even in the time that I gather you: for I will make you a name and a praise among all people of the earth, when I turn back your captivity before your eyes, saith the Lord.—Zeph. 3:20.

December 12. Bring ye all the tithes into the storehouse, that there may be meat in mine house, and prove me now herewith, saith the Lord of hosts, if I will not open you the windows of heaven, and pour you out a blessing, that *there shall* not *be room* enough *to receive it.*—Mal. 3:10.

December 13. Verily, verily, I say unto you, Except a corn of wheat fall into the ground and die, it abideth alone: but if it die, it bringeth forth much fruit.—John 12:24.

December 14. . . . We would see Jesus.— John 12:21.

December 15. As for me, I will behold thy face in righteousness: I shall be satisfied, when I awake, with thy likeness.—Psa. 17:15.

December 16. And Jesus stood still, and commanded him to be called. And they call the blind man, saying unto him, Be of good comfort, rise; he calleth thee.—Mark 10:49.

December 17. And Jesus said unto him, Go thy way; thy faith hath made thee whole. And immediately he received his sight, and followed Jesus in the way.—Mark 10:52.

December 18. But that ye may know that the Son of man hath power upon earth to forgive sins, (he said unto the sick of the palsy,) I say unto thee, Arise, and take up thy couch, and go into thine house.—Luke 5:24.

December 19. And the angel answered and said unto her, The Holy Ghost shall come upon thee, and the power of the Highest shall overshadow thee: therefore also that holy thing which shall be born of thee shall be called the Son of God.—Luke 1:35.

December 20. A light to lighten the Gentiles, and the glory of thy people Israel.—Luke 2:32.

December 21. The Spirit of the Lord *is* upon me, because he hath anointed me to preach the gospel to the poor; he hath sent me to heal the brokenhearted, to preach deliverance to the captives, and recovering of sight to the blind, to set at liberty them that are bruised,—Luke 4:18.

December 22. . . . The Lamb slain from the foundation of the world.—Rev. 13:8.

December 23. Glory to God in the highest, and on earth peace, good will toward men.—Luke 2:14.

December 24. And the angel said unto them, Fear not: for, behold, I bring you good tidings of great joy, which shall be to all people.—Luke 2:10.

December 25. For unto you is born this day in the city of David, a Saviour, which is Christ the Lord.—Luke 2:11.

December 26. . . . . The kingdoms of this world are become *the kingdoms* of our Lord, and of his Christ; and he shall reign for ever and ever. —Rev. 11:15.

December 27. And I heard a great voice out of heaven saying, Behold, the tabernacle of God *is* with men, and he will dwell with them, and they shall be his people, and God himself shall be with them, *and be* their God.—Rev. 21:3.

December 28. And God shall wipe away all tears from their eyes; and there shall be no more death, neither sorrow, nor crying, neither shall there be any more pain: for the former things are passed away.—Rev. 21:4.

December 29. He which testifieth these things saith, Surely I come quickly: Amen. Even so, come, Lord Jesus.—Rev. 22:20.

December 30. Brethren, I count not myself to have apprehended: but *this* one thing *I do,* forgetting those things which are behind, and reaching forth unto those things which are before,—Philip. 3:13.

December 31. I press toward the mark for the prize of the high calling of God in Christ Jesus. —Philip. 3:14.

ALPHABETICAL INDEX

☞ A CLASSIFIED INDEX, arranging the subjects according to their relation to the everyday life of the individual, begins on Page 11.

ALPHABETICAL INDEX—*Continued*

CPSIA information can be obtained
at www.ICGtesting.com
Printed in the USA
LVHW021538040921
696974LV00014B/1119